MOBILE IP
The Internet Unplugged

Prentice Hall Series in
Computer Networking and Distributed Systems
Radia Perlman, editor

Kaufman, Perlman, and Speciner	*Network Security:* *Private Communication in a Public World*
Solomon	*Mobile IP:* *The Internet Unplugged*
Taylor, Waung, and Banan	*Internetwork Mobility:* *The CDPD Approach*

MOBILE IP
The Internet Unplugged

JAMES D. SOLOMON

To join a Prentice Hall Internet Mailing list,
point to http://www.prenhall.com/mail_lists.

PTR Prentice Hall
Upper Saddle River, New Jersey 07458

Editorial/production supervision: *Joe Czerwinski*
Acquisitions editor: *Mary Franz*
Editorial assistant: *Noreen Regina*
Manufacturing manager: *Alexis Heydt*
Cover design director: *Jerry Votta*
Interior illustrations: *Lyena Solomon*

Prentice Hall books are widely used by corporations and government agencies for training, marketing, and resale.

The publisher offers discounts on this book when ordered in bulk quantities.
For more information contact: Corporate Sales Department, Phone: 800-382-3419;
Fax: 201-236-7141; E-mail:corpsales@prenhall.com.
Or write: Prentice Hall PTR, Corp. Sales Dept., One Lake Street, Upper Saddle River, NJ 07458

Printed in the United States of America

10 9 8 7 6 5 4 3 2 1

ISBN 0-13-856246-6

Prentice-Hall International (UK) Limited, *London*
Prentice-Hall of Australia Pty. Limited, *Sydney*
Prentice-Hall Canada Inc., *Toronto*
Prentice-Hall Hispanoamericana, S.A., *Mexico*
Prentice-Hall of India Private Limited, *New Delhi*
Prentice-Hall of Japan, Inc., *Tokyo*
Simon & Schuster Asia Pte. Ltd., *Singapore*
Editora Prentice-Hall do Brasil, Ltda., *Rio de Janeiro*

Моей драгоценной Леночке

(To my dearest Lyenochka)

Contents

PART 2   MOBILE IP   47

CHAPTER 4   Mobile IP Overview   47

CHAPTER 5   Mobile IP: The Gory Details   63

PART 3   APPLYING MOBILE IP   125

CHAPTER 7   Security Primer   125

CHAPTER 9 **Internet-Wide Mobility:**
A More Complicated Application **173**

CHAPTER 10 **Applying Mobile IP:**
A Service-Provider Perspective **199**

PART 4 **FUTURE TOPICS**   **247**

CHAPTER 12 **Mobility for IP Version 6**   **247**

CHAPTER 13 **Open Issues**   **273**

List of Figures

Foreword

Mobility, in all its many forms, is becoming the watchword of our society. Everything moves. Faster and faster.

When we started designing networking technologies, it was natural to assume that computers and communication equipment stayed put. Of course, we should have known better. Now, many computers move all the time. And many of them can communicate even while they are moving. The communications protocols that we use need to adapt.

One of the most common communication methods in use today is the IP suite of protocols, using IPv4, with TCP and UDP, and the extensive suite of applications that live on top of them. In light of the growth in movement, it was clearly necessary for the IP suite to be enhanced to cope with this.

A working group was formed within the Internet Engineering Task Force (IETF), and discussion began. Many solutions were proposed and argued. During this process Jim Solomon became involved in the activities.

The group continued to debate the alternatives, and some of the leaders moved on to other activities. Jim Solomon became co-chair of the work in the summer of 1994. He has led the group since then. With the help of his co-chairs, the group has produced a strong specification for how to address the needs. Out of the chaos of conflicting proposals has come an implementable, deployable solution. Because of both his understanding of the problems involved and his leadership in the community, Jim has been pivotal in bringing this about.

As a result, he is in a unique position to write the book you are holding. He has seen all of the issues. He understands the trade-offs that were made. In fact, as chair it was his job to understand all sides of the issues being discussed, not merely the one he liked. Thus, Jim has a thorough understanding of the protocol, the way it works, and the reasons for the decisions that were made. And this is communicated in this book. Further, because he has watched all the debates, and listened to the different ways people become confused about these protocols, Jim has included additional details and explanations precisely in those places where the reader is most likely to be left wondering about some aspects of the protocol.

As referred to above, mobility is becoming pervasive. At the simple end, you unplug your portable from the network at the office or on campus, and plug it back in at home. It has moved. Or you plug in from a hotel room telephone. Or from a cell phone, or the phone bank in the airplane. And more recently, we are seeing computers with radio or infrared links built right into them. They are mobile all the time. Clearly this is becoming an issue for developers of host communications software, builders of network elements, and the folks who have to build and maintain the networks we all use. They need information on what the technology is capable of, and how to use it. This book, like its author, addresses that problem squarely and capably.

Thus, you have a book which takes the reader from the elements of the Internet Protocol Suite through the problems of Mobility, and into the solution in progressively more detail. Thus, the book gives one the information to understand the Mobile IP solution space. And then Jim goes on to give the reader an understanding of where the technology is going. He covers the currently active work in expanding the application as well as telling the reader what we do not yet know how to do. Knowing where the pitfalls are is something everyone finds useful.

—Joel M. Halpern
Routing Area Director for the IETF
Director, Internetworking Architecture, Newbridge Networks, Inc.

Preface

*T*he dramatic improvement in size, weight, and sophistication of notebook computers; an increasing reliance on information available on computer networks, most notably the Internet; and the tremendous growth in the number of telecommuters and mobile workers, are driving the creation of standards for mobile computing and networking.

This book is about one such standard, Mobile IP, which allows a mobile node (e.g., a laptop or notebook computer) to change its location without the need to restart its applications or terminate any ongoing communication—something currently not accommodated by the Internet protocols. Mobile IP is an Internet standards-track protocol which enhances the existing Internet Protocol (IP) to accommodate mobility.

The book provides a complete guide to understanding Mobile IP at virtually any level of detail desired. It begins by describing the context within which Mobile IP operates. Then it describes the problems that Mobile IP is designed to solve, how it solves them, and how Mobile IP can be applied in a number of example configurations. The book also goes into considerable detail on the security implications of so applying Mobile IP and enumerates the technologies that can be used to combat existing and resulting security threats. The book also provides insight into the open issues in mobile computing and offers some possible solutions to the areas requiring further research.

The purposes of this book are threefold. The first is to demystify the Internet standards documents, or Request For Comments (RFCs), that define Mobile IP. Thus anyone with a casual, academic, or compelling need to understand this new technology will find the treatment of Mobile IP both accessible and thorough. The second purpose is to describe the administrative and security implications of Mobile IP to anyone considering its deployment. This group includes network administrators, corporate (network) security officers, network architects, and both wired and wireless service providers, among others. The third purpose is to help implementors understand what is not well explained, not explained at all, or explained incorrectly in the current standards documents.

The scope of this book is therefore limited to Mobile IP, its applications, and its security implications. This book does not duplicate information readily available in other works, such as detailed descriptions of all layers of the protocol stack. Specifically, the book does not provide a detailed look at every possible physical medium over which Mobile IP can run, since this information is available elsewhere and since Mobile IP is completely independent of such media.

Readers will appreciate the infrequent use of acronyms, the opposite of which plagues many works on computer networking. The book describes difficult topics in plain English and provides many examples and figures to illustrate its points. Also, the book stands on its own by providing enough background information for a reader to fully understand the nature of any given problem before solutions to that problem are investigated. Every attempt has been made to provide forward references to material not yet covered, such that readers will not be left hanging and wondering whether or not they have failed to understand a given section. Computer jargon is avoided at all costs and all terminology within the book is italicized and defined in a thorough glossary.

The book begins with a primer on computer networking, which provides an explanation of the protocol-layering models and the Internet Protocol (IP) in particular. Then it describes Mobile IP in detail, at a level which implementors will find extremely valuable. Then the book progresses through applications of Mobile IP while simultaneously addressing the security threats to users, their networks, and service providers. Then future topics, including mobility for version 6 of the Internet Protocol and some unresolved issues of Mobile IP, are described. Finally, a vision is offered of a world in which Mobile IP has been fully deployed.

Acknowledgments

*F*irst, I would like to thank all of the people at Prentice Hall for their confidence in me and for their professionalism. In particular, my acquisition editor, Mary Franz, is one of the most pleasant people to work with I've come across in years. Her optimism, enthusiasm, and sense of humor provided much-needed adrenaline boosts throughout this project. Thanks also to Radia Perlman for her help and encouragement, to production editor Joe Czerwinski, art director Jerry Votta, and administrator Noreen Regina for running such a tight ship.

Second, I would like to thank all of my reviewers, both formal and informal, for their careful analysis and very helpful comments: King Ables, Desireé Christensen, Bob Geiger, Steve Glass, Kent Leung, Gabriel Montenegro, Jason Moritz, Mike Pearce, Radia Perlman, Loren Rittle, Guy Romano, and Rocky Stewart. In particular I'd like to thank Loren Rittle for suggesting the organization of Part III—I might *still* be trying to arrange the applications and security chapters if not for his creative ideas.

Third, I'd like to thank my manager, Ken Zdunek of Motorola Inc., for sponsoring my participation in the Internet Engineering Task Force and for providing the computing and other resources I needed to write this book. Along these lines, I'd like to acknowledge my friends, colleagues, and co-chairs in the Mobile IP working group with whom I have enjoyed working over the past few years.

Finally, I would like to thank my dear wife, Lyena Solomon, for her patience, enthusiastic support, and encouragement—not to mention her wonderful illustrations and valuable editorial feedback. Also, I'd like to thank my family and friends for understanding the need to chain myself to a computer for six months in order to produce this work—and for welcoming me back into society once I had finished.

INTRODUCTION

C H A P T E R   **1**

Introduction

*I*magine going on a lengthy vacation or business trip that lasts an entire year. Since you will be away from home for a long time, you will need to make arrangements to have your mail delivered to you at your current address—a location which might change as often as every two weeks. How might you arrange to have your mail delivered to you under such conditions?

One solution is to send a change-of-address postcard to everyone who might send you some correspondence, such as utility companies, your credit card companies, your friends and relatives, and specifically not those inclined to send you junk mail. There are many problems with this solution, however. First, these postcards would have to be sent every time you moved to a new location. Second, you would have to be sure to send a postcard to every conceivable correspondent—otherwise someone might send an important notice to your home address months before you return home. Third, there is nothing to prevent some prank-ster from sending bogus change-of-address cards to your correspondents in order to redirect your mail to himself, your business rival, or to some other undesirable person or place.

A better solution is to leave a forwarding notice at your home post office. Then any mail that arrives for your home address would be forwarded by the postal system to your current care-of address. The advantage here is that you would only have one entity to keep informed of your current address, as opposed to every one of your potential correspondents. Presumably some security mecha-nism could be devised such that the post office would not change your forwarding address unless they could verify that you were who you claimed to be, and that you were indeed authorized to change that forwarding address.

True, some correspondence might be temporarily lost, if you moved while it was in transit from your home post office to your previous forwarding address. To solve this problem, you might arrange with your previous post office to forward any subsequently arriving mail to your current post office. Also, you might inform your correspondents that if they do not see a reply from you within a rea-sonable period of time then they should resend their letter to you.

If we change the word "letter" to "Internet Protocol data packet," change "forwarding" to "tunneling," and change "post office" to "Mobile IP-enhanced router," then the preceding discussion describes how Mobile IP works almost exactly. The more subtle details will take us about 300 pages to explain.

1.1 What Is Driving Mobile Communications?

In the last few years we have seen an explosion in the number of notebook com-puters and in the growth of the Internet. While notebook computers continue to improve with respect to size, weight, and capabilities, the Internet continues to grow at a mind-boggling pace.

In addition, we have also seen an increased reliance on network computing, with most organizations now having sophisticated networks that link their indi-vidual employees and their respective PCs and workstations. In some cases, information essential to conducting one's job can only be accessed via the net-work. Such information can be available either on an *intranet*, an organization's private network, or on the *Internet*, a public network linking corporations, uni-versities, nonprofit organizations, individuals, and government agencies world-wide.

Finally, more and more employees are becoming part of a mobile workforce. These include telecommuters, mobile salespersons, and other highly mobile indi-viduals. Such employees are increasingly requiring access to the information stored on the computers of their private intranets and on the global Internet.

The combination of these three forces—an increasingly mobile workforce, the increased reliance on network computing, and the improvements in portable computing technology—motivates the need for mobile computers to communi-cate with other computers, fixed and mobile.

The problem is that most network protocols—the complex rules that define how information is exchanged between two or more computers—were designed back in the days when almost all computers filled up large, climate-controlled rooms and, necessarily, did not move very often. As a result, many of these protocols fail to operate in the presence of rapidly moving computers.

This book describes Mobile IP, a solution to the problem of transferring information to and from mobile computers. Mobile IP is an Internet standards-track protocol being defined by the Internet Engineering Task Force. Unlike other technologies, Mobile IP is independent of the physical medium over which a mobile computer communicates. Mobile IP also allows a mobile computer to change its location without restarting its applications and without disrupting any ongoing communications. We will define all of these terms and concepts throughout Part I of this book.

1.2 What Background Do I Need to Understand This Book?

This book requires a basic background in computer science. Computer professionals with limited training in computer networking will find that they have the necessary background to understand the majority of the book. It also helps to have an elementary understanding of binary arithmetic, the way in which computers interpret and manipulate numbers.

This book provides tutorial information for those with limited backgrounds in computer networking, computer communications, and computer security. Specifically, this book requires no detailed understanding of Internet protocols or the cryptographic methods used to combat security threats. However, those possessing such knowledge will find that the material in this book is treated thoroughly and with a great deal of depth and breadth.

1.3 Who Is the Target Audience of This Book?

Every effort was made to take the Mobile IP specification documents and describe them in plain English. Thus, those seeking only an introduction to Mobile IP and the problems it was designed to solve will find the information they seek in an accessible and readable fashion.

Others seeking a detailed knowledge of Mobile IP will find such information in the book as well. Here we identify two explicit categories of individuals:

- Anyone considering deploying Mobile IP throughout their network will find the applications and security implications of doing so described in very intimate detail. This group includes network administrators, network managers, and corporate security officers on the one hand, and network architects of wireless and wired service providers on the other.

- Anyone considering implementing Mobile IP in hardware or software will also benefit from reading this book. This group includes engineers and managers employed by vendors of host software, protocol stacks, routers, network access equipment, and particularly manufacturers of local and wide-area wireless communications devices, access points, and infrastructure equipment. Such individuals will appreciate the explanations of the confusing, missing, and erroneous portions of the standards documents. These individuals will also find indispensable the context and applications for Mobile IP described in the book.

1.4 What Is the Purpose of This Book?

The main purpose of this book is to explain Mobile IP thoroughly, from the technology itself through its applications and security implications. Let's face it, it can be difficult to read standards documents and even more difficult to come away with any firm sense of the context in which a standard applies. *Mobile IP: The Internet Unplugged* provides this context for Mobile IP.

As suggested in the previous section, this book is also intended to clarify on behalf of implementors passages in the Mobile IP standards documents which are confusing, poorly worded, or downright wrong. It is also intended to help those considering deploying Mobile IP understand the security risks of doing so, along with explaining the methods for mitigating or eliminating those risks.

Another purpose is to provide a look within the working group within the Internet Engineering Task Force that is defining Mobile IP. Here we describe the "work in progress" for those without the time or the inclination to subscribe to the working group's mailing list or to attend the triennial meetings.

While this book gives a thorough treatment of Mobile IP—and those technologies that are necessary to place it in context—it specifically avoids long discussions of those things that are described elsewhere. For example:

- those wishing to understand the gory details of CDPD and other wireless link technologies should consider reading [Daye97] or [TaWaBa97];
- those wishing a treatment of computer networking which provides intimate details of *all* levels of the protocol stack should consider reading [Come95], [Stev94], or [Tane96]; and
- those seeking the mathematics behind specific encryption and authentication algorithms should consider reading [KaPeSp95] or [Schneier95].

A further intention of this book is to avoid belaboring the somewhat rocky and politically sensitive history of the Mobile IP working group. Rather, our focus is on Mobile IP as a technology and as the solution of choice for mobile computing. Instead of focusing on the politics of the Mobile IP working group, we instead direct our political comments at the policies of various government agencies—specifically those which have prevented the wide-scale adoption of privacy and commerce-enabling hardware and software.

1.5 What Notation Is Used throughout This Book?

Here is a quick guide to the notation used throughout this book:

- When you encounter a term in *italic font*, it is likely that the term has not yet been defined in the text, will be defined within a sentence or two, and most definitely appears in the glossary. Those places where italic font is used instead for emphasis will be clear by context.

- A term in Helvetica font is a field name of a packet header or extension.

- This book avoids acronyms as much as conceivably possible. For example, we do not abbreviate Mobile IP as "MIP," mobile nodes as "MNs," foreign agents as "FAs," etc. One acronym which is used throughout the book is IP which stands for the Internet Protocol. Not doing so would double the length of the book! Other acronyms used throughout the book include PPP, UDP, and TCP, but they are expanded numerous times to help the reader along.

- After much (wasted) time pondering the use of third-person singular pronouns, I have settled on the use of *he* and *him* for such purposes. This decision is based upon the following: first, using "*he or she*" and "*him or her*" in many or most instances is terribly awkward; second, using *it* instead of these other choices is ridiculous; and third, I share Charles Murray's opinion [Murr97a] that this problem would go away if authors simply agreed to use their own gender for such pronouns.

1.6 Are We Talking about IPv4 or IPv6?

The Internet currently consists almost entirely of nodes—hosts and routers—which implement version 4 of the Internet Protocol, which is written *IPv4*. The Internet is growing at such a rapid pace that a new version of the Internet Protocol was deemed necessary to accommodate some of the shortcomings of IPv4, such as a limit to the maximum number of addressable nodes. This new version, *IPv6*, is currently making its way through the Internet standards process and is expected to become widely deployed in the coming months and years.

   With few exceptions, this book discusses version 4 of the Internet Protocol (IPv4). Thus, we will drop the "v4" when talking about IPv4 and just use the acronym "IP." In those chapters where we discuss version 6 of the Internet Protocol, notably *Chapter 12, Mobility for IP Version 6*, or where there might be ambiguity, we will explicitly include the version number (e.g., "IPv4" vs. "IPv6").

1.7 How Can I Obtain RFCs and Internet Drafts?

The Request For Comments (RFC) series of documents, referenced often throughout this book, contain the official protocol standards of the Internet, as well as other interesting things. RFCs, as they are called, can be obtained in a number of ways.

Those with access to the World Wide Web can type the following location into their Web browser to obtain RFCs: ftp://ds.internic.net/rfc/rfc*NNNN*.txt, where *NNNN* is the actual number of the desired RFC. For example, [RFC 2002] can be retrieved from ftp://ds.internic.net/rfc/rfc2002.txt. One extremely useful document is the "index" of all published RFCs, which can be retrieved from ftp://ds.internic.net/rfc/rfc-index.txt.

Similarly, Internet Drafts, which are preliminary documents produced by the various working groups of the Internet Engineering Task Force, are available at ftp://ds.internic.net/internet-drafts/*document-name*, where *document-name* is the filename of the desired draft. For example, [draft-ietf-mobileip-firewall-trav-00.txt] can be retrieved from: ftp://ds.internic.net/internet-drafts/draft-ietf-mobileip-firewall-trav-00.txt.

In addition, RFCs and Internet Drafts can be obtained by E-mail. Simply send a message to "mailserv@ds.internic.net" with an empty subject and a body containing "FILE *filename*," where *filename* is the name of the desired file. For example, both of the above documents could be obtained with the following message:

```
To: mailserv@ds.internic.net
Subject:

FILE /rfc/rfc2002.txt
FILE /internet-drafts/draft-ietf-mobileip-firewall-trav-00.txt
```

Internet Drafts are only available for a period of six months after which they are revised, published as RFCs, or otherwise deleted. It should be understood that any reference to an Internet Draft within this book or anywhere else represents "work in progress." Such references are intended to provide an interested reader with a place to go for further information and also to give the original authors credit for their work. They are not meant to imply publication as an Internet standard of any kind.

Since Internet Drafts do indeed come and go, often without being published, there is a real possibility that a document referenced in this book will expire without being updated. In such a case, be sure to visit the Web site for this book at http://www.prenhall.com/solomon, where you can find these expired drafts.

Finally, further information about the Internet Engineering Task Force can be found at http://www.ietf.org/, and the Mobile IP working group's charter can be found at http://www.ietf.org/html.charters/mobileip-charter.html, along with links to the working group's current RFCs and Internet Drafts.

1.8 What Is the Roadmap for the Rest of This Book?

This book contains four parts arranged as follows:

1. Part I serves as the book's introductory portion. Chapter 1 sets out the purpose, target audience, and necessary background for the book. Then Chapter 2 provides a tutorial on computer networking for those unfamiliar with protocols, stacks, and the various methods by which information is moved through the Internet. Here we describe IP routing in detail, since Mobile IP's primary purpose is to overcome one of IP's shortcomings. Finally, Chapter 3 explains why a technology such as Mobile IP is necessary and why the existing solutions to the mobility problem in the Internet are unsatisfactory.

2. Part II explains Mobile IP itself in very fine detail. We begin in Chapter 4 with an overview of Mobile IP by defining the problem it solves and the scope of that solution. Then we present the requirements, goals, and assumptions behind the solution. Chapter 4 also introduces the terminology used by Mobile IP and walks through its operation at a high level. Chapter 5 then describes the three respective components of Mobile IP in detail: Agent Discovery, Registration, and Routing. Chapter 6 provides additional detail on tunneling, one of the technologies Mobile IP uses to route packets to mobile computers.

3. Part III describes how Mobile IP can be applied, and the benefits of doing so, in various situations. The security implications of each application are examined in detail. Chapter 7 give a security primer for those unfamiliar with computer security or with cryptography, the primary technology used to combat security threats. Chapter 8 shows a simple deployment of Mobile IP on an organization's campus network. We make things as simple as possible in this chapter by ignoring firewalls and connectivity to the Internet. Chapter 9 then makes things more difficult—and quite interesting—by introducing network firewalls into the picture. This leads to a discussion of secure firewall traversal in Mobile IP. Chapter 10 illustrates Mobile IP as the basis of a commercial service provider's business and addresses the concerns that are particular to service providers—the threats to the users having already been addressed in Chapters 8 and 9. Chapter 11 then shows two advanced applications of Mobile IP. First, it illustrates Mobile IP's ability to support multiple protocols (e.g., AppleTalk) and not just IP. Next, Chapter 11 shows how Mobile IP can provide connectivity for an entire mobile network, as opposed to just one mobile computer. Chapter 11 finishes by describing an application of Mobile IP that is invisible to the end-user, but is nonetheless useful.

4. Part IV describes the future of Mobile IP. Here, Chapter 12 provides considerable detail on Mobile IPv6, which provides mobility for the next version of the Internet Protocol. Then, Chapter 13 addresses three major open issues facing Mobile IP: performance of TCP, support for real-time traffic (e.g., audio and video), and service location. Chapter 14 then summarizes

the key points of the book and provides a "vision" of a world in which
Mobile IP has been widely deployed and of the things one will be able to do
when this state of affairs has been reached.

Computer Networking Tutorial

This chapter discusses the nature and mechanics of computer communications. First, we introduce the OSI Reference Model and compare it to the Internet model of communications. Next we examine the concept of *routing* and explore how the Internet moves information between its component networks. This exercise lays the foundation for the next chapter, where we show why the Internet model of routing necessitates something like Mobile IP.

Note that this chapter is by no means a complete guide to computer communications. For a more thorough treatment of the topic, see [Tane96], [Come95], or [Stev94]. If you already know the basics of computer networking and IP routing, then please feel free to skip this chapter and move on to the next one.

2.1 How Do Computers Communicate?

Computers communicate over a network by transmitting and receiving digital information. This information consists of binary digits, called *bits*, which take on the values zero or one. Bits are grouped into 8-bit chunks, called *bytes*,[†] which

---

[†] Bytes are sometimes called "octets" in other works and various standards documents.

can further be grouped into bundles called *frames* or *packets*, the latter of which we formally define in a subsequent section.

Before two computers can exchange packets, they must be connected by some form of physical *medium*, such as copper wire, optical fiber, or electromagnetic radiation (radio waves). Occasionally, the two computers will be connected by the same uninterrupted piece of physical wire or wireless link, in which case they can send packets directly. In most cases, however, the packets sent by a computer will have to traverse one or more intermediate switching devices in order to reach their final destination.

In practice, making two computers talk to each other can be very difficult, especially if they have different hardware, different operating systems, and different software applications. Making the computers talk to each other involves solving all of the problems suggested by the following questions:

- At what speed and over what physical medium will the computers communicate?
- If this medium is shared with several other computers, how do we determine whose turn it is to transmit?
- How will the computers be addressed, such that we can uniquely identify the sender and the intended recipient of each transmission?
- If the two computers are not directly connected, how will a suitable path be chosen from a packet's source to its destination?
- How can we detect errors in transmission, and fix them when they occur?
- In what digital format will the transmitted data be represented?

The branch of computer science which seeks to answer all of these questions is generally referred to as *computer networking*, or just *networking*. Rather than solve these problems simultaneously, computer scientists divide them into many individual problems that can be solved independently. Each such problem forms the basis of a *layer* of communications, with each layer being defined by a rigorously specified set of rules and procedures.

2.1.1 What Is a Protocol Layer?

Figure 2-1 shows the Open System Interconnection (OSI) reference model for computer networking as defined by the International Organization for Standardization (ISO). Each of the seven layers performs a specific set of functions and in turn provides a distinct set of services to the layer above it. The rules and procedures governing the operation of the various layers are called *protocols*.

Each protocol in this model is theoretically independent of the protocols in the layers above and below it. This allows for new technologies to be incorporated into a protocol layer without affecting the other layers—so long as the *service* provided by the new protocol is at least as rich in functionality as that of the old protocol it is replacing. While this is the theory, efficiency and other considerations tend to cause some degree of interdependency between the layers, as we will see throughout the later chapters of this book.

2.1.2 What Does Each Layer Do?

The functions performed by each of the protocol layers in Figure 2-1 are as follows:

1. The **physical layer** moves "raw" bits across a communications facility, or *medium*. A physical-layer protocol defines the electrical and mechanical characteristics of the medium, the bit rate, the voltages, etc.

2. The **data link layer** uses the raw bit-transmission facility provide by the physical layer to move *frames* from one computer to a *neighboring* computer on the same *link*. A frame consists of a small data link-layer *header* plus a network-layer *packet*. A data link-layer protocol defines methods for ensuring the reliability of each frame and also arbitrates access to those media types which are shared by many computers.

3. The **network layer** uses the frame-transmission facility provided by the data link layer to move *packets*[†] from their original source to their ultimate destination, traversing one or more intermediate links if necessary. A packet consists of a small network-layer header plus data from the higher layer(s). A network-layer protocol defines how network devices discover each other and how packets are routed to their final destination.

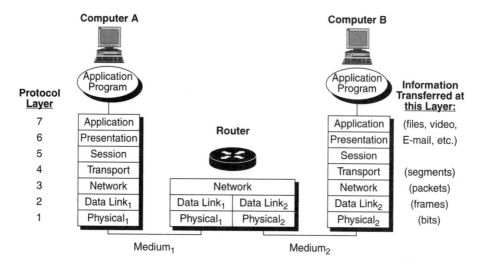

Figure 2-1 OSI Reference Model

[†] Packets are sometimes called "datagrams" in other works and various standards documents.

4. The **transport layer** is responsible for making reliable the end-to-end packet-transmission facility provided by the network layer. The data which flows across this reliable, end-to-end transmission facility is generally called a *stream*. Each individual transmission at the transport layer, called a *segment*, consists of a small transport-layer header plus data from a higher-layer protocol. Thus, a segment forms the payload portion of a network-layer packet. A transport-layer protocol defines the methods for detecting errors in the transmission of segments and for correcting them when they occur.[†]

5. The **session layer** takes the reliable *stream* provided by the transport layer and delivers rich, application-oriented services to the higher layers. Some session-layer protocols, for example, provide periodic "checkpoints," to which communications can be resumed in the event of a catastrophic network failure. This is useful when sending very large files over unreliable networks, where restarting the entire transmission from the beginning— after having already transmitted most of the file—would be extremely wasteful of network resources.

6. The **presentation layer** defines the syntax and semantics of the information being exchanged by an application. In English, this means that a presentation-layer protocol defines how the integers, text messages, and other data of an application are to be encoded and transmitted over the network. This allows all computers of varying hardware and operating systems to exchange information, regardless of their own particular method of storing such data.

7. The **application layer** provides the transfer of information that is specific to the computer program being run by a user. Some application-layer protocols define how electronic mail (E-mail) is to be exchanged. Some application layer protocols define how files are to be transferred from one computer to another, and some define how World Wide Web pages are to be fetched from a web server by a web client (browser).

A piece of hardware or software which implements a protocol is called a *protocol entity* (yes, this is an obnoxious term!). A protocol entity in one computer physically communicates with a corresponding protocol entity in another computer by using the services of the layer below it to transmit information across the network. Logically, however, we think of a protocol entity in one computer as talking directly to a corresponding protocol entity in another computer. Two protocol entities communicating with each other over a network are called *peers*.

For example, in Figure 2-1 the Network layer in Computer A logically communicates with the Network layer of the router. To do so, the Network layer

---

[†] Some transport-layer protocols provide what amounts to little more than a higher-level interface to the network layer. Such protocols tend not to be stream oriented nor do they necessarily provide any reliability. As we will see, the User Datagram Protocol is an example of this type of transport-layer protocol in the Internet.

makes use of the service provided by Data Link$_1$ to move packets across the link built of medium$_1$. Thus, the network layer entities in Computer A and the router are peers.

Protocols typically perform their magic by prepending a small header to the data they receive from the higher layer and transmitting the resulting information to their peer at the other side of the network. This small header contains information that helps the peer figure out how to process what it receives, and might include such things as protocol addresses, the length of the "data" portion, and a *checksum* used to detect and correct errors. At the peer, the small header is stripped off the received information, recovering the original data, which is then passed to the higher layer.

As a final note on terminology, the arrangement of protocols into a vertical set of boxes, as seen in Figure 2-1, is often called a protocol *stack* diagram. When each of the generic terms (e.g., "network-layer protocol") is replaced with the name of a specific protocol (e.g., "the Internet Protocol (IP)"), we call the resulting set of specific protocols a protocol *suite*. For example, the specific protocols which have been adopted by the Internet at all layers of the stack are collectively referred to as the TCP/IP Suite of Protocols.

2.1.3 Which Layers Are Relevant to This Book?

This book is primarily concerned with the network layer and the technologies which move packets from a source computer all the way to the ultimate destination. However, as described in *What Does Each Layer Do?* on page 11, the network layer relies on the service provided by the data link layer in order to move packets through the network. As such, some important characteristics of various links and their impact on the performance of transport-layer protocols will be discussed in *TCP Performance and Mobility* on page 273. Those readers interested in finding out more about other layers of the protocol stack are referred to [Tane96].

2.1.4 What Does the Network Layer Look Like?

The purpose of the network layer is to hide the specifics of individual links and to provide the transport layer with the illusion of one large, logical network. The network layer moves packets from the source computer all the way to the ultimate destination computer, traversing one or more links if necessary. A packet consists of a small network-layer header plus a segment of data passed down from the transport layer. Thus, looking down at the network layer, the transport layer sees a service which delivers segments from the source computer to the ultimate destination.

What Is a Node?

To accomplish their task, network-layer protocols assign one or more *logical addresses* to each network device, or *node*. By logical, we mean unrelated to any

physical addresses which might be necessary to implement a data link or physical-layer protocol (e.g., Ethernet addresses). The network layer defines two basic
categories of network devices, or nodes, as illustrated in Figure 2-2:

Hosts, which include PCs, workstations, mainframes, file servers, and other
types of computers.

Routers, which *forward* packets between hosts and other routers in order to
allow hosts not connected to the same link to communicate.

Forwarding is the process by which a router transmits a packet it has
received in order to move the packet closer to its ultimate destination.

What Is Routing?

Using special procedures called *routing protocols*, routers exchange information among themselves about the networks and hosts to which they are connected. This allows them to build tables, called routing tables, which are used to
select a path for any given packet from the source to the destination. We will
have more to say about routing protocols in *How Are Routing-Table Entries Created?* on page 26.

Hop-by-Hop vs. End-to-End

As Figure 2-2 shows, there can be more than one router along the path
between any two hosts. Each router makes only an individual decision as to
which is the *next* host or router (i.e., the next network *hop*) to which a packet
must be forwarded in order to reach its final destination. This method is called
hop-by-hop routing, to distinguish it from other technologies in which the entire
path from source to destination must be determined *before* any packets may be
sent.

Returning to Figure 2-1, we see that only the highest layers of the protocol
stack—the transport through application layers—are *end-to-end* protocols. By
this we mean that the protocol entities at these layers exist only in the ultimate
source and ultimate destination of the communication, such as the two comput-

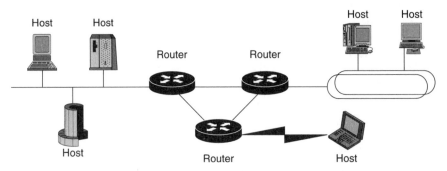

Figure 2-2 Network Entities: Hosts and Routers

ers shown in Figure 2-1. By contrast, the lower layers of the protocol stack—the physical through data link layers—are *hop-by-hop* protocols. The protocol entities at these layers may talk only to peer protocol entities in *neighboring* devices—those devices that are connected to the *same* link.

The network layer combines elements of both end-to-end and hop-by-hop protocols. On the one hand, network-layer packets are generated in one end-node and delivered to another end-node, which is the essence of end-to-end protocols. On the other hand, packets are examined by every router along the path between these end-nodes, which gives network-layer protocols a flavor of hop-by-hop protocols.

Routers vs. Bridges

Finally, to be completely rigorous, this book defines a *router* as a device which operates at the network layer. That is, a router forwards packets based upon information contained in their respective network-layer headers. In contrast, a device called a *bridge* operates at the data link layer. That is, a bridge relays frames based upon information contained in their respective link-layer headers.

As shown in Figure 2-3, a bridge is invisible to the network layer. For example, the network-layer software in both Host$_1$ and the Router have no idea that there is a Bridge separating them. Rather, the bridged medium appears as a single link to Host$_1$ and the Router. The Bridge relays frames between the two physical segments, as necessary, to convince Host$_1$ and the Router that they are directly connected to each other.

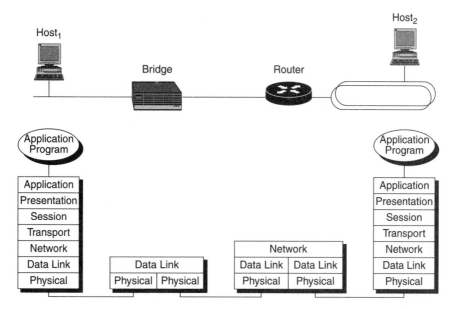

Figure 2-3 Bridges, Routers, and Hosts

2.2 What Is the Internet Protocol (IP)?

The Internet model of communications, as embodied in the TCP/IP suite of protocols, resembles but varies slightly from the OSI model. For instance, the Internet model generally groups the highest three layers of the OSI model together and considers them to be one layer, the application layer. However, for the purposes of this book, the two models can be considered to be identical.

The name given to the Internet's network-layer protocol is, not coincidentally, the *Internet Protocol (IP)* [RFC 791]. At the transport layer, layer 4, there are two protocols in wide use on the Internet: the *Transmission Control Protocol (TCP)* [RFC 793], which provides reliable, stream-oriented communications to the higher layers; and the *User Datagram Protocol (UDP)* [RFC 768], which provides connection-less communications to the higher layers without guaranteeing reliability. The combination of the Internet's reliable transport protocol (TCP) and its network protocol (IP) gives rise to the name of the Internet suite of protocols.

2.2.1 What Is ICMP?

The *Internet Control Message Protocol (ICMP)* [RFC 792] defines a set of error and control messages which provide indications that errors have occurred in the transmission of a packet. Other ICMP messages provide diagnostic information to a requesting node. A node which implements IP must also implement ICMP in order to claim compliance with Internet standards; thus when we speak of IP we are generally speaking about ICMP as well. Figure 2-4 shows the TCP/IP Reference model and shows the relationship between many common Internet protocols.

2.2.2 What Does IP Do?

IP, like all network-layer protocols, moves packets of information from the original source to the ultimate destination. This service is sometimes referred to as "end-to-end packet delivery." The reliability of the service provided by IP is called "best-effort," which means that IP will try very hard to deliver a packet to the destination, but IP makes *no guarantee* that the packet will arrive without error.

In essence, the service agreement that IP makes with higher-layer protocols can be stated as follows: "I will try my best to get packets containing your data to the intended destination. However, please note that there is a possibility that zero, one, or *many* copies of any given packet might arrive at the destination. Furthermore, any copy(s) which arrive might contain errors. If you don't find this quality of service acceptable, then you must take your own steps to guarantee that at most one copy of your data arrives at the destination error-free."

Thus, it is the job of the transport layer to provide a guarantee of error-free communications on an end-to-end basis, if an application requires this level of reliability. The *Transmission Control Protocol (TCP)* provides this reliable, end-to-end transmission of data in the Internet.

2.2.3 What Does an IP Packet Look Like?

An IP packet consists of a segment of data passed down from the transport or higher layer, plus a small *IP header* prepended to the data. The IP header, defined in [RFC 791], contains the fields shown in Figure 2-5. The most important fields in the IP header are the Source Address and the Destination Address. These addresses are similar in purpose to the respective addresses on a postal

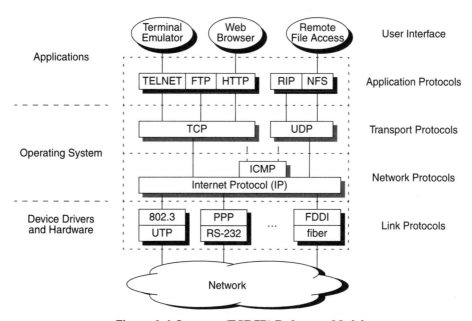

Figure 2-4 Internet (TCP/IP) Reference Model

0	1	2	3	
0 1 2 3 4 5 6 7	8 9 0 1 2 3 4 5	6 7 8 9 0 1 2 3 4 5 6 7 8 9 0 1		
Vers = 4 | IHL	Type of Service	Total Length		
Identification		Flags | Fragment Offset		
Time to Live | Protocol		Header Checksum		IP Header [RFC 791]
Source Address				
Destination Address				
IP Options ...				
Transport Layer (e.g., TCP) Header ...				
Application Layer (e.g., HTTP) Header ...				IP Payload
Application Layer Data (e.g., Web Page) ...				

Figure 2-5 IP Packet: Header and Payload

envelope—one provides the address of the sender, and one provides the address of the intended recipient.

IP Addresses

IP addresses are 32-bit (4-byte) numbers assigned to each network *interface* of a node. An interface is a generic term for the software and hardware through which a node attaches to a link. Nodes with multiple network interfaces, such as routers, have multiple IP addresses—one per interface.

Dotted-Decimal Notation

IP addresses are often written in "dotted-decimal" notation, where each of the four bytes is respectively written as a decimal integer separated by periods. For example, an IP address expressed as the hexadecimal number C0 13 F1 12 would be written in dotted-decimal notation as 192.19.241.18, because $C0_{(hex)} = 192_{(dec)}$, $13_{(hex)} = 19_{(dec)}$, $F1_{(hex)} = 241_{(dec)}$, and $12_{(hex)} = 18_{(dec)}$.

Network-Prefix and Host Portions

IP addresses have two components: the *network-prefix* portion and the *host* portion, as shown in Figure 2-6. A network-prefix is a sequence of bits which is identical for all nodes attached to the same link, which requires the host portion to be unique for each node on the same link. One can think of the network-prefix as identifying a link and the host portion as identifying a specific host or router connected to that link.

This rule is not without exceptions, however. Whereas it is common to have one network-prefix assigned to each link, there is nothing preventing multiple network-prefixes from being assigned to the same link. In this latter case, we can think of the physical link as being composed of multiple, virtual links wherein one network-prefix is assigned to each of these virtual links. In this way we can consider each link (physical or virtual) to be assigned exactly one network-prefix. Throughout this book we will ignore the case of multiple network-prefixes per link and assume only a single network-prefix. This simplifying assumption will not cause a loss of generality.

To illustrate the concept of network-prefixes, consider the IP address "129.61.18.26" whose network-prefix, we are told, consists of the leftmost 24 bits (3 bytes). In this case, $p = 24$ and $h = 8$, and therefore the network-prefix is "129.61.18" and the host portion is "26."

Prefix-Length

The *prefix-length* is defined as the number of bits which comprise the network-prefix portion of an IP address.[†] The number of bits in the host portion of

Figure 2-6 IP Address Semantics

an IP address is thus $(32 - prefix\text{-}length)$. Continuing the example above, the prefix-length of 129.61.18.26 is 24 bits. A convenient shorthand notation for an IP address and its prefix-length is *address/prefix-length,* which in our example would be written 129.61.18.26 / 24.

Other IP Header Fields

Other fields in the IP Header are briefly described as follows. The Version field tells which version of the Internet Protocol is represented in this packet. For IPv4, this field contains ... drum roll please ... 4! Future versions of the Internet Protocol will increment this field as appropriate. The IHL (Internet Header Length) field gives the length of the IP header, measured in 32-bit (4-byte) chunks. Thus, the minimum value for the IHL is 5 (times 4 equals 20 bytes) for an IP header without options.

The Type of Service field is used to specify how this packet is to be handled in networks which offer various service qualities (e.g., lowest delay, highest reliability, etc.). The Total Length gives the length of the entire IP packet—including the header itself—in bytes.

The Flags field and the Fragment Offset field are used to chop up large IP packets into small chunks, called *fragments*, for traversing networks that are unable to handle large IP packets. The Identification field is a unique value chosen by the sender to allow a recipient to reassemble a packet that had to be chopped up into fragments.

The Time to Live (TTL) field is used to limit the number of times an individual IP packet may be forwarded. Consider what would happen if a first router thought that the path to a destination was via a second router and vice-versa. When the first router received a packet for delivery to that destination, it would forward the packet to the second router, which would forward the packet back to the first router, which would forward the packet to the second router, etc. Without TTL, a packet caught in such a *routing loop* between these two routers would live for eternity. Routing loops are unfortunately rather common in large networks.

The Protocol field is used by the IP layer to determine *which* higher-layer protocol created the payload within the IP packet. Upon receipt of an IP packet, this field allows the IP software in the receiving node to pass the IP packet up the stack to the appropriate higher-layer protocol. For example, a Protocol field of 1 indicates ICMP, 6 indicates TCP, and 17 indicates UDP.

The Header Checksum field is used by a receiving node to verify that there was no error in transmission of the IP-header portion of the packet. That is, the Header Checksum is computed using only the fields in the IP header and specifi-

---

† Some TCP/IP software and some texts use the concept of *netmasks* instead of *prefix-lengths.* A netmask is a 32-bit binary number in which all 1-bits comprise the network-prefix portion and all 0-bits comprise the host portion of a corresponding IP address. Thus, a netmask of FF FF FF 00 (255.255.255.0 in dotted-decimal notation) would be equivalent to a prefix-length of 24, because each of the leftmost 24 bits of FF FF FF 00 is equal to 1.

cally is not computed using any of the IP payload. It is up to higher-layer protocols to provide a checksum which covers the payload of an IP packet.

IP Options

Following the fixed-length portion of the IP Header, as described above, are zero or more Options which may appear in the IP Header. Options are quite rare in IP packets, though they can be used to implement some rather interesting functionality. One such option, the Loose Source and Record Route option, will be described in *Why Use Tunneling Instead of Source Routing?* on page 99. Other options concern security, time-related data, and various diagnostic features.

2.2.4 How Does a Node Obtain an IP Address?

There are two ways that nodes can obtain their IP address(es)—manually and automatically. Manual assignment is common in corporate network environments where a network administrator is responsible for handing out IP addresses to the hosts and routers in the corporate network. Manual assignment generally involves typing the IP address (and other parameters, as we shall see in subsequent sections) into a node's configuration files or into the appropriate field of a graphical user interface, such as those that are found in many personal computers.

There are two common methods for assigning IP addresses to nodes automatically. The first is typically used when a user dials an Internet Service provider (ISP) using a modem, a telephone line, and a home Personal Computer. Here, the PC asks for an IP address to be assigned by the ISP's dial-in equipment during the *IP Control Protocol (IPCP)* [RFC 1661] phase of the *Point-to-Point Protocol (PPP)* [RFC 1332]. PPP is described in *How Does a Person Connect to Internet via PPP But without Mobile IP?* on page 202.

The other automatic IP address assignment method is termed the *Dynamic Host Configuration Protocol (DHCP)* [RFC 2131]. DHCP is often found in large corporate or university environments, where there are many nodes that come and go relatively rapidly. DHCP involves a node sending a request to a DHCP Server to lease an address for some period of time. DHCP is designed to coexist with its predecessor, the *Bootstrap Protocol (BOOTP)* [RFC 951], which also provides dynamic IP address assignment and is still being used in some environments.

2.3 How Does IP Routing Work?

In this section we will explore how nodes make forwarding decisions when presented with an IP packet for transmission. As we shall see, forwarding decisions are based upon fields within the IP packet header and based upon entries in the node's IP routing table.

In exploring IP routing we will first define an IP routing table and examine the fields which comprise an entry in the table. Next, we will define the rules for searching the routing table for an entry which matches the IP packet to be forwarded. With these rules in place, we will look at a few examples and finally conclude with some summary comments.

For now we ignore the question of how a node's routing table gets populated with entries. In fact, we will assume that they are created by "magic," and defer a discussion of the actual method until *How Are Routing-Table Entries Created?* on page 26.

2.3.1 What Is a Routing Table?

The description of routing tables and routing table entries which follows can be confusing—after all, there is a lot of information to absorb all at once. Don't worry if you get lost reading the next few paragraphs. There will be plenty of examples which illustrate these concepts and, hopefully, make them more clear, in the pages that follow.

As far as an individual node is concerned, IP packets fall into two categories: those for which the node itself is the ultimate destination and those for which any other node is the ultimate destination. A node determines if it is the ultimate destination by comparing the IP Destination Address field of a packet with each of its own IP address(es). If any of the addresses are equal, then the node is the ultimate destination of the packet. Any packets received over the network by a node for which it is the ultimate destination are *consumed*, i.e., passed to the higher-layer protocol indicated by the IP Protocol field within the IP header.

When a node receives a packet for which it is not the ultimate destination, then the node must figure out where to forward the packet in order to move the packet closer to its ultimate destination. This selection of a place to forward the packet is called "making a forwarding decision" or "routing a packet." This brings us to our definition of an IP routing table as a software data structure, conceptually organized as a table, that is used by a node to make forwarding decisions for packets not destined to the node itself.

Every IP node, whether a host or a router, has an IP routing table which it uses to make forwarding decisions. A forwarding decision must be made for every packet that is transmitted by a node. This include packets generated by the node itself (e.g., segments handed down from the transport layer) and packets received by routers which are to be forwarded along their respective paths to their final destinations.

In its simplest form, an *entry* in a routing table, or simply a *route*, has four columns: Target, Prefix-Length, Next Hop, and Interface. When a node has an IP packet to forward, it searches its routing table for an entry whose combination of Target and Prefix-Length fields matches the IP Destination Address in the packet header. If it finds a matching entry, the node forwards the packet to the node identified by the Next Hop field in that entry, via the link specified in the Interface field of that entry. A routing table entry is said to *match* an IP packet if the leftmost Prefix-Length bits of the entry's Target field are equal to those same bits in the packet's IP Destination Address field.

The Next Hop fields within a node's routing-table entries contain one of two possible values. For a Target that is not connected to one of the node's directly attached links, the Next Hop field contains the IP address of a router that can be used to reach that Target. Otherwise, the Next Hop field contains a special value indicating that the Target is connected to one of the node's directly attached links. In this latter case, we will use the notation "directly" throughout the example routing tables of this book.

2.3.2 What If There Is More Than One Matching Entry?

IP has very specific rules by which nodes must select one of possibly many matching routing-table entries. If a node has more than one matching route for a given destination, then the route with the largest Prefix-Length must be used to forward the packet. Confused? Let us look at an example.

Sample Routing Table

As an example, consider a node which needs to make a forwarding decision on a packet whose IP Destination Address is 7.7.7.1. The node's routing table contains the entries shown in Table 2-1:

Target / Prefix-Length	Next Hop	Interface
7.7.7.99 / 32	router 1	a
7.7.7.0 / 24	router 2	a
0.0.0.0 / 0	router 3	a

Table 2-1 Example Routing Table

For illustration purposes, the network-prefix portions of the Target fields—as determined by the respective Prefix-Length fields—are presented in **bold type** throughout this book. Similarly, we combine the Target and Prefix-Length fields into a single column, since these fields are so intimately related.

To search this routing table for matching entries we must compare, respectively, the leftmost Prefix-Length bits of each Target with that of the packet's IP Destination Address. Thus, we examine each entry in Table 2-1 as follows:

1. The first entry requires all 32 bits (4 bytes) of its Target and the IP Destination Address to be identical. Since 7.7.7.99 does not equal 7.7.7.1, then the first routing table entry does not match the IP packet.

2. The second entry requires only the leftmost 24 bits (3 bytes) of its Target and the IP Destination Address to be identical. Since the leftmost 24 bits of the Tar-

get are 7.7.7, and the leftmost 24 bits of the IP Destination Address are 7.7.7, then the second routing-table entry matches the IP packet.

3. The third entry requires zero (or more) bits of the Target and IP Destination Address to be identical. Equivalently stated, this entry matches all IP packets. Obviously, then, the third routing-table entry matches the IP packet.

Here we have two matching routes (the second and third entries). Since IP specifies that the matching route with the largest Prefix-Length must be used, the node in this example uses the second entry in its table to forward the packet, because 24 is larger than 0. Thus, the node forwards the packet to router 2 via interface "a."

Categories of Routing-Table Entries

This example illustrates the three basic categories of routing-table entries:

1. A *host-specific* route is a routing-table entry with a Prefix-Length of 32 bits. As the name implies, a host-specific route will provide a match for exactly one IP Destination Address; namely, the address specified in the Target field.

2. A *network-prefix* route is a routing-table entry with a Prefix-Length between 1 bit and 31 bits inclusive. As the name implies, a network-prefix route will provide a match for all IP packets whose Destination Address has the same network-prefix as the network-prefix of the Target field.

3. A *default* route is a routing table entry with a Prefix-Length of zero bits. As the name implies, a default route will provide a match for all IP packets. Because of the "largest matching prefix" rule, however, a default route will only be used if there are no matching host-specific or network-prefix routes for a packet's IP Destination Address.

Matching Rules Restated

Given these definitions, the rules for routing IP packets can be restated as follows:

1. If there is a host-specific route which exactly matches a packet's IP Destination Address, then this route must be used to forward the packet in preference to any matching network-prefix routes in the table.

2. Otherwise, if there is a network-prefix route which matches the network-prefix portion of the packet's IP Destination Address, then this route must be used to forward the packet in preference to any default route(s) (and any network-prefix routes of shorter prefix-length) which might be present in the table.

3. Otherwise (no matching host-specific or network-prefix routes), if there are one or more default routes, then one of these default routes can be used to forward the packet.

4. Otherwise (no matching routes at all), declare a routing error and send an *ICMP Unreachable* message to the source of the packet.

2.3.3 Routing Examples

Figure 2-7 shows a typical network configuration, which will serve as an example throughout this section. The figure shows two Ethernets which are connected via routers to an FDDI (Fiber Distribution Data Interface) ring which serves as a high-speed backbone.

The first thing we notice about Figure 2-7 is that every node has an IP address assigned to every one of its interfaces. Since the hosts shown in the figure have only one interface, then they have exactly one IP address. The routers, however, have two interfaces and thus require two IP addresses. Also note that all nodes on a link have identical network-prefix portions of their IP addresses on the interface which attaches to that link. Also shown in the figure are the routing tables for $Host_1$ and Router B.

In Figure 2-7, Ethernet A has been assigned a network-prefix of 1.0.0 (prefix-length = 24 bits), leaving 8 bits available to the host portion of the address. Normally, this would allow 256 individual nodes, because $2^8 = 256$. However, the binary values "all 0's" and "all 1's" (0 and 255, in decimal) have special meanings and therefore cannot be used in the host portion. This leaves 254 host numbers available for assignment to 254 individual nodes. Ethernet B and the Fiber Backbone also have network-prefixes whose prefix-lengths are 24 bits. Their network-prefixes are 2.0.0 and 3.0.0, respectively.

To see how IP routing works, let us consider a number of examples. For now we will consider only network-prefix routes and default routes. Further, as

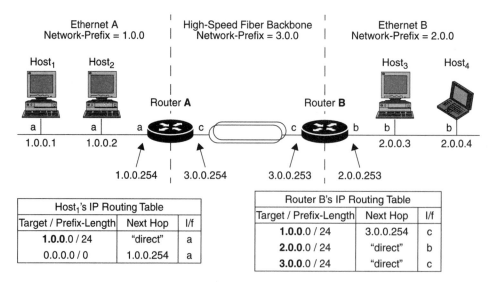

Figure 2-7 Example IP Network

before, we assume that the routing-table entries in the various nodes were created by "magic." The actual way they are created will be discussed in *How Are
Routing-Table Entries Created?* on page 26.

Hosts on the Same Link

Consider the case of $Host_1$ sending a packet to $Host_2$. Here we note that the
two hosts are connected to the same link (Ethernet A). The IP Source Address of
the packet is 1.0.0.1 and the IP Destination Address is 1.0.0.2. $Host_1$ begins by comparing the IP Destination Address with each of its own IP addresses. Since 1.0.0.1
does not equal 1.0.0.2, $Host_1$ knows that this packet is not destined for itself, and
thus it must make a forwarding decision in order to transmit the packet.

To make this forwarding decision, $Host_1$ begins searching its routing table
according to the rules in *What If There Is More Than One Matching Entry?* on
page 22. First, it finds no host-specific route whose Target exactly matches the IP
Destination Address (1.0.0.2). It does, however, find a network-specific route in the
first row of its table which matches all destinations whose network-prefixes are
1.0.0. This entry specifies that all such packets are to be sent "directly" to their
ultimate destination on the link identified by interface "a." Thus, $Host_1$ sends the
packet directly to $Host_2$ using interface "a" to transmit the packet.

Hosts on Different Links

Consider the case of $Host_1$ sending a packet to $Host_3$. Here we note that the
two hosts are not connected to the same link, and thus their communication will
involve one or more routers. In this example, the IP Source Address is 1.0.0.1 and
the IP Destination Address is 2.0.0.3. The steps involved are as follows:

1. As before, $Host_1$ recognizes this packet as being destined for some other
   node than itself and begins searching for a routing-table entry which
   matches the IP Destination Address. Since there are no matching host-specific
   or network-prefix routes, $Host_1$ searches for a default routing entry, which
   it finds. The default routing entry informs $Host_1$ to forward the packet to a
   Next Hop of Router A (1.0.0.254) on the link to which it attaches via
   interface "a." Thus, $Host_1$ forwards the packet to Router A.

2. When Router A receives the packet, it also sees that it is not the ultimate
   destination of the IP packet (because the IP Destination Address, 2.0.0.3 does
   not equal 1.0.0.254 nor does it equal 3.0.0.254). Thus Router A must make a
   forwarding decision and begins searching its routing table for a matching
   entry. Router A's IP routing table—not shown in the figure—has an entry
   which specifies that all Targets with network-prefix equal to 3.0.0 should be
   sent via interface "c" to a Next Hop address of Router B (3.0.0.253). So,
   Router A forwards the packet to Router B over the Fiber Backbone. (As an
   exercise, try to figure out what entries are needed in Router A's IP routing
   table. The answers are given in the footnote on the next page.[†])

3. When Router B receives the packet, it also sees that it is not the ultimate
   destination of the IP packet. Router B therefore consults its routing table

and finds a matching network-prefix route in the second row. This entry specifies that all IP destinations whose network-prefix is 2.0.0 should be delivered "directly" to their ultimate destination via interface "b." So, Router B transmits the packet via Ethernet B to Host$_3$.

2.3.4 IP Routing Summary

This section and the examples illustrate the important aspects of IP routing which can be summarized as follows:

- Each node makes its forwarding decision based *only* upon the Destination Address within the IP packet header. The Source Address is only examined when an error occurs, such as when a node is unable to forward a packet because no route is available to the destination.

- Routing decisions are typically based upon the network-prefix of the IP Destination Address, rather than the entire address. We will see *why* IP was designed this way in *Why is Routing Based on Network-Prefix?* on page 29. For now, it is only important to note that this is the case.

- Every node on the same link *must* have an identical network-prefix. The host portion of the IP address is used to differentiate among individual hosts on the same link.

This last point allows routing-table entries to be greatly simplified. Specifically, it allows the use of a single network-prefix route instead of as many host-specific routes as there are nodes on an individual link. For networks with hundreds of nodes on each of hundreds of links, the savings in routing table entries is quite dramatic by using network-prefix routes instead of host-specific routes.

2.4 How Are Routing-Table Entries Created?

Fundamentally, there are three ways in which a node's routing table can be populated with entries:

1. Statically, by manual configuration by a human;

2. Dynamically, through receipt of *ICMP Redirects*; or

3. Dynamically, by the automatic exchanging of routing information in the form of *routing protocols*.

We describe each of these methods briefly in the next three sections.

[†] The routing entries in Router A are: {**1.0.0**.0/24, "direct", a}, {**2.0.0**.0/24, 3.0.0.253, c}, and {**3.0.0**.0/24, "direct", c}.

Statically Configured Routing Entries

The routing tables of many hosts are configured manually by their primary user or by a network administrator. Usually this configuration results in two types of routes: network-prefix routes for all neighboring destinations (those connected to an attached link) and a default route for all other destinations. Hosts that are manually configured in this way can still listen for *ICMP Redirects* and participate in dynamic routing protocols to learn additional routes. These two dynamic mechanisms are described below.

Routers can also be configured manually with routing-table entries. However, such manual configuration becomes nearly impossible to manage when a network grows above a few tens or hundreds of links. On the other hand, some dynamic routing protocols can scale to accommodate networks with thousands of links and rapidly changing *topology*. We use the word topology to refer to the architecture, or layout, of network links and nodes, particularly the interconnection between hosts and routers.

ICMP Redirects

If a router determines that a neighboring host (i.e., a host on the same link) is using a non-optimal Next Hop to reach a destination, then the router can tell the host to use a different router as a Next Hop to that destination. The router does this by sending an *ICMP Redirect* message to the host. The redirect message contains the IP address of this "different router." Upon receipt of this message, the host modifies its routing table to contain an appropriate Next Hop for that destination.

The redirect message is defined such that it may be sent only when the router, source host, and "different router" are all neighbors. Furthermore, routers may send ICMP messages only to the original source of a packet—not to intermediate routers. Thus, *ICMP Redirects* do not provide a general mechanism that can be used by routers to dynamically learn paths to all of the destinations in a network. Such a mechanism is described in the next section.

Dynamic Routing Protocols

Dynamic routing protocols are considered to be part of the network layer, though they use IP—either directly or indirectly—to carry information between routers. A few common routing protocols, and their relationship to IP in the protocol stack, are shown in Figure 2-8. These include *Open Shortest Path First*

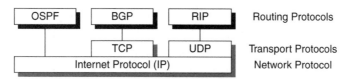

Figure 2-8 IP Routing Protocols

(OSPF) [RFC 1583], the *Border Gateway Protocol (BGP)* [RFC 1771], and the *Routing Information Protocol (RIP)* [RFC 1058] and [RFC 1723].

The specifics of how these protocols accomplish their function, and why some of them use IP directly and others use UDP or TCP, is beyond the scope of this book. Those with an interest in this topic should read the RFCs referenced above or one of several books listed in the chapter summary. However, for completeness, we very briefly describe the mechanics of dynamic routing protocols:

1. Someone, usually a network administrator, lays out a plan for a network by assigning IP network-prefixes to the various links.

2. Using this network-prefix plan, the routers in the network are manually configured with IP addresses on each of their respective interfaces. They are also configured with the prefix-length of each of the links to which they directly attach.

3. Routers discover who their neighboring routers are, either by manual configuration or by the methods specified by the routing protocol itself. A neighboring router is one that can be reached by sending a packet across exactly one link. (For example, all of the routers shown in Figure 2-2 and Figure 2-7 are respectively neighbors of each other.)

4. Routers periodically exchange information, in the form of *routing updates*, which consist of a list of routing entries. The entries contain: destination addresses, their associated prefix-lengths, and some measure of the distance to those destinations (e.g., number of network hops).

5. Routers place entries in their routing tables based upon the information gathered in each of the routing updates. In this way, the routers dynamically learn routes to the various destinations in the network.

It is important to note that IP in the presence of dynamic routing protocols is extremely robust. This is because most routing protocols allow routers to maintain multiple routes to the same destination. If one or more routers or links experience a temporary outage, IP can "route around the problem" and can generally do so very quickly. In fact, nodes and links fail quite regularly in the Internet, yet information continues to flow and much of the time the users are unaware that the failure has occurred.

Advertising Reachability

Finally, we note some terminology that will be used throughout this book. When a first router sends a routing update to a second router claiming that the first router is capable of reaching one or more destination addresses, we say that this first router is *advertising reachability* to these addresses.

For example, if a network administrator were to enable dynamic routing in Figure 2-7, then Router A would begin advertising reachability to network-prefixes 1.0.0 and 3.0.0, while Router B would begin advertising reachability to network-prefixes 2.0.0 and 3.0.0. Soon, Router A would learn that Router B is the best route to network-prefix 2.0.0, and Router B would learn that Router A is the best route to network-prefix 1.0.0.

2.5 Why is Routing Based on Network-Prefix?

In *How Does IP Routing Work?* on page 20, we learned that network-prefix routes can greatly simplify a node's IP routing table. The alternative to network prefix-based routing is host-specific routing. In host-specific routing, each node has a routing-table entry for each and every other host and router in the network. In the simple network we examined in *Routing Examples* on page 24, this would not be a problem. However, in the Internet, which contains hundreds of millions of hosts and routers, host-specific routing would clearly be unworkable. The reasons are primarily as follows:

1. Routers would need enough memory to hold tens of millions of routing-table entries. These tens of millions of entries would have to be searched for every packet that the routers are asked to forward. This would mean that routers would be spending most of their computing resources looking up routes and very little of their resources actually routing traffic.

2. As discussed in *How Are Routing-Table Entries Created?* on page 26, the routing updates exchanged between neighboring routers would need to contain **billions** of bytes in order to include information about every host and router in the Internet. If this were the case, then much of the Internet's link capacity would be consumed by routing updates, which would leave very little link capacity to move actual data traffic.

Thus, scalability is the main reason that IP routing is based upon network-prefixes. The maximum number of network-prefixes in the Internet is still a very large number (approximately 2 million, in IPv4), but this is much less than the maximum number of hosts (approximately 4 billion, in IPv4). While many people are aware of the Internet's alleged problem of running out of available IP addresses, few are aware of the more serious problem of "routing-table explosion," in which the memory capacity of current routers is being stretched to the limit. This is in part due to the phenomenal growth the Internet has experienced over the last decade. Imagine how chronic this problem would be without network prefix-based routing!

The preceding discussion is not meant to imply that host-specific routes are *never* used in Internet routing. Rather, the purpose is to show how important network-specific routing is to the scalability and health of the Internet, and how host-specific routes should be used sparingly and only under special circumstances.

2.6 How Can We Translate Names into Addresses?

IP addresses are 32-bit integers which are very easily manipulated by computers but they can be very hard for humans to work with. In the same way that it is easier to remember a friend's name than to remember his or her mailing address, humans prefer dealing with names of network devices rather than IP addresses.

In the Internet, the Domain Name System (DNS) is used to translate *hostnames* into IP addresses. For example, when you ask your favorite Web browser to fetch a document from, say, `http://www.lp.org/`, the first thing it must do is figure out the IP address of the computer whose hostname is `www.lp.org`. To do this, your computer sends a query to a name server, which returns the IP address of the desired host. Obviously, your computer must know the IP address of the name server itself before it can send such a query.

Generally, hosts obtain the IP address of their name server in the same way they obtain their own IP address. A common mechanism for this is manual configuration. In addition, *PPP IPCP Extensions for Name Server Addresses* [RFC 1877] and the *Dynamic Host Configuration Protocol (DHCP)* provide automated procedures by which a node can determine the IP address of a name server.

Today, most name servers are configured manually with their list of mappings between hostnames and IP addresses. There are currently no mechanisms widely deployed to automatically and securely update a name server, for example, when a host changes its IP address. However, the Internet Engineering Task Force is in the process of addressing this problem (see [RFC 2136] and [RFC 2065] for more information).

The Domain Name System is quite complicated and is also quite beyond the scope of this book. The important thing to remember is that the Domain Name System maps hostnames into IP addresses, and that the mapping between a given hostname and IP address is not expected to change very often. See [RFC 1034] and [RFC 1035] et seq. for the protocol specifications or [Come95] for a more accessible treatment of the Domain Name System.

2.7 How Can We Determine Link-Layer Addresses?

When a node has an IP packet to send to another node, it uses its IP routing table to determine the IP address of the Next Hop along the path to the ultimate destination. We have not yet said how the sending node determines the *link-layer address* of this Next Hop in order to transmit the IP packet within a link-layer frame. This section briefly describes this process.

2.7.1 What Is the Address Resolution Protocol?

The process of determining which link-layer address corresponds to a given IP address is called *address resolution*. The most common method for accomplishing this in the Internet is called the *Address Resolution Protocol (ARP)* [RFC 826]. ARP defines the *target* as the node whose link-layer address is sought and the *sender* as the node which seeks this information. Briefly, ARP works as follows.

1. The sender broadcasts an *ARP Request* message on the appropriate link. The Target IP Address field within this message contains the IP address of the node whose link-layer address is sought.

2. Each node receiving the *ARP Request* compares the Target IP Address field with its own IP addresses. If the Target IP Address equals one of the node's own IP addresses, then the node sends an *ARP Reply* message to the original sender, specifying the node's link-layer address.

Rather than repeat this process for every packet that a node sends, nodes store some number of IP-address / link-layer-address mappings in a data structure called an ARP cache. After some period of time the mappings are deleted, and the node must again go through the process of ARPing for a target. Deleting an old entry from an ARP cache is referred to as "aging" the ARP cache.

2.7.2 What Are Gratuitous and Proxy ARP?

In the previous section we saw how a node sends an *ARP Reply* upon receiving an *ARP Request* seeking its link-layer address. However, sometimes it is useful to have some designated node answer an *ARP Request* on behalf of another node that is currently or permanently unable to send *ARP Replies* itself. An example is when a mobile computer moves to a new link and can no longer receive *ARP Requests* sent by nodes on the previous link. Such an *ARP Reply* is called a *proxy ARP*, and the node sending it is said to be *proxy ARPing* for the other node.

Similarly, it is sometimes useful for a node to send an *ARP Reply* that is not prompted by any corresponding *ARP Request*. An example is when a new Ethernet network interface card is installed in a host, wherein the Ethernet (link-layer) address of this new card is different than the old one. Such a host might send several *ARP Replies* upon being powered on in order to inform other nodes on the link that the current mapping in their ARP cache needs to be modified to reflect the host's new link-layer address. Such an unsolicited *ARP Reply* is called a *gratuitous ARP*.

Proxy ARP and gratuitous ARP are essential to the proper operation of Mobile IP, as we will see in *How Are Packets Routed to and from Mobile Nodes?* on page 89.

2.8 Chapter Summary

This chapter showed how computer communications consists of a number of protocol layers, each of which relies on the services offered by the layer below it, to perform an increasingly more complicated set of functions. Specifically, we examined the OSI reference model which divides such communications into 7 layers. Of interest to this book is the network layer, layer 3, which maps to the Internet Protocol (IP) layer in the Internet's model of communications, known as the TCP/IP suite of protocols.

Next we examined the network layer in detail, seeing how it is responsible for moving a packet all the way from its original source to its ultimate destination, by picking a suitable path through an arbitrary topology of routers and links. We saw how Internet routing is based upon the network-prefix portion of a packet's IP Destination Address, which greatly improves the scalability of the Internet. Then we saw how all hosts connected to the same link must share a common network-prefix in their respective IP addresses. For more information on IP routing, see [Come95], [Stev94], or [Perl92].

We also saw how the Domain Name System in the Internet translates hostnames, which are easy for humans to work with, into IP addresses, which are needed by computers in order to send packets to each other. Finally, we saw how the Address Resolution Protocol can be used to determine a node's link-layer address when that node's IP address is known.

The Need for Mobile IP

*T*his chapter shows why a technology such as Mobile IP is required in the current Internet and what problems Mobile IP was designed to solve. We begin by showing why current Internet routing is incapable of delivering IP packets to computers that change their location, and why the existing solutions to this problem are unworkable in practice. Then we show some attractive properties of Mobile IP which make it desirable even in those circumstances where it is not absolutely required.

This chapter requires a basic understanding of computer networking in general, and IP routing in particular. It is strongly recommended that those without a strong background in these concepts read *Chapter 2, Computer Networking Tutorial*, before proceeding. As mentioned previously, the focus of this chapter and most of this book is on mobility for IP version 4, except for *Chapter 12, Mobility for IP Version 6*, where we discuss IPv6 mobility.

3.1 What Happens When a Node Changes Link?

As discussed in *Chapter 2, Computer Networking Tutorial*, IP nodes—hosts and routers—base their packet-forwarding decisions on information contained within the IP packet header. Specifically, routing decisions are made based upon the network-prefix portion of the IP Destination Address. This implies that all nodes

with interfaces on a given link must have identical network-prefix portions of
their IP addresses on those interfaces.

To see why this is the case, let's examine what happens if a host whose network-prefix has been assigned to one link, disconnects from that link and then
connects to a new link which has been assigned a different network-prefix. Such
a situation is shown in Figure 3-1.

In Figure 3-1, Host$_4$'s IP address has a network-prefix of 2.0.0, but Host$_4$ is
shown connected to a link whose network-prefix is 4.0.0. Also shown in the figure
are the entries in Router A's IP routing table. (We continue our practice of put-
ting the part of the Target which constitutes a "match" in **boldface type**.) The
first two entries in Router A's table are for the links to which Router A directly
connects. The last two entries are routes to network-prefixes 2.0.0 (via Router B)
and 4.0.0 (via Router C).

Following the procedure we described in *How Does IP Routing Work?* on
page 20, let's examine what happens when Host$_1$ tries to send a packet to Host$_4$:

1. Host$_1$ generates an IP packet in which the IP Source Address is 1.0.0.1 and
   the IP Destination Address is 2.0.0.4. The only match in Host$_1$'s routing table
   for this destination is a default route, which specifies a Next Hop of Router A
   (1.0.0.254) via Interface "a." Thus, Host$_1$ forwards the packet to Router A.

2. Router A finds an entry for Targets with network-prefix 2.0.0 in the third
   row of its routing table, which specifies a Next Hop of Router B (3.0.0.253)
   via Interface "c." Thus, Router A forwards the packet to Router B.

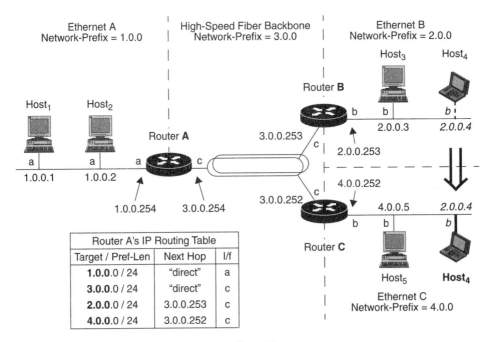

Figure 3-1 Host Movement

3. Router B has a "direct" route in its routing table for Targets with network-prefix equal to 2.0.0, so Router B transmits the packet via Interface "b" on Ethernet B. *However, the packet is undeliverable, because Host$_4$ is not connected to Ethernet B (where it is "supposed to be," based upon its network-prefix).* Router B will then send an *ICMP Host Unreachable* error message back to the source of the packet (Host$_1$).

In this example, we assumed that the routing-table entries of the various routers were populated by some sort of dynamic routing protocol (see *How Are Routing-Table Entries Created?* on page 26), and that Router B would necessarily be advertising reachability to the network-prefix 2.0.0. Notice how the packet was routed toward Router B in this example, precisely because Router B was advertising reachability to the network-prefix of Host$_4$'s IP address.

This turns out to be an important rule of IP routing: IP packets destined to a specific address will be routed toward the router(s) which advertise reachability to the network-prefix of that address.

Furthermore, if a node is not located on the link where its network-prefix says it's supposed to be located, then packets sent to that node will be undeliverable. Obviously, this means that such a node is incapable of communicating with any other nodes! As a corollary, a node may not move from one link to another if it wishes to communicate—without minimally changing the network-prefix portion of its IP address to reflect its new point-of-attachment to the network.

3.2 Can't You Solve This Problem with Host-Specific Routes?

In this section we examine host-specific routing as a possible solution to node movement and assess the practical implications of such a solution from the standpoint of scalability, robustness, and security.

3.2.1 How Might Host-Routes Solve the Problem?

Recall from *What If There Is More Than One Matching Entry?* on page 22 that a node must use the matching routing-table entry with the largest Prefix-Length when forwarding an IP packet. Equivalently stated, the node must use a matching host-specific route in preference to a matching network-prefix route, and should use a default route only if it has no matching host-specific or network-prefix routes.

Thus, the problem of delivering a packet to Host$_4$ in Figure 3-1 can be solved by placing host-specific routes in the routing tables of Router A, Router B, and Router C. As an exercise, stop reading and take a moment to figure out what these entries would look like. Done? Ok, here are the answers:

Router A: {Target / Prefix-Length = **2.0.0.4** / 32, Next Hop = 3.0.0.252, Interface = "c"};
Router B: {Target / Prefix-Length = **2.0.0.4** / 32, Next Hop = 3.0.0.252, Interface = "c"};
Router C: {Target / Prefix-Length = **2.0.0.4** / 32, Next Hop = "direct", Interface = "b"}.

In this way, the packet from Host$_2$ destined for Host$_4$ will be forwarded by Router A to Router C, which will then transmit the packet on Ethernet C, where it will be received by Host$_4$.

Before proceeding, and before my fingers and your eyes begin to ache, we need to introduce some new terminology. In an attempt to be consistent with Mobile IP terminology, we define the following:

A *home link* is the link on which a specific node *should* be located; that is, the link which has been assigned the same network-prefix as the node's IP address.

A *foreign link* is any link other than a node's home link—that is, any link whose network-prefix differs from that of the node's IP address.

Thus, the principles of IP routing we've discussed in previous sections can be written as follows: In the absence of host-specific routes, a node can receive packets only when it is connected to its home link. Similarly, a node connected to a foreign link—any link other than its home link—is incapable of communicating in the absence of host-specific routes.

3.2.2 Is This Solution a Good One?

It's time for some more terminology. We define *mobility* as the ability of a node to change its point-of-attachment from one link to another while maintaining all existing communications and using the same IP address at its new link. Furthermore, we define a *mobile node* as a node which is capable of mobility (i.e., a node which can change its point-of-attachment from one link to another while maintaining all existing communications and using the same IP address at its new link). Remote printing, remote login, and file transfers are some examples of applications whose communications are undesirable to interrupt when a mobile node moves from one link to another.

In *Why is Routing Based on Network-Prefix?* on page 29, we saw how host-specific routing is an unworkable solution for Internet routing *in general*. In the current section, however, we wish to determine whether or not host-specific routing is a reasonable solution for *mobility* in the Internet. Thus, we wish to determine whether host-specific routes employed *only* for "those mobile nodes not connected to their home links" is a reasonable solution in the context of the global Internet.

To make this determination, we need to get a handle on the number of host-specific routes that would be required to enable node mobility on the Internet. As we shall see, this number depends on the following:

1. the total number of mobile nodes we expect to see on the Internet;
2. the minimal number of nodes to which host-specific routes must be propagated on behalf of each mobile node;

3. the speed at which mobile nodes move from one link to another, and the number of host-specific routes which must be added, deleted, or modified each time a mobile node changes link.

In addition, we must determine whether the robustness of Internet routing, as described in *How Are Routing-Table Entries Created?* on page 26, would be somehow diminished with host-specific routing. Finally, as always, we must consider the security implications of this solution. In the next few sections we will attempt to provide qualitative measures for each of these quantities.

How Many Mobile Nodes?

With the dramatic increase in memory and CPU performance of notebook computers, along with the dramatic decrease in their size, weight, and power consumption, we expect highly mobile computers to become very prevalent in the future of the Internet. It is not unreasonable to expect that mobile nodes will number in the millions by the turn of the century. Thus, a workable solution for node mobility in the Internet is one which accommodates, at minimum, millions of mobile nodes.

How Many Routes Are Required for Each Mobile Node?

As a first step in approximating this number, let us take a look at Figure 3-2, which shows a node (Host$_2$) connected to a foreign link. The two sets of arrows depict the path that packets destined to Host$_2$ would take under the following two circumstances:

- A solid arrow shows the direction that a node would forward a packet if that node contained only a network-prefix route to Host$_2$'s *home link*.

- A dashed arrow shows the direction that a node *must* forward a packet in order to reach Host$_2$ at the *foreign link*.

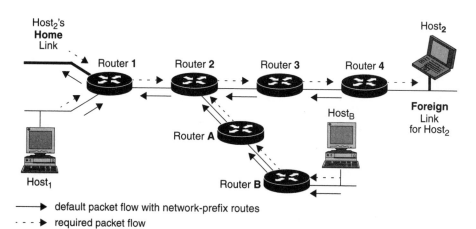

Figure 3-2 Routing Packets to a Mobile Node on a Foreign Link

Any node whose solid and dashed arrows point in different directions must be provided with a host-specific route to $Host_2$. In the figure, this includes: all hosts and routers on $Host_2$'s home link, Router 1, Router 2, Router 3, and Router 4. Note that Router A and Router B do not require host-specific routes.

Working through a few examples like this, we will soon see that, *at minimum,* all nodes along the path from a node's home link to its current foreign link must be provided with host-specific routes. In the global Internet, this could easily amount to hundreds of nodes, depending upon how far the foreign link is from the home link. Thus, each mobile node could result in the need to propagate hundreds of host-specific routes to other nodes in the Internet.

How Fast Will a Node Change Links?

Here we wish to determine how fast a mobile node can change its link and also the impact of each such change as measured by the number of host-specific routes which must be added, deleted, or modified. To get a handle on the latter, let's see what happens when $Host_2$, in Figure 3-2, moves to the link on which $Host_B$ is connected to Router B. In this case the following routing updates must be sent:

1. Router 3's host-specific route must be deleted;
2. Router 4's host-specific route must be deleted;
3. Router 2's existing host-specific route must be modified to have a new Next Hop of Router A;
4. Router A must be given a new host-specific route which points to Router B;
5. Router B must be given a new host-specific route which points to the new link.

In order to turn this example into a rule that can be applied in general, we need to define a new term. Of the nodes along the path from a mobile node's home link to *both* its old foreign link *and* its new foreign link, the one which is furthest from the home link is called the *branch point*. For example, Router 2 would be the branch point for $Host_2$ as it moved in Figure 3-2 from being a neighbor of Router 4 to being a neighbor of Router B.

As a general rule, then, the host-specific routes in nodes from the branch point to the old link must be deleted; new host-specific routes must be added from the branch point to the new link; and the host-specific route in the branch point itself must be modified to point toward the new link. In order to make this happen, suitable routing updates must be propagated to all of these nodes.

If mobile nodes change their points-of-attachment rapidly, as we would expect in the case of wireless links, then a good solution for Internet mobility is one which does not require a substantial number of routing updates each time mobile nodes change links.

Is This Solution Robust?

Furthermore, we note that if host-specific routes are propagated only to the minimal set of nodes (i.e., the routers along the path from the home link to the foreign link), then every single one of these routers and the links between them become single points-of-failure for sending packets to mobile nodes. That is, the Internet Protocol's ability to detect and route-around network failures is negated by using a minimal set of host-specific routes to accomplish node mobility. Any attempt to alleviate this problem necessarily involves propagating host-specific routes to a larger set of nodes than those along the path from the home link to the foreign link.

Is This Solution Secure?

One final observation deals with network security, and verifying the authenticity of routing updates containing the host-specific routes needed to accomplish node mobility. If a Bad Guy were to send routing updates that lied about a Good Guy's location, then that Good Guy would not be able to receive any of its packets.[†] This implies that some type of authentication is needed, which would most likely require enhancing an existing routing protocol. We will have more to say about this security threat in *Mobile Node Denial-of-Service* on page 160, but for now we simply note its existence and mention that Mobile IP is specifically designed to deal with this threat.

Conclusion

In summary, the following points make host-specific routes an unworkable solution to node mobility in the Internet:

- Minimally, host-specific routes must be propagated to all nodes along the path between a mobile node's home link and its foreign link.
- Some (in the worst case all) of these routes must be updated every time the node moves from one link to another.
- We expect millions of mobile nodes to be operating in the Internet within the coming years. Thus, we must multiply the number of host-specific routes suggested by the first two items by a million-or-so in order to determine the full impact of this solution.
- Unless host-specific routes are propagated to a much larger set of routers than the minimal set described in the first item above, then the Internet's ability to route around isolated node and link failures is negated by host-specific routing.
- There are serious security implications to using host-specific routes to accomplish node mobility in the Internet, which would require authentication and complicated key management protocols to address.

[†] A *Bad Guy* is someone performing an attack on a network, a computer, or a user.

Thus, host-specific routing has severe scaling, robustness, and security problems which make it an unacceptable solution to node mobility in the global Internet.

3.3 Why Not Just Change the Node's IP Address?

If host-specific routing is not an acceptable solution to node mobility, then how about simply changing the node's IP address as it moves from link to link? This is the question we set out to answer in this section, but first we briefly describe how this solution could work.

Recall that network-prefix routing requires all nodes on the same link to have the same network-prefix portion of their IP addresses. Thus, when a node moves from one link to another, minimally the network-prefix portion of its IP address must be changed to reflect the network-prefix that has been assigned to the new link. The node might be able to keep the host portion of its IP address, so long as no other node on the new link was using the same host portion; otherwise, the entire IP address would have to change. Once the node modified its IP address as described, it could begin communicating on the new link using its new IP address in all future communications.

3.3.1 Can Connections Survive a Changing IP address?

The two transport-layer protocols in wide use in the Internet are TCP (the Transmission Control Protocol) and UDP (the User Datagram Protocol). Both of these protocols have a nasty habit of using IP addresses as end-point identifiers. This turns out to be a show-stopper for a solution which requires a node's IP address to change, as we shall see.

Both TCP and UDP have the concept of *ports*. A port is a 16-bit (2-byte) integer which allows the receiving TCP and UDP protocol entities to determine which of many possible higher-layer applications is supposed to receive the data portion of any segment that arrives over the network. This allows many applications to be open simultaneously on a node and have the application traffic routed independently to the proper destination(s).

A TCP connection within a node is uniquely identified by the following four values: IP Source Address, IP Destination Address, TCP Source Port, and TCP Destination Port. In fact, the TCP Checksum field in each segment is computed using these four fields in addition to the data in the payload of the segment.

There is an enormous installed base of IPv4 nodes, all of which assume that these four quantities—source/destination address/port—will remain constant over the duration of a TCP connection. This installed base would simply drop its connections to a destination node whose IP address was to change. Thus, all ongoing communications between a mobile node and any of these existing nodes would have to be terminated, with new connections being initiated by the mobile node at its new address. Thus, by definition, changing a mobile node's address as it moves does not solve the problem of node mobility.

However, changing a node's IP address as it moves does solve a related problem, known as *nomadicity*. A nomadic node is one which must terminate all existing communications before changing its point-of-attachment, but then can initiate new connections with a new address once it reaches its new location. It is worth noting that there are existing mechanisms within the Internet suite of protocols to address node nomadicity, such as all of the automatic address-assignment mechanisms discussed in *How Does a Node Obtain an IP Address?* on page 20. These include the *Dynamic Host Configuration Protocol* and the *Point-to-Point Protocol's IP Control Protocol*.

3.3.2 How Do We Find a Node Whose IP Address Keeps Changing?

Nomadicity, as we've defined it in the previous section, not only requires a node to terminate and restart all communications every time the node moves but also suffers from another problem. Namely, there must be a way of "finding" a nomadic node whose address keeps changing. For example, consider the case where a fixed host wants to send an IP packet to a nomadic node. How does the host know what value to place in the IP Destination Address field of the IP packet header in order to send the packet to the nomadic node?

Generally, in the Internet, we assume that the fixed host knows the *hostname* of the nomadic node and that the hostname remains relatively constant. Thus, as mentioned in *How Can We Translate Names into Addresses?* on page 30, the fixed host would look up the nomadic node's hostname in a DNS name server in an effort to determine the node's IP address. There are two new problems, however, that must be dealt with:

1. The nomadic node's "IP address" entry in the Domain Name System must be updated every time the node changes link—i.e., every time the node changes its IP address. Otherwise, other nodes doing an address lookup would receive an old address rather than the nomadic node's current address.

2. A node which looks up a nomadic node's IP address must realize that the address returned from a name server is subject to change at any moment, and in fact might change quite rapidly.

The net result is a large increase in queries and updates to DNS name servers: first in the form of dynamic updates from nomadic nodes moving from link to link, and second in the form of more frequent queries from correspondents which realize that it is not safe to rely on a node's IP address remaining fixed for a significant period of time.

Another problem is related to securing these dynamic updates to the DNS. Once again, consider what happens when a Bad Guy lies to the DNS about the current IP address of a nomadic node—suddenly the nomadic node cannot be located by any potential correspondents. Thus, the authenticity of dynamic updates must be verified before they can be believed by a DNS server. Here we note that no such mechanism has been deployed in today's Internet, though proposals for fixing this problem are currently making their way through the Internet standards process.

In summary, changing a node's IP address does not provide a solution to node mobility, though it can be a useful solution to node nomadicity. Nomadicity, however, makes it next-to-impossible within the current Internet for another node to initiate contact with a nomadic node, because the first node can never be sure at what IP address the nomadic node can be reached.

3.4 Can't You Just Solve This at the Link Layer?

There are indeed link-layer solutions to node movement that have been devised for use with Internet-related protocols. This section briefly describes two of them and shows how they are not sufficiently general to solve the problem of node mobility on the global Internet.

3.4.1 What Are Some Existing Link-Layer Solutions?

In this section we will examine two link-layer mobility solutions which exist and, to some extent, are deployed in the Internet. One is a "wide-area" solution and the other is a "local-area" solution.

What Is CDPD?

CDPD stands for Cellular Digital Packet Data. I have always found "digital packet data" to be a curious choice of words, because it leaves me wondering just what the heck "analog packet data" might be. In any case, CDPD is a standard for sending IP packets over unoccupied radio channels within the analog cellular-telephone systems of North America.

CDPD differs from circuit-switched data in that the latter involves placing a telephone call between a cellular modem and a dial-up access server. The owner of the modem which places such a call is charged for the duration of connection, regardless of whether any actual data is transferred while the call is in progress. In CDPD, however, the radio channel is shared by many CDPD users, who compete for access to the channel only when they have actual data to transfer. (Recall that this is a function of the data link layer, as we saw in *What Does Each Layer Do?* on page 11.) Thus, in CDPD, the billing models tend to be based upon "amount of data transferred" as opposed to "duration of connection."

Obtaining CDPD service involves purchasing a CDPD modem for your computer and signing a service agreement with a CDPD service provider, or carrier. Since the various CDPD carriers are supposed to have roaming agreements in place, in theory you can use CDPD service in any geographic area where there is analog cellular coverage by a carrier that also provides CDPD service. Also in theory, this geographically disperse coverage makes CDPD a "wide-area" mobility solution.

When you sign up for CDPD service, the carrier provides you with an IP address for use throughout the CDPD network. Link-layer protocols—i.e., those below and invisible to IP—are responsible for ensuring that packets can be delivered to the carrier-provided IP address, anywhere within the CDPD network. Although conceptually similar to the Mobile IP approach, it is important to note that CDPD's protocols provide mobility only within the context of the CDPD system itself. This is why we have classified CDPD as a link-layer solution.

CDPD has a maximum speed of roughly 11 kilobits per second (kbps)—the maximum rate that would be seen by an actual user. One potentially attractive property of CDPD is its support for multiple protocols, although very few carriers actually provide service for network-layer protocols other than IP. (We show how Mobile IP can provide multiprotocol mobility in *Support for Other Protocols within the Mobile IP Framework* on page 219.)

CDPD service is not available currently in many markets, making it more of a "some-area" than a "wide-area" mobility solution. Some have criticized the CDPD specifications for requiring a network infrastructure which routes the *Connection-Less Network Protocol (CLNP)* [ISO8473], even when the network provides only IP service to the end-user. CLNP can represent a substantial administrative cost compared to that of running an IP-only network. The CDPD accounting and billing systems have likewise been criticized for their complexity.

Despite its criticisms, CDPD is an interesting technology for providing node mobility in the context of one particular medium. It can be quite useful for some applications in a number of different environments. For more information on CDPD, see [TaWaBa97].

What Is IEEE 802.11?

The Institute of Electrical and Electronics Engineers (IEEE) includes a body which produces protocol standards. One of the technologies they have standardized is for wireless local-area networks (wireless LANs), published in [802.11]. Simply stated, 802.11 is a much faster but a much more geographically constrained solution to node movement than is CDPD, supporting speeds in the 1 to 2 Megabit-per-second (Mbps) range.

802.11 defines a set of wireless transceivers (transmitters/receivers) which provide a bridge between the wireless medium and the wired infrastructure. A wireless network-interface device in a computer communicates with these transceivers as described in the 802.11 specification.

Link-layer protocols make the entire network of 802.11 transceivers appear to be one link as viewed by the network layer. Thus, mobility in 802.11 is invisible to the IP layer, as is the case for CDPD. However, any change of location that results in a node crossing a router boundary requires the node to change its IP address and, therefore, interrupts any ongoing communications. For this reason, many wireless LAN vendors currently support Mobile IP, while others have announced their intention to do so.

3.4.2 Why Aren't Link-Layer Solutions Sufficient?

There are several reasons why link-layer solutions are not sufficiently general to provide node mobility on the global Internet.

First of all, by definition, link-layer solutions provide node mobility only in the context of a single type of medium. For example, CDPD provides mobility when the mobile node moves from one CDPD cell to another. However, CDPD requires a mobile node to acquire a new IP address if the mobile node connects to another medium, such as a wired Ethernet. Thus, link-layer solutions such as CDPD and 802.11 enable only nomadicity between media of different types. (See *Why Not Just Change the Node's IP Address?* on page 40 for the difference between mobility and nomadicity, and why the former is preferable to the latter.)

Another problem with link-layer solutions is that they inherently necessitate N different mobility solutions for each of N possible media over which nodes might want to send IP packets. A single solution which works over all media types is to be preferred over multiple medium-specific solutions, if such a thing is architecturally possible. Mobile IP is such a solution.

Finally, link-layer solutions necessarily provide mobility within a limited geographic area. Local-area solutions such as 802.11 can provide mobility throughout a campus or a building, but are unusable once the node leaves this area. Wide-area solutions such as CDPD can provide much more geographically diverse areas in which coverage is available. However, the limited throughput of such systems makes a node prefer to be connected to another type of medium, if such is available—and CDPD does not provide mobility across different types of media.

Mobile IP, as we will see in *Chapter 4, Mobile IP Overview*, is unique in its ability to provide mobility over all types of media and, therefore, through an arbitrarily large geographic area. Using Mobile IP, a node can communicate using a fixed IP address wherever it can obtain a connection to the network.

3.5 What If I Only Need Nomadicity?

If all communications are initiated by the user of a mobile node, and the user does not mind shutting down his applications and re-starting them at a new location, then nomadicity is indeed sufficient and mobility is not absolutely required. The converse can be stated as follows: if other, fixed nodes must be able to initiate contact with a mobile node or the applications must not be re-started when a mobile node changes links, then mobility is required and nomadicity is not sufficient.

However, there are many reasons why mobility is preferable to nomadicity, even in those situations where it is not absolutely required. A few of these reasons are listed in this section, and most of them involve the virtues of using fixed IP address:

- Many applications have configuration databases which depend on IP addresses, as opposed to hostnames. In the presence of rapidly changing IP addresses, these applications would break.

- There is reason to believe that at some point in the future, servers (and not just clients) would need to become mobile. In this case, clients that know their servers only by their IP addresses will be incapable of locating them unless the servers have the mobility properties provided by Mobile IP.

- Some application vendors provide network-licensing systems which restrict access to only those nodes possessing specific ranges of IP addresses. Without Mobile IP, a nomadic node which changes link (and, necessarily, changes IP address) would no longer be able to obtain a license over the network to use these applications.

- Some security mechanisms provide access-privileges to nodes based upon their IP address. Mobile nodes employing Mobile IP allow such mechanisms to work in the presence of node mobility.

- Maintaining a pool of addresses for assignment to nomadic nodes can be difficult, and in some cases no assignment mechanism might be available. Mobile IP, which lets nodes keep their IP addresses as they move, does not exacerbate the problem of the limited availability of IPv4 addresses.

For these and other reasons, mobility as provided by Mobile IP can be extremely useful, even in those situations where it is not absolutely required.

3.6 Chapter Summary

This chapter began by showing why a node which changes from one link to another is incapable of communicating at the new location unless it changes its IP address to reflect the network-prefix that has been assigned to this new link. Next we showed why host-specific routing, which in some cases can eliminate this problem of IP routing, is not a workable solution in the context of the global Internet, owing to some severe scalability, robustness, and security concerns.

Then we explored why changing a node's IP address as it moves is undesirable, primarily because it forces the node to terminate any ongoing communications at the old link and then restart them at the new link. This led to a discussion of the difference between mobile computing and nomadic computing, and how it can be difficult if not impossible for other nodes to know at what address a nomadic computer can be reached at any given moment.

Next we examined a few link-layer solutions for mobility and found that they all share limitations in their geographic applicability and the media over which they can run. Finally, we showed how even in those instances where a node requires only nomadicity, the more subtle advantages offered by Mobile IP mobility can make network administration and other things much easier.

Thus, Mobile IP solves the following problems:

- if a node moves from one link to another without changing its IP address, it will be unable to receive packets at the new link; and
- if a node changes its IP address when it moves, it will have to terminate and restart any ongoing communications each time it moves.

Unlike host-specific routing and link-layer solutions, Mobile IP solves these problems in a secure, robust, and medium-independent manner whose scaling properties make it applicable throughout the entire Internet.

P A R T   2

MOBILE IP

C H A P T E R   4

Mobile IP Overview

*T*his chapter introduces Mobile IP as a technology that enables node mobility in the Internet. First we specify the problems that Mobile IP was designed to solve and delimit the scope of the solution. Next we examine the requirements and design goals of Mobile IP and then walk through the solution at a high level. Then, in *Chapter 5, Mobile IP: The Gory Details*, we will provide extensive detail on the workings of Mobile IP.

This chapter also introduces the terminology used throughout the rest of the book, so those not familiar with Mobile IP terminology are advised to read this chapter before moving on.

4.1 Is Mobile IP an Official Standard?

Mobile IP was approved by the Internet Engineering Steering Group (IESG) in June 1996 and published as a *Proposed Standard* in November 1996. A Proposed Standard is the first significant step in the evolution of a protocol from an Internet Draft into a full Internet Standard.

Mobile IP was produced by the *IP Routing for Wireless/Mobile Hosts (mobileip)* working group of the Internet Engineering Task Force (IETF), which was formed in June 1992. The Mobile IP standards documents include the following Request For Comments (RFCs):

- RFC 2002, which defines the Mobile IP protocol itself;
- RFCs 2003, 2004, and 1701, which define three respective types of tunneling used in Mobile IP;
- RFC 2005, which describes the applicability of Mobile IP; and
- RFC 2006, which defines the Mobile IP *Management Information Base (MIB)*. The Mobile IP MIB is a collection of variables within a node which implements Mobile IP that can be examined or configured by a manager station using version 2 of the *Simple Network Management Protocol (SNMPv2)* [RFC 1905].

Throughout this book, the term *Mobile IP* will generally refer to all of these documents which together form the standard technology for node mobility in the Internet.

4.2 What Problems Does Mobile IP Solve?

As we saw in *Why is Routing Based on Network-Prefix?* on page 29, the scalability of the global Internet depends upon network-specific routing, as opposed to host-specific routing. This, in turn, requires all nodes connected to the same link to share a common network-prefix portion of their IP address. If a node were to move from one link to another, then the network-prefix of its IP address would no longer equal the network-prefix assigned to its current link. As a result, network-prefix routing would fail to deliver packets to the node's current location.

In *Chapter 3, The Need for Mobile IP*, we showed that the currently available solutions to this problem—host-specific routing and changing the node's IP address—are not acceptable solutions for node mobility in the global Internet. Host-specific routing has severe scalability, robustness, and security concerns. Changing a node's IP address as it moves makes it impossible for the node to maintain any ongoing communications as it changes link.

Mobile IP is thus a solution for mobility on the global Internet which is scalable, robust, secure, and which allows nodes to maintain all ongoing communications while changing links. Specifically, Mobile IP provides a mechanism for routing IP packets to mobile nodes which may be connected to any link while using their permanent IP address.

4.3 What Is the Scope of the Mobile IP Solution?

When a source computer wants to send a packet to a destination computer, the source does not know or care where the destination is located—it just wants its packets to be delivered to the proper recipient. This is the function of the *network layer*, Layer 3 of the Open Systems Interconnection (OSI) Model. The network layer is responsible for dynamically selecting a path from the original source of a packet to its ultimate destination. In the Internet, the network-layer protocol is named, not coincidentally, the *Internet Protocol (IP)*.

IP accomplishes very little by itself. Typically, one or more *routing protocols* are necessary to move packets around a complex network. Routing protocols are used by routers to exchange information about the location of the various destinations and links which comprise the Internet. Examples of routing protocols include *Open Shortest Path First (OSPF)*, the *Routing Information Protocol (RIP)*, and the *Border Gateway Protocol (BGP)*.

Mobile IP is a *network-layer* solution to node mobility in the Internet. By this we mean that Mobile IP accomplishes its task by setting up the routing tables in appropriate nodes, such that IP packets can be sent to mobile nodes not connected to their home link. In fact, Mobile IP can be considered to be a routing protocol which, unlike the examples listed above, has a very specialized purpose. As we will see, the purpose of Mobile IP is to allow IP packets to be routed to mobile nodes which could potentially change their location very rapidly.

4.3.1 Over What Media Types Can Mobile IP Operate?

As a network-layer protocol, Mobile IP is completely independent of the media over which it runs. This is in keeping with the design philosophy behind the Internet Protocol itself, which was designed to be independent of the underlying characteristics of the links over which it runs. As before, we use the term *media* to refer to the physical-layer protocols over which a data link and network-layer protocol are run.

Thus, a mobile node employing Mobile IP can move from one type of medium to another without losing connectivity. For example, Mobile IP allows a notebook computer to disconnect from a wired Ethernet and switch to a wireless LAN interface without experiencing a disruption in network service. We use the term *heterogeneous mobility* to refer to this ability of a mobile node to move between different media types while retaining its ability to communicate.

Of course, Mobile IP also allows a mobile node to move from one network link to another of the same media type (e.g., in a different location) and retain its connectivity. A technology which allows movement among network connections of the same media type is said to provide *homogenous mobility*.

As we saw in *What Are Some Existing Link-Layer Solutions?* on page 42, existing technologies, such as CDPD and IEEE 802.11, provide only homogenous mobility. Both of these allow mobility within their own respective networks but not between networks of differing media. Mobile IP is unique in its ability to accommodate heterogeneous mobility in addition to homogenous mobility.

4.3.2 Is Mobile IP a Complete Mobility Solution?

Mobile IP solves the primary problem of routing IP packets to mobile nodes, which is an enormous first step in providing mobility on the Internet. However, a complete mobility solution would involve enhancements to other layers of the protocol stack as well.

For example, in *How Can TCP Performance Be Improved for Mobile Nodes?* on page 278 we examine a number of changes that could be made to TCP in order to improve the performance of applications in a mobile environment. Also, it would improve throughput and delay performance if there was a standard mechanism which allowed a network-interface card to communicate "up the stack" to provide the applications with the characteristics of the current link. For example, information such as raw bandwidth, signal-to-noise ratio, and congestion indications would allow TCP and applications to behave in a more intelligent fashion when problems occur with the data link.

Thus the scope of the Mobile IP solution is simply the specification of those mechanisms which are necessary to route packets to mobile nodes at the network layer. Other technologies, including modifications to TCP and to applications, are specifically outside the scope of Mobile IP.

4.4 What Are the Requirements for Mobile IP?

The requirements which drove the design of Mobile IP are as follows:

1. A mobile node must be able to communicate with other nodes after changing its link-layer point-of-attachment to the Internet.

2. A mobile node must be able to communicate using only its home (permanent) IP address, regardless of its current link-layer point-of-attachment to the Internet.

3. A mobile node must be able to communicate with other computers that do not implement the Mobile IP mobility functions.

4. A mobile node must not be exposed to any new security threats over and above those to which any fixed node on the Internet is exposed.

Let us look at each of these requirements in detail.

In *What Happens When a Node Changes Link?* on page 33, we showed how network-prefix-based routing mechanisms, such as those employed on the Internet, are incapable of delivering packets to a node which is not connected to its home link. Mobile IP was specifically created to allow nodes to communicate on any link to which they might connect. The first requirement is simply another way of stating this fact.

Also in *Why Not Just Change the Node's IP Address?* on page 40, we mentioned how changing a node's IP address was one way to allow packets to be routed to it as it moves. However, we showed how this would force the node to terminate all on-going communications at the old link and re-start them when it connects to the new link. Also, we noted the difficulty in establishing contact with a node whose address changes as it moves from link-to-link. Thus, the second requirement specifically rules out any solution which calls for changing a node's IP address as it moves.

Further, we noted the fact that in many cases it is desirable that a node's IP address remain fixed for other reasons. Notably, certain network services are based upon IP address, such as software licenses and access privileges. These are some of the additional reasons why it is desirable for a node to retain its IP address regardless of its location.

The next requirement—that Mobile IP require no protocol changes to existing fixed hosts and routers—recognizes that it is horribly naive to assume that the massive installed base of IPv4 hosts and routers can be upgraded to support mobility functions. Thus, it is required that Mobile IP implementation be limited only to the mobile nodes themselves and the few nodes which provide special routing functions on their behalf.

The final requirement recognizes that mobile computing implies new security threats, and that these threats must be addressed by Mobile IP. Specifically, Mobile IP is designed to prevent trivial denial-of-service attacks, which would be possible if there were no authentication of the messages by which a mobile node reports its current location. See *Mobile Node Denial-of-Service* on page 160 for a complete discussion of this topic.

4.5 What Are the Design Goals for Mobile IP?

Mobile computing and wireless communications are a natural match. Notebook computers have liberated computing from the desktop, but the wired networks from which they obtain connectivity still limit when and where they can be used. Some wireless networks allow computers to communicate at any time and at any place. However, many such networks are expensive, slow, or both.

Routing protocols, Mobile IP included, require the transmission of routing updates between the various nodes in the network. In order to make Mobile IP suitable for use over a wide range of wireless links, one of the design goals was to make the size and the frequency of these updates as small as possible.

Another design goal was to make it as simple as possible to implement mobile node software. This increases the number of nodes which can potentially make use of Mobile IP, especially memory and processing-constrained devices such as pagers, smart cellular telephones, and personal organizers, in addition to fully functional notebook computers.

Finally, as mentioned in *Why is Routing Based on Network-Prefix?* on page 29, the perception in the Internet community is that the Internet is running out of available IPv4 addresses. Thus, another goal of Mobile IP was to avoid solutions which require mobile nodes to use multiple addresses, or which require large pools of addresses to be made available for use by mobile nodes, unless absolutely necessary.

4.6 What Assumptions Does Mobile IP Make?

Mobile IP's fundamental assumption is that *unicast* packets—those destined to a single recipient—are routed without regard to their IP Source Address. That is, Mobile IP assumes that unicast packets are routed based only upon the IP Destination Address and typically only the network-prefix portion of that address. In *Denial-of-Service Revisited* on page 209 we will see how this assumption, though theoretically valid, might not necessarily be operationally valid under certain circumstances.

A more subtle assumption made by Mobile IP is somewhat metaphysical in nature. Mobile IP assumes that the Internet (equivalently, a private intranet) "exists," and that it is capable of delivering packets between any pair of nodes in the network. Mobile IP's concern is not with *which* dynamic routing protocols are being employed in the Internet and *how* the Internet's routing architecture scales to accommodate millions of hosts and routers ... only that it *does* use such protocols and that it *can* scale to such a size.

Mobile IP, therefore, assumes that some very smart people in the various working groups of the Routing Area of the Internet Engineering Task Force are capable of solving these routing problems. All Mobile IP requires is an infrastructure of routers and links that is capable of routing packets to any node which is connected to its home link—exactly what the Internet Protocol, by definition, provides. This allows us to abstract a portion of the Internet as a *cloud*, which reminds us that the *presence* of routers and links is important for Mobile IP, but not their specific topology.

4.7 Where Does Mobile IP Reside?

Mobile IP defines three functional entities where its mobility protocols must be implemented (note that all terms in *italic font* will be defined eventually in this chapter and/or the glossary):

1. **Mobile Node**—a *node* which can change its point-of-attachment to the Internet from one *link* to another while maintaining any ongoing communications and using only its (permanent) IP *home address*.

2. **Home Agent**—a *router* with an interface on the mobile node's *home link* which:

   a. the mobile node keeps informed of its current location, as represented by its *care-of address*, as the mobile node moves from link to link;

   b. in some cases, *advertises reachability* to the *network-prefix* of the mobile node's *home address*, thereby attracting IP packets that are destined to the mobile node's *home address;*[†] and

c. intercepts packets destined to the mobile node's *home address* and *tunnels* them to the mobile node's current location; i.e, to the *care-of address*.

3. Foreign Agent—a *router* on a mobile node's *foreign link* which:

a. assists the mobile node in informing its home agent of its current *care-of address*;

b. in some cases, provides a *care-of address* and *de-tunnels* packets for the mobile node that have been *tunneled* by its home agent; and

c. serves as a default *router* for packets generated by the mobile node while connected to this *foreign link*.

Figure 4-1 illustrates these entities and shows their relationships. Those familiar with the Mobile IP specification document [RFC 2002] will notice slightly different terminology being employed in this book—namely, home/foreign *link* instead of home/foreign *network*. The word *link*, in this context, is more descriptive and therefore a better choice than *network,* which is inherently vague.

Before describing how Mobile IP works, we provide brief definitions of the other terminology introduced above. The intention here is to describe the purpose of the various elements and addresses but not to describe how they are assigned. The assignment mechanism will be described in *At a 10,000-Foot Level, How Does Mobile IP Work?* on page 57.

Tunneling

A *tunnel* is the path followed by a first packet while it is encapsulated within the payload portion of a second packet, as seen in Figure 4-2. Also shown

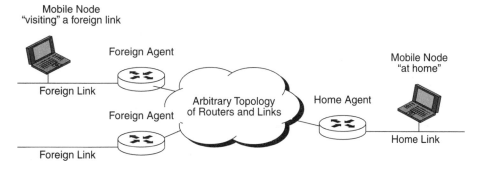

Figure 4-1 Mobile IP Entities and Relationships.

[†] Alternatively, some other router may advertise reachability to the network-prefix of a mobile node's home address.

is an example of the home agent tunneling a packet to a foreign agent in order to deliver the packet to a mobile node. The symbol ⬭ will be used to denote an IP tunnel throughout the figures of this book.

Home Address, Home Link, and Home Agent

A mobile node's *home address* is an IP address assigned to the mobile node "permanently;" i.e., for as long a time as an address would be assigned to any stationary host or router. The home address *does not* change as a mobile node moves from link to link. Rather, a mobile node's home address would change only for the same reasons, and under the same circumstances, as the address of a stationary host or router would change (e.g., if the entire network required renumbering).

The mobile node's home address is closely related to the mobile node's home agent and therefore its home link. Specifically, the network-prefix of the mobile node's home address *defines* its home link. That is, a mobile node's home link is that link which has been assigned the same network-prefix as the network-prefix of the mobile node's home address. A mobile node's home agent is a router that has at least one interface on the mobile node's home link.

With very few exceptions, a mobile node communicates with all other nodes using only its home address. That is, a mobile node's home address is the IP Source Address of all packets sent by the mobile node and the IP Destination Address of all packets sent to the mobile node. This requires a mobile node's home address to be placed in the "IP address" field of its entry in the Domain Name System, such that other nodes looking up the mobile node's hostname will find the mobile node's home address. See *How Can We Translate Names into Addresses?* on page 30 for more information on the Domain Name System.

Finally, we note that a mobile node's home link need not be a physical link composed of some physical medium. Rather, the home link can be a virtual link

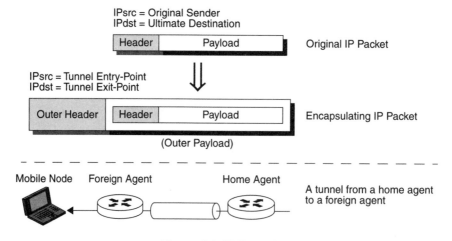

Figure 4-2 IP Tunneling

that exists only as software within the mobile node's home agent. The home agent can be considered to have a virtual interface through which it attaches to this virtual home link. Such a mobile node can never "connect" to its virtual home link and therefore will never be "at home." Instead, the mobile node can physically connect only to foreign links and will always be "away from home."

Care-of Address, Foreign Link, and Foreign Agent

A care-of address is an IP address associated with a mobile node that is visiting a foreign link. Since this is one of those definitions that is completely accurate, but conveys absolutely no useful information, let us try to define a care-of address by examining its properties:

- A care-of address is specific to the foreign link currently being visited by a mobile node.

- A mobile node's care-of address generally changes every time the mobile node moves from one foreign link to another.

- Packets destined to a care-of address can be delivered using existing Internet routing mechanisms; i.e., no Mobile IP-specific procedures are needed in order to deliver packets to a care-of address.

- A care-of address is used as the exit-point of a tunnel from the home agent toward the mobile node.

- A care-of address is almost never used as the IP Source or Destination Address in a mobile node's conversations with other nodes.† Specifically, the care-of address will never be returned by a Domain Name Server when another node looks up the mobile node's hostname.

Once again, we will defer the discussion of how a mobile node acquires a care-of address, and from whom, until we walk through the protocol itself in *At a 10,000-Foot Level, How Does Mobile IP Work?* on page 57.

There are two conceptual types of care-of addresses:

1. A *foreign agent care-of address* is an IP address of a foreign agent which has an interface on the foreign link being visited by a mobile node. A foreign agent care-of address can be any one of the foreign agent's IP addresses, so long as the foreign agent has at least one interface on the foreign link. Thus, the network-prefix of a foreign agent care-of address need not equal the network-prefix that has been assigned to the foreign link. A foreign agent care-of address can be shared by many mobile nodes simultaneously.

2. A *collocated care-of address* is an IP address temporarily assigned to an interface of the mobile node itself. The network-prefix of a collocated care-of address must equal the network-prefix that has been assigned to the for-

---

† The exceptions involve message exchanges which are part of Mobile IP itself, such as those used to obtain a care-of address from a *Dynamic Host Configuration Protocol (DHCP)* server as well as certain *Address Resolution Protocol (ARP)* messages.

eign link being visited by a mobile node. This type of care-of address might be used by a mobile node in situations where no foreign agents are available on a foreign link. A collocated care-of address can be used by only one mobile node at a time.

Summarizing, a care-of address is an IP address that is close to a mobile node's visited, foreign link. By *close* we mean that the care-of address is at most one network "hop" away from the visited foreign link. The care-of address is either an address of a foreign agent with an interface on this foreign link or an address that has been assigned temporarily to an interface of the mobile node itself. The care-of address is used by the home agent to deliver packets to a mobile node while it is visiting a foreign link; specifically, the care-of address is an exit-point of an IP tunnel from the home agent toward the mobile node.

4.7.1 Can Agents Be Hosts or Must They Be Routers?

By definition, a *router* is a network device that implements IP and that forwards packets not explicitly addressed to itself. This is in contrast to a *host,* which sends and receives packets but does not forward packets of which it is neither the original source nor the ultimate destination. By definition, then, home agents and foreign agents *are* routers.

However, one can implement a home agent and a foreign agent on a computer that "looks" more like a conventional host than it does a conventional router. For example, one can implement a home agent on a PC, but once it starts tunneling packets to mobile nodes, it then "becomes" a router, simply by virtue of the fact that it is forwarding packets not explicitly addressed to itself.

Zombie Alert!

The argument as to whether agents are hosts or routers is one of the most frequent zombies to rear its ugly head on the Mobile IP working group's electronic mailing list. A zombie, as in horror movies, is something that keeps living even after it appears to be finished (i.e., dead). This particular zombie has been sleeping pretty quietly since the publication of the IPv6 specification document [RFC 1883] which defined the terms *host* and *router* with a high degree of precision (see the definitions in the previous paragraph). The Mobile IP community owes the IPNGWG working group a tremendous debt of gratitude in this regard!

4.7.2 Who Owns the Mobile Nodes and the Agents?

Generally speaking, there is a close administrative relationship between the owner of a mobile node and the owner of that mobile node's home agent. For example, the same company that provides mobile nodes for its employees, in the form of notebook computers, will also have network administrators responsible for operating the home agents of those mobile nodes. Thus, a mobile node, its home agent, and, therefore, its home link are generally operated by the same administrative entity. (However, we will see examples where the home agent is actually owned by a service provider in *Chapter 10, Applying Mobile IP: A Service-Provider Perspective.*)

In contrast, no such relationship need exist—and in practice often will not exist—between the owner of a mobile node and its home agent on the one hand, and the owner of a foreign agent on the other. In an intranet environment (i.e., within a single corporate or educational institution's network), one would expect the same entity to own and operate mobile nodes, home agents, and foreign agents. However, a foreign agent may be located on any of the individual educational or commercial networks which comprise the global Internet, in which case the foreign agent will be owned by an entity entirely separate from the owner of a mobile node and its home agent.

Summary

In this section we defined the entities which cooperate to provide node mobility on the Internet—the mobile node, the home agent, and the foreign agent—and mentioned that only these three entities are required to implement any of the Mobile IP protocols. We also introduced some terminology which we will need in the next section to understand how Mobile IP works. Namely, we showed how a mobile node has two addresses that are relevant to its mobility— the home address, a permanent address which it uses to communicate with other nodes; and a care-of address, a temporary address used by its home agent to tunnel packets toward the mobile node when it is visiting a foreign link.

4.8 At a 10,000-Foot Level, How Does Mobile IP Work?

The functions, nodes, and protocols of Mobile IP are all interrelated, which makes them hard to describe without an annoying number of forward and backward references. The purpose of this section, therefore, is to illustrate Mobile IP at a very high level. Then in *Chapter 5, Mobile IP: The Gory Details*, we will explore each component in great detail.

So, with no further ado, here is how Mobile IP works:

1. Home agents and foreign agents advertise their presence on any attached links by periodically multicasting or broadcasting special Mobile IP messages called *Agent Advertisements.*

2. Mobile nodes listen to these *Agent Advertisements* and examine their contents to determine whether they are connected to their home link or a foreign link. *While connected to their respective home links, mobile nodes act just like stationary nodes—that is, they make use of no other Mobile IP functionality.* The rest of the steps which follow, therefore, assume that a mobile node has discovered that is connected to a foreign link.

3. A mobile node connected to a foreign link acquires a care-of address. A foreign agent care-of address can be read from one of the fields within the for-

eign agent's *Agent Advertisement*. A collocated care-of address must be acquired by some assignment procedure, such as the *Dynamic Host Configuration Protocol*, the *Point-to-Point Protocol's IP Control Protocol*, or manual configuration.

4. The mobile node *Registers* the care-of address acquired in step 3 with its home agent, using a message-exchange defined by Mobile IP. In the registration procedure, the mobile node asks for service from a foreign agent, if one is present on the link. In order to prevent remote denial-of-service attacks, the registration messages are required to be authenticated. See *Mobile Node Denial-of-Service* on page 160 for a complete discussion of this topic.

5. The home agent or some other router on the home link advertises reachability to the network-prefix of the mobile node's home address, thus attracting packets that are destined to the mobile node's home address. The home agent intercepts these packets, possibly by using proxy ARP (see *What Are Gratuitous and Proxy ARP?* on page 31), and tunnels them to the care-of address that the mobile node registered in step 4.

6. At the care-of address—at either the foreign agent or one of the interfaces of the mobile node itself—the original packet is extracted from the tunnel and then delivered to the mobile node.

7. In the reverse direction, packets sent by the mobile node are routed directly to their destination, without any need for tunneling. The foreign agent serves as a router for all packets generated by a visiting mobile node.

These steps are illustrated in Figure 4-3, which shows the case of a mobile node connected to a foreign link and using a foreign agent care-of address. The case of a mobile node visiting a foreign link and using a collocated care-of address is very similar but introduces some new wrinkles, which are best deferred until *Chapter 5, Mobile IP: The Gory Details*. As stated in step 7 above, all packets generated by the mobile node are sent directly to their destination, with the foreign agent serving as the mobile node's default router.

Mobile IP in Reverse Order

The preceding overview was presented in the chronological order in which events in Mobile IP occur. As an aid to understanding, we will now explore the components of Mobile IP in reverse order, showing the end-result and working backward to determine what must occur in order to reach that result.

First of all, a packet destined to a mobile node's home address cannot be delivered to the mobile node when it is connected to a foreign link, unless all the routers along the path from the home link to the foreign link are given host-specific routes. In the absence of such host-specific routes, some other mechanism is required in order to deliver packets to a mobile node that is visiting a foreign link. Mobile IP uses tunneling as this delivery mechanism.

Thus, Mobile IP requires there be an address which is "near" a visiting mobile node (in a network sense) which can serve as the exit-point of the tunnel.

1. Home agents and foreign agents periodically broadcast *Agent Advertisements* which are received by all nodes on the link.

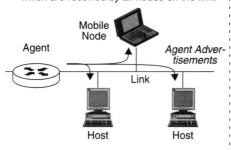

2. Mobile nodes examine *Agent Advertisements* and determine whether they are connected to their home or a foreign link.

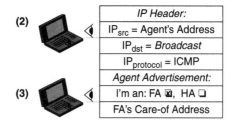

IP Header:
IP_{src} = Agent's Address
IP_{dst} = *Broadcast*
$IP_{protocol}$ = ICMP
Agent Advertisement:
I'm an: FA ☒, HA ☐
FA's Care-of Address

3. Mobile nodes connected to a foreign link obtain a care-of address from the *Agent Advertisement.*

4. Mobile node registers its care-of address with its home agent.

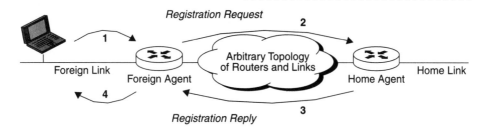

Registration Request

Registration Reply

5a. Home agent or other router advertises reachability to mobile node's home address…

5b. … thus attracting packets destined to the mobile node's home address.

Routing Update:
"I can reach all destinations with network-prefix equal to mobile node's home address."

5c. Home Agent intercepts packets destined to the mobile node's home address and tunnels them to the mobile node's care-of address.

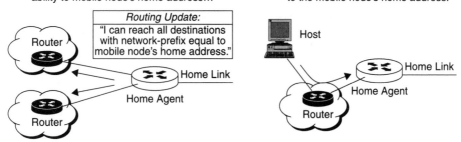

6. Foreign Agent removes original packet from the tunnel and delivers the original packet to the mobile node over the foreign link.

Figure 4-3 Delivering Packets to a Mobile Node on a Foreign Link.

Also, the address of this exit-point should be reachable via existing routing mechanisms. That is, it must not require any Mobile IP-specific functionality to deliver tunneled packets to the exit-point; otherwise a circular dependency results.

The care-of address provides this tunnel exit-point and must be at most one network "hop" away from the mobile node's foreign link. In the case of a foreign agent care-of address, the care-of address is exactly one hop away; in the case of a collocated care-of address, the care-of address is zero hops away (it is collocated with the mobile node itself).

Since every tunnel must have an entry-point in addition to an exit-point, a node must be identified which can serve as this entry-point. A router connected to the mobile node's home link—the home agent—*is* this tunnel entry-point. In order for the home agent to tunnel packets destined to a mobile node, though, the home agent must be able to intercept such packets. To do this, the home agent or some other router on the home link advertises reachability to the network-prefix of the mobile node's home address. In some cases (e.g., when the home agent has only a single interface) the home agent uses proxy ARP to intercept these packets.

With the home agent able to intercept packets destined to the mobile node's home address, the home agent must also know the exit-point of the tunnel. This is the function performed by Mobile IP's authenticated Registration procedure, wherein the mobile node informs its home agent of its current care-of address. First the mobile node must determine that it is connected to a foreign link and second it must acquire a care-of address, before it can register this care-of address with its home agent.

Mobile IP Agent Discovery aids mobile nodes in performing these last two functions. It is accomplished by having both home agents and foreign agents periodically multicast or broadcast Mobile IP *Agent Advertisements*, which mobile nodes can receive and inspect to determine their current link and any agents available on that link.

If the mobile node discovers that it is connected to its home link, it behaves just like any fixed node in that it makes use of no additional Mobile IP functionality. In the case of a foreign link, the mobile node reads a care-of address from one of the fields within a foreign agent's *Agent Advertisement*; registers the care-of address with its home agent; and begins receiving packets from the foreign agent via a tunnel from the home agent to the care-of address.

4.9 Chapter Summary

This chapter showed that Mobile IP is a network-layer solution to mobility and suggested that other mechanisms, outside the scope of Mobile IP, could help to provide a more complete mobility solution in some circumstances. Unlike some other technologies, Mobile IP allows node mobility across media of similar or dissimilar types.

Next we examined the requirements of Mobile IP, the most important of which is enabling a mobile node to communicate using only its home address while changing its point-of-attachment to the Internet. Additionally, we noted the requirement that Mobile IP not require any hardware or software changes to the existing, installed base of IPv4 hosts and routers—other than those nodes specifically involved in the provision of mobility services. We also mentioned that a mobile node must provide strong authentication when it informs its home agent of its current location, to prevent remote denial-of-service attacks of the form described in *Mobile Node Denial-of-Service* on page 160.

Finally, we walked through Mobile IP itself by defining the three entities which cooperate to realize the solution: mobile nodes, foreign agents, and home agents. We saw how mobile nodes that are attached to their home link—a link whose network-prefix equals the network-prefix of the mobile node's home address—work just like any fixed host or router, making use of no additional Mobile IP functionality.

For a mobile node connected to a foreign link, Mobile IP uses tunneling to deliver packets that are destined to the mobile node's home address. The tunnel's purpose is to bury an original packet destined to the mobile node's home address (an unroutable address) within a packet destined to the care-of address (a routable address), in order to get the original packet close to the mobile node. Then, at the care-of address, the original packet is extracted from the tunnel and is delivered to the mobile node.

Tunneling requires a mobile node to report its current care-of address to its home agent, in a procedure called Registration. This necessitates a procedure called Agent Discovery which enables mobile nodes to determine their current location and obtain a care-of address on a foreign link.

Thus, the Mobile IP solution involves three basic functions—Agent Discovery, Registration, and Packet Routing—which we explore in their entirety in the next chapter: *Chapter 5, Mobile IP: The Gory Details.*

Mobile IP: The Gory Details

This chapter describes in detail the three major components of Mobile IP:

- Agent Discovery, the process by which a mobile node determines its current location and obtains a care-of address;
- Registration, the process by which a mobile node requests service from a foreign agent on a foreign link and informs its home agent of its current care-of address; and
- the specific mechanisms by which packets are routed to and from a mobile node that is connected to a foreign link.

The purpose of this chapter is to provide a detailed, conceptual understanding of Mobile IP, but not at a level of detail that would be necessary to write software to implement mobile nodes, home agents, and foreign agents. However, this chapter provides a very sound conceptual framework which greatly aids implementation efforts. As always, the specification documents themselves [RFCs 2002-2006] provide the "official word" on all details with respect to Mobile IP implementation *except* where those specifications are in error and explicitly noted as such in this book.

Although Mobile IP can operate over any data link-layer protocol, the interaction between Mobile IP and the *Point-to-Point Protocol (PPP)* can be confusing. Thus, we defer a discussion of how Mobile IP operates over PPP until *How Do Mobile IP and PPP Interact?* on page 205, where we can cover all of the subtleties in one section. Note, however, that all of the principles in this chapter also apply to Mobile IP-over-PPP.

This chapter assumes basic familiarity with the goals, requirements, and scope of Mobile IP, as well as its components and terminology. Readers not possessing such knowledge are strongly encouraged to read *Chapter 4, Mobile IP Overview*, before proceeding.

Finally, this chapter ignores most of the important administrative considerations for Mobile IP, such as how a mobile node is assigned a home address, how a mobile node knows the address of its home agent, and how the Mobile IP functions are configured and enabled on a mobile node, home agent, and foreign agent. Because they tend to be application-specific, these very important administrative concerns are discussed throughout the chapters of *Part 3, APPLYING MOBILE IP*.

5.1 What Is the Mobile IP Design Philosophy?

Mobile IP was explicitly designed with *extensibility* in mind. Specifically, all of the protocol messages defined by Mobile IP consist of a small, fixed-length portion followed by one or more extensions. The extensions allow virtually any useful information to be carried by the existing protocols. This provides a framework for people to innovate and to provide interesting new applications for Mobile IP that its designers might not have envisioned. An example of this is described in *Mobile IP as a Layer-2, Tunnel-Establishment Protocol* on page 235.

With one exception, the extensions in Mobile IP all have the same format. Namely, they consist of the following three fields:

- a Type field, which, like a name, distinguishes the extension from other extensions of different kinds;
- a Length field, which measures the size of the Data field in bytes; and
- a Data field, which contains the actual information to be sent from the source to the destination.

The Type and the Length simply assist the recipient in interpreting the "meat" of the extension, which is contained in the Data field. This specific format is often called TLD[†] encoding (Type-Length-Data) and is present in many Internet protocols as well as the protocol standards produced by other organizations.

The one exception to the Type-Length-Data format is the One-Byte Padding Extension, which has a Type field but no Length or Data fields. This extension can be appended to a message of odd length to form an even-length message for those operating systems and networking software packages that refuse to transmit a message of odd length.

[†] Some texts use "Value" instead of "Data" for the name of the third field, in which case the acronym is "TLV" instead of "TLD."

5.2 What Is Agent Discovery?

This section describes Agent Discovery, the process by which a mobile node:

- determines whether it is currently connected to its home link or a foreign link;
- detects whether it has moved from one link to another; and
- obtains a care-of address when connected to a foreign link.

The rest of this section describes how mobile nodes, foreign agents, and home agents cooperate to accomplish these functions. We also explore the options available to a mobile node when it connects to a link where the functions described below are not available.

5.2.1 What Messages Comprise Agent Discovery?

Agent Discovery consists of two simple messages. The first, *Agent Advertisements*, are used by agents (home, foreign, or both) to announce their capabilities to mobile nodes. Specifically, *Agent Advertisements* are periodically transmitted as multicasts or broadcasts to each link on which a node is configured to perform as a home agent, foreign agent, or both. This allows a mobile node that is connected to such a link to determine whether any agents are present and, if so, their respective identities (IP addresses) and capabilities.

Messages of the second type, *Agent Solicitations*, are sent by mobile nodes that do not have the patience to wait around for the next periodic transmission of an *Agent Advertisement*. The sole purpose of an *Agent Solicitation*, then, is to force any agents on the link to immediately transmit an *Agent Advertisement*. This is useful in those situations where the frequency at which agents are transmitting is too low for a mobile node that is moving rapidly from link to link.

Because of key management difficulties, the Agent Discovery messages—*Agent Advertisements* and *Agent Solicitations*—are not required by Mobile IP to be authenticated. We have much more to say about the security considerations of Mobile IP and about key management throughout the chapters of *Part 3, APPLYING MOBILE IP*.

Those of us who read far too many Internet RFCs will recognize that *Agent Advertisements* and *Agent Solicitations* are conspicuously reminiscent of *Router Advertisements* and *Router Solicitations*, as defined in *ICMP Router Discovery Messages* [RFC 1256]. In fact, Mobile IP uses these exact message formats and extends them as necessary to accomplish Agent Discovery.

Agent Discovery Message Formats

Agent Solicitations, as defined by Mobile IP, are identical to *ICMP Router Solicitations*, except for one very arcane difference (*Agent Solicitations* must have their IP Time to Live field set to 1). An *Agent Solicitation* is shown in Figure 5-1. There is not much to say about *Agent Solicitations*—when a home agent or a foreign agent receives one, it should immediately respond by transmitting an *Agent Advertisement*. A Type field of 10 distinguishes the *Agent/Router Solicitation* from all other types of ICMP messages.

Similarly, *Agent Advertisements* are formed by appending one or more of the extensions defined by Mobile IP [RFC 2002] to the *ICMP Router Advertisement* message defined in [RFC 1256]. The Mobility Agent Advertisement Extension must be included by agents, as shown in Figure 5-2. The Prefix-Length Extension is optional, as described in *How Does a Mobile Node Determine That It Has Moved?* on page 69. The next few paragraphs highlight the various fields in the *Agent Advertisement*.

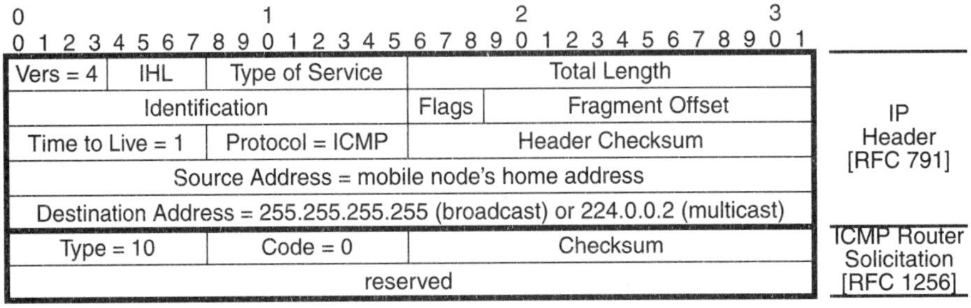

Figure 5-1 Agent Solicitation Message

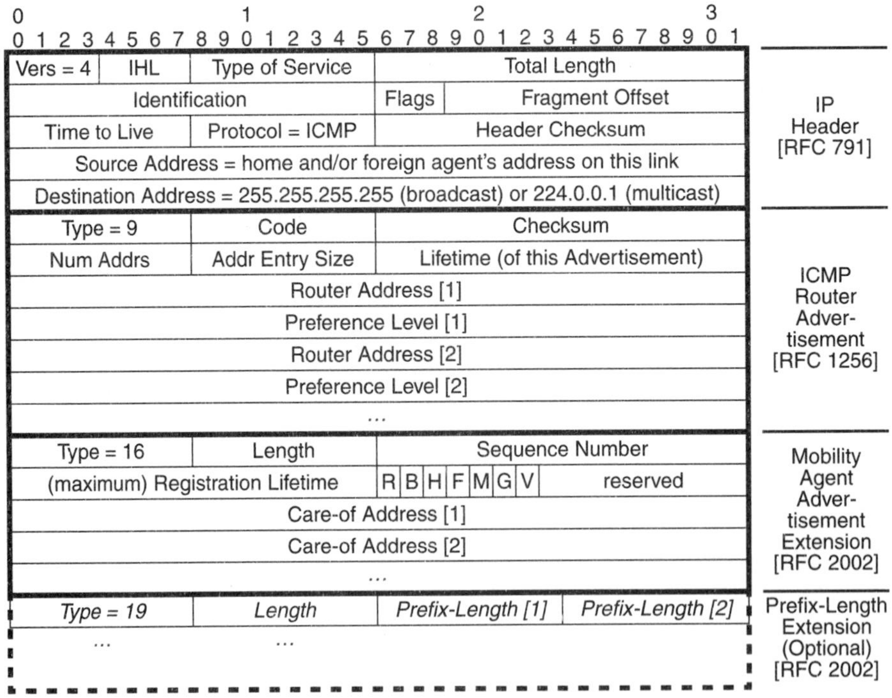

Figure 5-2 Agent Advertisement Message

IP Header Fields

The IP header of an *Agent Advertisement* is used by a mobile node to determine whether it is connected to its home link or a foreign link as follows:

1. If the network-prefix of the IP Source Address equals the network-prefix of the mobile node's home address—specifically, if the IP Source Address equals the address of the mobile node's home agent—then the mobile node is connected to its home link. If the mobile node is returning to its home link (i.e., it was previously connected to a foreign link), then it deregisters with its home agent, as discussed in *What Is Registration?* on page 72. Also, the mobile node might need to broadcast several gratuitous ARPs, as described in *How Does a Home Agent Intercept Packets?* on page 92.

2. Otherwise, the mobile node is not connected to its home link and it should invoke its "move detection" algorithm (see *How Does a Mobile Node Determine That It Has Moved?* on page 69) to determine whether it has moved to a new link since the last time it received an *Agent Advertisement*. If the mobile node determines that it has moved to a new link, then it acquires a new care-of address (as described below in *Mobility Agent Advertisement Extension Fields*) and registers with its home agent, as discussed in *What Is Registration?* on page 72.

ICMP Router Advertisement Fields

A Type field equal to 9 identifies the ICMP message as an advertisement. Implementations of ICMP Router Discovery are supposed to ignore received advertisements whose Code field is anything but 0. Thus, Mobile IP home agents and foreign agents can use a different value for the Code field to prevent any nodes other than mobile nodes from using them as routers. Specifically, home agents and foreign agents use the value 16 for this purpose. Otherwise, they use a Code of 0 to allow all nodes on the link to use them as routers.

The Checksum, as always, is used to check whether the message was received without error. The Lifetime field (which has absolutely nothing to do with the unfortunately named Registration Lifetime field within the Mobility Agent Advertisement Extension) is an indication of how frequently this agent sends advertisements. The Lifetime field is primarily used for "move detection," and thus we defer further discussion of it until *How Does a Mobile Node Determine That It Has Moved?* on page 69.

The Num Addrs field and the Addr Entry Size field tell, respectively, how many Router Address / Preference Level pairs are listed and how many bytes each pair contains. For IP addresses, Addr Entry Size equals 8 (4 bytes for the address plus 4 bytes for the preference). If the IP Total Length field is longer than would be expected, based upon the Num Addrs and Addr Entry Size fields, then the additional portion of the received message is interpreted as extensions. If one such extension is the Mobility Agent Advertisement Extension (described in the next section), then the received message is an *Agent Advertisement*. Otherwise, the received message is an *ICMP Router Advertisement*.

Since all of these fields—Num Addrs, Addr Entry Size, Router Address, and Prefer-ence Level—have more to do with routing than with the process of Agent Discov-ery, we defer further discussion of them until *How Are Packets Routed to and from Mobile Nodes?* on page 89.

Mobility Agent Advertisement Extension Fields

As with all Mobile IP extensions, the Type field identifies the kind of exten-sion. A Type field of 16 identifies the extension as a Mobility Agent Advertisement Extension. As described in *What Is the Mobile IP Design Philosophy?* on page 64, the Length field gives the number of bytes in the Data portion of the extension, not counting the Type and Length fields themselves.

An agent resets the Sequence Number field to zero when it reboots and incre-ments the Sequence Number field in each successive transmission of an *Agent Advertisement*. The Sequence Number field therefore allows a mobile node to deter-mine if its foreign agent has rebooted. If so, a mobile node should assume that the foreign agent no longer knows of its existence, and it should therefore rereg-ister with that foreign agent as described in *What Is Registration?* on page 72.

The Registration Lifetime (not to be confused with the Lifetime field in the *ICMP Router Advertisement* portion of the message) and the R, M, G, and V bits are related to registration and routing, and thus we defer further discussion of these fields until *What Is Registration?* on page 72 and *How Are Packets Routed to and from Mobile Nodes?* on page 89.

The F and H bits identify the sender of the advertisement as a foreign agent, a home agent, or both. Advertisements sent by a foreign agent have the F bit set to 1. Similarly, home agents set the H bit to 1. An agent that is both a home agent (for some mobile nodes) and a foreign agent (for other mobile nodes) sets both the F and the H bits to 1 in its advertisements. The B bit is set by a foreign agent to indicate that it is too busy to accept additional registrations and, therefore, that a mobile node should select a different foreign agent with which to register.

Finally, a mobile node on a foreign link can acquire its care-of address directly from the Care-of Address field(s) of an *Agent Advertisement*. If multiple care-of addresses are listed, then any one of them can be used by a mobile node. If a mobile node selects a care-of address from an *Agent Advertisement* sent by a specific foreign agent, then the mobile node must register via *that* foreign agent, as specified in *What Is Registration?* on page 72.

Prefix-Length Extension Fields

As always, the Type and Length fields specify the kind and the size of an extension, respectively. The Prefix-Lengths contained in the Data portion of the extension are used by a mobile node to perform "move detection," which we describe in the next section.

5.2.2 How Does a Mobile Node Determine That It Has Moved?

There are two ways by which mobile nodes can determine that they have moved from one link to another. In this section we assume that there is at least one agent present on every link to which the mobile node might connect. Then, in *Move Detection without Advertisements* on page 71, we discuss what happens when there are no agents present and, therefore, a mobile node hears no advertisements on its current link.

Move Detection Using Lifetimes

The first method uses the Lifetime field within the *ICMP Router Advertisement* [RFC 1256] portion of an *Agent Advertisement*. This field effectively tells the mobile node how soon it should expect to hear another advertisement from that same agent. Because advertisements can be lost, especially when sent over error-prone, wireless links, home agents and foreign agents send advertisements faster than the Lifetime field requires—approximately three times as fast, as recommended by [RFC 2002].

If a mobile node is registered with a foreign agent, and fails to hear an advertisement from that agent within the specified Lifetime, then the mobile node can assume that it has moved to a different link or that its foreign agent is terribly confused or broken. In either case, the mobile node would be wise to register with the next foreign agent from which it receives an *Agent Advertisement* and to send an *Agent Solicitation* if no such advertisement is forthcoming.

Move Detection Using Network-Prefixes

The second method for move detection uses network-prefixes. Here we assume that the mobile node is registered with a foreign agent on some link and has recorded the *Agent Advertisement* by which it discovered that foreign agent. Now we assume that the mobile node receives an *Agent Advertisement* from a second foreign agent—i.e., one whose advertisements are sent from a different IP Source Address.

Because it is possible to have multiple foreign agents on the same link, the mobile node must determine if it received the two advertisements on the same or different links. If they were received on the same link, then the mobile node need not register with the new foreign agent. Otherwise (the advertisements were received on different links), the mobile node has changed location and should register with a foreign agent on the new link. Registration is described in *What Is Registration?* on page 72.

To determine whether two advertisements were received on the same link, the mobile node computes the network-prefix(es) of the respective advertisements. This computation can be performed only if both *Agent Advertisements* contained the Prefix-Lengths Extension. Those of you who might have allergic reactions to mathematical formulations might wish to skip over the next paragraph, in which we describe exactly *how* the network-prefix(es) can be determined from a received *Agent Advertisement*.

A valid Prefix-Length Extension must contain exactly one Prefix-Length for every Router Address listed in the *ICMP Router Advertisement* portion of the *Agent Advertisement*. Assuming that there are N such Router Addresses, then *Network-Prefix [i]* is determined by the leftmost *Prefix-Length [i]* bits of *Router Address [i]*, for each integer i between 1 and N. That is, *Network-Prefix [1]* equals the leftmost *Prefix-Length [1]* bits of *Router Address [1]*, *Network-Prefix [2]* equals the leftmost *Prefix-Length [2]* bits of *Router Address [2],*and so on. The network-prefix(es) assigned to the link are the various, computed values of *Network-Prefix [i]*.

Using the method described in the previous paragraph, a mobile node computes the network-prefix(es) of the two advertisements and compares them. If they differ, then the mobile node concludes that the two advertisements were received on different links. Otherwise, the mobile node concludes they were received on the same link. In the case of a mobile node comparing a newly received advertisement with that of the foreign agent with which it is currently registered, the mobile node should register with a foreign agent on the new link if it determines that it has moved.

Otherwise, if an advertisement is received from another agent on the same link, the mobile node concludes that it has not moved. In such a case, the mobile node need not register with this new agent—unless, of course, it has not received an advertisement within the specified Lifetime from the foreign agent with which it is currently registered. This implies that the mobile node still employs the first method of move detection—involving Lifetimes—to see if its current foreign agent is no longer available. If it is no longer available, then the mobile node should register with a new foreign agent.

5.2.3 What Does a Mobile Node Do If It Hears *No* Advertisements?

Trying to Communicate on the Home Link

If the mobile node is connected to a link but receives no *Agent Advertisements* (even after sending a number of *Agent Solicitations*), then it can try several things in an effort to communicate. The first thing it can do is assume it is connected to its home link *and* that its home agent is currently dead (otherwise, the home agent would be sending *Agent Advertisements*). In this case, the mobile node simply attempts to communicate as if it were connected to its home link, for example, by sending an *ICMP Echo Request* message to the default router it uses when connected to its home link. If the default router responds, then the mobile node is most likely connected to its home link and can proceed to communicate as specified in *How Are Packets Routed When a Mobile Node Is at Home?* on page 90.

DHCP and Manual Configuration on Foreign Link

Otherwise, if there is no response from the default router, then the mobile node can assume that it is connected to some foreign link. In this case, the mobile node can attempt to obtain an address from a *Dynamic Host Configuration Protocol (DHCP)* [RFC 2131] server. If this is successful, then the mobile node can use this address as a collocated care-of address and register with its home agent, as specified in *What Is Registration?* on page 72.

Otherwise, if there is no response from a DHCP server, then the human using the mobile node can manually configure an IP address for use as a collocated care-of address. Failing this, then the mobile node is basically out of luck and nothing can be done. We note that this final case is not a deficiency of Mobile IP, because a conventional node in a similar situation—neither DHCP server nor manual configuration by a human available—would likewise be unable to communicate.

Move Detection without Advertisements

Assuming that a mobile node is able to obtain a collocated care-of address, the mobile node still must be able to determine when it moves from one agent-less link to another. There are two ways that a mobile node might infer that such movement has occurred. The first is to note whether any forward progress has recently been made in any of its open TCP connections. If not, then the mobile node might conclude that it has moved since the last time it registered.

Also, the mobile node can put its network-interface driver into "promiscuous mode." In this mode, the mobile node examines *all* packets on the link, not just packets destined to itself. If none of the packets flying across the link have network-prefixes that equal the mobile node's current care-of address, then the mobile node might infer that it has moved to a new link from the one on which the care-of address was obtained. If so, the mobile node should acquire a new care-of address and register with its home agent. Of course, the mobile node must also know the prefix-length of the various links in order to determine if the network-prefix of its current care-of address is equal to that of the addresses on its current link.

Note that both of these methods—TCP progress monitoring and promiscuous link examination—require some form of assistance from layers other than the network layer. In this context, "network layer" means IP and ICMP. This is one example in which help from the transport layer and the link layer can provide a more complete solution to mobility than that afforded by the network layer alone.

5.2.4 Summary

In this section we described Agent Discovery, the process by which mobile nodes determine whether they are connected to their home link or a foreign link, and discover the agent(s) that are present on their current link. Specifically, mobile nodes listen for *Agent Advertisements*, which are periodic transmissions sent by home agents and foreign agents. The mobile node can request an advertisement by sending an *Agent Solicitation*. Because of key management difficulties, Agent Discovery messages are not required to be authenticated.

Also, we saw how Agent Discovery provides two mechanisms by which mobile nodes can determine whether or not they have moved since the last time they registered. The first method uses Lifetimes and can be used by a mobile node in all situations. The second method uses network-prefixes and requires agents to include the Prefix-Lengths Extension in their *Agent Advertisements*.

Finally, we saw how Agent Discovery provides a method for mobile nodes on foreign links to acquire a care-of address. To do so, a mobile node simply reads a care-of address directly from an *Agent Advertisement* sent by a foreign agent on the link. If a mobile node connects to a link on which no advertisements are being sent, the mobile node can use transport and link-layer indications to determine its current location, and then acquire a care-of address using DHCP or manual configuration.

5.3 What Is Registration?

This section describes Mobile IP Registration. A mobile node *registers* whenever it detects that its point-of-attachment to the network has changed from one link to another. Also, because these registrations are valid only for a specified Lifetime, a mobile node reregisters when it has not moved but when its existing registration is due to expire. Mobile IP Registration is the process by which a mobile node:

- requests routing services from a foreign agent on a foreign link;
- informs its home agent of its current care-of address;
- renews a registration which is due to expire; and
- deregisters when it returns to its home link.

This section describes all of these processes in detail. Some of the more subtle capabilities of Registration are also described which allow a mobile node to:

- have multiple, simultaneous care-of addresses registered with its home agent, wherein the home agent tunnels a copy of packets destined to the mobile node's home address to each of the multiple care-of addresses;
- deregister a specific care-of address while retaining others; and
- dynamically ascertain the address of a potential home agent, if the mobile node has no prior knowledge of its home agent(s).

Mobile IP Registration follows Mobile IP Agent Discovery as described in *What Is Agent Discovery?* on page 65. When a mobile node detects that it is connected to its home link, it deregisters with its home agent and begins acting like any fixed host or router (i.e., it uses no additional Mobile IP functionality).

When the mobile node detects that it is connected to a foreign link, it acquires a care-of address and registers this care-of address with its home agent, possibly via a foreign agent (if there is one on the foreign link). The rest of this section describes how mobile nodes, foreign agents, and home agents cooperate to accomplish these registration functions.

5.3.1 What Messages Comprise Registration?

Mobile IP Registration consists of the exchange of two messages: a *Registration Request* and a *Registration Reply*. A registration message is carried within the data portion of a *User Datagram Protocol (UDP)* [RFC 768] segment, which is in turn placed within the payload portion of an IP packet. Figure 5-3 shows this protocol relationship. As was the case with Agent Discovery, the Registration messages consist of a short, fixed-length portion followed by one or more variable-length extensions.

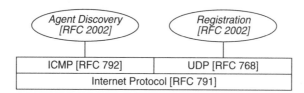

Figure 5-3 UDP as Registration Transport

Registration Scenarios

Before delving into a detailed description of the fields of *Registration Requests* and *Replies*, let us first examine how the messages are used and under what circumstances. A "registration" consists of an exchange of a *Registration Request* and a *Registration Reply* between a mobile node and its home agent, possibly involving a foreign agent as well. The three most common scenarios for registration are as follows:

1. A mobile node registers on a foreign link using a foreign agent's care-of address:

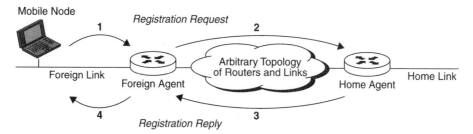

2. A mobile node registers on a foreign link using a collocated care-of address (perhaps because no foreign agent is present on the foreign link):

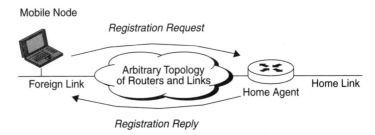

3. A mobile node deregisters upon returning to its home link:

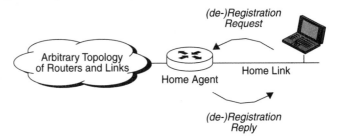

Other, more obscure scenarios are possible but are deferred until *What's the Deal with the 'R' Bit?* on page 88.

Registration Protocol

A *Registration Request* message is sent by a mobile node to begin the registration process. As illustrated above, in some instances the *Registration Request* is sent directly to the mobile node's home agent. In other cases, it is sent via a foreign agent, which examines the *Registration Request* and, if it finds nothing objectionable, relays it to the mobile node's home agent.

The home agent receives the *Registration Request* and sends back to the mobile node a *Registration Reply,* which, among other things, tells the mobile node whether or not its attempted registration was successful. As illustrated above, the *Registration Reply* sent by the home agent takes the reverse path of the *Registration Request* which prompted it.

If a mobile node does not receive a *Registration Reply* within a reasonable period of time (in response to one of its *Registration Requests*), then the mobile node retransmits the *Registration Request* a number of times until it does receive a *Reply.* As per sound protocol design principles, the time between each successive retransmission by the mobile node is required to be longer than the previous time, up to some preconfigured maximum period of time.

Registration Message Formats

Figure 5-4 shows a *Registration Request* message, complete with the IP header, the UDP header, and extensions. Figure 5-5 shows only the fixed-length portion of a *Registration Reply*—the only portion that differs from a *Registration Request*. Each of these registration messages is required to contain the Mobile-Home Authentication Extension, the purpose of which is to prove that the message was actually sent by the node that claims to have sent it. We describe why such proof is important in *How Does a Node Know Who Really Sent a Registration Message?* on page 84.

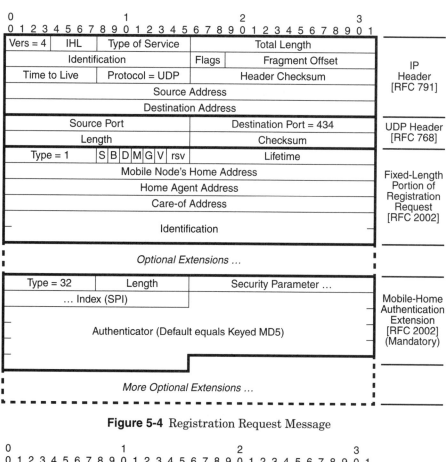

Figure 5-4 Registration Request Message

Figure 5-5 Registration Reply (fixed portion only)

"Bindings"

Before describing the fields in the *Registration Request* and *Reply* messages, it is convenient to introduce some new terminology. Recall that the primary purpose of registration is for a mobile node to inform its home agent of its current care-of address(es)—the address(es) to which the home agent tunnels packets for delivery to the mobile node. The home agent, therefore, must contain a table that maps a mobile node's home address into the mobile node's current care-of address(es). An entry in this table is called a *binding entry,* and, therefore, we say that the primary purpose of registration is to create, modify, or delete a mobile node's binding entry(s) at its home agent. Note that a binding, and thus a registration, is only valid for a specified Lifetime, and that a mobile node must re-register if this lifetime is near expiration.

IP Header Fields

The IP header fields were described in *What Does an IP Packet Look Like?* on page 17. The challenge in filling out these fields in Mobile IP registration is determining what to put in the Source Address and Destination Address fields. We provide plenty of detail on this in *How Do Nodes Process Registrations?* on page 77.

UDP Header Fields

A mobile node selects whatever value it wants for the Source Port field and always sets the Destination Port field to 434, the value reserved for Mobile IP registration messages. Generally, foreign agents and home agents reverse the values of the port fields when sending replies. The UDP Length field provides the size of the UDP Payload (i.e, the Mobile IP fields) measured in bytes, and the Checksum field allows a receiving node to determine if an error occurred in transmission.

Mobile IP Fields

The Type field identifies the message as either a *Registration Request* (1) or a *Registration Reply* (3). The mobile node sets the S bit to 1 in the *Registration Request* to ask that its home agent create or delete a binding for the specified care-of address without affecting any other existing bindings. This feature allows the creation (or deletion) of multiple, simultaneous bindings for the mobile node at its home agent.

The B, D, M, G, and V bits have more to do with routing than with registration per se and are described in detail in *How Are Packets Routed to and from Mobile Nodes?* on page 89. For completeness, though, we mention their purpose here. The B bit is set to 1 by a mobile node to request that the home agent provide it (via a tunnel) a copy of broadcast packets that occur on the home link—normally, a home agent only tunnels packets destined exclusively to the mobile node (such packets are called unicast packets). The D bit informs the home agent which entity is performing decapsulation; i.e., where the exit-point of the tunnel is located. The D bit is set to 1 for a collocated care-of address and is set to 0 for a foreign agent care-of address.

The M and the G bits request that the home agent use *Minimal Encapsulation* [RFC 2004] or *Generic Routing Encapsulation* [RFC 1701] respectively, instead of *IP in IP Encapsulation* [RFC 2003] for tunneling. Finally the V bit is set to 1 if the mobile node and foreign agent can support Van Jacobson Header Compression [RFC 1144] across the foreign link.

The Code field in a *Registration Reply* tells the mobile node whether its attempted registration was accepted or rejected. Some values of the Code field indicate success—i.e., that the registration was accepted by the home agent or the foreign agent. Other values indicate failure—that the registration was rejected by the home agent or the foreign agent—and the reason for the failure. Some example reasons include authentication failures, administrative prohibitions, lifetime too long, and home agent unreachable.

A mobile node sets the Lifetime field in a *Registration Request* to the number of seconds it would *like* its registration (binding entry) to last before it expires. The Lifetime field in the corresponding *Registration Reply* tells the mobile node how long the registration *actually* lasts before it expires—that is, the maximum length of time that was permissible to the home agent or the foreign agent. A Lifetime of zero indicates that the mobile node wishes to deregister (i.e., delete) the specified care-of address whereas a Lifetime of $FFFF_{(hex)}$ indicates that the care-of address should be registered for infinity.

The Mobile Node's Home Address and Home Agent Address fields are pretty self-explanatory, except that there is an interesting use for the Home Agent Address field that is described in *How Can a Mobile Node Learn the Address of a Home Agent?* on page 82. The Care-of Address field is set to the specific care-of address being registered or deregistered by the mobile node. In the special case where the mobile node wishes to deregister *all* care-of addresses in *all* of its current bindings—such as when the mobile node returns to its home link—the Care-Of Address field is set to the mobile node's home address, and the Lifetime is set to 0.

The Identification field—chosen by the mobile node to be unique for each attempted registration—serves two purpose. First, it allows the mobile node to match *Registration Requests* with the corresponding *Replies*, further allowing the mobile node to know which one of many possible outstanding requests has been accepted or rejected. The second purpose is to prevent a Bad Guy from saving a copy of a mobile node's *Registration Request* and replaying it at a later time. The uniqueness of the Identification field, along with the mandatory Mobile-Home Authentication Extension, prevents this from occurring. We have more to say about security in *How Does a Node Know Who Really Sent a Registration Message?* on page 84.

5.3.2 How Do Nodes Process Registrations?

In this section we walk through the processing performed by mobile nodes, foreign agents, and home agents when they receive or generate registration messages.

When Should a Mobile Node Register?

A mobile node always begins the registration process when it detects that it has moved from one link to another. There are other circumstances under which it should register, even if it has not changed links. For example, the mobile node should reregister when it detects that its current foreign agent has rebooted (as determined by the Sequence Number field in its foreign agent's advertisements). Also, the mobile node should reregister when its current registration is due to expire soon.

How Does a Mobile Node Send a Registration Request?

The mobile node uses the information it learned through Agent Discovery to determine which of the "Registration Scenarios" discussed in the previous section applies, and it builds its *Registration Request* accordingly. Table 5-1 shows how a mobile node selects the fields of a *Registration Request* in each of the three common scenarios. The Identification field and the Authentication Extension(s) are discussed in *How Does a Node Know Who Really Sent a Registration Message?* on page 84.

For a mobile node, the trickiest part about registration is figuring out the Link-Layer Destination Address of the frame in which it places the *Registration Request* message for transmission on its current link. On the home link this is easy—the mobile node uses the *Address Resolution Protocol (ARP)* to determine the home agent's link-layer address, and sends the frame accordingly.

On foreign links, however, it is very dangerous for a mobile node to transmit ARP frames that contain its home address. This is because other nodes on the foreign link will get terribly confused if they place the mobile node's home address into their respective ARP tables, especially if these nodes attach to multiple links. Therefore, as a rule, a mobile node must never send an ARP frame containing its home address on a foreign link.

When registering via a foreign agent, then, the mobile node should record the foreign agent's link-layer address from the Link-Layer Source Address field of that foreign agent's *Agent Advertisements*. The mobile node should use this address as the Link-Layer Destination Address of the frame which carries the *Registration Request* message.

Finally, it is assumed that the same method by which a mobile node acquires a collocated care-of address will also provide the mobile node with the IP address of a default router on the foreign link (see *Selecting a Router on a Foreign Link* on page 95 for details). This router will be the "first hop" for the *Registration Request* (and for all other packets generated by the mobile node while the mobile node is connected to this link). In this situation, the mobile node may ARP for its default router's link-layer address, provided that the mobile node's *ARP Request* message contains its care-of address and not its home address.

Once the mobile node figures all of this out, it transmits the *Registration Request* and waits to receive a *Registration Reply*. If it hears no *Reply* within a reasonable period of time, then the mobile node retransmits the *Registration*

Fields	Mobile Node Registering with Foreign Agent Care-of Address	Mobile Node Registering with Collocated Care-of Address	Mobile Node deregistering upon Returning to Home Link
Link-Layer Header:			
Source Address	mobile node's link-layer address		
Destination Address	copied from Agent Advertisement	obtained via ARP using care-of address[a]	obtained via ARP using home address
IP Header:			
Source Address	home address	care-of address	home address
Destination Address	foreign agent	home agent[a]	home agent
UDP Header:			
Source Port	*can be anything*		
Destination Port	434		
Registration Request:			
Type	1		
S bit	1, if this registration should not affect existing bindings; 0, otherwise		0
B bit	1, if mobile node wants a copy of broadcasts on the home link; 0, otherwise		0
D bit	0	1	0
M bit	set according to the mobile node's requirements for tunneling and header compression *and* the foreign agent's support for same	set according to the mobile node's requirements and support for tunneling and header compression	0
G bit			0
V bit			0
rsv	0		
Lifetime	copied from Agent Advertisement	whatever the mobile node wants	0
Mobile Node's Home Address	mobile node's IP home address		
Home Agent's Address	home agent's IP address		
Care-of Address	copied from Agent Advertisement	collocated care-of address obtained via DHCP or manually	mobile node's home address
Identification	chosen in accordance with style of replay-protection used between mobile node and home agent		
Extensions:			
	Mobile-Home Authentication Extension is required.		

Table 5-1 Fields in Registration Request as Set by Mobile Node

[a]If the mobile node is registering with a collocated care-of address via a foreign agent (as described in *What's the Deal with the 'R' Bit?* on page 88, then the Link-layer Destination Address and the IP Destination Address fields are set to the foreign agent addresses as respectively learned from the *Agent Advertisement*.

Request until it does. The next section examines how foreign agents process *Registration Requests* they receive from mobile nodes.

How Does a Foreign Agent Process a Registration Request?

In this section we assume that the mobile node is registering via a foreign agent—otherwise, the *Registration Request* would be sent directly to the mobile node's home agent, bypassing the foreign agent altogether. Upon receipt of a *Registration Request*, the foreign agent applies a sequence of validity checks. If any of them fail, then the foreign agent rejects the registration by sending a *Registration Reply* to the mobile node with a Code field indicating the cause of the rejection. Some reasons that a foreign agent might reject a registration are as follows:

- The mobile node included a Mobile-Foreign Authentication Extension which included an invalid Authenticator field—i.e., the mobile node failed authentication at the foreign agent. (See *How Does a Node Know Who Really Sent a Registration Message?* on page 84.)

- The mobile node requested a Lifetime which exceeds the maximum value permitted by the foreign agent.

- The mobile node requested a type of tunneling that is not supported by the foreign agent.

- The foreign agent has insufficient resources to handle any additional mobile nodes.

If all is well with the mobile node's *Registration Request*, then the foreign agent *relays* it to the mobile node's home agent. Here, *relaying* is distinguished from *forwarding*, the latter being what a router does with a packet (i.e., simply copying the packet from one interface to another, making only very minor modifications to the IP header along the way). In contrast, the foreign agent "consumes" the original IP and UDP headers that contained the *Registration Request* and creates new ones for transmission to the home agent. The new (relayed) UDP/IP packet contains the same payload as did the original packet. The IP Destination Address of the new packet is read from the Home Agent field of the *Registration Request,* and the IP Source Address is the IP address of the foreign agent on the interface over which it will transmit the packet.

Before relaying the *Registration Request*, the foreign agent records certain information that it will need to ultimately send a *Reply* to the mobile node and to route packets on behalf of the mobile node (assuming the registration is successful). Specifically, the foreign agent records the Link-Layer Source Address, IP Source Address, and UDP Source Port, as well as the Home Agent Address, the Identification field and the requested Lifetime. We show how these fields are used in future sections.

How Does a Home Agent Process a Registration Request?

Upon receipt of a *Registration Request*, a home agent performs a set of validity checks not unlike those performed by a foreign agent. If the *Registration Request* is invalid for any reason—most notably, because of an authentication failure—the home agent sends a *Registration Reply* to the mobile node with a suitable Code field indicating the reason for the failure. In such a case, the home agent does not modify the mobile node's binding entry(s) in any way.

If the *Registration Request* is valid, then the home agent updates the mobile node's binding entry(s) according to the specified Care-of Address, Mobile Node's Home Address, Lifetime, and S fields, as specified in Table 5-2. Depending on the

Registration Request Fields:			Result
Care-of Address	**Lifetime**	**S Bit**	
any address ≠ home address	> 0	0	Replace all of the mobile node's existing bindings (if any) with a new binding for the specified care-of address.
any address ≠ home address	> 0	1	Create a binding for the specified care-of address, leaving any other existing bindings for the mobile node unmodified.
any address ≠ home address	0	1	Delete the mobile node's binding for the specified care-of address, leaving any other existing bindings unmodified.
mobile node's home address	0	any	Delete all of the mobile node's bindings.
mobile node's home address	> 0	any	Call the manufacturer of the mobile node because the mobile node is broken.

Table 5-2 Binding Updates at Home Agent

request, the home agent either begins tunneling packets to the specified care-of address or ceases all tunneling on behalf of the mobile node. Also, the home agent sends gratuitous or proxy ARPs as specified in *How Does a Home Agent Intercept Packets?* on page 92.

Finally, the home agent sends a *Registration Reply* to the mobile node indicating that the registration was successful. The IP Source and Destination Address and the UDP Source and Destination Port in the *Registration Reply* are simply reversed from the respective fields in the *Registration Request*.

How Does a Foreign Agent Process a Registration Reply?

Here, again, we assume that the mobile node is registering via a foreign agent—otherwise, the *Registration Reply* would be sent directly to the mobile node from the home agent, bypassing the foreign agent altogether. Upon receipt of a *Registration Reply*, the foreign agent—you guessed it—performs a series of validity checks.

If the *Reply* is found to be invalid in any way, then the foreign agent generates a new *Registration Reply* containing a suitable rejection Code field and sends it to the mobile node. Here we consider a valid *Reply* to be one that is legitimate in the eyes of the foreign agent. This has nothing to do with the particular value of the Code field in the *Reply* in which the home agent indicates whether or not it was pleased with the prompting *Registration Request*. In contrast, we consider an invalid *Reply* to be one which fails the foreign agent's criteria for being a legitimate *Registration Reply*. For example, an invalid *Reply* is one which is malformed, contains an unrecognized extension, or fails home-agent-to-foreign-agent authentication.

The foreign agent cannot simply relay to the mobile node an invalid *Reply* from the home agent for a number of reasons, most notably because the Code field is probably misleading or wrong. For example, if the foreign agent receives a *Reply* that is malformed or contains an unknown extension, then the Code field should indicate this fact when the *Reply* is ultimately received by the mobile node. If the foreign agent were simply to change the Code field, then the Authenticator within the Mobile-Home Authentication Extension would become invalid. This is why the foreign agent must generate a new *Registration Reply*, in which it can set the Code field to an appropriate value without breaking the Authenticator.

If the *Registration Reply* is valid, then the foreign agent updates its list of known, visiting mobile nodes and relays the *Registration Reply* to the mobile node, using some of the fields it recorded from the original *Registration Request* to transmit the *Reply*. At this point, the foreign agent begins de-tunneling packets sent to the mobile node and begins acting as a default router for packets generated by the mobile node. See *How Are Packets Routed to and from Mobile Nodes?* on page 89 for details.

How Does the Mobile Node Process a Registration Reply?

Upon receipt of a *Registration Reply*, the mobile node performs its own sequence of validity checks. If the *Reply* is valid, then the mobile node examines the Code field to examine whether the registration was accepted or rejected by the home agent (and foreign agent, if applicable).

If the Code field indicates rejection, then the mobile node can attempt to repair the error that caused the rejection and attempt a new registration. Common reasons for rejection include excessive Lifetimes (i.e., greater than the foreign agent will permit) and invalid Identification fields (where the home agent was expecting a different value, under the style of replay protection in effect). See *How Does a Node Know Who Really Sent a Registration Message?* on page 84 for further information about the Identification field.

If the Code field indicates acceptance, then the mobile node adjusts its routing table as appropriate for the current link and begins (or continues) communicating. (See *How Are Packets Routed to and from Mobile Nodes?* on page 89 for details of how this communication occurs.) Also, the mobile node stops retransmitting its *Registration Requests*.

5.3.3 How Can a Mobile Node Learn the Address of a Home Agent?

Generally, the mobile node is manually configured with the address of its home agent at the same time it is configured with its home address, the network-prefix of its home address, the address of a Domain Name System server, etc. However, in this section we describe a way in which a mobile node that has not been configured with the address of its home agent can dynamically ascertain this address using the Mobile IP Registration protocol.

The procedure, illustrated in Figure 5-6, works as follows:

1. The mobile node forms its home-link-directed, IP broadcast address by setting to 1 all of the bits in the host portion of its home address. That is, the broadcast address has the form `network-prefix.11…11`. The mobile node supplies this home-link-directed broadcast address in the Home Agent Address field of its *Registration Request*.

2. If a foreign agent is involved in the registration, the foreign agent relays the *Registration Request* to the home-link-directed broadcast address, simply by using the Home Agent Address field of the *Registration Request* to determine the address to which the request must be relayed. If the mobile

Registration Request is broadcast to all nodes on the home link, where it is received by all home agents. The Home Agent field contains the home link-directed broadcast address.

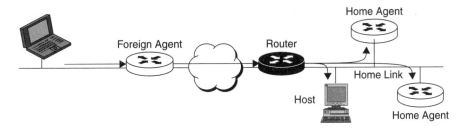

All home agents reject the registration by sending a Registration Reply in which the Code field equals 136 and the Home Agent field contains their unicast IP address.

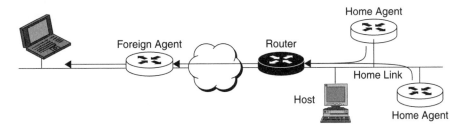

The Mobile node collects the replies and registers with one of the home agents which responded to the original request. The home agent accepts the new request and sends a reply.

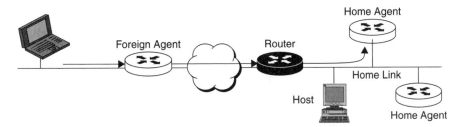

Figure 5-6 Ascertaining a Home Agent Address Dynamically

node is registering without a foreign agent, then the mobile node uses this home-link-directed broadcast address as the IP Destination Address of the packet containing its *Registration Request*.

3. The *Registration Request* is emitted as a broadcast on the home link, where it is received by all nodes on the link—specifically, by all home agents. A home agent which receives this registration and is willing to act as a home agent for the mobile node must nonetheless reject the registration, but it does so in a special way. Namely, the home agent returns a *Registration Reply* with a Code field containing 136 (Denied by home agent, Unknown home agent address) and a Home Agent Address field containing the unicast address—not the home link-directed broadcast address—of the home agent. In fact, all such home agents that are willing to serve the mobile node reject the registration in this way.

4. The mobile node ultimately collects these rejected *Registration Replies* and looks for ones containing Code 136 and a unicast Home Agent Address field. The addresses in these Home Agent Address fields are then the IP addresses of home agents that are willing to serve as the mobile node's home agent. The mobile node then may attempt a new registration, using the unicast address of one of these home agents in a *Registration Request*.

5.3.4 How Does a Node Know Who *Really* Sent a Registration Message?

Mobility in general and Mobile IP in particular pose several challenges in the area of security. The security implications of Mobile IP are addressed throughout *Part 3, "APPLYING MOBILE IP."* In this section we briefly describe a security threat which is solved within the framework of Mobile IP registration, deferring the particulars to *How Does Mobile IP Prevent This Denial-of-Service Attack?* on page 161.

The Mobile IP registration procedure provides a particular area of vulnerability because it is used to inform the home agent where to tunnel packets on behalf of a mobile node. Specifically, a Bad Guy could simply send a bogus *Registration Request* to a mobile node's home agent and cause all packets to be tunneled to the Bad Guy instead of to the mobile node's legitimate care-of address. Aside from allowing the Bad Guy to see a copy of every packet destined to the mobile node, this also prevents the mobile node from receiving any packets, and therefore from communicating.

To prevent such attacks (called denial-of-service attacks), Mobile IP requires all registration messages between the mobile node and the home agent to be authenticated. Authentication is a process by which a sending node proves its identity to a receiving node, often by making use of a secret value known only to the sender and receiver. A primitive form of authentication involves sending a username and password between a user and a remote node. This form of authentication is primitive because it is trivial to "snoop" on the wire and read the username and password as the packets containing this information are sent across a network.

In contrast, Mobile IP requires "strong authentication" between the mobile node and home agent—the kind that can't be broken simply by examining the packets that go by. We have more to say on this in *What Do We Mean by Authentication, Integrity Checking, and Non-Repudiation?* on page 132, but for now we simply note that Mobile IP authentication is strong (very difficult to break) and provides protection against replay attacks. This latter attack is when a Bad Guy records an authentic message that was previously transmitted and replays it at a later time. Mobile IP uses the Identification field in the *Registration Request* and *Reply* to protect against such replay attacks.

One final note with respect to denial-of-service attacks has to do with the prospects of doing "route optimization" in Mobile IP. As we describe in *How Are Packets Routed to a Mobile Node on a Foreign Link?* on page 90, packets sent to a mobile node are first routed to its home link and then tunneled to the care-of address by the home agent. Potentially, it could be more efficient for the node who originally sent the packets to tunnel them directly to the care-of address, without waiting for them to be routed first to the home link. The denial-of-service attacks described above turn out to be *the* major problem to be solved in doing this optimized routing to mobile nodes. We examine this in detail in *Why the Triangle Route?* on page 101.

5.3.5 How Can a Mobile Node Provide Additional Information to a Foreign Agent or its Home Agent?

The Mobile-Home Authentication Extension mentioned in *How Does a Node Know Who Really Sent a Registration Message?* on page 84 is one of many possible extensions that can be carried by Mobile IP registration messages. Mobile IP allows any useful extension to be defined and included in *Registration Requests* and *Replies*. The only other extensions defined by [RFC 2002] are:

- the Mobile-Foreign Authentication Extension; and
- the Foreign-Home Authentication Extension.

These extensions are used to authenticate a mobile node to a foreign agent and a foreign agent to a home agent, respectively (and vice versa). We show an interesting use for Mobile IP extensions when we discuss multiprotocol service in *Support for Other Protocols within the Mobile IP Framework* on page 219.

5.3.6 What If the Mobile Node Is Ping-Ponging Back-n-Forth Between Wireless Cells?

The area over which the signal from a wireless transmitter can be accurately received is referred to as its *coverage area*. The coverage area, or cell, of a transmitter rarely looks like the nice little hexagons drawn in many network diagrams. Instead, the cells generally overlap each other, as shown in Figure 5-7.

In fact, the situation is even worse than this, because the shapes of the cells tend to vary (unpredictably) with time. This variation makes it possible for a mobile node which is receiving a first transmitter to lose contact with that transmitter and begin receiving the signal from a second transmitter—all without moving an inch. If each wireless cell were its own link, each having been assigned a unique network-prefix, then the mobile node could potentially be changing links very rapidly, despite remaining completely still. This would generate a tremendous number of Mobile IP Registrations, since the mobile node must register every time it changes link.

There are two solutions to this problem of rapid mobility across wireless cells. One is outsidethe scope of Mobile IP and involves link-layer mechanisms. The other uses Mobile IP's simultaneous binding capability. Each of these is briefly described below.

Link-Layer Solution

The link-layer solution involves making the cells of a wireless network form "a few" large links, each containing many cells. Recall from our definitions that a bridge is a network element which makes several media segments appear as one link (as viewed by the network layer). The use of bridges in this way prevents every change of cell from likewise being a change of link, and therefore requiring a new Mobile IP Registration. Rather, link-layer-specific mechanisms are used to accomplish "handoffs" between cells that are part of the same link—then Mobile IP is used to accomplish mobility between cells that are part of different links. We show an example of this in *Motorola's iDEN™: A Case Study* on page 213.

Simultaneous Bindings

The second solution uses Mobile IP's simultaneous binding capability to reduce the number of registrations. Recall that the S bit in the *Registration Request*—if set to 1—indicates to the home agent that the mobile node wishes to create a binding for the specified care-of address, but wishes to leave all existing bindings unmodified. For example, if a mobile node has registered a care-of address on a first link, and then registers another care-of address on a second

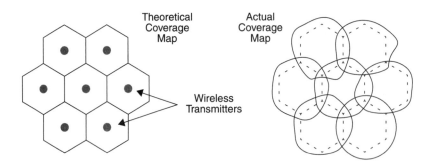

Figure 5-7 Wireless Coverage: Theory vs. Reality

link, its home agent will then have two bindings for the mobile node—one for each of these respective care-of address.

Recall that packets sent to a mobile node's home address are intercepted by its home agent and tunneled to its care-of address. In actuality, the home agent tunnels a copy of such packets to every one of the care-of addresses that have been registered by the mobile node—i.e., to every one of the care-of addresses in the mobile node's current bindings. Thus, to continue the above example, the mobile node's home agent would tunnel a copy of every packet to both the first care-of address and the second care-of address.

Now consider a mobile node that is physically located at the border between two wireless cells, as shown in Figure 5-8. If the mobile node is moving back-n-forth between the two cells, it can register a care-of address on both links. Then the mobile node simply receives a tunneled packet from the transmitter in whichever cell it happens to be receiving at the current moment. The other packet (sent by the other transmitter) will likely be lost, though there is also a chance that it, too, will be received by the mobile node. In either case, recall that IP does not guarantee that exactly one copy of a packet will arrive at its ultimate destination—in fact, TCP/IP implementations are specifically required to accommodate the receipt of zero, one, or multiple copies of an IP packet.

Thus, the simultaneous-binding feature of Mobile IP can be used to prevent large numbers of registrations by a mobile node that is on the border between two wireless cells. Support for this feature is optional by home agents, however. A home agent which does not support multiple simultaneous bindings does not reject a *Registration Request* in which this feature is requested. Rather, it sends a *Registration Reply* with the Code field set to 1, indicating to the mobile node that its registration has been accepted, but that simultaneous mobility bindings are unsupported by this home agent (and, therefore, that the mobile node's existing bindings have been deleted).

It is unclear whether this feature of Mobile IP has any applicability in the real world, however. Most wireless systems with overlapping coverage areas tend to be architected as suggested earlier in this section. Namely, numerous cells tend to be grouped together into confederations which form a single link as viewed by the network layer (IP), with a mobile node using link-layer handoffs to maintain connectivity as it moves within a single confederation of cells.

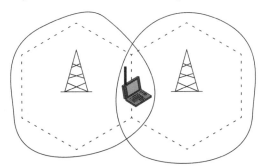

Figure 5-8 Mobile Node Bordering Two Cells

In many cases, different (i.e., neighboring) confederations use completely different portions of the RF (radio-frequency) spectrum, meaning that is difficult or impossible for a mobile node to concurrently maintain connectivity with two cells that are in different, respective confederations. This makes it essentially impossible for the mobile node to receive tunneled packets from a first cell at one point in time and from a second cell very soon thereafter. Thus, there is serious doubt as to whether this feature of Mobile IP will still be around as the protocol advances to the next step along the Internet standards track.

5.3.7 What's the Deal with the 'R' Bit?

One of the more poorly understood features of Mobile IP is the "Registration Required," or R bit, within the Mobility Agent Advertisement Extension of a foreign agent's *Agent Advertisements*. Implementors should note that [RFC 2002] is essentially wrong in almost every place it attempts to explain the operation of this feature. Thus, this section explains how the various entities are required to behave in the presence of the R bit, and shows some real-world applications where it can be essential.

Commercial service providers, by definition, require payment for the services they provide. Consider such a provider that makes (e.g., wireless) foreign links and foreign agents available to its customers. Before allowing a mobile node to use these foreign links and foreign agents, the service provider will generally demand that the mobile node provide authentication, in order for the provider to determine whether the owner of the mobile node is one of his customers. Here we note that Mobile IP Registration—in the form of its various authentication extensions—provides a very convenient mechanism for such authentication.

When a mobile node uses a foreign agent care-of address, the mobile node is required to register via the foreign agent whose care-of address it is using. However, if the mobile node acquires and uses its own collocated care-of address, then the mobile node would not ordinarily be required to register via a foreign agent. How, then, might the service provider—who might be most concerned about the cost of the (e.g., wireless) foreign link—authenticate the mobile node as a precondition of allowing the mobile node to communicate using that service provider's links?

This is the purpose of the R bit, which, if set to 1, informs a mobile node that it must register via a foreign agent—even if it is using a collocated care-of address. *A mobile node that ignores this warning will have its packets dropped on the floor by the service provider's equipment!* Of course, the use of the R bit only makes sense if service providers have control over their foreign links and can configure their foreign agents to route packets only on behalf of those nodes which have successfully registered. Such a situation is illustrated in Figure 5-9.

In the absence of the R bit, one would not expect a mobile node that is using a collocated care-of address to register via a foreign agent. After all, the foreign agent is not the tunnel exit-point and, therefore, does not de-tunnel packets for the mobile node. Rather, the foreign agent—if it is also a standard IP router—will

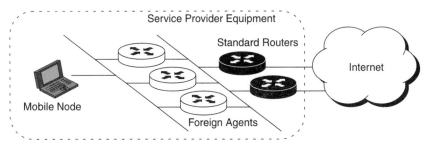

Figure 5-9 All Paths to Internet Controlled by a Commercial Service Provider

merely *route* IP packets to the mobile node's collocated care-of address (as opposed to de-tunneling them and delivering the inner packet to the mobile node).

So what does a foreign agent *do* when a mobile node registers with it using a collocated care-of address? The foreign agent most certainly does not de-tunnel packets for the mobile node, because the tunnel exit-point is by definition the care-of address. Rather, the foreign agent becomes a "standard router" for the mobile node and simply forwards packets from an incoming network interface to the interface connected to the mobile node's foreign link. Note that these packets are indeed tunneled packets that the home agent has encapsulated for delivery to the mobile node.

This discussion illustrates the difference between a foreign agent on the one hand, and the care-of address on the other. A foreign agent is a router on the foreign link which in some cases provides both routing and de-tunneling services to a mobile node (when the mobile node uses the foreign agent's care-of address) and in other cases provides only routing services to the mobile node (when the mobile node uses a collocated care-of address). The R bit provides a method for a foreign agent to communicate to a mobile node that it *must* register via that foreign agent, even when the mobile node uses a collocated care-of address—otherwise, the foreign agent will refuse to route packets on the mobile node's behalf.

The obvious question to ask, though, is: Why would the mobile node not just use a foreign agent care-of address on those links where a foreign agent is sending *Agent Advertisements*? It turns out that there are reasons relating to security and multiprotocol support that would cause a mobile node to prefer a collocated care-of address to a foreign agent care-of address. These reasons are discussed in *Requirements for Secure Firewall Traversal in Mobile IP* on page 181 and *Support for Other Protocols within the Mobile IP Framework* on page 219, respectively.

5.4 How Are Packets Routed to and from Mobile Nodes?

The first two sections in this chapter describe the methods by which mobile nodes determine their current location (Agent Discovery) and how they communicate this location to their home agent (Registration). In the current section we describe the third major topic area of Mobile IP—the procedures by which packets are routed to and from mobile nodes, depending upon their current location.

There are two primary cases we must consider: a mobile node connected to its home link and a mobile node connected to a foreign link. In the case of a foreign link, there are two secondary cases to consider: a mobile node using a foreign agent care-of address and a mobile node using a collocated care-of address.

5.4.1 How Are Packets Routed When a Mobile Node Is at Home?

By definition, packets destined to a mobile node's home address are routed to the mobile node's home link as a result of the normal functioning of network-prefix routing. Thus, no special routing procedures are required to deliver packets to a mobile node that is connected to its home link. This implies that the rules for routing packets to a mobile node which is connected to its home link are identical to the rules for routing packets to any conventional IP host or router.

In addition, no special rules are needed to route packets generated by a mobile node that is connected to its home link. Like any host or router, such a mobile node uses its routing table to select an appropriate Next Hop for any packet it generates. Similarly, no special rules are needed for populating with entries the routing table of a mobile node while it is connected to its home link.

Some mobile-node implementations store a copy of the mobile node's "home routing table entries"—i.e., those entries present in the routing table when the mobile node is connected to its home link—in order to quickly restore these entries when the mobile node returns from a foreign link to its home link. However, implementors should note that the routing topology might have changed since the mobile node was last connected to its home link (e.g., a new default router could have taken the place of the previous default router) and the mobile node's "home routing table entries" would need to be adjusted accordingly.

5.4.2 How Are Packets Routed to a Mobile Node on a Foreign Link?

In this section we describe how unicast packets—those with a single destination (as opposed to multiple destinations)—are routed to and from a mobile node that is connected to a foreign link. Broadcast and multicast packet routing is more complicated and is described in *Can Mobile Nodes Send/Receive Broadcasts/Multicasts?* on page 102.

The procedures for routing packets to a mobile node that is connected to a foreign link can be summarized as follows:

1. A router on the home link, possibly the home agent, advertises reachability to the network-prefix which equals that of the mobile node's home address.

2. Packets destined to the mobile node's home address are therefore routed toward its home link and specifically toward the mobile node's home agent.

3. The home agent intercepts packets destined to the mobile node, assuming the mobile node has registered one or more care-of addresses, and tunnels a

copy to each such care-of address (see *Chapter 6, Tunneling*). See *How Does a Home Agent Intercept Packets?* on page 92 for the method by which home agents intercept these packets.

4. At each care-of address—an address of a foreign agent or an address collocated within the mobile node itself—the original packet is extracted from the tunnel and delivered to the mobile node.

The two cases—a foreign agent care-of address and a collocated care-of address—are shown in Figure 5-10. In both cases, the home agent receives a packet destined to one of its mobile nodes and looks up the corresponding bindings. The home agent then tunnels the packet to the care-of address, not knowing or caring whether the mobile node or a foreign agent is the tunnel exit-point. Thus, in both cases, the encapsulated (inner) packet is from the "Host" in Figure 5-10 to the mobile node's home address, and in both cases the encapsulating (outer) packet is from the home agent to the care-of address.

In the case of the foreign agent care-of address, when the foreign agent receives the tunneled packet, it removes the encapsulating (outer) packet to recover the encapsulated (inner, original) packet. It then sees that the IP Destination Address is that of a registered mobile node, looks up the appropriate interface, and sends the packet to the mobile node. In the case of the collocated care-of address, the mobile node performs similar processing upon receiving the tunneled packet. The mobile node removes the outer packet to recover the original packet, and ultimately passes the contents of the original packet up the stack to the higher-layer protocol.

All home agents and foreign agents are required to implement *IP in IP Encapsulation* [RFC 2003] for tunneling purposes. In addition, they may implement *Minimal Encapsulation within IP* [RFC 2004] and *Generic Routing Encapsulation (GRE)* [RFC 1701]. Mobile nodes which are capable of operating with a collocated care-of address have identical requirements with respect to tunneling.

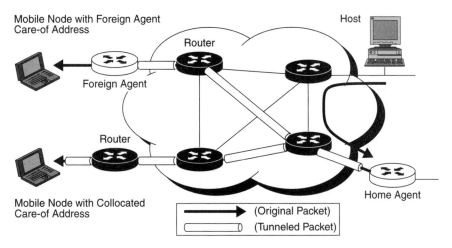

Figure 5-10 Routing Packets to Mobile Nodes on Foreign Links

How Does a Home Agent Intercept Packets?

There are two ways in which a home agent can intercept packets destined to the home address of a registered mobile node. The first method is by advertising reachability to the mobile node's home address, which generally applies only to home agents that are routers with multiple interfaces. In such a case, a packet destined for a mobile node might arrive at the home agent through some interface other than the one through which it connects to the home link. Here the home agent intercepts the packet by virtue of being the Next Hop through which other hosts and routers reach Targets on the home link—i.e., as a natural consequence of IP routing.

The other method involves the use of gratuitous and proxy ARP. Consider a host on a mobile node's home link that tries to send a packet to the mobile node. If the home link uses ARP for address resolution (e.g., Ethernet) then the host will broadcast an *ARP Request* message in order to determine the mobile node's link-layer address. However, if the mobile node is currently registered on a foreign link, then it is impossible for the mobile node to receive this *ARP Request,* because ARP messages are never forwarded by routers.

Rather than have the *ARP Request* go unanswered, the mobile node's home agent—which must have an interface on the home link—sends an *ARP Reply* to the host specifying the *home agent's* link-layer address as corresponding to the mobile node's IP home address. This proxy ARP causes the host to send IP packets to the home agent while the mobile node is away from its home link. Thus, proxy ARP is the second method by which the home agent can intercept packets destined for a mobile node's home address.

However, if a mobile node was recently connected to its home link and sent *ARP Replies* specifying its own link-layer address, then it is possible that some nodes on the home link might still have this address in their ARP cache. Thus, when a mobile node registers on a foreign link and the home agent has no existing bindings for the mobile node, the home agent must send a number of gratuitous ARPs on behalf of the mobile node in order to update these ARP caches. The gratuitous ARPs specify the home agent's link-layer address as corresponding to the mobile node's IP home address just like the proxy ARPs described in the previous paragraph.

When the mobile node returns to its home link, it must likewise update these ARP caches to contain the mobile node's link-layer address as corresponding to the mobile node's IP home address (instead of the home agent's link-layer address). The mobile node does this by sending a number of gratuitous ARPs upon returning to its home link. Similarly, when a mobile node deregisters with its home agent, the home agent must cease sending proxy ARPs for the mobile node and begin allowing the mobile node to answer *ARP Requests* itself.

Routing Table Integration via Virtual Interfaces

Recall that IP routing tables entries have at least four fields: Target, Prefix-Length, Next Hop, and Interface. Usually, the Interface field contains a pointer to a chunk of software called a *device driver*. The device driver hides the specific char-

acteristics of the network interface hardware and the lower-layer protocols from
the IP layer, which, frankly, could not care less about such details. Thus, the Interface field is said to point to a "physical interface," because, ultimately, the device
driver will invoke the hardware which transmits bits on some physical medium.

The trick to integrating tunneling into a routing table is to define something called a *virtual interface*. Unlike the physical interfaces described in the
previous paragraph, a virtual interface is a chunk of software which does not
ultimately transmit bits on a physical medium. In our case, the virtual interface
is going to perform tunnel encapsulation or decapsulation, depending on the circumstance. Figure 5-11 illustrates a virtual interface as it might look in a home
agent. An example routing table that would correspond to this figure is shown in
Table 5-3.

Target / Prefix-Length	Next Hop	Interface
7.7.7.0 / 24	"direct"	1
default / 0	6.6.6.254	2
7.7.7.1 / 32 (e.g., a mobile node's home address)	1.1.1.1 (e.g., the mobile node's care-of address)	α

Table 5-3 Routing Table for Home Agent in Figure 5-11

Let's examine what happens when a packet arrives for the home agent that
is destined to the mobile node's home address (7.7.7.1). The packet arrives via
one of the physical interfaces (e.g., Physical Interface 2) and gets passed up the
stack to the IP routing software. The routing software must now consult the
routing table to make a forwarding decision. The "best" match (i.e., the longest-
matching prefix) is the host-specific route to the mobile node's home address—
the last entry in Table 5-3. So the home agent "forwards" the packet to a Next Hop
of the mobile node's care-of address (1.1.1.1) via Interface α.

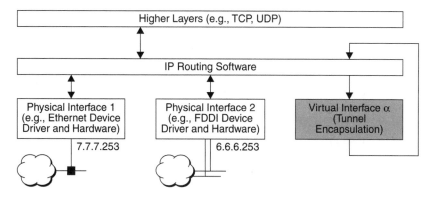

Figure 5-11 Encapsulation via Virtual Interface in Home Agent

Thus the IP Routing software invokes the Interface α software and passes to it the IP packet and the Next Hop. When the software which implements interface α gets invoked, it encapsulates the original IP packet within a new IP packet whose Source Address is that of the home agent and whose Destination Address is the Next Hop, or the mobile node's care-of address. When the virtual interface finishes building the outer packet, it now is in possession of a (new) IP packet. As is always the case, this packet must be submitted to the IP Routing Software in order for it to choose a Next Hop and outgoing Interface. Thus, the virtual-interface software invokes the IP routing software again.

The encapsulating (outer) packet, upon being presented to the IP Routing Software, has a Destination Address equal to the mobile node's care-of address (1.1.1.1). The only match in the table for this is the default route in the second entry. This time, the route specifies a Next Hop of 6.6.6.254 via Interface 2 (which is a physical interface). Thus, the IP Routing Software invokes the device driver for Interface 2, which builds an FDDI frame and sends it across the fiber ring to the node whose address is 6.6.6.254 (to be further routed to 1.1.1.1).

Host-specific routes pointing to virtual interfaces are an elegant way for home agents to integrate the special processing required by Mobile IP into their existing IP routing tables. A similar entry is required at the foreign agent for a visiting mobile node. The foreign agent's routing table would look something like the one shown in Table 5-4 (see also Figure 5-12).

Target / Prefix	Next Hop	Interface
5.5.5.0 / 24	"direct"	1
1.1.1.0 / 24	1.1.1.254	2
7.7.7.1 / 32	"direct"	1

Table 5-4 Routing Table for Foreign Agent in Figure 5-12

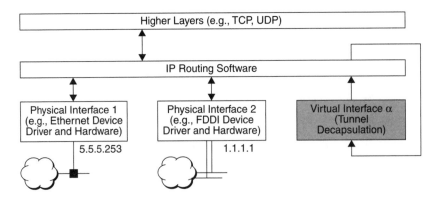

Figure 5-12 Virtual Interface: Decapsulation in Foreign Agent

Continuing the example, when the tunneled packet arrives at the foreign agent (over one of the physical interfaces), it is passed to the IP routing software. The IP routing software sees that the (outer) packet's destination is one of the foreign agent's addresses—namely, the address it advertises as a care-of address. Thus the IP software "consumes" the packet by passing it—header and payload—to the "higher layer." The higher layer, read from the IP Protocol field, is IP itself in the case of a packet tunneled using *IP in IP Encapsulation*. Thus the IP software passes the packet to the "higher layer" which handles all IP packets whose IP Protocol fields equal IP—namely, its virtual-interface software.

Where in home agents it performs encapsulation, the virtual-interface software in foreign agents performs decapsulation. The virtual-interface software strips off the encapsulating (outer) IP header and passes the payload—namely, the encapsulated (inner, original) IP packet—up to the IP routing software. To the IP routing software, this original IP packet looks as if it arrived over virtual interface α. The IP routing software now finds itself with an IP packet whose Destination Address does not match any of the foreign agent's IP addresses—which means that the routing table must be consulted in order to select a Next Hop and an outgoing Interface.

The packet that was passed up by the virtual-interface software is the original IP packet, whose Destination Address is the mobile node's home address. The best match for this address is, of course, the host-specific route (the third entry in Table 5-4). This specifies that such packets are to be delivered directly to the mobile node via physical Interface 1. So, the foreign agent hands the packet over to the software which implements the Ethernet device, and the packet is transmitted over the foreign link to the mobile node.

5.4.3 How Do Mobile Nodes Send Packets?

Selecting a Router on the Home Link

As mentioned in *How Are Packets Routed When a Mobile Node Is at Home?* on page 90, a mobile node connected to its home link functions just like any other fixed host or router with respect to packet routing. In fact, we would expect a mobile node on its home link to have identical entries in its IP routing table as other nodes connected to that home link. These routing table entries are typically created via the same means by which nodes obtain their IP address. Examples include manual configuration, DHCP, and PPP's IPCP (the interaction between Mobile IP and PPP is described in *How Do Mobile IP and PPP Interact?* on page 205).

Selecting a Router on a Foreign Link

When a mobile node is connected to a foreign link, it must have a way to determine a router that can forward packets generated by the mobile node. In this section we describe some mechanisms available to the mobile node for selecting such a router. There are two cases to consider: a mobile node that registers via a foreign agent and a mobile node that registers directly with its home agent.

With a Foreign Agent

If a mobile node registers via a foreign agent, whether or not the mobile node is using the foreign agent's care-of address (see *What's the Deal with the 'R' Bit?* on page 88), then [RFC 2002] provides the mobile node with two primary alternatives for its choice of router:

1. the foreign agent itself, as specified by the IP Source Address of that agent's periodically transmitted *Agent Advertisements*; and

2. any router whose address appears in the Router Address fields within the *ICMP Router Advertisement* [RFC 1256] portion of any node's *Agent Advertisements* or *Router Advertisements*.

The first alternative implies that the foreign agent with which a mobile node is registered must be willing and able to serve as a router for all packets generated by that mobile node. As indicated by the second alternative, this is different from saying that the mobile node must *choose* that foreign agent as its router; rather, Mobile IP requires that the foreign agent must provide this routing function *if* the mobile node so desires.

The second alternative states that a mobile node can select any router whose address is listed in the Router Address fields of either a foreign agent's *Agent Advertisements* or of any "plain" router sending *ICMP Router Advertisements*. However, a mobile node is not allowed to send *ARP Requests* containing its home address on a foreign link. Mobile nodes can, however, determine the link-layer address of routers by recording the source link-layer address of their respective advertisements. Therefore, this second alternative—where a mobile node selects the Router Address with the highest Preference Level (as described in [RFC 1256])—is useful only in those situations where the mobile node can determine the router's link-layer address without sending *ARP Requests* containing its home address. One such situation is when the mobile node uses a collocated care-of address and can use that address within its ARP messages. The bottom line is that mobile nodes using a foreign agent care-of address should just use their foreign agent as a router and be done with it!

All packets generated by a mobile node are sent to the router it selects from the available alternatives, as described above. This implies that the mobile node configures its routing table as shown in Table 5-5. If the mobile node has just

Target / Prefix-Length	Next Hop	Interface
0.0.0.0 / 0 (default)	(the selected router address)	(the interface through which the mobile node connects to the foreign link)

Table 5-5 Mobile Node's Routing Table When Connected to a Foreign Link

moved from its home link to this foreign link, it is wise for the mobile node to store a copy of the routing table entries it uses on its home link such that they can be restored when the mobile node again returns to its home link.

Without a Foreign Agent

A mobile node that registers a collocated care-of address on a foreign link that does not contain a foreign agent also has two alternatives for selecting a router. First, if there is a router on the link sending *ICMP Router Advertisements*—as distinctly opposed to a foreign agent sending *Agent Advertisements*—then the mobile node can use any of the addresses listed in the Router Address fields of the advertisement as the address of a router. The mobile node uses the same procedures described in *With a Foreign Agent* on page 96 to select an address from those listed in the advertisement.

If there is no such router sending advertisements, then the mobile node must rely on the same mechanism by which it acquired its collocated care-of address to provide the address of a suitable router. DHCP, one method by which the mobile node can acquire a collocated care-of address, can also provide all sorts of useful information to the mobile node including the address of a router. Similarly, PPP's IPCP can provide the mobile node with the IP address of the node at the other end of the PPP link, which the mobile node can use to forward all of its packets. Finally, manual configuration—whether or not it was used by the mobile node to acquire its collocated care-of address—can be used to provide the mobile node with the address of a router.

Determining the Link-Layer Address of the Router

As we discussed in *How Does a Mobile Node Send a Registration Request?* on page 78, a mobile node must not transmit an *ARP Request* containing its home address on any foreign link. Doing so would likely cause nodes on the foreign link to be incapable of communicating with the mobile node after it moves to a different link.

However, a mobile node that has acquired a collocated care-of address may transmit *ARP Requests* that contain this care-of address. With these rules in mind, let us see how a mobile node determines the link-layer address of its router on a foreign link.

Routers Sending Advertisements

When a mobile node uses its foreign agent as its router, then the mobile node simply records the Link-Layer Source Address fields from the respective frames that carry the foreign agent's *Agent Advertisements*. This address can then be used as the Link-Layer Destination Address in the frames which carry IP packets generated by the mobile node (including the mobile node's *Registration Request* message).

If the mobile node is using a router that it discovered by receiving *ICMP Router Advertisements* sent by that router, then the mobile node should also record the Link-Layer Source Address field of those advertisements. This address is

then used as the Link-Layer Destination Address of frames which carry IP packets
generated by the mobile node.

Routers Not Sending Advertisements.

If the mobile node uses any other router—that is, any router other than one
sending advertisements—then the mobile node must learn the link-layer
address of that router using other means. In the case of PPP links, this is unnecessary because there is no link-layer address per se in PPP. On other media, such
as Ethernet, the only method available to the mobile node is generally ARP.

Thus, if the mobile node is using a collocated care-of address, then the
mobile node can ARP for its router using its care-of address as the Sender Protocol
Address in its *ARP Requests*. However, if the mobile node has no such collocated
care-of address, then short of some magical form of meditation, the mobile node
is basically out-of-luck.

Actually, the mobile node could put its network interface into "promiscuous
mode" and try to deduce the link-layer address of its router by examining the
packets that are sent on the network. This deduction is not advised, however. A
mobile node using a foreign agent care-of address should simply use its foreign
agent as a router, since it is trivial for the mobile node to obtain the foreign
agent's link-layer address.

5.4.4 Doesn't This Assume That IP Packets Are Routed without Regard to Their Source Address?

Mobile IP, as described in [RFC 2002], does indeed assume that IP unicast
packets (i.e., those with a single destination, as opposed to multicast packets) are
routed based solely on their IP Destination Address and without regard to their IP
Source Address. However, new attacks being waged on the Internet by Bad Guys
might cause Internet Service Providers to implement policies which invalidate
this assumption.

Specifically, Internet Service Providers are being advised by the Internet
Architecture Board (IAB) to filter packets by Source Address and discard those
whose Source Address appears to be coming from the "wrong" place. Packets fit-
ting this description are those whose Source Addresses have network-prefixes that
do not match any of the network-prefixes assigned to the links that are known to
exist in the direction from which the packets arrived.

This type of filtering, called network ingress filtering, presents a very large
problem for Mobile IP. This is because packets sent by mobile nodes connected to
a foreign link are exactly the type of packets that fit the above description and
that network ingress filtering is designed to block! The Mobile IP working group
has recognized this problem and is addressing it using "reverse tunneling,"
which we describe in more detail in *What Does Mobile IP Do about Ingress Filtering?* on page 211.

5.4.5 Why Use Tunneling Instead of Source Routing?

To this point we have examined two methods for overcoming the deficiency of network-prefix routing that makes it unable to deliver packets to mobile nodes that are connected to foreign links. The first method, host-specific routing, had severe problems related to scalability, security, and robustness. The second method, protocol tunneling, is the approach adopted by Mobile IP. There is also a third alternative, source routing, that could potentially be used to modify the path that a packet would normally follow under network-prefix routing. In this section, we examine why this approach was rejected in favor of tunneling, at least in the context of IPv4 mobility.

What Is Source Routing?

We begin our discussion of source routing by showing how it could be employed to deliver packets to mobile nodes connected to a foreign link. IP Version 4 defines an IP Header Option called the Loose Source and Record Route Option. This option lists one or more intermediate destinations that a packet containing the option must visit along its journey to its final destination.

As an example, consider a source host that wants to send a packet to a destination host, but also wants that packet to visit a specific router along the path from source to destination. The source host places the address of the "next intermediate destination"—the router—in the IP Destination Address field and puts the destination host's IP address within the Loose Source and Record Route Option. The packet will then be routed, generally using network-prefix routing, to the router specified in the IP Destination Address field.

When the router receives the packet, it inspects the options and realizes that it is only an intermediate destination. It then grabs the next address in the Loose Source and Record Route Option—the destination host—and forwards the packet to the Next Hop along the path to the destination host. Before forwarding the packet, the router "records" its own IP address within the Loose Source and Record Route Option. Specifically, the router records its IP address on the interface over which it forwards the packet.

When the packet arrives at the destination host, it inspects the options and determines that it is the ultimate destination of the packet. Therefore, the destination host "consumes" the packet by passing it to the higher-layer protocol indicated by the IP Protocol field. The option specifies that when a destination host responds to a source host that included the Loose Source and Record Route Option in its packets, that destination host should include a "reversed" source routing option in the response packets. In this example, the original destination host would include a Loose Source and Record Route Option specifying the same router as an intermediate destination when sending packets back to the original source host.

How Could Source Routing Be Used in Mobile IP?

Charles Perkins, then of IBM [Perk93], and Dave Johnson of Carnegie Mellon University [John93] separately proposed similar, clever schemes by which loose source routing could be used to implement node mobility on the Internet. Simplifying greatly, their proposals work as follows. Whenever a mobile node has a packet to send to a correspondent, the mobile node includes a Loose Source and Record Route Option in the packet specifying its current care-of address as an intermediate destination. Then, when the correspondent replies to the mobile node, it reverses the source route and the packet is routed to the mobile node via its care-of address.

The mobile node still requires a home agent, though, for correspondents that do not know the mobile node's current care-of address. For these correspondents, packets to the mobile node are sent normally, in which case they are routed to the home link, where they are intercepted by the home agent and loose-source routed to the mobile node via the care-of address. Obviously, then, the mobile node would still be required to register its care-of address with its home agent, for the same reasons described in *When Should a Mobile Node Register?* on page 78.

Why Isn't Source Routing a Good Solution?

There are three primary reasons why source routing was rejected by the Mobile IP working group as a solution. The first reason is that the Loose Source and Record Route Option, despite having been defined in the original IPv4 specification [RFC 791], is rarely, if ever, implemented correctly in IPv4 hosts (though routers do tend to implement it correctly). Some nodes simply drop all packets that contain this option (or any other option, for that matter). Others actually crash (!) upon receiving IP packets containing options. Finally, few, if any, implementations actually reverse the source route, even though this was a requirement of the IPv4 specification.

The second reason is that IP packets containing options require additional processing by every router along the path from source to destination—not just the routers listed in the source-routing option! This is because the options must be parsed by each router to see if they contain an option that might be relevant to that router before it forwards the packet. Conversely, packets that do not contain options—a fact that can be determined quickly by examining the IP Header Length field—can generally be routed very quickly, often in hardware, which allows current router technology to route IP packets at pretty blazing speeds. A packet containing any IP option can experience as much as a 10-to-1 performance penalty in some commercial routers. This was deemed to be an unacceptable performance penalty, especially when compared with tunneling which requires only two routers to do "special" processing—the home agent and the tunnel exit-point (either a foreign agent or the mobile node itself).

The final reason that loose-source routing was deemed unacceptable relates to security. As we described in *How Does a Node Know Who Really Sent a Registration Message?* on page 84, a Bad Guy could send a packet to a mobile node's correspondent specifying some bogus care-of address as an intermediate destination in a loose-source route. This would cause the correspondent to reverse the source route, specifying this bogus care-of address as an intermediate destination in its replies. At this point, the mobile node is cut off from communicating with this correspondent, and the Bad Guy gets to see a copy of all packets sent by that correspondent to the mobile node. This problem could be eliminated with the proper use of authentication, but it has the same key management problems as does route optimization, which we describe in the next section.

5.4.6 Why the Triangle Route?

Packets that are sent by a correspondent to a mobile node connected to a foreign link are routed first to the mobile node's home agent and then tunneled to the mobile node's care-of address. However, packets sent by the mobile node are routed directly to the correspondent, thus forming a triangle as shown in Figure 5-13. The question we wish to address in this section is: Why doesn't the mobile node inform correspondents of its care-of address and have them tunnel directly to the mobile node, bypassing the home agent? This optimized routing is potentially more efficient in terms of delay and resource consumption than is triangle routing, because, in general, the packets will have to traverse fewer links on their way to their destination.

The main obstacle to route optimization relates to security. For a correspondent to tunnel directly to a mobile node, the correspondent must be informed of

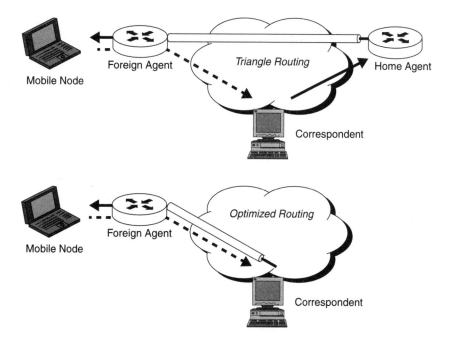

Figure 5-13 Triangle Routing vs. Optimized Routing

the mobile node's current care-of address. Note the similarity between this and
Mobile IP Registration, the purpose of which is to inform a mobile node's home
agent of the mobile node's current care-of address. Without strong authentication in the messages that inform a mobile node's correspondent of its current
care-of address, trivial denial-of-service attacks—of the nature we described in
How Does a Node Know Who Really Sent a Registration Message? on page 84—
would be possible to perform with respect to correspondents.

Specifically, a Bad Guy need only send a bogus registration to the mobile
node's correspondent in order to cut off all communication between the two
nodes. This is the challenge presented by any attempts to optimize the routing in
Mobile IP. It is conceivable that a network administrator could configure a secret
key between a mobile node and its home agent, in order to protect the registration messages against forgeries. It is not practical, however, to likewise distribute keys between a mobile node and every other node with which it might
correspond. In the absence of automated mechanisms, distributing keys between
a mobile node and its correspondents is simply unworkable. We examine the
challenges presented by key distribution in more detail in *Chapter 7, Security
Primer*.

Route Optimization in Mobile IP is "work in progress." While there is some
isolated interest in this topic, the majority of the working-group members view it
as a very low-priority work item. This is probably because route optimization
provides significant savings in resources only when the mobile node is far from
its home agent and near its correspondent. In most situations, the mobile node or
the correspondent is close to the home agent, implying that the network
resources to be saved by direct tunneling are small in comparison to the authentication and key distribution necessary to do it securely. See [draft-ietf-mobileip-
optim-05.txt] for more information on route optimization in Mobile IP.

5.4.7 Can Mobile Nodes Send/Receive Broadcasts/Multicasts?

In the preceding sections we described how unicast packets are routed to
mobile nodes. Unicast packets are those with a single destination. In this section
we describe how mobile nodes can send and receive both multicast and broadcast
packets when connected to a foreign link. Multicast packets are those with multiple destinations—namely, those nodes that have "joined" the multicast group.
Broadcast packets are those delivered to all nodes—all nodes, that is, on a single
link or on many such links, depending upon the type of broadcast.

Broadcasts

IP broadcasts packets are, by definition, those with an IP Destination Address
which specifies a broadcast address. IP broadcast addresses are those with host
portions that are all binary 1's; that is, they have the form `network-pre-
fix.11…11`. Broadcasts packets with this type of Destination Address will be termed
prefix-specific broadcasts, since they are delivered to all nodes which have an

address with a matching network-prefix. In the special case where the prefix-length is 0 bits, that is, when the address is all binary 1's (255.255.255.255), we call this a link-specific broadcast, since it is delivered only to those nodes on the link on which it is sent. Equivalently stated, prefix-specific broadcasts may traverse one or more routers before being delivered to their destinations, while a link-specific broadcast may not.

A mobile node can obtain a copy of broadcasts that are transmitted on its home link, even when the mobile node is currently connected to a foreign link. The mobile node requests that its home agent forward all broadcasts—both prefix-specific and link-specific—by setting the B bit in its *Registration Requests*. This instructs the home agent to deliver a copy of all such broadcasts via a tunnel to the mobile node. The exact delivery mechanism depends upon whether the mobile node is using a foreign agent care-of address or a collocated care-of address.

Receiving Broadcasts with a Collocated Care-of Address

A mobile node with a collocated care-of address receives broadcast packets in exactly the same way as it receives unicast packets. Namely, its home agent tunnels the broadcast packet to the mobile node's collocated care-of address, the mobile node de-tunnels the packet, and the mobile node passes the encapsulated (inner) broadcast packet to the higher layer. A mobile node using a collocated care-of address must set the D bit to 1 in its *Registration Requests*, to inform its home agent that the mobile node itself is decapsulating packets. The reason for this will become clear in the next section.

Receiving Broadcasts with a Foreign Agent Care-of Address

A mobile node with a foreign agent care-of address receives broadcast packets far differently from the way in which it receives unicast packets. Consider what would happen if the home agent simply tunneled broadcast packets to the foreign agent's care-of address. The foreign agent would de-tunnel the packet and then have absolutely no clue what to do with it, because the IP Destination Address of the encapsulated (inner) packet would be a broadcast address and the foreign agent would not know which mobile node was supposed to receive it. Thus, the foreign agent would not know on which interface to transmit the de-tunneled broadcast packet.

For this reason, a home agent must use *nested encapsulation* (multiple levels of encapsulation) to deliver broadcast packets to mobile nodes which have registered a foreign agent care-of address. First, the home agent encapsulates a broadcast within a first encapsulating packet with IP Source Address equal to the home agent's address and IP Destination Address equal to the mobile node's home address. Then, the home agent encapsulates this first encapsulating packet within a second packet with IP Source Address equal to the home agent's address and IP Destination Address equal to the care-of address.

In this way, when the doubly-encapsulated packet arrives at the care-of address, the foreign agent decapsulates (once) and sees a unicast packet whose Source Address is the home agent's address and whose Destination Address is the mobile node's home address. Note that this packet looks like any other unicast packet that the home agent might tunnel for delivery to the mobile node. Therefore, the foreign agent looks in its routing table and sends the packet to the mobile node over the appropriate link. Note further that this unicast packet contains the encapsulated broadcast packet, which must be de-tunneled by the mobile node before being passed to the higher-layer protocol.

A mobile node with a foreign agent care-of address must set the D bit to 0 in its *Registration Requests*. The home agent uses the setting of the D bit to determine whether it must use nested encapsulation to deliver broadcasts as described in this section, or whether it must use a single level of encapsulation to deliver broadcasts as described in the previous section. Implementors should note that a mobile node that sets the B bit to 1 in order to receive broadcast packets must be capable of de-tunneling packets, regardless of whether the mobile node uses a foreign agent or collocated care-of address.

Sending Broadcasts

The way in which a mobile node sends broadcasts is independent of whether it has a collocated or a foreign agent care-of address. However, transmission of broadcasts by mobile nodes does depend upon the type of broadcast, as specified by the following three cases:

1. If the destination is a link-specific broadcast (255.255.255.255) intended for the mobile node's foreign link, then the mobile node simply transmits the packet on the foreign link, using the link-layer broadcast address to deliver the frame containing this packet to all nodes on the link.

2. If the destination is a link-specific broadcast (255.255.255.255) intended for the mobile node's home link, then the mobile node must tunnel this packet to its home agent. The encapsulating (outer) packet has an IP Source Address equal to the mobile node's home address, and the IP Destination Address is the mobile node's home agent.

3. If the destination is a prefix-specific broadcast (network-prefix.11...11), then the mobile node has two alternatives. First, it can tunnel the packet to its home agent as in item 2 above. Second, the mobile node can transmit the packet normally, sending it in a link-layer frame whose Link-Layer Destination Address is that of its router, just like any unicast packet transmitted by the mobile node. However, some intermediate routers might be configured to filter broadcast packets, in which case a mobile node will be better off tunneling such packets to its home agent.

Thus, mobile nodes can participate in broadcasts either as senders or receivers, simply by setting the appropriate bits (B and D) in their *Registration Requests* and using the procedures described above.

Multicasts

IP multicasts are, by definition, those packets with IP Destination Addresses whose four leftmost bits are "1110"—that is, they have the form `1110.multi-`

cast-group. In dotted-decimal notation, the range of IP multicast addresses, also known as Internet Class D Addresses, is therefore 224.0.0.1 through 239.255.255.255.

Any node can send a packet to a multicast group, simply by building an IP packet in which the IP Destination Address is set to the group's multicast address. Senders do not need to be *members* of a group in order to send multicasts to the receivers of that group. A node joins (becomes a member of) a multicast group, and therefore becomes a receiver of the packets sent to that group, by sending special messages to *multicast routers*. A multicast router is a router that is capable of routing multicast packets.

The messages that nodes use to join multicast groups are defined by the *Internet Group Management Protocol (IGMP)* [RFC 1112]. Specifically, nodes send *IGMP Host Membership Reports* to express their desire to join multicast groups. IGMP, like ICMP, is considered to be part of the network layer. Also like ICMP, IGMP messages are carried within the payload portion of IP packets.

Multicast routers use special *multicast routing protocols* in order to exchange reachability information about the individual members of each group. In doing so, each multicast router computes a *delivery tree* that describes how multicast packets are to be routed to members of each group. Multicast routing delivers packets using special algorithms which prevent packets from being duplicated unless they absolutely have to be. This is the whole point of using IP multicast; otherwise, one could simply send a unique IP unicast to each and every member of the group. (For more information on IP multicast, see [Come95], [Stev94], or [Perl92].)

Unlike IP unicast and IP broadcast packets, IP multicast packets are routed based upon both the IP Destination Address (i.e., the group address) *and* the IP Source Address (i.e., the address of the sender). The IP Source Address must be *topologically correct*; that is, the network-prefix of the IP Source Address must equal the network-prefix of the link on which the IP multicast is originated. Equivalently stated, a node which sends a multicast packet must be connected to its home link. Obviously, this causes problems for mobile nodes that are currently connected to a foreign link. We show how Mobile IP deals with this problem in the next few sections.

Mobile Nodes as Senders of Multicasts on a Foreign Link

A mobile node that is connected to a foreign link must not send multicast packets directly on that link using its home address as the IP Source Address; otherwise, multicast routers will not be able to deliver the packets to all of the group's receivers. Such a mobile node has two options for sending multicasts. First, the mobile node can tunnel them to its home agent, in exactly the same way as specified for broadcast packets in *Sending Broadcasts* on page 104. This method requires the mobile node's home agent to be a multicast router; that is, the home agent must be capable of forwarding IP multicast packets.

Alternatively, a mobile node that has a acquired a collocated care-of address can use that address as the IP Source Address of its multicast packets and send them directly on the foreign link. This method requires that one or more multicast routers be present on the foreign link. Further, this method is only useful if the multicast application does not use the IP Source Address of multicast packets as the *identity* of the sender, since a mobile node's care-of address (and hence the IP Source Address) changes when it moves.

Mobile Nodes as Receivers of Multicasts on a Foreign Link

Recall that a receiver must send *IGMP Host Membership Reports* on its attached link to inform a neighboring multicast router that the node wishes to receive multicasts for a specific group. A mobile node that is connected to a foreign link has two options available if it wishes to receive multicasts.

The first option is for the mobile node to tunnel IGMP packets to its home agent—which, of course, assumes that its home agent is also a multicast router. The home agent then adds the mobile node to the multicast delivery tree. To actually deliver multicast packets, the home agent tunnels them to the mobile node. The form of these tunneled packets depends on whether the mobile node is using a foreign agent care-of address or a collocated care-of address, and the mechanism is exactly the same as we saw for broadcast packets in *Receiving Broadcasts with a Foreign Agent Care-of Address* on page 103 and *Receiving Broadcasts with a Collocated Care-of Address* on page 103.

This first option, in which the mobile node joins the multicast delivery tree by way of its home agent, is useful in those situations where the multicast group is administratively restricted to a specific set of links owned, for instance, by a single corporation. In such a case, multicast packets tunneled to the mobile node by its home agent can be encrypted, authenticated, or both if the mobile node is currently connecting via a public, untrusted link. We examine the full implications of such security arrangements in *Chapter 9, Internet-Wide Mobility: A More Complicated Application*.

The second option for a mobile node that wishes to receive multicasts is for the mobile node to send *IGMP Host Membership Reports* directly on the foreign link. This, of course, assumes that there is at least one multicast router present on the foreign link. If the mobile node has a collocated care-of address, then the mobile node should use this address as the IP Source Address of its IGMP packets, though a mobile node with a foreign agent care-of address may use its home address to send these packets. The reason the latter is permissible is that the IGMP messages merely inform the neighboring multicast router that there *is* a receiver present—the multicast router normally does not care about the identity of the receiver.

This second option, in which the mobile node joins the multicast delivery tree by way of a multicast router on a foreign link, might be more efficient than joining by way of its home agent. This would be the case when there are many receivers of a single multicast group simultaneously connected to the same link. In the first method, each such receiver would obtain a private copy of the multicast via a tunnel from its home agent, which further implies many transmissions on the foreign link. In the second method, the multicast router transmits each individual multicast packet only once on the foreign link.

Finally, a mobile node that joins a group via a router on a foreign link must rejoin that group when it moves to a new link, if it wishes to remain a member of that group.

Summary

Using the procedures illustrated in this section, a mobile node can participate in the same multicast and broadcast communications when connected to a foreign link as when connected to its home link. Specifically, a mobile node connected to a foreign link can send and receive both broadcast and multicast packets, in addition to unicast packets. This fulfills the overriding philosophy of Mobile IP which is to provide for the mobile node the same connectivity it enjoys on its home link, regardless of its current point-of-attachment to the Internet.

5.4.8 How Does Van Jacobson Compression Work?

TCP plus IP headers are 40 bytes (total) in length; thus, it is very desirable to compress out the redundant or nonuseful header information when transmitting them over slow, bandwidth-limited links. The Internet standard mechanism for doing this is commonly referred to as "Van Jacobson Header Compression," named for the primary inventor and author of the technique. TCP/IP Header compression is documented in [RFC 1144].

Because Mobile IP is a natural match for wireless computing, and wireless links tend to be the very kinds of links that are slow or bandwidth-limited, it is very desirable for the mobile node and foreign agent to be able to compress TCP/IP headers. Thus, Mobile IP allows the mobile node and the foreign agent to negotiate the use of Van Jacobson header compression as part of the Mobile IP Registration procedure.

Specifically, a mobile node which desires header compression sets the V bit within its *Registration Requests*, but only when registering with a foreign agent which indicated support for header compression by setting the V bit in its *Agent Advertisements*. Unfortunately, the Mobile IP specification is silent on what happens once the mobile node has successfully registered in this fashion.

As [RFC 1144] implies, header compression requires the link layer to be able to distinguish between compressed packets and uncompressed packets. Thus, header compression in the context of Mobile IP can be performed only over those foreign links employing link-layer protocols that define a standard mechanism for transmitting such compressed and uncompressed packets.

PPP is one such data-link-layer protocol, which, we should note, has its own mechanism for negotiating the use of Van Jacobson Header Compression. (PPP is discussed in *How Does a Person Connect to Internet via PPP But without Mobile IP?* on page 202.) Most of the common Local Area Network protocols over which IP is run—Ethernet, FDDI, Token Ring—do not have separate link types defined for distinguishing compressed IP packets from uncompressed ones. However, CDPD and several other wireless media do have link-layer protocols that can make such a distinction.

Assuming the presence of a link layer which can distinguish between compressed and uncompressed IP packets, the following information can be used by mobile-node and foreign agent implementors to determine how to compress TCP/IP headers sent between these two nodes on the foreign link.

First of all, [RFC 1144] requires a "physical link treated as two, independent, simplex links (one each direction)" in order to perform correctly. Thus, a mobile node that has successfully negotiated the use of header compression with a foreign agent (during registration) must use that foreign agent as a router for all packets that it generates. This provides the bidirectional traffic flow across a single link required by [RFC 1144].

Also, header compression as defined in [RFC 1144] uses the concept of "compression slots" to make TCP/IP compression very efficient, even when data is flowing over multiple, simultaneous TCP connections. Using the advice in [RFC 1144], both the mobile node and the foreign agent should assume that the number of compression slots is 16, since there is no protocol mechanism defined within the scope of Mobile IP for the mobile node and foreign agent to negotiate a different number of slots.

Finally, since PPP's *Internet Protocol Control Protocol (IPCP)* [RFC 1332] likewise provides a mechanism to negotiate the use of Van Jacobson Header Compression, mobile nodes that connect to foreign agents over PPP links should not set the V bit in their *Registration Requests*. Doing so would be redundant and ambiguous. Such mobile nodes should allow the PPP compression software to do the header compression and decompression. Likewise on the foreign agent.

5.5 Chapter Summary

This chapter described in detail the three component technologies of Mobile IP:

1. *Agent Discovery* is the method by which a mobile node determines whether any home agents, foreign agents, or both are present on its current link and by which the mobile node determines whether it is connected to its home link or a foreign link. Agent Discovery also provides a mechanism for a mobile node to determine when it has moved from one link to another and further provides a way for a mobile node to obtain a foreign agent care-of address. Agent Discovery consists of two messages—*Agent Solicitations* and *Agent Advertisements*—that are derived from, and are very similar to, the corresponding messages defined in *ICMP Router Discovery* [RFC 1256].

2. *Registration* is the method by which a mobile node requests routing and possibly de-tunneling services from a foreign agent (if present) and by which a mobile node informs its home agent of its current care-of address(es). Registration is also the method by which a mobile node renews a registration which is due to expire and further provides a way for a mobile node to deregister when it returns to its home link. The registration procedure also provides a way for a mobile node to dynamically ascertain the address of a home agent, if the mobile node has no prior knowledge of its

home agent. Registration consists of two messages—*Registration Requests* and *Registration Replies*—that are exchanged between a mobile node, possibly a foreign agent, and the mobile node's home agent. All registration messages are required to contain the Mobile-Home Authentication Extension to guard against denial-of-service attacks which would otherwise be trivial to perform.

3. Finally, Mobile IP defines the rules for routing any type of packet—unicast, multicast, and broadcast—to and from mobile nodes that are connected to a foreign link. Packets sent by a mobile node are routed directly to their destination without the need for tunneling, except for certain multicast and broadcast packets. Packets sent to a mobile node are routed to its home agent where a copy is tunneled to each care-of address that has been registered by the mobile node. At the care-of address, the original packet is extracted from the tunnel and delivered to the mobile node.

In the next chapter we examine tunneling in more detail, since tunneling is such an integral part of Mobile IP.

Tunneling

*T*his chapter provides additional information about tunneling, since tunneling plays such an important role in Mobile IP. We begin with a primer on IP Fragmentation, since fragmented IP packets affect which type of encapsulation methods can be used by a tunnel entry-point. Then we describe in detail the three types of tunneling used by Mobile IP: *IP in IP Encapsulation*, *Minimal Encapsulation*, and *Generic Routing Encapsulation (GRE)*.

6.1 What Is IP Fragmentation?

Many link layers and the hardware over which they run place an upper limit on the size of a frame that they are capable of transferring. This limit, called the *link MTU (Maximum Transfer Unit)*, in turn limits the maximum size of an IP packet that may be transferred within a single frame. An IP packet which is larger than the link MTU of the link over which it is to be forwarded must be *fragmented* before it may be transmitted. Fragmentation is the process by which a large IP packet is chopped up into smaller pieces—fragments—in order for the smaller pieces to fit within a link's MTU.

Fragmentation can occur when two hosts, each of which is directly connected to a link with large MTU, communicate via routers which themselves are connected via links with small MTU. To prevent fragmentation in such cases,

IPv4 recommends—and IPv6 requires—hosts to discover the *path MTU* between the source and destination. The path MTU is the smallest of the individual link MTUs comprising the path between the source and the destination. IPv4 hosts can discover the path MTU using the procedure defined in [RFC 1191], which we briefly describe in *How Does IPv4 Path MTU Discovery Work?* on page 113.

6.1.1 How Does Fragmentation Work?

IP fragmentation is performed either by the original source of a packet or by a router along the path to the ultimate destination. The fragments are created in such a way as to be reassembled at the ultimate destination of the original packet. The exception is fragmentation that occurs within a tunnel, where the tunnel fragments are reassembled at the tunnel's exit-point, which, in fact, is the ultimate destination of the *tunneling* packet.

Which Packets Are Fragmented?

A node with an IP packet to transmit—either a host generating the packet or a router forwarding the packet—compares the size of the packet with the MTU of the link over which the node's routing table specifies the packet should be transmitted. If the packet is too large to fit within the link MTU—as determined by the IP Total Length field—then the packet is fragmented.

The exception to this rule is IP packets which have the Don't Fragment bit set to 1 within the IP header. A node might set the Don't Fragment bit in order to perform Path MTU discovery as defined in [RFC 1191]. If such packets would otherwise need to be fragmented, then they are instead discarded, and an ICMP message is sent to the original source of the packet. The ICMP message is of Type *Destination Unreachable,* where the Code field is set to indicate that fragmentation was needed but the Don't Fragment bit was set.

Fragmentation Procedure

When a node has a packet to transmit which must be fragmented it performs the following procedure (see Figure 6-1):

1. It chops up the payload portion of the packet into chunks (fragments) of as large a size as possible such that each resulting fragment—including an IP header—will fit within a single link-layer frame. The size of the fragment must be an integer multiple of 8 bytes, because of the way the size is encoded within the resulting IP header. (The final fragment need not be an integer multiple of 8 bytes and is likely to be of different size than the rest.)

2. It prepends a copy of the original IP header to each of the payload fragments to form IP fragments. For each resulting IP fragment, the node must:

   a. make sure the IP Identification field of all fragments is identical;

   b. set the IP Fragment Offset field of each fragment to allow the reassembler to figure out the ordering of the fragments;

c. set the IP Total Length field to be the length of the individual IP fragment—*not* that of the total, original IP packet; and

d. set the IP More Fragments bit to 0 for the last fragment and set it to 1 for all other fragments, including the first one.

The fragmenting node transmits each fragment using the normal IP routing procedure to select a Next Hop. When the fragments arrive at the destination, they are reassembled as follows:

- fragments with same IP Source Address, Destination Address, Protocol, and Identification fields are placed within the same *reassembly buffer*, where they accumulate until all individual fragments of the same original packet have arrived;

- the Fragment Offset field, along with the More Fragments and the Total Length fields, are used to determine the order in which the fragments are reassembled and also to determine when all the fragments have arrived;

- when the last fragment arrives, the original packet is recovered, the reassembly buffer is freed, and the original packet is further processed as if it had arrived unfragmented (often being passed to the higher-layer protocol indicated by the IP Protocol field); and

- if all of the fragments do not arrive within a reasonable period of time, the buffer is freed, and whatever fragments have arrived are discarded.

6.1.2 How Does IPv4 Path MTU Discovery Work?

In this section we briefly describe *Path MTU Discovery* [RFC 1191] for IPv4. We do so for two reasons: first, because it is intimately related to fragmentation; and second, because *IP in IP Encapsulation* [RFC 2003] defines specific behavior for tunnel entry-points in order to support it, which we describe in *Building an Encapsulated Packet* on page 115.

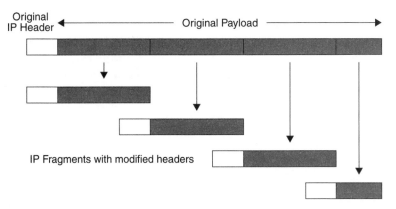

Figure 6-1 IP Fragmentation

Prior to [RFC 1191], a sending IPv4 node selected an MTU based upon the location of the destination. If the destination was connected to the same link (as determined by the routing table), then the link MTU was also used as a path MTU. If the destination was connected to some other link, then the smaller of the link MTU of the sender and 576 bytes—the size of a packet that all IPv4 nodes must be capable of receiving—was used as a path MTU. In many instances, this resulted in path MTUs which were either too large or too small, depending upon the circumstances.

The method defined in [RFC 1191] works as follows:

- a sender assumes the path MTU to be the link MTU of the link over which it forwards packets to reach a destination;

- the sender transmits all IP packets to the destination with the Don't Fragment bit set;

- any router along the path which would ordinarily be required to fragment the packet—because its Next Hop link has an MTU less than the Total Length of the packet—sends an *ICMP Destination Unreachable* message of Code "fragmentation needed and DF set" to the sender, and discards the original packet;

- upon receipt of these ICMP messages, the sender reduces its estimate of the path MTU and begins sending smaller packets to that destination;

- when no more ICMP messages of the above type are received by the sender, then it has discovered the path MTU for that destination.

[RFC 1191] proposes an enhancement to the existing *ICMP Destination Unreachable* message of Code "fragmentation needed and DF set" originally defined in [RFC 792]. Specifically, the router generating the message includes the "Next-Hop MTU" for the link which caused the router to generate the message. In this way, the original sender knows exactly how much to reduce its estimate of the path MTU each time it receives one of these ICMP messages.

6.2 What Is IP in IP Encapsulation?

IP in IP Encapsulation, as defined in [RFC 2003], is the Internet-standard method for encapsulating an entire IPv4 packet within the payload portion of another IPv4 packet. As described in *How Are Packets Routed to a Mobile Node on a Foreign Link?* on page 90, Mobile IP home agents and foreign agents are required to implement *IP in IP Encapsulation* in order to perform the home-agent-to-care-of address tunnel.

6.2.1 Building an Encapsulated Packet

IP in IP Encapsulation is rather straightforward. A first IP packet is placed within the payload portion of a new IP packet, and the fields of the encapsulating (outer) IP header are set as follows:

- the Version is set to 4;
- the Type of Service (TOS) bits are copied from the inner IP header;
- the Source Address and Destination Address are set to the entry-point and the exit-point of the tunnel, respectively;
- the Internet Header Length (IHL), the Total Length, and the Checksum are recomputed for the outer header;
- the Identification, Flags, Fragment Offset are set as specified by [RFC 791] for any IP packet. Specifically, a unique value is placed within the Identification field, and the Flags and Fragment Offset are set in accordance with whether or not the resulting, encapsulated packet needs to be fragmented. The Don't Fragment bit of the outer header is always set to 1 if the inner IP header has the Don't Fragment bit set to 1, which allows Path MTU Discovery to work properly in the presence of IP tunnels (see *How Does IPv4 Path MTU Discovery Work?* on page 113);
- the Protocol field is set to 4 to indicate that the payload is itself an IP packet (header plus payload); and
- the Time to Live field is set to a value large enough to deliver the encapsulating packet to the tunnel exit-point.

The Time to Live field of the encapsulated (inner) IP header is decremented by the tunnel entry-point if the packet is being forwarded, for example, from some physical interface into the tunnel. Similarly, upon being decapsulated, the Time to Live field of the encapsulated (inner) IP header is decremented by the tunnel exit-point if the packet is being forwarded, for example, from the tunnel to a physical interface.

Thus, tunnels implemented using *IP in IP Encapsulation* appear as a single, virtual link to packets that pass through them. For example, a packet that arrives at a first router, passes through a tunnel which begins at that first router, emerges from the tunnel at a second router, and is further forwarded toward its ultimate destination, will have its IP Time to Live field decremented twice, exactly as if the tunnel were a single link connecting these two routers.

6.2.2 Relaying ICMP Messages

The *Internet Control Message Protocol (ICMP)* [RFC 792] defines a set of messages which provide diagnostic information and report error conditions. ICMP messages generated by a host or router in response to an IP packet are sent to the original source of that packet and generally provide useful information to that source.

However, ICMP messages generated in response to a tunneled packet are sent to the entry-point of the tunnel, not necessarily to the original source of the encapsulated (inner) packet. In many circumstances, however, it is useful to inform the original source of the inner packet when an ICMP message is generated within a tunnel. Thus, [RFC 2003] defines the behavior of a tunnel entry-point necessary to *relay* certain ICMP messages to this original source. We now describe how this works.

Soft State

As specified in [RFC 792], ICMP messages sent to the source of an offending IP packet contain an ICMP header and some portion of the original, offending IP packet. This portion of the offending packet is only required to be the IP header plus a minimum of 8 bytes of the payload. Unfortunately, 8 bytes is not enough to contain the Source Address and Destination Address of the inner packet in the case when the offending packet is an encapsulating packet. This would ordinarily make it impossible for the tunnel entry-point to determine *which* node was the source of the original (inner) packet.

However, by maintaining information called *soft state*, a tunnel entry-point can make this determination upon receipt of an ICMP message from within the tunnel. Soft state is a set of variables that describe the current characteristics of the tunnel. These variables include:

- Path MTU of the tunnel;
- the length of the tunnel, measured in "hops"; and
- whether or not the end of the tunnel is reachable.

The entry-point updates its soft state based upon ICMP messages *it* receives from routers within the tunnel. For example, if the entry-point sets to 1 the Don't Fragment bit in the encapsulating (outer) header and receives an *ICMP Destination Unreachable* message of Code "fragmentation needed and DF set," then the entry-point knows to decrease its estimate of the tunnel path MTU.

Similarly, if the entry-point receives an *ICMP Time Exceeded* message of Code "time to live exceeded in transit," then it knows that the value it is using for the Time to Live field within the encapsulating (outer) IP header is too small and therefore that it must increase its estimate of the length of the tunnel.

If the tunnel entry-point receives an *ICMP Destination Unreachable* message of Code "net/host/protocol unreachable," then the entry-point knows that the exit-point of the tunnel is currently unreachable, owing probably to some permanent or temporary routing failure.

Using Soft State to *Relay* ICMP Messages to the Original Sender

A tunnel entry-point uses these soft-state variables to generate ICMP messages to the original source of a packet *at the time it encapsulates that packet for delivery into the tunnel*—not necessarily at the time the entry-point (later) receives an ICMP message from within the tunnel.

For example, consider a packet arriving at a home agent which is to be tunneled to a mobile node's care-of address. The home agent examines the Total Length of the packet to see if it exceeds the soft-state measurement of the tunnel's Path MTU. If so, then the home agent knows that the packet must be fragmented in order to reach the tunnel exit-point. If the packet also has its Don't Fragment bit set to 1, then the home agent immediately generates an *ICMP Destination Unreachable* message of Code "fragmentation needed and DF set," and discards the original packet.

Note that the home agent does not wait for an ICMP message to be generated within the tunnel for *this* packet, before sending an ICMP message to the original source. Rather, the home agent relies on its previous knowledge of the tunnel's path MTU—as represented by its tunnel soft state—to immediately generate the unreachable message to the original packet's source.

[RFC 2003] goes into considerable detail as to which messages from within the tunnel should and which should not be relayed to the original source of the inner packet. Since the purpose of this book is to provide additional insight into the standards documents—not to repeat them verbatim—we refer the interested reader to [RFC 2003] for the details of handling all possible ICMP messages at a tunnel entry-point.

6.2.3 Preventing Recursive Encapsulation

Recursive encapsulation is defined as the process by which a routing loop causes tunneled packets to reenter the same tunnel (an additional time) before exiting [draft-ietf-ipngwg-ipv6-tunnel-07.txt]. In such a case, each encapsulation adds another IP header, with its own Time to Live, causing the packet to grow in size and to circulate through the network indefinitely. Note that this is different from *nested encapsulation*, where a packet enters a first tunnel and then enters a second tunnel. In the case of nested encapsulation, the encapsulated packets ultimately reach their tunnel exit-points—not so for recursive encapsulation.

GRE, which we describe in *What Is Generic Routing Encapsulation (GRE)?* on page 121, and IPv6 tunneling both have explicit mechanisms for preventing recursive encapsulation. IPv4 tunneling, as defined in [RFC 2003], has no such mechanism. Rather, IPv4 tunnel entry-points use the following tests to determine whether a packet is likely to be undergoing recursive encapsulation:

1. If the tunnel entry-point is itself the IP Source Address of the original (possibly encapsulated) packet, then the tunnel entry-point should assume the presence of recursive encapsulation. *Note that this test applies only to packets that arrive from some node other than the entry-point itself through one of its external network interfaces.*

   Specifically, recall that a home agent must use nested encapsulation to deliver a broadcast packet to a mobile node which uses a foreign agent care-of address. Here the inner tunnel is from the home agent to the mobile node's home address and the outer tunnel is from the home agent to the care-of address.

If the rule above were applied to the first (inner) encapsulating packet, then the home agent would be forbidden from generating the second (outer) encapsulating packet, since the IP Source Address of both packets would be the same; namely, that of the home agent.

2. If the IP Source Address of the (possibly tunneled) original packet is the same as the tunnel exit-point, as determined from the entry-point's routing table, then the tunnel entry-point should assume the presence of recursive encapsulation. This case represents a router which thinks that a packet should be tunneled to that packet's original source, which seems strange indeed.

6.2.4 Summary

IP in IP Encapsulation [RFC 2003] provides a standard method of encapsulating IPv4 packets within the payload portion of another IPv4 packet. Unlike *Minimal Encapsulation*, examined in the next section, *IP in IP Encapsulation* works in all cases, whether the original IP packet is fragmented or not.

IP in IP Encapsulation requires more overhead—20 bytes versus 8 or 12— than *Minimal Encapsulation*. By maintaining soft state, tunnel entry-points can relay ICMP messages generated within the tunnel to the original source of an offending packet.

6.3 What Is Minimal Encapsulation?

Minimal Encapsulation within IP, as defined in [RFC 2004], is an optional form of tunneling which can be used in Mobile IP. The purpose of *Minimal Encapsulation* is to decrease the number of additional bytes that are needed to implement a tunnel. It does this by removing the redundant information carried by both the encapsulating (outer) IP header and the encapsulated (inner) IP header in *IP in IP Encapsulation* [RFC 2003].

6.3.1 Building an Encapsulated Packet

An original IP packet is tunneled using *Minimal Encapsulation* as follows (see Figure 6-2):

1. A Minimal Forwarding Header (see Figure 6-2) is inserted between the original IP header and the original IP payload.
2. The original IP header is modified as follows:

    a. the Protocol field is set to 55, which identifies the (new) payload as a minimally encapsulated, tunneled packet;

    b. the Source Address and the Destination Address are replaced by the addresses of the entry-point and the exit-point of the tunnel, respectively;

    c. the Internet Header Length (IHL), the Total Length, and the Checksum are re-computed for the new header and payload; and

    d. the Time to Live field is decremented if the entry-point is routing the original packet from some (e.g., physical) interface to the tunnel interface. Conversely, if the entry-point is also the source of the original packet, then the Time to Live field is not decremented.

3. The Minimal Forwarding Header is filled in as follows:

    a. the Protocol field is copied from the Protocol field of the original IP header;

    b. the Original Source Address Present (S) bit is set to 0 if the tunnel entry-point is identical to the source of the original IP packet—otherwise, it is set to 1;

    c. the Header Checksum is computed over the Minimal Forwarding Header (after the rest of the header has been assembled);

    d. the Original Destination Address field is copied from the IP Destination Address of the original packet; and

    e. if the tunnel entry-point is not the original source of the packet, then the Original Source Address field is copied from the IP Source Address of the original IP packet. Otherwise, this field is not present in the tunneled packet.

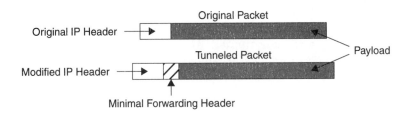

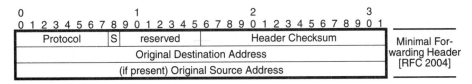

Figure 6-2 Minimal Encapsulation

Thus, the size of a Minimal Forwarding Header, and hence the overhead of a tunnel implemented via *Minimal Encapsulation*, is either 8 or 12 bytes, depending on whether the entry-point is also the source of the original packet.

6.3.2 Fragmentation

The procedure for decapsulating a minimally encapsulated packet involves restoring the original IP header from the fields within the Minimal Forwarding Header. As Figure 6-2 shows, there is no place within the Minimal Forwarding Header to store information about the original packet with regard to fragmentation. As a result, a tunnel entry-point must use *IP in IP Encapsulation* in order to tunnel those original packets which are already fragmented.

Equivalently stated, *Minimal Encapsulation* cannot be used when an original packet is already fragmented. In contrast, an encapsulating (outer) packet may be fragmented in order to traverse a tunnel with a small path MTU, but an original packet that is already fragmented cannot be tunneled via *Minimal Encapsulation*.

6.3.3 Time to Live and Tunnel Length

Recall that *IP in IP Encapsulation* makes the tunnel appear as a single virtual link to an original packet. The packet's Time to Live field is decremented only upon entry into the tunnel and exit from the tunnel. In contrast, *Minimal Encapsulation* exposes an original packet to every link between the entry-point and the exit-point, at least from the perspective of Time to Live.

Equivalently stated, an original packet traversing a *Minimal Encapsulation* tunnel will have its Time to Live decremented at every router between the entry-point and the exit-point. Thus, a situation might arise where a minimally encapsulated packet (where Time to Live is decremented at each router within a long tunnel) might not be able to reach a destination that *would* be reachable via *IP in IP Encapsulation* (where Time to Live is decremented only at the entry-point and exit-point of the same long tunnel). *Mobile-node implementors should take note of this fact when deciding whether to request Minimal Encapsulation during Registration.*

6.3.4 Relaying ICMP Messages

Procedures for relaying ICMP messages to original senders are the same for *Minimal Encapsulation* as they are for *IP in IP Encapsulation*. Implementations of *Minimal Encapsulation* should still maintain soft state, because the size of the Minimal Forwarding Header (8 or 12 bytes) still means that ICMP messages from within the tunnel will not contain the IP address of the original source—except in the degenerate case where the tunnel entry-point is the same as the original source of the packet.

6.3.5 Preventing Recursive Encapsulation

The procedures for preventing recursive encapsulation in *Minimal Encapsulation* are the same as for *IP in IP Encapsulation*. See *Preventing Recursive Encapsulation* on page 117 for more information.

6.3.6 Summary

In summary, *Minimal Encapsulation* can save a few (usually 8) bytes over *IP in IP Encapsulation* but carries with it the following disadvantages:

- it does not work when an original packet is already fragmented;
- it results in the Time to Live of the original packet being decremented at every router within the tunnel, which increases the chance that a mobile node cannot be reached if its home agent uses *Minimal Encapsulation*; and
- its mysteriously chosen packet layout does not put the Original Source Address in an area that guarantees it will be returned by an ICMP message within the tunnel, implying that a tunnel entry-point still has to implement soft state in order to relay such messages to the original source of the packet.

For these reasons, Mobile IP implementors should concentrate on making *IP in IP Encapsulation* work correctly and in accordance with [RFC 2003] and forget about *Minimal Encapsulation*.

6.4 What Is Generic Routing Encapsulation (GRE)?

Generic Routing Encapsulation (GRE) [RFC 1701] is the final tunneling method accommodated by Mobile IP. GRE supports other network-layer protocols in addition to IP. It allows a packet of a first protocol suite to be encapsulated within the payload portion of a packet of a second protocol suite. This is in contrast to *IP in IP Encapsulation* and *Minimal Encapsulation*, both of which support only IP.

6.4.1 Multiprotocol Encapsulation

Consider the case of a network-layer packet of a first protocol suite that is to be encapsulated for delivery within a network-layer packet of a second protocol suite. [RFC 1701] calls the inner packet the *payload* packet and the outer packet the *delivery* packet. If we further consider the possibility of P different types of payload packets and D different types of delivery packets, then we would normally require $D \times P$ documents which specify how to encapsulate all of the various payload packets within all of the various delivery packets.

However, with GRE we need only $P + D$ documents—P documents describing how to encapsulate the various payload packets within GRE, and D documents specifying how to encapsulate GRE within the various delivery packets. If

P and *D* are large, as they are in organizations which have many protocols running on their networks, then GRE provides a more manageable solution.

Figure 6-3 illustrates the GRE encapsulation process. A GRE header is placed between the payload packet and the delivery packet, and the fields of the GRE header are filled in as specified in [RFC 1701]. The case in which the payload and delivery packets are both IPv4 packets, as would be the case for a tunnel from a home agent to a foreign agent in Mobile IP, is shown in Figure 6-3.

6.4.2 Preventing Recursive Encapsulation

Unlike *IP in IP Encapsulation* and *Minimal Encapsulation*, GRE provides explicit protection against recursive encapsulation. Figure 6-3 shows the GRE header. The minimum length of a GRE header is 4 bytes, if none of the optional fields are present.

Of particular note is the Recur field in the GRE header, which is a counter that keeps track of the number of additional encapsulations which are allowed. A router which is considering further tunneling a GRE-encapsulated packet examines this field before doing so. If the Recur field is not zero, then the packet may be further encapsulated and the Recur field in the new GRE header is decremented by one. Otherwise, if the Recur field has already reached zero, then the packet must not be further encapsulated (and will likely be discarded).

A similar mechanism has been proposed to prevent recursive encapsulation in IPv6. [draft-ietf-ipngwg-ipv6-tunnel-07.txt] defines a Destination Option for this purpose. (An overview of IPv6 is provided in *How Does IPv6 Differ from IPv4?* on page 248.) The IPv6 tunneling draft also warns implementors about *loopback encapsulation,* where a router recursively encapsulates a packet to itself without the packet ever being emitted through a physical interface. Such a condition can

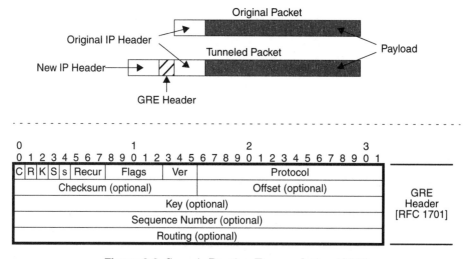

Figure 6-3 Generic Routing Encapsulation (GRE)

cause the router to crash or to infinitely process the same packet, or both. Implementors should take precautions in order to prevent such a tunnel from being configured in a node.

6.4.3 Summary

GRE's support for multiprotocol tunneling and its explicit prevention of recursive encapsulation makes it attractive for certain applications. In *Support for Other Protocols within the Mobile IP Framework* on page 219 we show one such application in which GRE is used by Mobile IP to enable mobile nodes to receive packets of multiple protocol suites in addition to IP when those mobile nodes are connected to a foreign link.

6.5 Chapter Summary

This chapter began with a description of IP fragmentation, the process by which an IP packet is chopped up into smaller chunks, called fragments, in order to traverse links with Maximum Transfer Unit (MTU) smaller than the Total Length of the IP packet. This provided the necessary background to understand IP tunneling in detail.

Next we described *IP in IP Encapsulation*, the mandatory Mobile IP tunneling mechanism which must be supported by all home agent and foreign agent implementations, as well as by those mobile nodes which support operation with collocated care-of addresses. *IP in IP Encapsulation* works whether or not an original packet is already fragmented.

Finally, we described *Minimal Encapsulation* and *Generic Routing Encapsulation (GRE)*, two types of tunneling which may also be supported by Mobile IP implementations. *Minimal Encapsulation* works only when an original packet is not fragmented, while *Generic Routing Encapsulation* supports multiprotocol encapsulation and has explicit mechanisms for preventing recursive encapsulation.

3

APPLYING MOBILE IP

C H A P T E R **7**

Security Primer

*T*his chapter gives an introduction to computer and network security. Here we define the nature of computer and network security and provide an introduction to the technologies used to combat security threats. We also investigate the Internet-related protocols that employ these technologies. This provides the foundation necessary to understand the security implications of applying Mobile IP in various situations, which we investigate in subsequent chapters. For a complete treatment of computer security, see [KaPeSp95] or [Schneier95].

In this chapter and throughout this book, we borrow from [KaPeSp95] the term "Bad Guy" to describe an individual who might try to steal information, deny or steal service, or otherwise perform some type of attack on a computer or network. A "Good Guy," in contrast, is someone who is doing something that he or she is properly authorized to do.

7.1 What Do We Mean by *Security*?

When computer scientists and network managers talk about *security*, they are generally referring to the science (though some would call it an art) of protecting computers, network resources, and information against unauthorized access, modification, and/or destruction. This generally involves four related topics, the definitions of which have been paraphrased from *Security Architecture for the Internet Protocol* [RFC 1825]:

- *confidentiality*—transforming data such that it can be decoded only by authorized parties;

- *authentication*—proving or disproving someone's or something's claimed identity;

- *integrity checking*—ensuring that data cannot be modified without such modification being detectable; and

- *non-repudiation*—proving that a source of some data did in fact send data that he might later deny sending.

Broadly speaking, the technology employed to accomplish all of these security features is called *cryptography*. In the remainder of this section, we will define cryptography and show how it can be used to accomplish the functions listed above.

7.2 What Is Cryptography?

Solutions to the problems raised by security generally fall into two categories: *cryptographically strong* solutions and *you-are-kidding-yourself* solutions. A you-are-kidding-yourself solution is one which a Bad Guy can defeat simply by looking at the contents of packets as they fly across a network or by using simple decoding methods.

In contrast, a cryptographically strong solution is one that cannot be broken without spending more money trying to defeat it than the value to be gained by defeating it in the first place! (For example, it would not make sense, even for a Bad Guy, to purchase $10 million worth of computers in order to break a security system that allowed him to steal $100 from an Automatic Teller Machine once he was successful.) This book will deal only with cryptographically strong solutions.

Cryptography is the science of transforming data in seemingly bizarre ways to accomplish surprisingly useful things. It is practiced by a frighteningly intelligent breed of mathematicians, called cryptographers. Many have a peculiar habit of giving very complicated answers to what would appear to be simple questions. A sample dialogue goes something like this:

> *Person of Average or Better Intelligence: "If I did this, that, and the other thing, would that then be secure?"*

Cryptographer: "It is computationally infeasible that your security mechanism could be broken within the relevant lifetime of the data you wish to protect, assuming that computing power continues to improve at or near its current rate of growth."

Person of Average or Better Intelligence: "Huh?"

This is not to imply that cryptographers are deceptive. To the contrary they are quite good at telling us what is *not* secure. However, it is very difficult for anyone, even the best of cryptographers, to *prove* that *no* one will *ever* find a way to break a given security scheme.

Nonetheless, cryptography, when properly applied, can provide all of the security features mentioned in the opening part of this section—namely, confidentiality, authentication, integrity checking, and non-repudiation. We will see examples of all of these features later in this chapter.

7.2.1 Cryptographic Systems

A cryptographic system consists of two fundamental components: a complicated mathematical function, called an *algorithm*, and one or more secret or public values, called *keys*. A key is a chunk of binary data that is (supposed to be) known only to the parties which wish to communicate securely. In contrast, an algorithm is usually published and is available to anyone who wants to read it. This state of affairs is fortunate, because it is relatively easy to generate a new chunk of binary data (a key) but difficult to devise new cryptographic algorithms.

A *strong* cryptographic algorithm is one that has withstood the attempts of really smart mathematicians to *break* it. An algorithm is said to be broken when someone figures out a weakness or a flaw that can be exploited by Bad Guys to do bad things. When an algorithm is broken to the point at which it can be easily defeated, then it ceases to be useful. Algorithms are considered to be good ones when many smart people have tried to break them, over long periods of time, without being successful.

A good key is one that is known only to the appropriate person(s), is not easily guessable, and is sufficiently long. Specifically, a key should be long enough to withstand brute-force attacks in which a Bad Guy simply tries every possible key until he finds the right one. A cryptographic system is not considered to be secure unless it uses a strong algorithm, avoids pitfalls such as those described in Chapter 9 of [KaPeSp95], and chooses and manages keys carefully.

Various government agencies, however, are urging the computer and networking industries to adopt their so-called "Clipper" proposals, all of which are based on the opposite premise. Some of these proposals involve keeping the algorithms themselves secret rather than exposing them to peer-review within the cryptographic community. In addition, various government agencies would keep copies of everyone's keys, though presumably these keys could be obtained only through a court order.

As you can imagine, these proposals have been resisted strongly within the cryptographic community. The Internet Architecture Board (IAB) and the Internet Engineering Steering Group (IESG)—two organizations involved in the Internet standards process—have gone on record as officially opposing such proposals, as have most of my colleagues in the Internet Engineering Task Force. See [RFC 1984] for more information on this important topic. (The irony of the cited reference's document number is hereby acknowledged.)

Throughout this book, we will assume that all algorithms are known to everyone, including Bad Guys, but that the keys (or pairs of keys) are known only to those who are *supposed* to know them—i.e., the parties that wish to communicate securely. Also, we will steer clear of any discussion of the mathematics behind cryptography and instead concentrate on its uses. See [KaPeSp95] or [Schneier95] for a discussion of such mathematics.

7.2.2 Secret-Key versus Public-Key Algorithms

Cryptographic algorithms fall into two broad categories:

1. A *secret-key* algorithm is one in which the same key—a secret key—is used by both the sender and the receiver, who must work very hard to keep the value of the key, well, secret.

2. A *public-key* algorithm is one which uses a pair of (related) keys—one used by the sender and one used by the receiver. One of the keys in the pair is kept secret (the private key) and the other is widely published (the public key).

Because secret-key algorithms involve both parties performing computations using the same key, they are often called "symmetric algorithms." However, we will use the term "secret-key algorithms" throughout this book. Also, because public-key algorithms generally involve the use of different keys by the various parties, they are often called "asymmetric algorithms." However, we will use the term "public-key algorithms" throughout this book.

One of the primary challenges in cryptography is distributing keys in a secure fashion (i.e., without their falling into the wrong hands). The best cryptographic algorithms in the world are useless if a Bad Guy is able to obtain a copy of the key or keys that were used to protect some data. As we will see in *How Can We Manage Keys Securely?* on page 139, it is easier to perform key distribution for public-key algorithms than it is for secret-key algorithms.

On the other hand, secret-key algorithms tend to be faster than public-key algorithms, as measured by the amount of time it takes a computer to perform the necessary calculations, for a given level of protection. Therefore, secret-key algorithms are often used to protect the actual data, even when public-key technology is used to distribute keys. All of this is probably quite confusing, but it will become more clear as we look at how cryptographic algorithms are actually used to provide various types of security in the next few sections.

7.3 What Do We Mean by *Confidentiality*?

Individuals who wish to communicate over a public network in such a way as to prevent all others from reading their data, desire a security property called *confidentiality*. *Encryption algorithms* are a specific subset of cryptographic algorithms which are commonly used to provide confidentiality. These algorithms are usually used as in the following example (see Figure 7-1):

- Howard wishes to send a message to Dominique that only she can read. The message, in its plain, unscrambled form, is called *plaintext*.

- Howard *encrypts* the plaintext message using an *encryption algorithm* and a *key*. The output of the encryption algorithm is called *ciphertext*.

- Howard transmits the ciphertext message over the network to Dominique. Any host or router in the network is able to inspect the ciphertext, but only the nodes which possess the key can recover the original, plaintext message.

- Dominique, who possesses the proper key, *decrypts* the ciphertext message, using the inverse of the encryption algorithm used by Howard, to produce the original, plaintext message.

- Dominique reads the plaintext message hoping that it contains something interesting or useful, considering all of the trouble that she and Howard have just gone through.

We now examine in more detail how systems employing encryption can be built both from secret-key algorithms and from public-key algorithms.

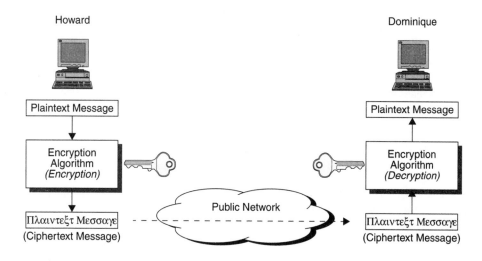

Figure 7-1 Confidentiality Using Encryption

7.3.1 Secret-Key Encryption

Secret-key encryption is easier to understand than public-key encryption because only one key is involved—*the* secret key. If Howard and Dominique wish to communicate confidentially using a secret-key encryption algorithm, then they both need to agree on a secret value to use as a key. We will explore ways in which this might occur in *How Can We Manage Keys Securely?* on page 139, but for now we assume that this agreement happens magically—i.e., without any information being sent over a network (where a Bad Guy might intercept it).

In addition to agreeing on the secret key, Howard and Dominique must also agree on a secret-key encryption algorithm to use. It bears repeating that the strength of an algorithm depends upon its mathematical characteristics but not upon hiding the identity of the algorithm itself. For this reason, Howard's and Dominique's choice of algorithm need not be kept secret, though there is no reason to make a Bad Guy's job any easier by telling him what algorithm they are using.

Once Howard and Dominique have agreed on a secret key and an encryption algorithm, they can exchange encrypted messages that only the other person can decrypt. Symbolically, this can be written as follows:

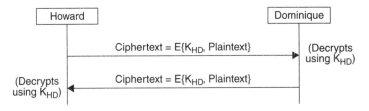

Here, K_{HD} is the key shared by Howard and Dominique (we use their initials as subscripts to remind us who knows the value of the key). Also, E{stuff} is used to denote an encryption operation whose inputs are the stuff in braces. In this case, the encrypted message (the ciphertext) is produced using the secret key (K_{HD}) and an original, Plaintext message.

Howard sends private messages to Dominique by encrypting them using K_{HD}, which she decrypts using the same exact key. Likewise, Dominique sends private messages to Howard by encrypting them using K_{HD}, and Howard also uses K_{HD} to decrypt these messages.

7.3.2 Public-Key Encryption

Public-key encryption is more difficult to understand than secret-key encryption because there are more keys involved. In public-key systems, each individual has a pair of keys—a public key that is widely published and a private key that is kept secret. The public key and the private key are mathematically related in a very important way. However, it is impossible to determine one if we only know the other. That is, it is *extremely* difficult to figure out someone's private key, even if we know that individual's public key.[†]

If Howard and Dominique wish to communicate confidentially using a public-key encryption algorithm, then each one needs to know the other person's public key. Note that one of the wonderful properties of public keys is that they can be sent over a network in the clear (i.e., in plaintext form). In fact, public keys have the exact opposite security requirements as do private keys and (shared) secret keys: whereas a secret key cannot be guarded too strongly, a public key cannot be published too widely! We will see why this is the case in *How Can We Manage Keys Securely?* on page 139.

In addition to learning each other's public keys, Howard and Dominique must agree on a public-key encryption algorithm to use. As with secret-key algorithms, the strength of a public-key algorithm depends upon its mathematical characteristics but not upon hiding the identity of the algorithm itself. For this reason, Howard's and Dominique's choice of algorithm need not be kept secret, though—again—there is no reason to make a Bad Guy's job any easier by telling him what algorithm they are using.

Once Howard and Dominique have obtained each other's public keys and agreed on an encryption algorithm, they can exchange encrypted messages that only the other person can decrypt. Symbolically, this can be written as follows:

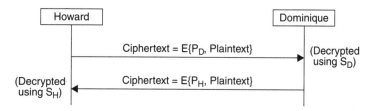

Here, P_D is Dominique's public key and P_H is Howard's public key. We will use 'S' for private keys because they must be kept Secret (we cannot use 'P' because we already used that letter for public keys). This turns out to be a reasonable choice, because private keys are also used to produce digital signatures, as we will see in *Digital Signatures* on page 137.

Thus, Howard sends confidential messages to Dominique by encrypting them using Dominique's public key (P_D). As shown in the figure, Dominique decrypts the messages using her private key (S_D). Recall that only Dominique knows the value of her private key. Similarly, Dominique sends confidential messages to Howard by encrypting them using Howard's public key (P_H). Howard decrypts the messages with his private key (S_H).

Public-key encryption algorithms tend to be slow in comparison to secret-key algorithms, as measured by the amount of time it takes a computer to perform the calculations required to do encryption and decryption. However, as

---

[†] OK, not impossible, but it would take so long that the information that subsequently could be obtained would be of little value.

has been hinted previously, it is much easier to distribute keys for public-key algorithms than for secret-key algorithms.

For this reason, encryption systems are frequently built using a hybrid approach, where public-key algorithms are used to distribute temporary secret keys (called session keys), which are in turn used to perform secret-key encryption of the actual messages. This is the strategy used in *Pretty Good Privacy (PGP)* [Stall95], upon which many E-mail applications that support encryption are based.

7.4 What Do We Mean by *Authentication, Integrity Checking*, and *Non-Repudiation*?

Our primary purpose in this section is to discuss authentication, but as we will see, the technology used to accomplish authentication is generally the same as that used to provide integrity checking and non-repudiation as well. Thus, it makes sense to discuss all of these security features together, which we do in the remainder of this section.

7.4.1 What Is Authorization?

One of the purposes of a computer network is to provide a way to share resources among many users. These resources must generally be protected against unauthorized access. For example, most users want to protect their files from being modified by other users. Similarly, users want to protect their electronic mail from being read by other users.

A computer which contains shared resources is usually called a *server,* and access to its resources is controlled by application or operating-system software. Server software allows a user to access a resource only after checking that the user has permission to do so—a process called *authorization*. Authorization is not terribly useful, however, unless the server also requires the user to *prove* his identity before authorizing him to do something. Otherwise, a Bad Guy could falsify his identity in order to gain access to someone else's information.

7.4.2 What Is Authentication?

Authentication is this process of proving someone's or something's claimed identity. Authentication usually involves challenging a person to prove that he has physical possession of something (e.g., a smartcard or a driver's license) or that he has knowledge of something (e.g., a password or his mother's maiden name). Authentication protocols define the message flows by which this challenge and response are sent and received by the parties being authenticated.

An ATM (Automatic Teller Machine) is a common example of a computer which authenticates a user before granting him access to a resource (cash). Most ATMs authenticate a person by requiring him to prove that he has *both* physical possession of something (his ATM card) *and* knowledge of something (his Personal Identification Number). His bank usually authenticates him before authorizing the ATM machine to distribute any money. In this way, a person is only allowed to withdraw money from his own bank account.

7.4.3 Strength of Authentication Systems

Authentication systems fall into the same two categories discussed previously: *you-are-kidding-yourself* authentication and *cryptographically strong* authentication. In this book we will be concerned only with cryptographically strong authentication, the kind that cannot be defeated simply by snooping on packets that fly across a network. It is worth noting, however, that username/password-based authentication systems fall into the you-are-kidding-yourself category. Let us see why this is the case.

A common Internet application that uses username/password-based authentication is the remote login program named TELNET [RFC 854]. When someone uses TELNET to login to a remote computer, he must type his username and password before the remote system allows the login. The problem is that the username and password are transmitted over the intervening network as plaintext. Any Bad Guy along the path can record the username and password and subsequently use them to gain access to the same remote computer. Unfortunately, username/password-based authentication is nearly ubiquitous in modern computer networks.

Cryptographically strong authentication, on the other hand, can be so hard to break that it can be upheld as a legally binding, digital equivalent of a handwritten signature! As was the case with encryption, strong authentication can be implemented with either secret-key algorithms or public-key algorithms. We will briefly describe their operation in the next two sections.

7.4.4 Secret-Key Authentication

Secret-key authentication systems fall into two categories. The first is built from the same exact algorithms that are used to implement secret-key encryption, as we described in *Secret-Key Encryption* on page 130. The second uses a completely separate category of cryptographic algorithms known as *message digests*. We will briefly describe how these two methods work.

Authentication via Secret-Key Encryption

If Howard and Dominique wish to authenticate each other using a secret-key encryption algorithm, then, as before, they must agree on a specific algorithm to use and they must both have knowledge of a shared, secret key. Once again, we defer a discussion of how they obtained these keys until *How Can We Manage Keys Securely?* on page 139. Assuming that they share a key and have agreed on a secret-key encryption algorithm, then Howard authenticates Dominique by asking her to encrypt a specific number and vice versa, as show in the following exchange:

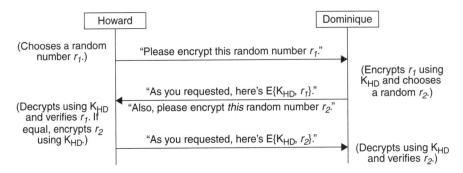

Thus, Howard picks a first random number (r_1), remembers it, and sends a copy of it to Dominique. Dominique receives r_1 and encrypts it using their shared, secret key K_{HD}. She picks a second random number (r_2) and sends it to Howard along with the encrypted value of r_1 (denoted as $E\{K_{HD}, r_1\}$). Howard decrypts $E\{K_{HD}, r_1\}$ and compares the result with what he originally sent to Dominique. If the two values are identical, then whoever sent the message to Howard must have known the value of the key K_{HD}; that is, the sender of the message has proven that he or she "knew something"—namely, the value of the key. Since Dominique is the only person besides Howard that knows the key, then Howard concludes that Dominique is the only person who could have sent that message. Thus, this operation authenticates Dominique to Howard.

The rest of the message exchange is designed to authenticate Howard to Dominique, who included her own randomly chosen number (r_2) in the second message. Howard encrypts r_2 using the key K_{HD} (which is written $E\{K_{HD}, r_2\}$) and sends the result to Dominique, who verifies the encryption in the same manner as Howard did previously. If the decrypted value equals r_2, then Dominique is positive that Howard sent the message. Thus, the exchange shown above accomplishes mutual authentication. It also, however, contains a flaw which can be exploited by a Bad Guy to break the authentication. Here we simply acknowledge the existence of this flaw and refer interested readers to Chapter 9 of [KaPeSp95] for the details.

Authentication and Integrity Checking via Secret Keys and Message Digests

The other way in which secret keys can be used to provide authentication is through a special set of cryptographic algorithms known as *message-digest*[†] *algorithms*. A message-digest algorithm takes an arbitrarily large chunk of data (i.e., a message) and computes from it a fixed-length (smaller) chunk of data called a *message digest*.

[†] These are also called hash functions and one-way transforms in the literature.

As an analogy, we can think of the original message as a human being and the message digest as that person's fingerprint. Just as it is extremely difficult (impossible?) to find two human beings with the same fingerprint, it is extremely difficult to find two original messages that when run through a message-digest algorithm produce the same message digest.

As with encryption algorithms, the strength of a message-digest algorithm depends upon its mathematical properties—the difficulty of finding different messages that produce the same message digest—but not upon keeping the algorithm itself a secret. Thus, we assume that a Bad Guy can determine what message-digest algorithm is being used and that some other piece of information must be kept secret from him in order for a message-digest algorithm to accomplish anything useful. We now describe how this works.

If Howard and Dominique wish to authenticate each other using a message-digest algorithm, then, as before, they must agree on a specific algorithm to use and they must both have knowledge of a single, secret key. Assuming that they share a key and have agreed on a message-digest algorithm, then Howard authenticates Dominique by asking her to compute the message digest of an appropriate value (e.g., the current time and date) plus the shared, secret key, as shown in the following exchange:

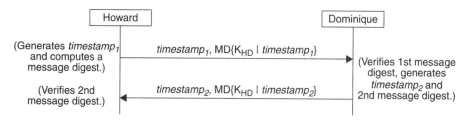

Thus, Howard generates a first *timestamp* (a piece of data that encodes the current time and date), appends it to the secret key, and computes a message digest of the result. Here, MD{stuff} denotes a message digest computed from stuff, and so MD{K_{HD} | *timestamp$_1$*} means a message digest computed from the secret key K_{HD} concatenated with *timestamp$_1$*. Howard sends his timestamp (*timestamp$_1$*) and the message digest to Dominique.

Dominique verifies the message digest by similarly appending the received timestamp (*timestamp$_1$*) to her copy of the secret key (K_{HD}) and computing her own version of the message digest. If her message digest is identical to the one she received, then she knows that Howard must have sent the message, because it would be virtually impossible for anyone to compute the message digest without knowing the key. Similarly, Dominique generates her own timestamp (*timestamp$_2$*), appends it to the secret key (K_{HD}), and computes a 2nd message digest which she sends to Howard along with *timestamp$_2$*. Howard then verifies the received message digest using the same procedure as Dominique used to verify his message digest. Thus, this exchange provides mutual authentication of Howard and Dominique.

Integrity Checking

Now consider what would happen if Howard were to send a message (e.g., "Buy 1000 shares of stock"), a timestamp, and a message digest (computed over the message, the timestamp, and the secret key) to Dominique. If Dominique verified the message digest, as described above, then she can be sure of two things—first, that Howard indeed sent the message; and second, that the message had not been modified in transit. Both of these things result from the property of message-digest algorithms that makes it extremely difficult to modify the input to the message-digest algorithm (in this case, the message, timestamp, and secret key) without also changing the output of the algorithm (i.e., the resulting message digest).

In this example, if a Bad Guy modified the message (e.g., changed the word "Buy" to the word "Sell"), then the verification that Dominique performs would detect the modification. Also, since the Bad Guy does not know the secret key, it is impossible for him to compute a new message digest that would pass the verification test performed by Dominique. This process, of verifying that a message has not been modified in transit, is called *integrity checking*.

Replay Protection

Another thing we notice is that the presence of the timestamp prevents a Bad Guy from making a copy of a packet sent by Howard and then sending that same packet to Dominique at a later date (e.g., to get her to sell an additional 1000 shares of stock). If Dominique were to receive such a packet, she could inspect the timestamp to see if it was "reasonably close" to her measure of the current time and date. If not, she would discard the packet. Thus, timestamps can provide another security feature known as *replay protection* which, as the name implies, prevents a Bad Guy from storing a copy of a valid packet and sending it at a later time in order to do bad things.

7.4.5 Public-Key Authentication

Public-key authentication systems also fall into two categories. The first is roughly analogous to the method we described in *Authentication via Secret-Key Encryption* on page 133 except, of course, a public-key encryption algorithm is used instead of a secret-key algorithm. Owing to the similarity, we will forgo a discussion of this method and simply note its existence. The second type of public-key authentication system uses *digital signatures*, which we now describe.

Recall that in public-key cryptography each person (or computer) has two mathematically related keys—a private key, which is known only to that person, and a public key, which is known to as many people as possible. As we described in *Public-Key Encryption* on page 130, Howard sends Dominique a confidential message by encrypting the message using Dominique's public key. Only the person who possesses the corresponding private key—namely, Dominique—can decrypt the message, but anyone who possesses her public key can send her a confidential message.

Thus, public-key encryption has the following semantics: "Everyone has access to Howard's public key so everyone can send him an encrypted message; however, only Howard can decrypt (read) those messages because only Howard has access to the corresponding private key." For authentication, however, we want the opposite semantics: "Everyone has access to Howard's public key so everyone can *verify* a message in which he provides authentication; however, only Howard can *generate* authentication that proves him as the sender of a message because only Howard has access to the corresponding private key." As this discussion suggests, public-key authentication is the same as public-key encryption but with the roles of the keys reversed.

Digital Signatures

Thus, if Howard wants to authenticate himself to Dominique, he performs a public-key transformation on some plaintext message using his *private* key. He then sends the resulting, authenticated ciphertext to Dominique as shown in the following figure:

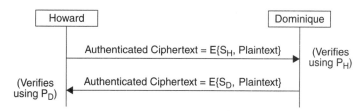

We write the authenticated ciphertext as $E\{S_H,$ Plaintext$\}$, where E stands for encryption and S_H is Howard's private key. ('S' is used to denote a private key, because 'P' is used for public keys and we need another letter. 'S' is the first letter of "secret," which reminds us that the private key is kept secret from everyone but its owner.)

Dominique verifies the message by performing an associated public-key transformation on the received ciphertext using Howard's public key (P_H). If this transformation produces the expected result, then Dominique knows that only the person who possesses the corresponding private key could have produced the received ciphertext. Since Howard is the only person who has this private key, then this system authenticates Howard to Dominique. Similarly, when Dominique wishes to authenticate herself to Howard, she performs a public-key transformation on a plaintext message using her private key, which Howard verifies using her public key.

If we pause for a moment to ponder the significance of this exchange, we notice that performing these public-key operations using one's own private key, in order to provide authentication, is a lot like signing something with a handwritten signature. Thus, performing these public-key transformations on a plaintext message with a private key is called *signing* the message, and the resulting ciphertext is called a *digital signature.*

Public-Key Authentication Using Digital Signatures and Message Digests

Public-key operations such as those used to produce digital signatures are computationally expensive, especially for large messages. In contrast, message digests tend to be relatively inexpensive to compute. Therefore, the general method of signing a large message is first to compute a message digest of the message and then sign the resulting message digest. Since it is assumed that it is impossible to find two messages with the same message digest, signing the message digest is as good as signing the original message.

Thus, if Howard wants to digitally sign a large plaintext message before sending it to Dominique, he computes a message digest of that plaintext message, denoted MD(plaintext), and signs the result. Howard then sends the signed message digest, denoted $E\{S_H, MD(plaintext)\}$, along with the original, plaintext message to Dominique. Upon receipt, Dominique performs the appropriate signature-verification transform using Howard's public key (P_H) and compares the result with a message digest she computes over the received, plaintext message. If they are equal, then she knows that Howard sent the message and that the message has not been modified in transit. Thus digital signatures in conjunction with message digests can provide both authentication and integrity checking.

Digital Signatures and Non-Repudiation

In addition, digital signatures have another extremely interesting property. Recall that with secret-key cryptography, two or more parties must know the value of a secret key in order for anything useful to be accomplished. Specifically, a receiver uses the same secret key to verify an authenticated message as the sender used to produce the message. However, public-key cryptography does not possess this property; namely, the only person that knows the value of a private key is that person himself!

Thus, where two or more parties could have generated an authenticated piece of data using secret-key cryptography (e.g., a message digest computed over both a plaintext message and a secret key), only one individual can generate a digital signature—the person possessing the private key. This means that a digital signature can be used as proof that a person authenticated a certain message.

For example, consider if Howard wanted to purchase 1000 shares of a promising stock. He could send a message to his broker to that effect and authenticate the message using a digital signature. If Howard later wished to claim that he never sent such a message (e.g., because the stock plummeted in value), then his broker could produce the digitally signed purchase order as proof that Howard did indeed place the order. At this point, there is absolutely nothing that Howard can do to disprove this evidence supplied by his broker! Well, yes, Howard could claim that someone, somehow, stole a copy of his private key, but that is Howard's problem, not his broker's.

Thus digital signatures provide another security feature called *non-repudiation*. As we saw in the previous example, a digital signature can be generated only by the party that has a private key, meaning that the owner of that private key cannot later claim that he did not produce a digital signature. A digital signature computed over a plaintext message that also contains a timestamp is an extremely powerful device in that it can provide all of the things we've talked about in this section: authentication, integrity checking, replay protection, and non-repudiation!

With this understanding of secret-key and public-key cryptography, it is now time to explore the methods by which keys can be distributed to the parties that are supposed to know them, without being obtainable by Bad Guys. This is the topic of the next section.

7.5 How Can We Manage Keys Securely?

Recall that a cryptographic system is considered to be secure only if it uses a strong algorithm, avoids certain pitfalls, and chooses and distributes key(s) carefully. A well-*chosen* key is one that is not easily guessable and is sufficiently long. A well-*managed* key is one that is known only to the appropriate person(s). The challenge of *key management* is to make sure that no one other than the intended person(s) can obtain the appropriate key(s), particularly when keys must be distributed to various individuals over a network. Specifically:

- if two parties wish to communicate securely using secret-key cryptography, then only those two parties are able to obtain a copy of their shared, secret key; and

- if two parties wish to communicate securely using public-key cryptography, then each individual is able to obtain the other person's public key authentically; i.e., each is able to determine that they have indeed obtained the other person's public key and not one substituted by a Bad Guy.

Key management in secret-key cryptography is extremely difficult to do securely. However, if we can figure out a way to manage public keys securely, then we can always encrypt a secret key using a public-key encryption algorithm before sending it over the network. Thus, if we can solve the easier problem of distributing public keys securely, then we can also solve the harder problem of distributing secret keys securely.

7.5.1 Challenges in Public-Key Management

Key distribution in public-key cryptography would seem to be very easy. After all, a person's public key can be given to anyone and therefore can be sent over a network as plaintext. So what's the problem? Well, consider what could happen if Howard sent a message to Dominique containing a copy of his public key. A Bad Guy could intercept the message and substitute his own public key for Howard's. When the message gets to Dominique, she might use the enclosed key to encrypt a confidential message that she believes can only be read by Howard. However, she is really encrypting the message using the Bad Guy's public key. This means that Howard cannot decrypt the message but the Bad Guy can!

This illustrates the fundamental challenge of distributing public keys, which can be stated as follows: "Anyone can lie about the value of anyone else's public key." Thus, public key distribution is not as easy as it seems, though there are ways to distribute public keys securely. The solution involves authenticating the message that contains the public key, or authenticating the key itself. This is of course a chicken-and-egg problem—how can two parties authenticate the key-exchange messages if they do not share keys in the first place? In the next few sections we discuss ways in which this authenticated key exchange can take place.

7.5.2 Manual Methods

One way Howard can obtain Dominique's public key securely is for her to send it to him electronically (e.g., by electronic mail) and then for Howard to call her on the phone to verify the contents. This works if he already knows Dominique and can recognize her voice on the phone. While this works very well, it gets a little cumbersome when there are many people, each of whom needs to exchange public key values. Thus, automatic methods have far better scalability. We will examine some of these methods in the next few sections.

7.5.3 Trusted Third Parties

Another way to obtain a public key is from a third party that sends it in the form of a *public-key certificate*. In its simplest form, a public-key certificate is someone's public key that has been digitally signed by someone else, usually a trusted party called a *certificate authority*. Certificates are generally minted by an authority "off line" but because they are digitally signed they can be retrieved "on line" from any convenient place, such as a Web page, a directory, or directly from the person to whom the certificate applies.

Thus, if Howard wants to obtain Dominique's public key securely, he can request that she send her public-key certificate to him. Among other things, the certificate contains Dominique's public key signed by the certificate authority, which is written $E\{S_{CA}, P_D\}$. Assuming that Howard can obtain the certificate authority's corresponding public key (P_{CA}), then he can verify the signature—and hence the value of Dominique's public key—using the methods that are described in *Public-Key Authentication Using Digital Signatures and Message Digests* on page 138.

Now all we need is a way to obtain the public key of the certificate authority, without which we cannot verify any of the certificates it provides. Usually this is done by some manual method, as described in the previous section. For example, some software packages, notably World Wide Web browsers, come preconfigured with a list of certificate authorities and their corresponding public keys. Others have noted that a company which mints certificates could take out an advertisement in several major newspapers in which they publish their public key. This does not guard against some Bad Guy at the newspapers from substituting his own public key for that of the certifying authority before the edition goes to press. However, everyone knows that there are no Bad Guys working for any large, major newspapers, so this threat is not as large as it might be in a world where not all journalists and editors had impeccable ethics and high moral standards.

It would be detrimental to scalability if every possible public key were provided by a single certificate authority. Therefore, certificate authorities are usually arranged in some sort of hierarchy. The certificate authority at the top of the hierarchy simply provides public-key certificates for the public keys of the authorities immediately beneath it, and so on, until we reach the bottom of the hierarchy, where the certificate authorities at this level provide public-key certificates for actual users. In this way, a user might have to traverse several layers of hierarchy to reach a certificate authority for which he already has a copy of its public key.

7.6 What Security Protocols Are Used in the Internet?

There are numerous security protocols and cryptographic algorithms in use throughout portions of the global Internet. A complete treatment of these protocols and algorithms is beyond the scope of this book (see [KaPeSp95] or [Schneier95] for such a treatment). Therefore, we will confine our discussion to those protocols that provide solutions to the security problems introduced by mobility in general and Mobile IP in particular. Specifically, we confine our discussion to the IP-layer security and key management protocols.

The *Security Architecture for the Internet Protocol* [RFC 1825] defines a framework for security at the IP layer. Two companion documents, [RFC 1826] and [RFC 1827], define the specific packet formats for IP-layer authentication and encryption respectively. Other documents [draft-ietf-ipsec-isakmp-07.txt] and [draft-ietf-ipsec-isakmp-oakley-03.txt] define the protocols for setting up *security associations* and performing key management. We describe these protocols and their applications in this section.

7.6.1 What Is a Security Association?

A security association is central to the IP-layer security model. It is an agreement between two nodes that specifies how the sender will cryptographically transform data before transmitting it to the receiver. A security association can be thought of as a row in a table that contains, among other things, the columns shown in Table 7-1. That is, a security association contains all of the information necessary for a receiver to know how to decrypt a message or verify the authentication contained in that message. Security associations are "one-way" in nature, which implies that two of them are necessary for two-way communications—one for each direction.

Security Parameters Index	Authentication Algorithm	Authentication Key(s)	Replay Protection	Encryption Algorithm	Encryption Key(s)
01234567	e.g., Keyed MD5	(a secret key)	timestamp	-	-
89ABCDEF	-	-	-	e.g., RSA	(public/private key)

Table 7-1 An Example Security-Association Table

Two nodes might have several different types of security requirements. For example, they might have some data to exchange which requires strong authentication. They might have other data to exchange that requires strong confidentiality. Still other data that is not sensitive might require no cryptographic protection at all.

Therefore, two nodes can have multiple security associations, each applicable to a certain sensitivity level of data. A sending node informs the receiving node which of the many possible security associations has been used in the creation of a given packet by including in the packet an identifier called a Security Parameters Index. This identifier is simply an integer which specifies which "row" of its security-association table a receiver should use to interpret the received packet.

The integer value to be used as a Security Parameters Index is chosen by the receiver at the same time that the algorithms, keys, and other parameters of the security association are negotiated between the two parties. Namely, all of this occurs during key distribution, which can be done manually or by an automated key-management protocol such as the one described in [draft-ietf-ipsec-isakmp-07.txt].

7.6.2 What Is the IP Authentication Header?

The *IP Authentication Header* [RFC 1826] provides authentication, integrity checking, and possibly non-repudiation of the IP header and payload. The *Authentication Header* is usually placed between the IP header and the upper-layer header (e.g., TCP) in order to protect the entire packet against being modified in transit and to authenticate the sender. The *Authentication Header* provides no means for encrypting data—this functionality is provided by the *IP Encapsulating Security Payload* which is described in the next section.

The format of the *IP Authentication Header* is shown in Figure 7-2. The Next Header field is used to identify the protocol or header which follows the *Authentication Header*. The Next Header can be an IPv6 extension header (which we discuss in *IPv6 Extension Headers* on page 249); an upper-layer header, such as TCP or UDP; or IPv6 or IPv4 itself in the case of a tunnel. This latter case turns out to be very useful for Mobile IP, as we will see in *How Can Mobile Nodes Traverse the Firewall without Compromising the Corporate Network?* on page 180.

The Length field specifies the size of the Authentication Data field measured in 32-bit words. The Security Parameters Index field (see *What Is a Security Association?* on page 141) tells the receiver how to interpret and, therefore, how to verify, the message digest or digital signature present in the Authentication Data field. That is, the Security Parameters Index tells the receiver which of many possible security associations was used to compute the value in the Authentication Data field.

7.6.3 What Is the IP Encapsulating Security Payload?

The *IP Encapsulating Security Payload* [RFC 1827] provides confidentiality and possibly authentication and integrity checking of the IP payload. It is used similarly to the *Authentication Header*, being placed between the IP and upper-layer header or between two IP headers in the case of a tunnel.

The generic *Encapsulating Security Payload* packet-format is not very interesting. It consists of a 32-bit Security Parameters Index field followed by a bunch of encrypted stuff that is specific to the encryption algorithm being employed. It is much more useful to look at a specific example of the *Encapsulating Security Payload*. One such example is provided in Figure 7-3, which shows the payload as defined for the Triple Data Encryption Standard (Triple-DES) encryption algorithm. The payload format is defined in [RFC 1851], whereas Triple-DES itself is described in [Tuchman79].

In Figure 7-3, the shaded fields are encrypted before being transmitted, while the unshaded fields are sent as plaintext. The Security Parameters Index field provides identical functionality to what we have seen previously. A randomly

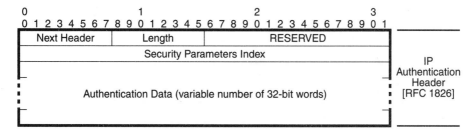

Figure 7-2 IP Authentication Header

chosen Initialization Vector is common in many encryption algorithms and is used to ensure that identical plaintext messages produce different encrypted, ciphertext messages (see [KaPeSp95] for details).

Following these two plaintext (unencrypted) fields is the encrypted payload. The encrypted payload consists of an Upper-Layer Header and User Data (the actual information being transmitted from the source to the destination) followed by some padding and a Next Header field. As before, the Next Header field identifies the protocol or header contained in the Upper-Layer Header and User Data fields.

Random data can be placed in the Padding field to make it very difficult for a Bad Guy to guess the length of the "real" data that is being protected by encryption. This is useful for small messages that are common in many remote login programs, some of which are only a few bytes in length. Finally, the Pad Length field tells the receive how many Padding bytes were added to the original payload.

7.6.4 Other Security Protocols in the Internet

There are many other security protocols used in the Internet. We mention some of them below and provide references for those interested in finding out more about them:

- *Secure SHell (SSH)* and *Secure CoPy (SCP)* provide secure remote login, command execution, and file transfer in the Unix {{tm}} environment. See [draft-ietf-tls-ssh-00.txt] for more information about SSH.

- SOCKS provides a general mechanism for secure, application-layer, firewall traversal. We discuss firewalls in *What Are Firewalls?* on page 147. See [RFC 1928] for more information about SOCKS.

- The *Secure Sockets Layer (SSL)* [draft-ietf-tls-ssl-version3-00.txt] and the *Secure HyperText Transfer Protocol (S-HTTP)* [draft-ietf-wts-shttp-04.txt] are frequently used to provide confidentiality and authentication for the World Wide Web (WWW) and for other applications.

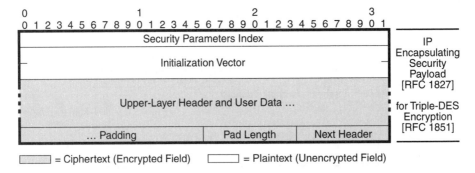

Figure 7-3 IP Encapsulating Security Payload (Triple-DES)

7.6.5 What Is ISAKMP/Oakley?

The *Internet Security Association and Key Management Protocol (ISAKMP)* [draft-ietf-ipsec-isakmp-07.txt] provides a framework by which two parties can negotiate security parameters and set up security associations. The *Oakley Key Determination Protocol* [draft-ietf-ipsec-oakley-01.txt] can be used to establish session keys between these parties. The combination of these two protocols—as defined in [draft-ietf-ipsec-isakmp-oakley-03.txt]—accomplishes simultaneous key establishment and security-parameter negotiation. This integrated protocol, referred to as ISAKMP/Oakley, provides authentication, integrity checking, and confidentiality of the key-exchange process. This means that two parties using ISAKMP/Oakley can be certain to whom they are talking and can be confident that a Bad Guy cannot derive any useful information by eavesdropping on their packet exchange.

It is important to note that ISAKMP/Oakley is only useful where a pre-existing security relationship exists. For example, Howard and Dominique could certainly use ISAKMP/Oakley to negotiate the use of Triple-DES encryption and a corresponding shared secret key. However, they cannot be sure that they are actually talking to each other—i.e., they cannot authenticate their ISAKMP message exchange—unless, for example, they can obtain each other's public key in a secure fashion. One such way they can do this is by manual configuration or by using a certificate authority as described in *Challenges in Public-Key Management* on page 139.

For completeness, we note that Howard can indeed send to Dominique his public-key certificate as part of the ISAKMP protocol exchange and vice versa. The important point to note, however, is that ISAKMP does not provide the means by which Howard can generate a public key and have it certified by some authority, nor the means by which someone else (such as Dominique) can obtain a public-key certificate from such an authority. This latter problem is being addressed by the Simple Public Key Infrastructure working group of the Internet Engineering Task Force (see [draft-ietf-spki-cert-req-00.txt] and [draft-ietf-spki-cert-structure-01.txt] for more information).

7.6.6 What Is SKIP?

Simple Key-Management For Internet Protocols (SKIP) [draft-ietf-ipsec-skip-07.txt] is an alternative key-management protocol for use with IP-layer security. While ISAKMP/Oakley currently requires two nodes to exchange several protocol messages before they may begin communicating securely, SKIP supports a concept called *inline-keying*. This property of SKIP allows a node to establish session keys with another node in the very same packets that are used to exchange user data. As we will see in *How Can Mobile Nodes Traverse the Firewall without Compromising the Corporate Network?* on page 180, inline-keying is very valuable to Mobile IP.

SKIP is based upon the *Diffie-Hellman* public-key agreement system. Thus, we must first understand Diffie-Hellman in order to understand SKIP. The next section describes Diffie-Hellman and the following section describes how SKIP uses Diffie-Hellman to realize inline-keying.

What Is Diffie-Hellman?

As defined in [DifHel76], Diffie-Hellman allows two nodes to derive a shared secret key for use in secret-key cryptography as follows:

1. Each node generates a random, secret value which it keeps private;
2. Each node computes a public value, derived mathematically from the random, secret value, and sends this public value to the other node;
3. Each node mathematically combines the public value received from the other node with its own random, secret value.

Miraculously (actually, due to the mathematical properties involved in the derivation of the public and secret values), the two nodes end up with the same exact combined values in step 3 which they can use as a shared, secret key. What makes this exchange useful is the fact that the secret portions are not disclosed to anyone and, therefore, only these two nodes can compute the combined value (which they can use subsequently as a key).

Diffie-Hellman has a major vulnerability, though. It most certainly allows two nodes to establish a shared, secret key in a secure fashion. However, by itself it does not allow a node to figure out *with whom* it is establishing that secret key! For example, a Bad Guy on the path between two nodes could fool them into each establishing a key with the Bad Guy instead of with each other.

One way in which this vulnerability can be defeated is by having the two nodes send "certified" public values to each other. These certified public values are equivalent to the public-key certificates we described in *Challenges in Public-Key Management* on page 139. A receiving node verifies the certificate in order to determine the identity of the node sending the public value. In this way, two nodes can establish secret keys and be sure with whom they are establishing them.

How Does SKIP Use Diffie-Hellman?

SKIP uses these certified, or authenticated, public values to realize key management. With SKIP, every node on the Internet has a Diffie-Hellman secret value which it keeps private and a certified public value that is stored in a directory somewhere. For example, the certified public values can be stored in Domain Name System servers. A node sends a secure packet—one that is encrypted, authenticated, or both—to another node as follows:

- The source node combines its own secret value with the destination node's public value to derive a shared, secret key.
- From this shared, secret key, the source node derives two other keys using a sequence of encryption and message-digest operations.

- The source node uses these two keys to respectively authenticate and/or encrypt the packet contents in conjunction with the *IP Authentication Header* and the *IP Encapsulating Security Payload*.

- The source node sends the authenticated and/or encrypted packet to the destination node along with a SKIP header which informs the destination node how to derive the two respective keys.

- The destination node uses information in the SKIP header to determine the certified public value to use for the sender. The destination node combines that sender's public value with its own secret value to derive the shared, secret key.

- The destination node uses other information in the SKIP header to determine the appropriate sequence of encryption and message-digest operations required to derive the encryption and authentication keys.

- The destination node uses these keys to decrypt or validate the contents of the received packet.

One very important observation is that the source node requires no prior communication with the destination node before it can send a secure packet to it. All that is required is for the two nodes to obtain each other's certified public values from the directory. Alternatively, the two nodes can be manually configured with these public values.

Thus, SKIP provides inline-keying by including information needed to derive keys within packets containing user data. This, combined with the ability of SKIP to "name" public values independently of the IP Source Address in the packet, makes it attractive as a way for mobile nodes in Mobile IP to traverse firewalls that protect their private networks (see *How Can Mobile Nodes Traverse the Firewall without Compromising the Corporate Network?* on page 180). Before we can possibly understand what this means, though, we must first define what we mean by a firewall, which we do in the next section.

7.7 What Are Firewalls?

> *"Usually, a firewall's purpose is to keep the jerks out of your network while still letting you get your job done." — Marcus J. Ranum [Ranum95]*

In this section we describe firewalls as a common mechanism to guard against security threats in the Internet. We begin with a brief history of the Internet and why firewalls have come into existence. Then we examine three primary categories of firewalls.

7.7.1 What Is the *Highly Abridged* History of Firewalls?

The global Internet grew out of research funded by the U.S. Government's (Defense) Advance Research Projects Agency. In its early days, the so-called ARPANET connected universities, military installations, and other public and private research organizations. The purpose was to share data and facilitate remote collaboration among colleagues in different locations.

The TCP/IP protocols were developed as part of this initial research. IP, ICMP, UDP, and TCP were published as Internet standards in 1980 and 1981. The global Internet has been growing exponentially ever since, in terms of both the amount of traffic carried and the number of hosts and networks that are connected. The robustness, scalability, and performance of this technology makes it one of the most amazing technological achievements in history.

As word began to spread about the utility of the Internet, corporations and individuals began connecting throughout the 1980s and 1990s. Specifically, companies began connecting their own private networks to the Internet to allow their employees to gather or share information with customers and suppliers.

Not everyone wanted to accomplish such productive things, however. Some took great pleasure in breaking into these private networks in order to steal proprietary information or wreak havoc in other assorted ways. This gave birth to the need to protect a network from unauthorized access while still providing legitimate users with access to the information available on the Internet. This in turn led to the field of computer security and the use of Internet firewalls.

A *firewall* is a device or a set of devices which separates a trusted, private network from an untrusted, public network such as the Internet (see Figure 7-4). A firewall protects a private network from intrusion by Bad Guys, but, as the quote at the beginning of this section illustrates, it should not prevent people on the inside from exchanging information with others on the public network. In the next few sections we describe the three primary types of firewalls along with their advantages and disadvantages.

7.7.2 What Is a Packet-Filtering Router?

The simplest type of firewall is a router that has been configured by a network administrator to prevent certain classes of packets from being forwarded. The goal is to configure the router in such a way as to forward all of the packets generated by Good Guys but reject all packets generated by Bad Guys. In prac-

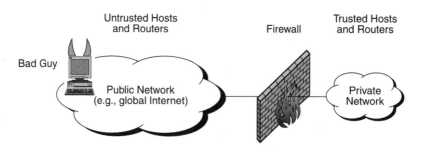

Figure 7-4 Firewall Reference Model

tice, this can be extremely difficult, because unfortunately the Bad Guys do not place warning labels on their packets.

A packet-filtering router is shown in Figure 7-5. It determines whether or not to forward a given packet by looking at the packet's header fields. Based upon these header fields the packet is classified according to a set of *rules* that are part of the router's configuration. These rules specify whether certain packets may be forwarded or whether they must be discarded. Rules are also known as *Access Control Lists* or ACLs (pronounced ack´-els). Packets that are discarded because of an ACL are said to be *filtered* or *screened*.

An example Access Control List might be as follows:

- forward all packets belonging to connections initiated by internal machines;
- forward all packets belonging to electronic mail connections initiated by outside machines;
- forward all Domain Name Service messages;[†] and
- discard all other packets.

A router configured in this way would examine the IP Source Address and Destination Address fields along with the TCP and UDP header fields of a packet in order to determine whether or not the packet may be forwarded. We also note that in this example, no UDP/IP packets (other than those associated with the Domain Name Service) are allowed to be forwarded through the router. Many routers are unable to maintain application-layer information necessary to allow UDP/IP packets to pass through without compromising network security.

Packet-filtering routers are attractive because they are fast and because they are largely independent of applications. They are fast because they perform relatively simple processing. They are independent of applications because they do not have to be upgraded or replaced when a new application comes along. This is in contrast to application-layer relays, which we examine in the next section. Finally, packet-filtering routers can be an inexpensive solution because most private networks already have a router of some sort which they use to connect to the Internet.

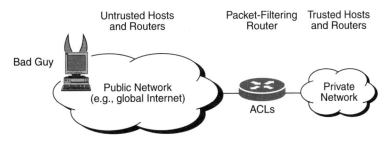

Figure 7-5 Packet-Filtering Router as Firewall

[†] DNS messages are carried within UDP segments.

The problem with packet-filtering firewalls is that they are extremely difficult to configure correctly. Access Control Lists must frequently be written in an obscure syntax without the help of graphical user interfaces. Any mistake in an ACL can leave the private network vulnerable to attack by a Bad Guy. Often, there is no way to verify that a set of ACLs is correct until it is too late—i.e., after the private network has already been compromised.

There are other problems with packet-filtering routers, too. Because they are by definition routers, the IP addresses of the machines in the private network are visible to the public network, making those machines more vulnerable to attack than they might otherwise be. Also, a good security system has the ability to log suspect activity, and routers generally have little or no disk space on which to record such events. Finally, they do not support certain security policies, such as requiring users to be authenticated before being allowed to communicate outside the firewall.

Nonetheless, packet-filtering routers are quite common on the Internet, even though they are relatively vulnerable to attack. In fact, it seems like every time a network administrator "finally" figures out the right set of ACLs, a Bad Guy figures out a new way to break into the private network. This leads many private networks to install more restrictive firewalls, such as the application-layer relays we describe in the next section.

7.7.3 What Is an Application-Layer Relay?

Because Bad Guys have found clever ways to break into networks "protected" by packet-filtering routers, network administrators have moved to more restrictive firewall architectures. One such architecture involves network devices called application-layer relays, which we describe in this section.

A typical configuration involving an application-layer relay is shown in Figure 7-6. Here, a host in the private network sets up a connection to the firewall and sends application-layer data to the firewall. The firewall then relays this application-layer data over a new connection that it sets up to the ultimate destination host. The two routers in the figure are configured with ACLs which allow packets only to and from the relay host. Specifically, the routers do not

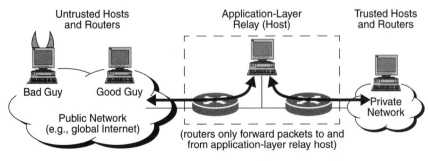

Figure 7-6 Application-Layer Relay as Firewall

allow any packets to flow directly between the private network and the public network.

Application-layer relays are able to enforce more sophisticated security policies because they understand not only packet headers but also, by definition, the applications themselves. In addition, they are often easier to configure and they are able to hide from the public network the addresses of nodes within the private network. Because they can be built with plenty of disk capacity, they have the ability to provide full auditing and logging capability. In addition, they can support such policies as requiring users to authenticate themselves before communicating with hosts outside the firewall (see SOCKS [RFC 1928] for more information about authenticated firewall traversal).

Application-layer relays are normally slower than packet-filtering routers, however, simply because they have much more work to do. Specifically, application-layer relays must process packets at all of the protocol layers and might have very many TCP connections open at any given time. Also, by definition, an application-layer relay must specifically support an application before it can be used across the firewall. Typically, new applications are available to users well before the firewall catches up and is able to relay the associated traffic. An application-layer relay is thus "visible" to end users, who either must have firewall-aware applications or must modify their behavior in order to use their existing applications.

Another problem with application-layer relays is that they prevent even legitimate mobile users from enjoying the same connectivity they enjoy when connected to the private network. This is because some applications that are in use in the private network might not be supported by the firewall and possibly because the firewall does not work symmetrically in both directions.

Thus, some people "poke holes" in their application-layer relays to allow such mobile workers to access the resources in their private networks. This, however, leaves the private network vulnerable to the same types of attacks that can be waged against networks "protected" by packet-filtering routers. The solution to this problem is to introduce cryptography into the picture. This leads us to the third major type of firewall, which we refer to as secure tunnelers.

7.7.4 What Is a Secure Tunneler?

A secure tunneler, for our purposes, is a firewall of the application-layer relay type that also provides a cryptographically secure method for authorized users to access a private network across a public network. Figure 7-7 shows the components of such a firewall, which might or might not be physically implemented as a single network device. The firewall processes packets that arrive from the public network as follows:

- if the packet is tunneled to the firewall and has valid authentication (and usually encryption), it is de-tunneled and routed "transparently" to the destination node within the private network;

- otherwise, the packet is submitted to the application-layer relay and is processed accordingly.

The secure tunnel shown in the figure is implemented using the *IP Authentication Header* and/or the *IP Encapsulating Security Payload*. The policy mentioned above allows authorized users—specifically, those who provide authentication to the firewall—to access resources as if they were directly connected to their private network. Unauthorized users—those incapable of providing such authentication—have their packets subjected to the application-layer relay, which allows nodes in the private network to access information as in the previous section but keeps intruders out of the private network.

Secure tunnelers can also be used to build *Virtual Private Networks (VPNs)* across a public network such as the Internet, as shown in Figure 7-8. A Virtual Private Network functions as a single, secure, logical network while being composed of many physical networks of varying levels of trust. The secure tunnel shown in the figure protects the two physical private networks from being accessed by intruders while additionally providing confidentiality. This keeps a Bad Guy from eavesdropping on data exchanged between the two networks.

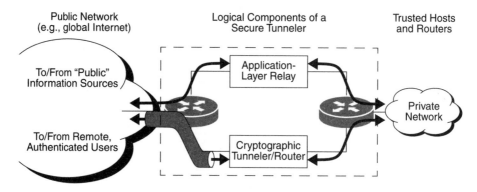

Figure 7-7 Secure Tunneler as Firewall

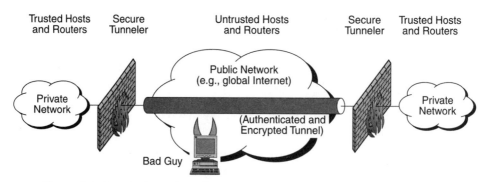

Figure 7-8 Secure Tunneling Firewalls Providing a Virtual Private Network

7.8 Chapter Summary

This chapter defined computer and network security and described the technology commonly used to provide such security, namely, cryptography. We saw how cryptographic algorithms fall into two broad categories: secret-key and public-key algorithms.

We then examined how secret-key and public-key technology could be used to provide a number of security properties, such as confidentiality, authentication, and integrity checking. We saw how digital signatures using public-key technology could also provide non-repudiation.

Next we examined the Internet protocols that provide a mechanism for IP-layer security. The two main protocols are the *IP Authentication Header* and the *IP Encapsulating Security Payload*. We saw how the concept of a security association was central to the IP-layer model of security as implemented in these two protocols. Finally, we gave an overview of the challenges and the protocols used to implement key management within the Internet: ISAKMP/Oakley and SKIP.

Finally this section concluded with a discussion of firewalls, which are used to protect a private network from unauthorized access by nodes on the public portion of the Internet. We saw how firewalls fall into three basic categories: packet filtering routers, application-layer relays, and secure tunnelers.

With this foundation of network security we are now prepared to examine applications of Mobile IP in detail. The technology introduced in this section will be combined in various ways to combat the security threats present on networks that deploy Mobile IP, whether or not those threats have anything to do with Mobile IP per se. In the next three chapters we describe these applications, identify the resulting security threats, and identify methods for protecting against these threats.

Campus Mobility: A Simple Mobile IP Application

This chapter investigates a simple application of Mobile IP within a single campus environment. The term "campus" is used loosely to refer to anything ranging from a few rooms in a single building to an entire university or corporate campus. The important characteristic is that the network, particularly the routing infrastructure, is completely under the control of a single administrative authority. Specifically, we assume that the network is *not* connected to the global Internet.

First we describe the application of Mobile IP in such a campus and the benefit derived from doing so. Then we examine the challenging piece of the puzzle, namely, the security implications of such a deployment. We analyze the security threats from the standpoint of the mobile user and of the operator of the network. In the next chapter we make the problem more difficult by allowing connectivity to the global Internet.

8.1 What Is the Model for This Application?

In this section we describe exactly what it means to deploy Mobile IP on a campus intranet. Specifically, we will describe the location of home agents and foreign agents and how mobile nodes gain access to their services. Then in the rest of this chapter we examine the security threats faced by such a network and offer protections against these threats.

8.1.1 What Is a Campus Intranet?

An *intranet* is a private network based upon TCP/IP protocols which is either a portion of the global Internet (usually secured against intrusion by a firewall) or a private network which is not connected to the global Internet at all. A *campus intranet* is therefore a private network that provides connectivity for all the computers on an organization's premises. In this chapter we assume that a campus intranet is not connected to the global Internet. A corporate building containing such a network is shown in Figure 8-1. This could be one of many buildings on a large, corporate campus or a few rooms belonging to a single company within a shared office-building.

Here, each department of the company has its own local area network (LAN) consisting of some physical medium over which that department's hosts can communicate. To make things interesting, we assume that there are two types of media deployed throughout the campus: wired Ethernet and some type of wireless LAN product (e.g., ATT WaveLAN, Proxim, etc.). In Figure 8-1, hosts are shown as square boxes, each of which is connected to the LAN. Unoccupied LAN ports, or *network jacks*, are shown as a vertical line without an associated host. These might be located in, for example, conference rooms, where an employee might wish to connect a notebook computer to the network.

Each departmental LAN is connected to a router that minimally routes IP packets. Each router is connected over a high-speed fiber backbone, which in turn allows all departments to share information. Also, we assume that all hosts are wholly owned by the enterprise and, therefore, we assume that under normal circumstances these hosts can be trusted. (We relax this assumption in *Chapter 9, Internet-Wide Mobility: A More Complicated Application*, which presents a much more challenging security problem.)

8.1.2 How Is Mobile IP Deployed?

The network of Figure 8-1 is transformed into one which supports Mobile IP by upgrading all of the routers to be both home agents and foreign agents and by installing mobile-node software on the hosts. Alternatively, we could upgrade one or more hosts on each LAN to be home agents and foreign

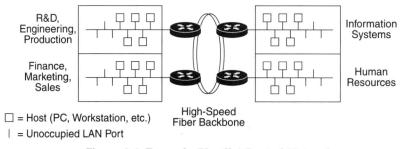

Figure 8-1 Example (Vanilla) Routed Network

agents. The resulting network, with each router performing both home agent and foreign agent functionality, is shown in Figure 8-2.

Specifically, the functions that must be performed by a network administrator are summarized as follows:

1. Mobile node software is installed on every host computer that is relatively portable. Obvious examples of such hosts are notebook computers. Conversely, it does not make a lot of sense to install mobile-node software, or at least to enable it, on a workstation that weighs nearly 100 pounds including monitor. It is hard to imagine such a workstation changing location rapidly enough to benefit from Mobile IP.

2. Foreign agent and home agent software is installed on all of the routers in the campus. Alternatively, foreign agent and home agent software can be installed on various personal computers and workstations throughout the network, at least one on each link.

3. Each mobile node is assigned a home link, a home address, and a home agent in a straightforward manner. For example, the Ethernet segment that runs through the cube walls and the floor of the R&D Department would be the home link of the mobile nodes owned by the engineers in that department. Similarly, their mobile nodes would be given IP home addresses whose network-prefix is equal to the network-prefix assigned to that link. Finally, the router that connects to that link would become the mobile node's home agent.

4. As required by Mobile IP's authenticated registration procedure, a shared secret key is configured between each mobile node and its home agent, respectively.

The Mobile IP *Management Information Base (MIB)* [RFC 2006] can greatly assist network administrators in managing the mobile nodes, foreign agents, and home agents on the network. The MIB defines a set of variables which can be examined or modified remotely using a network-management application employing version 2 of the *Simple Network Management Protocol (SNMPv2)* [RFC 1905].

For example, the MIB allows an administrator to configure a mobile node's home address and authentication key into that mobile node's home agent. Of

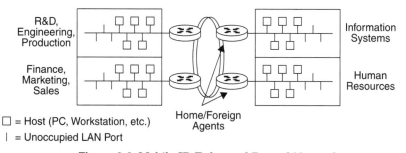

Figure 8-2 Mobile IP-Enhanced Routed Network

course, the secure version of SNMP should be used for such operations; otherwise, the keys would be sent as plaintext over the network, where they can be intercepted easily. Other operations that can be performed by the MIB include monitoring the agents for authentication failures and security violations, which can indicate whether the mobile node and home agent are both using the same method of replay protection (i.e., timestamps versus nonces). Similarly, an administrator can modify such configuration parameters as the maximum lifetime in registrations permitted by foreign agents and home agents.

This "campus intranet" application of Mobile IP is straightforward and simple to implement. The MIB makes this application relatively easy to manage. We now examine the utility of such a deployment and then move on to the fun part of analyzing its security implications.

8.1.3 Why Should I Harass My Network Administrators to Deploy Mobile IP In This Way?

Mobile IP as deployed above would allow an employee to carry his notebook computer anywhere in the campus, plug into any available network jack (or communicate wirelessly), and have access to all of the information available to him when he is connected to his desk.

For example, when questions come up in meetings, a person with a notebook computer can consult his electronic mailbox or a Web page to find the answers, resolving such issues immediately rather than postponing important decisions or wasting time arguing without readily obtainable facts.

Such notebooks need not be rebooted or reconfigured when they are unplugged from their home link and connected into an available network jack in the conference room. Also, the applications need not be restarted because Mobile IP allows the notebook computer to retain its IP address as it moves throughout the campus.

8.1.4 What Is the Security Model for This Chapter?

In the sections which follow we examine the security threats to a campus that has deployed Mobile IP as described above. Note that a security threat is a threat *from someone*. Therefore, it is important to characterize the source of such threats and the steps that should be taken to minimize them.

We use the term *security model* to describe the assumptions we make about who is allowed to access the network and under what circumstances. In this chapter we assume that physical access to the network is strictly controlled. By this we mean there are security guards, name badges, and all of the typical mechanisms you find in any reasonably large corporation to prevent unauthorized individuals from connecting computers to the network, either wirelessly or through a wired network jack. We also assume that network administrators are the only ones who are allowed physical and network access to the routers.

Note also that this model represents prudent practice for any organization which is serious about protecting its computers and the information stored on them. Further, we note that this model has nothing to do with Mobile IP per se—the same physical security requirement applies to all campus intranets, whether they support Mobile IP or not.

If physical access to a network is perfectly controlled, there are far fewer security threats facing that network. However, physical security is never perfect, and therefore we wish to examine ways of mitigating the attacks that might happen when someone compromises the physical security of the campus. We examine such threats in the next few sections.

8.2 Insider Attacks

This threat has nothing to do with Mobile IP per se, but for completeness we note that mobile nodes and the network itself are quite vulnerable to attack from "insiders"—i.e., those individuals who are *supposed* to be trustworthy employees. A survey conducted by Ernst & Young and *InformationWeek* [Viol96] suggests that roughly twice as many successful attacks on corporate networks are waged by insiders as by outsiders who somehow break into these networks.

Generally, these insider attacks involve a disgruntled employee gaining access to sensitive data and then forwarding it, either electronically or physically, to a competitor. It is worth noting that the only way to mitigate such attacks is to:

- enforce strict controls on *who* can access *what* data (e.g., there is no reason to allow Human Resources employees to access the latest integrated-circuit design stored on the engineering department's computers);

- use strong authentication of users and computers to enforce these access controls—specifically, eliminate plaintext username/password-based, you-are-kidding-yourself authentication in favor of cryptographically strong authentication; and

- encrypt all data transfer on an end-to-end basis between the ultimate source and the ultimate destination machines to prevent eavesdroppers from stealing information as it flows through the network.

These steps do not prevent a disgruntled employee from disclosing to competitors information which he has been authorized to access. However, these steps do prevent someone in a first department disclosing the information contained in a second department, etc. Once again we note that the threat we are describing in this section is not specific to Mobile IP—nor is it exacerbated by Mobile IP in any way. It is important that these threats be understood, however, in the context of trying to provide a secure private-network environment.

8.3 Mobile Node Denial-of-Service

In this section we describe a denial-of-service attack that could be waged upon any mobile node, had Mobile IP not been designed to prevent such attacks from the beginning. It is important to note that this attack is not necessarily specific to the current chapter, in which we are discussing a campus deployment of Mobile IP. Rather, this attack applies to any deployment and configuration of mobile nodes, foreign agents, and home agents. Nonetheless, we discuss it in this chapter because this is our first opportunity to explore the threats faced by a mobile node.

8.3.1 What Is a Denial-of-Service Attack?

Generally speaking, a denial-of-service attack is something that a Bad Guy does in order to prevent someone from getting useful work done. In the context of computer networking, a denial-of-service attack usually takes one of the following forms:

- A Bad Guy sends a tremendous number of packets to a host (e.g., a Web server) that brings the host's CPU to its knees attempting to process all of the packets. In the meantime, no useful information can be exchanged with the host while it is processing all of the nuisance packets.

- A Bad Guy somehow interferes with the packets that are flowing between two nodes on the network. Generally speaking, the Bad Guy must be on the path between the two nodes in order wreak any such havoc.

Mobile IP itself cannot do much about nuisance packets, though in *Chapter 10, Applying Mobile IP: A Service-Provider Perspective*, we will see how a common solution to this problem invalidates one of Mobile IP's primary assumptions about IP routing. We explore this in detail in *Denial-of-Service Revisited* on page 209.

The threat presented by the second form of denial-of-service attack, where a Bad Guy prevents packets from flowing between two legitimate nodes, would potentially be worsened by mobility if Mobile IP had not been designed to deal with this threat from the beginning. In the rest of this section we will describe the nature of this security threat and see how Mobile IP addresses it.

8.3.2 What Type of Denial-of-Service Attacks Does Mobile IP Prevent?

Recall that one of the primary purposes of Mobile IP Registration is for the mobile node to inform its home agent of its current care-of address—the address to which the home agent will subsequently tunnel all packets destined to the mobile node's home address. Consider what would happen if a Bad Guy were to generate a bogus *Registration Request*, specifying his own IP address as the care-of address for a mobile node (see Figure 8-3). Then, all packets sent by correspondent nodes would be tunneled by the mobile node's home agent to the Bad Guy. There are two obvious problems with this:

1. The Bad Guy gets to see a copy of every packet destined to the mobile node.
2. The mobile node has been cut off from all communications, because it cannot receive any packets.

Note how trivial it is for the Bad Guy to perform this attack—he merely sends a bogus *Registration Request* to the mobile node's home agent. Compare this situation with that of fixed hosts and routers. In the case of fixed hosts, a node must generally be on the path between two corresponding hosts in order to cut off their traffic flow completely. In the case of mobility, however, a node could wage the described denial-of-service attack from anywhere in the network. Thus, this represents an added security threat which the Internet Architecture Board required the designers of Mobile IP to address.

8.3.3 How Does Mobile IP Prevent This Denial-of-Service Attack?

The solution to this threat is to require cryptographically strong authentication in all registration messages exchanged by a mobile node and its home agent. As described in *What Do We Mean by Authentication, Integrity Checking, and Non-Repudiation?* on page 132, strong authentication means that it is next-to-impossible for a Bad Guy to generate a bogus *Registration Request* without the home agents being able to recognize it as a forgery.

Mobile IP allows a mobile node and home agent to use whichever authentication algorithm(s) they choose. However, all implementations must support the default algorithm of "Keyed MD5." This authentication method uses the *MD5 Message-Digest Algorithm* [RFC 1321] to provide secret-key authentication and integrity checking of the type we described in *Authentication and Integrity Checking via Secret Keys and Message Digests* on page 134.

Specifically, Mobile IP authentication using Keyed MD5 works as follows (see Figure 8-4). A mobile node generates a *Registration Request*, consisting of the fixed-length portion and the Mobile-Home Authentication Extension. The mobile node fills in all of the fields of the request and extension except for the Authentica-

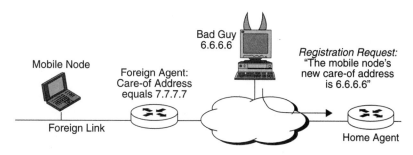

Figure 8-3 Lying about a mobile node's care-of address.

tor field, which is left blank. Then the mobile node computes an MD5 [RFC 1321] message digest over a sequence of bytes that includes:

- the shared, secret key which is known only to the mobile node and its home agent;
- the fixed-length portion of the *Registration Request* message;
- all extensions, up to and including the fields of the Mobile-Home Authentication Extension (i.e., the Type, Length, and Security Parameters Index fields) but not including the Authenticator field itself; and
- the shared, secret key again.

The output of the MD5 computation is a 16-byte message digest that the mobile node places within the Authenticator field of the Mobile-Home Authentication Extension. This completes the assembly of the *Registration Request* message, which the mobile node then sends to its home agent as described in *How Does a Mobile Node Send a Registration Request?* on page 78.

When the message arrives at the home agent, it performs largely the same processing as the mobile node performed in assembling the message. Specifically, the home agent computes its own message digest using the shared, secret key and the fields of the received *Registration Request*. It then compares the computed message digest with the one received within the Authenticator field from the mobile node. If they are equal, then the home agent knows that the mobile node indeed sent the *Registration Request* and that the message had not been modified in transit. Thus, the Mobile IP authentication extensions provide both authentication and integrity checking.

The exact inverse of the procedure described above happens when the home agent returns a *Registration Reply* to the mobile node. The home agent computes

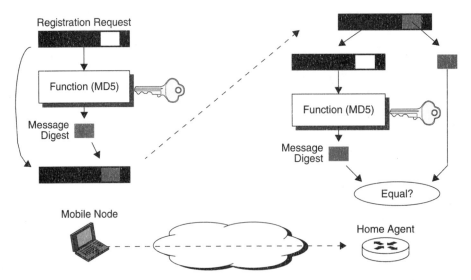

Figure 8-4 Authentication of Registration Messages via Keyed MD5

a message digest of the *Registration Reply* and the secret key and includes this message digest within the Authenticator field of the *Registration Reply*. The mobile node verifies the message digest to authenticate the home agent and to check the integrity of the reply.

8.3.4 What about Replay Attacks?

The Mobile-Home Authentication Extension prevents the denial-of-service attack described above. However, it is not enough by itself, because a Bad Guy could obtain a copy of a valid *Registration Request*, store it, and then "replay" it at a later time, thereby registering a bogus care-of address for the mobile node. To prevent this replay attack from happening, the mobile node generates a unique value for the Identification field in each successive attempted registration. The Identification field is generated in such a way as to allow the home agent to determine what the next value should be. In this way, the Bad Guy is thwarted because the Identification field in his stored *Registration Request* will be recognized as being out-of-date by the home agent.

Mobile IP specifies two ways in which the Identification field can be chosen in order to prevent these replay attacks. The first uses timestamps, wherein the mobile node uses its current estimate for the date-and-time-of-day in the Identification field. If this estimate is not sufficiently close to the home agent's estimate of the current time, then it rejects the mobile node's registration and at the same time provides the mobile node with enough information to synchronize its clock to the home agent's clock. Then, any future Identification values generated by the mobile node will be within the home agent's tolerance.

The other method uses *nonces*, which are reminiscent of the random-number challenges we saw in *Authentication via Secret-Key Encryption* on page 133. In this method, the mobile node specifies to the home agent the value that the home agent must place in the lower half of the Identification field in the next *Registration Reply* that it sends to the mobile node. Similarly, the home agent specifies to the mobile node the next value it must use in the upper half of the Identification field in its next *Registration Request*. If either node receives a registration message in which the Identification field does not match this next, expected value, then the message is rejected in the case of the home agent or ignored in the case of the mobile node. The rejection mechanism allows the mobile node to synchronize to the home agent in case it has stale information about which value to use in the Identification field and vice versa.

8.3.5 Summary

Mobile IP registration has built-in prevention of denial-of-service attacks of the type described in this section. Specifically, it is impossible for a Bad Guy to lie to a mobile node's home agent about that mobile node's current care-of address, because all registration messages provide authentication of the message's source, integrity checking, and replay protection.

8.4 Theft of Information: Passive Eavesdropping

A serious threat faced by the mobile node and other hosts on the network is theft of information. Theft of information occurs when a Bad Guy eavesdrops on someone else's packets in order to learn confidential or proprietary secrets that might be contained in those packets. As we saw in *What Do We Mean by Confidentiality?* on page 129, encryption is the most common mechanism used to protect data against being examined by unauthorized parties. In this section we describe two ways in which encryption can be employed to protect the confidentiality of data being sent and received by a mobile node and other nodes on the network.

8.4.1 Nature of the Threat

Given the security model of this chapter (see *What Is the Security Model for This Chapter?* on page 158), it is logical to ask who might be able to gain access to unauthorized information, since we have already determined that physical access to the campus must be secured in order for this deployment to be practical.

There are always people who will be given access to the campus intentionally, such as vendors, customers, job candidates and repair technicians. The problem is that physical security is seldom perfect, and unauthorized people are often unintentionally allowed to access the campus as well. We note that wireless links can provide a serious vulnerability, in that someone need not physically be connected to the network in order to gain access to the information being sent across that link.

In addition, it is sound engineering practice to anticipate problems and try to deal with them before they occur. Such is the approach we take in this section. We acknowledge the imperfect nature of physical security and take steps to secure the campus network. Our assumption is that unauthorized persons will inevitably gain wired or wireless access to the network infrastructure, and we must therefore take steps to protect the network from such individuals.

8.4.2 Link-Layer Encryption

In the campus mobility example of this chapter we assume two categories of media by which a mobile node might connect to a foreign agent or its home agent: wired Ethernet and wireless LANs (local area networks). In this section we describe a way to prevent a Bad Guy from stealing information that flows between a mobile node and its foreign agent in the particularly vulnerable case of wireless links. In the next section we describe a preferable method that works regardless of physical medium and protects data at all points in the enterprise, not just over a mobile node's foreign link.

An illustration of link encryption is given in the first panel of Figure 8-5. Here the mobile node and the foreign agent encrypt all packets they exchange over the foreign link. We also assume that key management for the encryption is performed without disclosing the keys to any unauthorized parties. In this way, all frames transmitted on the link contain encrypted packets that only the mobile node or the foreign agent can decrypt.

Link encryption is particularly important when the foreign link is a wireless LAN. It is easier to eavesdrop on a wireless link because a Bad Guy does not have to physically connect to the link to be able to receive packets. It is therefore important to encrypt packets sent over a wireless link, to prevent a Bad Guy from eavesdropping. For this reason, many vendors who sell wireless LAN network interfaces build encryption into their products or make it available as an option.

Other vendors do not provide such encryption and claim that their products are "secure" against eavesdropping because their physical-layer protocols are difficult to decode. Such claims are unfortunate, because the consensus of many cryptographers is that the information transmitted by these products is relatively easy to break, especially when compared to strong encryption algorithms. The name for this is "security through obscurity," and while it might be the latter it most certainly is not the former!

Of course, many of these vendors are responding to the policies of various governments which limit the use or the export of products containing strong encryption. For many companies, the cost of supporting two different products— one containing encryption for the domestic market and one without encryption for export—can be a losing proposition from a business perspective. Therefore, many companies opt to make a single product without encryption which can be sold in all markets, leaving users vulnerable to the types of attacks described in this and other sections. See [RFC 1984] for more information about this topic.

8.4.3 End-to-End Encryption

As always, the "right thing to do" for those concerned about the confidentiality or integrity of their data is to perform end-to-end encryption. This means encrypting and decrypting the data at the ultimate source and ultimate destination of the communications as opposed to merely encrypting over the last (or first) link.[†] The virtues of end-to-end encryption are many:

- the data is protected against eavesdropping at all points in the network, rather than being protected only on the foreign link;

- the data is protected regardless of the medium employed on the foreign link (it can be difficult to find products that implement certain link technologies that also implement encryption);

- resources are only expended at the ultimate source and destination rather than at (potentially) many locations, preventing the communication from incurring unnecessary delay;

[†] This is not to say that link encryption is bad; rather, it is to say that end-to-end encryption is better.

- such a solution extends naturally to accessing a private network over a public infrastructure without compromising the confidentiality of the data on the private network (we will see examples of this in *Chapter 9, Internet-Wide Mobility: A More Complicated Application*).

The second frame of Figure 8-5 shows end-to-end encryption used to prevent theft-of-information. As shown in the figure, link encryption does not protect against a Bad Guy eavesdropping on the packets along the path between the correspondent node and the foreign agent—only against a Bad Guy eavesdropping on the foreign link itself. In contrast, end-to-end encryption provides no such vulnerabilities. A Bad Guy who eavesdrops at any point of the conversation in the second panel of Figure 8-5 will see only ciphertext that he is incapable of decrypting.

Some examples of Internet-based applications that provide such end-to-end encryption include SSH (Secure remote [Unix] SHell), SCP (Secure remote file CoPy), and SSL (Secure Sockets Layer as used by many secure sites and browsers in the World Wide Web). The *Encapsulating Security Payload* [RFC 1827] can provide end-to-end encryption for other application programs that do not support encryption themselves. This encrypts not only the application-layer data and protocol header but also the transport-layer header as well, which prevents a Bad Guy from determining *which* application is being run, let alone the data exchanged as part of that application.

1. Link Encryption to secure data exchanged only on the foreign link:

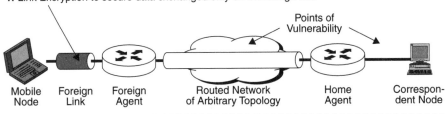

Mobile   Foreign   Foreign   Routed Network   Home   Correspon-
Node   Link   Agent   of Arbitrary Topology   Agent   dent Node

2. End-to-End Encryption through IP Encapsulating Security Payload: no obvious vulnerabilities!

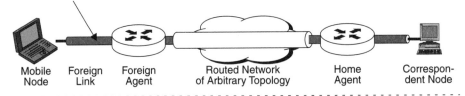

Mobile   Foreign   Foreign   Routed Network   Home   Correspon-
Node   Link   Agent   of Arbitrary Topology   Agent   dent Node

Legend:

🬋🬋🬋 Encrypted Tunnel or Link Encryption   **Figure 8-5** Confidentiality
🬋🬋🬋 Unencrypted, Mobile IP Tunnel   through Link Encryption vs.
▬▬▬ Plaintext Data Packets   End-to-End Encryption.

8.5 Theft of Information: Session-Stealing (Takeover) Attack

A session-stealing attack is one in which a Bad Guy waits for a legitimate node to authenticate itself and start an application session, then takes over the session by impersonating the identity of the legitimate node. Usually, the Bad Guy must send a tremendous number of nuisance packets to the legitimate node in order to prevent it from realizing that its session has been hijacked.

8.5.1 Session-Stealing on the Foreign Link

The nature of the threat in this section is similar to the passive-eavesdropping case. Namely, we assume that a Bad Guy has been able to slip through the physical security of the campus and is within the range of the wireless transmitters/receivers operating on a mobile node's foreign link. Equivalently, we could assume that the Bad Guy has physically connected to an Ethernet-based foreign link. The session-stealing attack is waged as follows:

- the Bad Guy waits for a mobile node to register with its home agent;
- the Bad Guy eavesdrops to see if the mobile node has any interesting conversations taking place (e.g., a remote login session to another host or a connection to its remote electronic mailbox);
- the Bad Guy floods the mobile node with nuisance packets, bringing the mobile node's CPU to its knees; and
- the Bad Guy steals the session by sourcing packets that appear to have come from the mobile node and by intercepting packets destined to the mobile node.

The user of the mobile node might realize that something is not right, because his applications will stop functioning. However, the user probably has no idea that his sessions have been hijacked because there is no indication on his screen that something like this has occurred. We note that the Bad Guy could also take over the sessions of any conventional hosts that happen to be connected to the same link as the mobile node. Such conventional hosts include those that do not implement Mobile IP or, equivalently, other mobile nodes that are connected to their home link.

The method of preventing this attack is the same as that used to prevent passive eavesdropping. Specifically, we minimally require link-layer encryption between the mobile node and its foreign agent. As before, we prefer end-to-end encryption between the mobile node and its correspondent node, but we defer this discussion until *Session-Stealing Elsewhere* on page 168.

Encryption prevents session-stealing attacks for the following reason. If link encryption is employed between the mobile node and the foreign agent, then each will respectively expect all packets received from the other to be encrypted. This means that each of these nodes will in turn decrypt all received packets in

order to recover the plaintext. Note that only the mobile node and the foreign
agent possess the necessary keys to both encrypt and decrypt the data they
exchange.

It is therefore impossible for the Bad Guy to generate ciphertext that will
decrypt to anything other than gibberish at the mobile node and foreign agent,
because the Bad Guy cannot obtain the appropriate key(s). Additionally, a good
encryption scheme provides a method by which a decrypting node can determine
whether the recovered plaintext is gibberish or whether it is legitimate.

An obvious way of implementing this latter feature is to provide both
encryption and integrity checking of the data. Then, upon decryption, if the data
does not pass the integrity check, then the receiving node knows that it is gibberish. As described in [Bellovin96], encryption without authentication has some
serious vulnerabilities so it is wise to both encrypt *and* authenticate sensitive
data. In any case, the important point is that encryption, properly applied,
makes the session-stealing attack described in this section impossible.

8.5.2 Session-Stealing Elsewhere

If the Bad Guy does not have access to the foreign link (e.g., the link is
wired or the Bad Guy is out of range of the wireless transmitter and receiver), it
is still possible for him to wage a session-stealing attack. Of course, this requires
the Bad Guy to have access to the network somewhere along the path between a
mobile node and its correspondent node.

Here again we assume that the Bad Guy has compromised the campus's
physical security mechanisms and has been able to establish a physical connection to the network. We further assume that the Bad Guy might slip into a conference room in order not to be noticed and might connect a computer to a
network jack in that room. After all, it would be difficult for a Bad Guy to go
unnoticed in a room where there were plenty of legitimate employees milling
around, at least during normal business hours.

Once again, what we have described here is not new to Mobile IP. However,
we acknowledge that conference rooms might not have network jacks installed in
them if Mobile IP had not been deployed on the campus. Nonetheless, this is a
realistic situation that might occur on a campus and we treat it accordingly.

The session-stealing attack in this instance is similar to the case described
in the previous section for session-stealing on the foreign link. The differences
are as follows:

- link-layer encryption employed only on the foreign link provides no useful
  protection; and
- the Bad Guy could potentially steal any session whose packets traverse the
  link to which the Bad Guy connects, not only those sessions related to
  mobile nodes.

The method by which the Bad Guy wages the attack is identical to that of
the previous section. Namely, he eavesdrops on the conversations until he finds

one interesting enough to hijack, then attacks one of the end-points with nuisance packets, and finally assumes the identity of the attacked end-point.

Once again, encryption is the way to prevent such attacks. Clearly link-layer encryption employed only over the foreign links is *not* sufficient. End-to-end encryption is required to protect the data at all points in the network. Such encryption, as before, can be implemented with the *Encapsulating Security Payload* or with application-layer encryption as we saw in *End-to-End Encryption* on page 165.

8.6 Other Active Attacks

This section describes the final category of active attack that might be waged by a Bad Guy on the private network on the campus of this chapter. Unlike the previous sections, here we describe an attack that does not involve the Bad Guy passively monitoring or actively stealing an existing session. Rather, the type of attack we wish to examine is one where the Bad Guy connects to a network jack, figures out an IP address to use, and tries to break into the other hosts on the network.

The nature of the threat here is the same as in *Session-Stealing Elsewhere* on page 168; namely, a Bad Guy slips past the physical security on the campus and ducks into an unoccupied conference room, pleasantly finding several network jacks available in that room. The attack proceeds as follows:

1. The Bad Guy figures out the network-prefix that has been assigned to the link to which the network jacks are connected. There are a number of methods by which he might make this determination:

    a. he listens for Mobile IP *Agent Advertisements* and uses the Prefix-Lengths Extension to uniquely determine the network-prefix(es);

    b. he listens to packets on the link belonging to various other nodes and by careful examination of the IP Source and Destination Addresses deduces the network-prefix of the link; or

    c. he has enough *chutzpah* to send packets to a *Dynamic Host Configuration Protocol (DHCP)* server which, owing to lax security policies or errors in configuration, tells him exactly what he wants to know—and might even assign him an IP address!

2. The Bad Guy guesses a host number to use, which, along with the network-prefix determined in step 1, gives him an IP address to use on the current link. One way in which the Bad Guy can determine an unused host number is to listen to packets for a while and pick one that does not appear to be in use. Another is to pick a host number, send a few *ARP Request* messages containing the resulting IP address, and see if the messages go unanswered. If so, then there is a good chance that the selected host number is not being used.

3. The Bad Guy proceeds to try to break into the hosts on the network, for example, by attempting to log into the Unix machines and guessing username/password pairs until he is successful. We note here that it is simply astounding how many networks contain host accounts with trivially guessable passwords and therefore how often such attacks are successful! (Ideally, passwords should be at least eight characters long, should contain at least one or more punctuation characters or spaces, and should not be written on a piece of paper and taped to a computer monitor.)

The way in which the network can protect against some attacks is by making it impossible for the Bad Guy to communicate with other nodes in the network from such a network jack. This requires the following safeguards:

- All publicly accessible network jacks (e.g., those in conference rooms) must connect to a foreign agent that has been configured to enforce the policy associated with the R bit in its *Agent Advertisements*. Recall that such a foreign agent will refuse to route packets on behalf of any node on the link which has not successfully registered with that foreign agent. (See *What's the Deal with the 'R' Bit?* on page 88.)

- There must not be any nodes, mobile or otherwise, connected to such a link whose sessions can be hijacked. The simplest policy which provides such protection is to remove all nonmobile nodes from the link and require all legitimate mobile nodes to use (minimally) link-layer encryption.

In this way, it will be impossible for the Bad Guy to successfully register with the foreign agent because it will have no way of generating an authentic *Registration Request* that will be affirmatively answered by a home agent somewhere on the network. Thus, no such active attack is possible by a Bad Guy under the configuration outlined above.

It is important to note that a foreign agent with the R bit set as described above provides better protection from attackers than does a router providing connectivity for such a conference room. Thus, in some ways, Mobile IP can provide slightly better security if it is deployed carefully.

8.7 Summary/Conclusions

In this chapter we described a simple deployment of Mobile IP on an individual corporate campus. Our deployment consisted of upgrading all of the routers in the campus to be both home agents and foreign agents and of upgrading all reasonably portable hosts to be mobile nodes. Then we assigned home addresses to all of the mobile nodes based upon the user's department and configured Mobile IP authentication keys between the mobile nodes and their respective home agents.

Our security model in this chapter was based upon the assumption of securing physical access to the campus and hence the network. However, we noted that physical security is never perfect and that prudence dictates that we take reasonable precautions to protect the mobile users, the private network, and the data contained therein.

The way we protected the internal data—and this is not necessarily specific to Mobile IP—was to minimally perform link encryption over the foreign link and preferably end-to-end encryption. Such a network is very robust against all kinds of active and passive attacks that can be waged by Bad Guys.

Finally, we described a denial-of-service attack in which a Bad Guy lies to a mobile node's home agent about the mobile node's current care-of address. Also, we saw how Mobile IP is specifically designed to prevent this type of attack through a combination of the Mobile-Home Authentication Extension and the Identification field. Together, these fields provide authentication, integrity checking, and replay protection for all *Registration Requests* and *Replies*.

Internet-Wide Mobility: A More Complicated Application

*I*n the previous chapter we made life easy by considering a private, campus intranet that was not hooked to the global Internet and whose mobile nodes were allowed to move only within the campus environment. In the current chapter, however, we investigate a more complicated application of Mobile IP. This application allows a user to move anywhere throughout the entire Internet without exposing his private network to additional security threats. We also show a method by which a company can make available foreign agents for use by its customers, vendors, and other guests, all without compromising the security of that company's network.

This chapter also introduces the complications that firewalls introduce to Mobile IP—specifically, the problem of mobile nodes getting packets past the firewall when they are outside of the private network boundary. While the basic technology described in this chapter is relatively mature, we note that firewall traversal is an active work item within the Mobile IP working group of the Internet Engineering Task Force.

9.1 What Is the Model for This Application?

In this section we describe how we intend to deploy Mobile IP in order to enable Internet-wide mobility. First we describe the location of home agents and foreign agents and show how mobile nodes gain access to their services. Then we examine the security threats faced by such a network and offer protections against these threats.

9.1.1 What Are Our Assumptions and Requirements?

As mentioned in the introduction, we made every possible simplifying assumption we could in the previous chapter. In this chapter we do the exact opposite. Once again we assume the existence of a corporate intranet which contains sensitive data that must be kept confidential. This time, however, we allow this private network to be connected to the global Internet, as shown in Figure 9-1. As always, connecting to the Internet requires some sort of firewall to protect the corporate network against unauthorized access.

The requirements driving our deployment of Mobile IP, and the topological placement of home agents and foreign agents with respect to the firewall, are as follows:

- The corporate network must be safe from intrusion; that is, there must be a firewall between the corporate network and the global Internet.

- Authorized mobile nodes—those belonging to employees of the corporation—must not suffer any loss of connectivity to resources inside the firewall, even when connected to a foreign link that is outside the firewall.

- The corporate network must not be exposed to any new security threats over and above those that face any network connected to the Internet (through a firewall).

- A visitor must be able to communicate with the global Internet (and presumably his own private network) from "public" areas such as conference rooms, training facilities, etc.

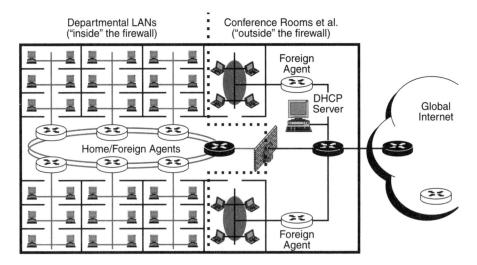

Figure 9-1 Mobile IP Deployment with Global Mobility

This final requirement is certainly desirable in that it allows a visitor to the campus—e.g., a vendor, a customer, or a consultant—to connect to the Internet using Mobile IP in order to reach his private network.

9.1.2 How Can Mobile IP Be Deployed to Fulfill These Requirements?

Figure 9-1 shows how we can deploy Mobile IP in such a way as to fulfill all of the requirements listed in the previous section. As in the previous chapter, we have departmental LANs composed of possibly many types of media, which are connected to routers that have been upgraded to support both home agent and foreign agent functionality. These agents are connected by a high-speed fiber backbone as before.

As Figure 9-1 shows, some of the network devices are "inside" the firewall and some are "outside" the firewall. *Inside* refers to devices in the private portion of the network that are protected against intrusion. *Outside* refers to the rest of the global Internet—i.e., those devices from which the firewall protects the private network. The departmental LANs, including conventional hosts, home/foreign agents, and certain mobile nodes, are all inside the firewall. We therefore require strict physical security to be enforced with respect to who is allowed to enter a department's room, floor, factory, etc.

On the other hand, all publicly accessible network jacks, such as those found in conference rooms and waiting areas, are outside the firewall. As such, physical security need not be as strictly enforced in such areas. The network jacks in these public areas are connected to foreign agents, which provide the standard Mobile IP support facilities described below.

All mobile nodes—both those owned by the corporation and those owned by anyone else—may plug into the network in these public areas. Mobile nodes owned by employees of the corporation are assigned to home agents and home links within those employees' departmental LAN just as in the previous chapter. Mobile nodes belonging to visitors will have home agents and home links on some network that is outside the firewall, presumably reachable through the global Internet.

Most likely, a visitor's mobile node which connects to a network jack in a conference room of Figure 9-1 will be on the outside of his own firewall, just like the mobile nodes owned by the corporation's employees. Foreign agents are provided at these locations in order for mobile nodes to perform move detection, obtain care-of addresses, and select a default router. Also, these foreign agents will serve as a relay agent for those mobile nodes which wish to obtain a collocated care-of address from a DHCP server. The R bit is turned off on these foreign agents, because the administrators of the network need not enforce an access-control policy on this network (which is outside the firewall).

9.1.3 Why Is It Done This Way?

The primary motivation for the architecture shown in Figure 9-1 is to keep all mobile nodes outside the firewall. Only authorized mobile nodes which can authenticate themselves to the firewall will be allowed to communicate with hosts on the protected portion of the corporate network. All others will be allowed to access the global Internet. Finally, this deployment adds no security risks over and above those faced by any organization that connects to the Internet.

One profound observation about this deployment is the presence of the firewall that separates the mobile nodes in the conference room from the corporation's own home agents (and home links) on the inside. This requires a method for packets to and from authorized mobile nodes to *traverse* the firewall. The challenge in this chapter is to specify such a mechanism that does not compromise the security of the corporate network.

With this description of the Mobile IP deployment, we now analyze the security threats to the corporate network and to that corporation's mobile nodes. First we revisit the threats discussed in the previous chapter, then we move on to the hard part of devising protocols by which mobile nodes can securely traverse a firewall without compromising the security of their private network.

9.2 Which Threats Are Largely the Same As Before?

Many of the threats facing the mobile node, the corporate network, or both based upon the deployment outlined above happen to be identical to those in the previous chapter. We will not spend a lot of time on these identical threats, but for completeness we summarize them here:

- The corporation always faces threats from insiders—those who are supposed to be trustworthy employees. To protect against an insider divulging secret or proprietary information, an organization should restrict access to information to those absolutely requiring that information.

- Mobile nodes always face the threat of trivial denial-of-service attacks where a Bad Guy lies to the mobile node's home agent about the mobile node's current care-of address. As we saw in the previous chapter, Mobile IP prevents such attacks through the use of cryptographically strong authentication as part of the registration procedure.

- Passive eavesdropping and active takeover attacks are still faced by mobile nodes that do not use encryption. The deployment in the current chapter mandates the use of encryption whenever the mobile node is outside the firewall, making such attacks impossible in this circumstance. Mobile nodes should additionally use encryption when inside the firewall to prevent such attacks at all times.

- A Bad Guy who gained access to the "restricted" portion of the campus, i.e., where there are network jacks connected to the departmental LANs inside the firewall, could wreak all sorts of havoc on the machines within the private portion of the network. For this reason, physical access to such areas must be strictly controlled.

With respect to this last item, note that a Bad Guy who gains access to the network jacks in the conference rooms cannot wreak any such havoc, because he is outside the firewall. It should now be clear why we placed such publicly accessible areas outside the firewall.

Note that when the corporation's mobile nodes are plugged into a network jack in these conference rooms, the mobile nodes are "on the Internet" with no firewall to protect them against attacks! This is a severe new vulnerability that we had not encountered in the previous chapter. We describe this vulnerability, and the protection against same, in the next section.

9.3 How Do We Protect a Mobile Node That Is Outside the Firewall?

In this section we describe the threats to a mobile node that is currently outside of its firewall and offer protections against these threats. A mobile node in such a situation is just like any other node on the Internet with no firewall to protect it. It is therefore vulnerable to passive eavesdropping attacks, active session-stealing (takeover) attacks, etc.—all the attacks described in the previous chapter.

In this case, however, the mobile node has no firewall to protect it from the millions of other nodes on the Internet. Therefore, the magnitude of the threat is far greater than before. Thus we require very strong methods to protect the mobile node from these threats. Our solution is based upon VPN technology, which we describe in the next few sections.

9.3.1 VPNs Revisited

Recall our discussion of Virtual Private Networks (VPNs) in *What Is a Secure Tunneler?* on page 151. A VPN consists of two or more physical private networks that are separated by a public network and function as a single private network. VPNs are built from authenticated and encrypted tunnels between secure tunneling firewalls at the border of each physical network. The firewall protects its network by admitting only those packets that have been authenticated and encrypted by one of the other firewalls.

An example VPN is shown in Figure 9-2. The two firewalls look like normal routers (or bridges) to the other routers within their respective private networks. To see how this works, let us consider what happens when $Host_1$, which is in one physical portion of the VPN, sends a packet to Host$_2$, which is in another physical portion of the VPN:

1. Host$_1$ builds an IP packet with its own IP address as the Source Address and Host$_2$'s IP address as the Destination Address.

2. Host$_1$ sends the packet which is ultimately forwarded to the firewall on the left of Figure 9-2 via conventional IP routing.

3. The firewall prepends an *IP Encapsulating Security Payload* header to the original IP packet and encrypts the original IP header and payload. Here we assume that the encryption algorithm—or a separate algorithm—provides authentication and integrity checking in addition to confidentiality.

4. The firewall places the resultant *Encapsulating Security Payload* header plus encrypted original packet within the payload portion of a new IP packet. The new IP packet has a Source Address of the leftmost firewall and a Destination Address of the rightmost firewall (again, see Figure 9-2).

5. The new packet is transmitted over the Internet, where it is ultimately received by the firewall on the right of Figure 9-2.

6. The firewall consumes the outermost IP packet header and examines the *IP Encapsulating Security Payload* header. The Security Parameters Index field within that header informs the firewall how to process the received ciphertext. The firewall proceeds to decrypt and verify the authentication and integrity of the packet.

7. If the packet is authentic (i.e., if the authenticator is valid), then the firewall removes the *IP Encapsulating Security Payload* header to recover the original IP packet.

8. The firewall forwards the packet, which is ultimately delivered to Host$_2$ via conventional IP routing.

Note how all of the hosts and routers within the VPN—i.e., within the physical portions of the private network—are protected from all of the hosts and routers on the Internet by the firewalls. These firewalls allow only packets containing strong authentication to pass through. If the authentication and encryption keys are managed carefully, then there is no way that nodes outside of the VPN—i.e.,

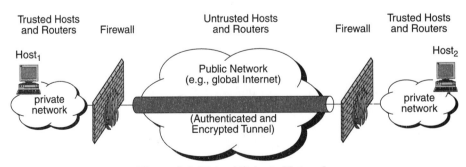

Figure 9-2 Virtual Private Network

nodes on the public portion of the Internet—can generate the authentication required to penetrate the private network. We now show how VPN technology can be used to protect a mobile node on the public portion of the Internet.

9.3.2 Mobile Nodes as a Special Case of VPNs

In this section we show how a special case of Virtual Private Networks can be used to protect mobile nodes when they are connected to the public portion of the Internet and when they have no firewall to protect them from various attacks. The solution involves extending the VPN with a tentacle to encompass the mobile node itself, as shown in Figure 9-3. The "firewall" shown protecting the mobile node is not a separate hardware device; rather, the "firewall" is a software module running on the mobile node, probably somewhere within its operating system.

The mobile node in Figure 9-3 can be considered to be a single-node private network with an integrated firewall; i.e., a private network that contains exactly one device—the mobile node and the firewall software. With this analogy in mind, we see that the mobile node and the other private networks shown in the figure form a VPN just like that described in the previous section.

The software that implements the mobile node's internal "firewall" has the same policy as the physical firewalls. Specifically, the mobile node only admits packets that contain valid authenticators. The authenticator can be within an *IP Encapsulating Security Payload* or an *IP Authentication Header* just as described in the previous section. Any packet not containing such authentication is discarded by the mobile node with no further processing.

Similarly, the physical firewalls shown in the figure treat the software "firewall" in the mobile node as they would any other trusted firewall. Specifically, they will admit those packets that have been authenticated by the mobile node via an *Encapsulating Security Payload* or an *Authentication Header*. In this way, the mobile node is able to communicate with all hosts and routers within the rest of the VPN—i.e., within any of the physical, private networks—without compromising the security of those networks.

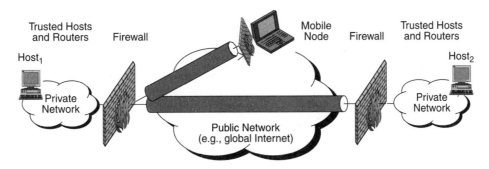

Figure 9-3 Protecting a Mobile Node with VPN Technology

It is important to note that a mobile node in such a configuration extends the security boundary of the physical private network. Specifically, if a Bad Guy is able to mount a successful attack on the mobile node, it is very likely that he will also be able to use the mobile node to attack other hosts in the private network. Thus, it is extremely important for network administrators to ensure that all such mobile nodes have software on them that discards packets that are not authenticated by the appropriate firewall(s). In addition, it is desirable that this software be configured in such a way as to prevent less knowledgeable employees from disabling this security feature.

What we have just described is a conceptual framework both for protecting mobile nodes that are on a public network and for providing them with secure access to their private networks. In this high-level discussion we have intentionally omitted several important details. Specifically, we have not answered the following questions:

- How does a mobile node establish the authenticated and/or encrypted tunnel to the firewall?

- Does the mobile node establish this tunnel before or after it registers with its home agent?

- Is the mobile node's home agent inside or outside the firewall?

- How do we establish keys between the mobile node and its firewall?

- How do the mobile node and the firewall agree on a set of encryption and/or authentication algorithms to use?

- How does the mobile node know whether it is inside or outside the firewall? (Only in the latter case does it need to set up a secure tunnel with the firewall.)

In the following sections we describe two solutions to the problems suggested by these questions. The first is an existing implementation using SKIP. The second uses ISAKMP/Oakley and is "work in progress" within the Mobile IP working group of the Internet Engineering Task Force. This second discussion represents a snapshot of the current thinking on this topic.

9.4 How Can Mobile Nodes Traverse the Firewall without Compromising the Corporate Network?

In this section we describe two methods by which mobile nodes that are within the public portion of the Internet can traverse a firewall that protects their private network from unauthorized access. First, we describe the model, the assumptions, and the requirements of the solutions. Then we describe these two solutions in subsequent sections.

9.4.1 What Are the Assumptions and Requirements for Firewall Traversal?

In this section we describe the assumptions and requirements for our solution to the firewall-traversal problem for mobile nodes. The following list has been adapted from the Mobile IP working group's requirements document [draft-ietf-mobileip-ft-req-00.txt] for firewall traversal.

Assumptions for Secure Firewall Traversal in Mobile IP

We make the following assumptions for firewall traversal:

1. The mobile node's private network is protected from intrusion by a firewall of the secure tunneling type. The firewall implements the *IP Authentication Header*, *IP Encapsulating Security Payload*, and either SKIP or ISAKMP/Oakley for key management.
2. The mobile node's foreign link is on the "public" portion of the Internet, meaning that there are no firewalls between the mobile node's foreign link and the firewall protecting the mobile node's private network.

The first assumption implies that the firewall's admission policy is based solely upon the authenticity and integrity of packets received from the outside. Specifically, this means that the firewall need not know anything about Mobile IP.

The second assumption implies that the mobile node is connecting via a foreign link which is not itself separated from the Internet by a firewall. Examples of such situations are dial-up connections to Internet Service Providers, and Ethernet connections at university campuses and terminal rooms at trade shows or conferences. Note how our proposed deployment in Figure 9-1 is consistent with this latter assumption.

Requirements for Secure Firewall Traversal in Mobile IP

The requirements we place upon our solution are as follows:

1. *The solution must protect the mobile node and the private network from passive eavesdropping and active takeover (session-stealing) attacks.* Minimally, this requires an encrypted tunnel between the mobile node and the firewall. As recommended in [Bellovin96], we also require authentication of this encrypted tunnel.
2. *The solution must work for organizations that have private addresses on their networks.* By private addresses we mean those that are not advertised to the rest of the Internet, either because they are "officially" unroutable addresses (i.e., those defined in [RFC 1918]) or because they are legitimately owned by some *other* organization or service provider. Unfortunately, there are many organizations that use such addresses. Complicating matters is the fact that these same organizations often configure their routers to discard packets that carry "external" addresses—those which may

exist on the public portion of the Internet but which are not permitted within the private network. The firewall traversal solution must also work in private networks that have such policies. Generally, this will require "burying" such addresses within a tunnel when they would otherwise have appeared as either the Source Address or Destination Address of an IP packet.

3. *The solution must not require the firewall to implement or understand Mobile IP.* Specifically, the solution must not require the firewall to pass packets that are not authenticated but are destined to UDP Port 434 (the Mobile IP registration port). Thus, our solution must not require any modifications to the standard policies that would be implemented on secure tunneling firewalls. Similarly, we must not require the firewall to itself be a mobile node's home agent.

4. *Our solution must not require a mobile node to be reachable at its home address.* A chicken-and-egg problem would result if we were to relax this requirement. Consider that the firewall will not let packets from the mobile node into the private network until the mobile node has authenticated itself to the firewall. However, the firewall cannot send a response packet to the mobile node's home address unless the mobile node has already registered, implying that the mobile node has already sent a *Registration Request* through the firewall to its home agent, and so on.

5. *Our solution must minimally work with collocated care-of addresses and it would be desirable if it also worked with foreign agent care-of addresses.* Foreign agent care-of addresses are problematic, owing to the "application-layer relay" function they perform, especially during Mobile IP registration. Specifically, the *IP Authentication Header* protects fields in the IP packet header itself. It is impossible for a mobile node to know in advance what some of the values for those fields will be when the foreign agent relays its *Registration Request*. Thus, it is impossible for a mobile node to compute an authenticator that will not be invalidated by this relay function. We note that possible solutions to this problem—such as permitting the firewall to pass *Registration Requests* that do not contain authentication that can be verified by that firewall—are inconsistent with requirement 3 above.

6. *Our solution must work in the presence of additional firewalls between the mobile node's home agent and the firewall at the perimeter of the private network.* Many organizations segment their internal, private networks with additional firewalls which, for example, prevents finance employees from accessing the data in the engineering computer systems and vice versa. Thus, our solution should permit such a network configuration and work in the presence of these firewalls. It is important to note that this requirement is consistent with *assumption* number 2 in the previous section, in that we assume all firewalls are controlled by the network administrators of the mobile node's private network and that none of these firewalls belong to other organizations.

These are the requirements and assumptions driving the design of a general mechanism by which mobile nodes can traverse firewall(s) protecting their private networks. We now describe two such mechanisms: one using SKIP for key management and the other using ISAKMP/Oakley.

9.4.2 Firewall Traversal Using SKIP

This section describes a method by which mobile nodes can traverse firewalls protecting their private networks wherein those firewalls implement SKIP for key management. The technology described here was developed by Gabriel Montenegro and Vipul Gupta of SUN Microsystems and documented in [draft-montenegro-firewall-sup-00.txt]. It is important to note that the method described below is not "science fiction"—rather, it has actually been implemented by these two gentlemen and is running in their laboratory.

Reference Model

The reference diagram for SKIP-based firewall traversal is shown in Figure 9-4. Here we see a mobile node on the public portion of the Internet with only one firewall separating it from its home agent and private network. The firewall implements the *IP Authentication Header, Encapsulating Security Payload,* and SKIP.

In order to simplify the discussion, we ignore the possibility of multiple firewalls separating the mobile node from its home agent and just consider the single firewall shown in Figure 9-4. Furthermore, of the possible levels of encryption and authentication that might be in use, we ignore all of them except the encrypted and authenticated tunnel between the mobile node and the firewall. End-to-end encryption and authentication between the mobile node and its correspondent node is certainly possible, and it layers nicely on top of the secure tunnel between the mobile node and the firewall. It is ignored, however, since including it would confuse the discussion.

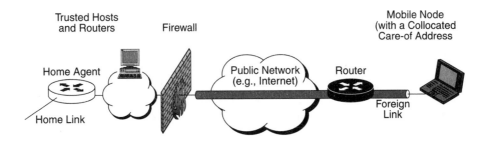

Figure 9-4 Reference Diagram for Firewall Traversal

Administrative Considerations

In order for the mobile node to be able to traverse the firewall securely, the following administrative functions need to be performed (e.g., by an organization's network or security manager):

- The mobile node must be configured with a method for obtaining the firewall's Diffie-Hellman public value (see *How Does SKIP Use Diffie-Hellman?* on page 146 for details). This configuration can manifest itself in two ways: a direct method in which the mobile node is configured with the firewall's actual Diffie-Hellman public value; or an indirect way in which the mobile node is provided with a means for verifying the authentication within the firewall's certified public value. For simplicity, we assume the former.

- Identical arguments apply with respect to the firewall obtaining the mobile node's Diffie-Hellman public value. We assume manual configuration which might occur at the same time the firewall is configured with the knowledge that this particular mobile node is legitimately allowed to traverse the firewall if it provides valid authentication.

- The mobile node and firewall must have hardware or software installed that implements at least one common secret-key authentication algorithm and one common secret-key encryption algorithm. In this section we assume Keyed MD5 authentication [RFC 1828] and Triple-DES encryption [RFC 1851], respectively.

- The mobile node must be configured with a range of IP addresses that are known to be "within" the private network. This allows the mobile node to know whether it is currently connected to its private network or the public portion of the Internet. The nice thing about placing this responsibility with the mobile node is that the user can always be consulted in case the mobile node guesses incorrectly and is unable to communicate.

- The home agent must also be configured with this range of IP addresses known to be within the private network. This allows the home agent to determine that a mobile node is attempting to register a care-of address outside of the private network. In this case, a home agent must modify its normal forwarding function in order to deliver tunneled packets to the firewall before the firewall can forward them toward the care-of address.

With these administrative functions accomplished, we now assume that the mobile node has connected to some foreign link on a public network and must perform its normal Mobile IP functions: determining its current location, acquiring a care-of address, and registering that care-of address with its home agent. We describe the method by which this occurs in the next section.

Registration Procedure

In this section we describe how a mobile node registers with its home agent once it has connected to a foreign link in the public portion of the Internet. As per our *Reference Model* on page 183, we assume that there is only one firewall separating the mobile node from its home agent. The registration process proceeds as follows:

1. The mobile node connects to the foreign link and obtains a collocated care-of address via DHCP, PPP's IPCP, or manual configuration, as described in *DHCP and Manual Configuration on Foreign Link* on page 71.

2. The mobile node consults its list of addresses known to be within the private network and determines that its current care-of address is in the public portion of the Internet; i.e., the mobile node determines that it is outside the private network and therefore must traverse the firewall.

3. The mobile node registers the care-of address with its home agent. Because the mobile node has an external care-of address, it must securely tunnel its *Registration Request* to the firewall. The building of this tunneled *Registration Request* message is the interesting part of this discussion and where this chapter differs so profoundly from previous ones. We therefore describe how the *Registration Request* message is built in its own section. See Figure 9-5 for an illustration of this message, and see *How Does a Mobile Node Build a Tunneled Registration Request?* on page 187 for the details of how the message is built. Here we briefly summarize the components of the final message before it is forwarded by the mobile node to its default router. These components are as follows:

   a. an outer IP packet header, accomplishing the tunnel to the firewall;

   b. a SKIP header, which informs the firewall of the identity of the mobile node and allows the firewall to determine the encryption and authentication algorithms which have been used by the mobile node;

   c. an *Authentication Header*, which is used to authenticate the mobile node to the firewall and provides integrity checking for the entire contents of the packet;

   d. an *Encapsulating Security Payload* which is used to encrypt the "data" portion of this message—namely, a "normal" *Registration Request*; and

   e. the encrypted *Registration Request* message, including the (inner) UDP/IP headers, the fixed-length portion of the request, and the Mobile-Home Authentication Extension.

4. The mobile node forwards this securely tunneled *Registration Request* message to its default router, and the message is ultimately delivered to the firewall.

5. The firewall uses the fields in the SKIP header to determine the identity of the mobile node and to further determine how the mobile node has authen-

ticated and encrypted the packet. Here we note that SKIP provides a way for the mobile node to inform the firewall that its identity, and hence its Diffie-Hellman public value, is based upon its home address, not the IP Source Address of the packet (which is set to the mobile node's care-of address).

6. The firewall validates the authenticator contained within the *IP Authentication Header* and then decrypts the contents of the *IP Encapsulating Security Payload* to recover the "normal" *Registration Request* message. If the authenticator is invalid, the firewall logs the error and discards the packet with no further processing.

7. The firewall inspects the decrypted *Registration Request* to find that the IP Source Address—the mobile node's care-of address—is an external address. If the firewall belongs to an organization that uses private addresses and whose routers drop packets containing external addresses, then the firewall tunnels the *Registration Request* to the home agent. We assume here that there is no need for the firewall to provide authentication or encryption in this tunneled packet. If, on the other hand, the organization uses public addresses, then the firewall can simply forward the *Registration Request* toward the home agent without any need for further tunneling.

8. The home agent receives the *Registration Request* and processes it according to the rules set forth in Mobile IP. Specifically, it verifies the mobile node's identity by validating the Mobile-Home Authentication Extension.

9. Assuming that the request is valid, the home agent returns a *Registration Reply* to the mobile node as always. Once again, if the organization is using private addresses, the home agent must determine whether the IP Destination Address—the mobile node's care-of address—is an external address. If so, the home agent must tunnel the packet to the firewall. One way for the home agent to make this determination is for the mobile node to include a new Firewall Traversal Extension in its *Registration Request*. Inclusion of this extension would provide the home agent with an explicit notification that the mobile node is outside the firewall.

10. When the *Registration Reply* reaches the firewall, it recognizes the IP Destination Address—the mobile node's care-of address—as an address with which it has an existing security relationship. The firewall then securely tunnels the *Registration Reply* to the mobile node in largely the same way as the mobile node tunneled the *Registration Request* to the firewall. Specifically, the tunneled message consists of an outer IP header, SKIP header, *Authentication Header, Encapsulating Security Payload* header, and the encrypted *Registration Reply*.

11. The mobile node uses the SKIP header to determine the identity of the firewall and to determine how to decrypt the packet and validate the authenticator within the *IP Authentication Header*. If the authenticator fails, the mobile node logs the error and discards the packet without further processing. Otherwise, the mobile node processes the decrypted *Registration Reply* according to the rules set forth in Mobile IP. Specifically, the mobile node

verifies the home agent's identity by validating the Mobile-Home Authentication Extension.

Once this registration process completes, the home agent begins attracting packets destined to the mobile node's home address and tunneling them to the care-of address as always. We describe how data packets flow between the mobile node and the private network in *Data Flow* on page 192. First we describe how the mobile node builds the *Registration Request* message mentioned in step 3 above.

How Does a Mobile Node Build a Tunneled Registration Request?

In step 3 of the previous section, we gave a high-level overview of how the mobile node sends a *Registration Request* to its home agent via a secure tunnel to the firewall. In this section we describe how the mobile node builds this packet before forwarding it to a default router. The ultimate result is shown in Figure 9-5, which provides reference for the entire discussion which follows.

Building the "Normal" Registration Request

The mobile node first builds a "normal" *Registration Request* message, as described in *How Does a Mobile Node Send a Registration Request?* on page 78. As always, this message contains a UDP/IP header followed by the fixed-length portion of the *Registration Request* and the Mobile-Home Authentication Extension. The "normal" *Registration Request* will ultimately be encrypted and placed within the payload of an *Encapsulating Security Payload* header. It appears shaded in the lower portion of Figure 9-5. Here we note that the IP Source Address is the mobile node's care-of address.

Building the (Outer) IP Header, the Keys, and the SKIP Header

The mobile node generates the outer (tunneling) IP header in a straightforward manner. The mobile node places the tunnel entry-point—its care-of address—in the Source Address field and the tunnel exit-point—the firewall's IP address—in the Destination Address. The IP Protocol field is set to 57, which identifies the next header as a SKIP header.

Next the mobile node generates the specific keys that it will ultimately use to authenticate and encrypt the tunneled message. For complete details on these functions, see [draft-ietf-ipsec-skip-07.txt], which describes the following key derivation process:

1. The mobile node combines its own Diffie-Hellman secret value with the firewall's public value to create a shared secret key, which we denote K_{MF} (the subscripts refer to the mobile node and the firewall, respectively).

2. The mobile node generates a random number to use as a key for protecting the current packet. We call this key K_P.

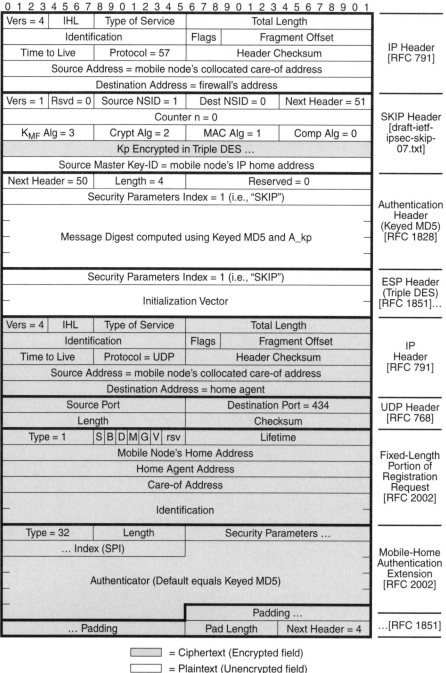

Figure 9-5 Registration Request Securely Tunneled to Firewall

3. From K_P, the mobile node generates the specific authentication key A_K_P and specific encryption key E_K_P, using various operations involving message digests as described in [draft-ietf-ipsec-skip-07.txt].

The mobile node proceeds to build the SKIP header and fills in the fields as follows (see Figure 9-5). The Source Name Space ID (Source NSID) field is set to 1 to inform the firewall that the identity of the node sending the packet is not that specified by the IP Source Address of the packet but, rather, is that specified within the Source Master Key-ID field. Since we presume that the mobile node's identity is its IP home address, the mobile node places its home address in the Source Master Key-ID field. The Destination Name Space ID (Dest NSID) field is set to 0 to inform the firewall that the IP Destination Address of the (outer) IP packet is also the identity of the firewall. The Next Header field is set to 51 to denote that an *Authentication Header* follows the SKIP header.

The Counter n field, which can be used to change the Diffie-Hellman values used to compute K_{MF}, is set to 0. The K_{MF} Alg field is set to 3, which informs the firewall how to recover K_P and ultimately how to recover A_K_P and E_K_P, the two keys used to authenticate and encrypt the packet respectively. The Crypt Alg and MAC Alg fields are set to values that indicate which actual encryption and authentication algorithm are used to protect the packet contents—in this case, Triple-DES (2) and Keyed MD5 (1), respectively. The Comp Alg field indicates which, if any, compression algorithm has been applied to the data before encryption and authentication. Finally, K_P is encrypted using the algorithm specified by the K_{MF} Alg field and placed in the named field.

To further illustrate the significance of the fields in the SKIP header, let us examine how the firewall processes the SKIP and (outer) IP header to ultimately recover the *Registration Request*:

1. The firewall uses the Source NSID and the Source Master Key-ID field to determine that this packet has been sent by a mobile node whose Diffie-Hellman public value is associated with the mobile node's IP home address—not the care-of address that appears as the Source Address of the (outer) IP packet header.

2. The firewall combines its own Diffie-Hellman secret value with the mobile node's public value to create the shared secret key, K_{MF}.

3. The firewall uses the K_{MF} Alg field to determine *how* to decrypt K_P, the latter of which is contained in the SKIP header in encrypted form. Specifically, the K_{MF} Alg field tells the firewall which secret-key encryption algorithm to use to decrypt K_P. The actual key to use in this decryption operation is K_{MF}, as computed in the previous step.

4. The firewall also uses the K_{MF} Alg field to determine the sequence of operations by which it recovers A_K_P and E_K_P from the decrypted value of K_P, the latter of which is computed in the previous step.

5. The firewall uses the Crypt Alg and MAC Alg fields, along with E_K_P and A_K_P, to decrypt and verify the packet contents as contained within the *Encapsulating Security Payload* and the *Authentication Header,* respectively.

Building the Encapsulating Security Payload and Authentication Header

Once the mobile node has built the "normal" *Registration Request*, the tunneling (outer) IP header, and the SKIP header, it proceeds to build the *Encapsulating Security Payload* and *Authentication Header*. Once this completes, the mobile node assembles all of the pieces and transmits the packet.

The *Encapsulating Security Payload* is built according to the rules in [RFC 1851]. The Security Parameters Index field is set to 1 to indicate that the encryption algorithm is specified in the SKIP header. A suitable Initialization Vector is placed in the appropriate field and the Next Header field is set to 4 to indicate that the encrypted payload is an IP packet (header plus payload). At this point, the entire payload is encrypted using Triple DES with the secret key E_K_p. The encrypted fields are shaded in Figure 9-5.

At this point the mobile node assembles all of the headers and payloads together as shown in Figure 9-5, and proceeds to fill in the fields of the *Authentication Header*. Once again, the Security Parameters Index field is set to 1 to indicate that the authentication algorithm is specified in the SKIP header. The Next Header field is set to 50 to indicate that an *Encapsulating Security Payload* header follows. Finally, a message digest is computed over the entire packet except for a few fields in the outer IP header which may change along the path between the mobile node and the firewall (e.g., the Time to Live field). The message digest is computed using MD5 with the secret key A_K_p.

Finally, this (minimally) 156-byte behemoth is forwarded by the mobile node to its default router over the foreign link. The securely tunneled packet is ultimately routed to the firewall where it verifies the authentication, decrypts the contents, and passes the "normal" *Registration Request* to the home agent.

Summary

This section described how a mobile node builds the securely tunneled *Registration Request* message and sends it to the firewall. Our purpose was to illustrate how all of the individual pieces—SKIP, *Authentication Header*, and *Encapsulating Security Payload*—fit together. In future sections we will not provide nearly this level of detail with respect to the fields within the individual packet headers. Rather, we will devise a shorthand notation to denote which headers are present and highlight the contents only of the interesting fields.

Shorthand Notation

Packet diagrams such as the one in Figure 9-5 are useful tools for understanding how all of the security protocols fit together. However, such diagrams quickly get unwieldy for describing packet contents under many different circumstances as data flows between the various entities. Therefore, we now introduce a shorthand notation for describing packet headers and the interesting fields contained within them.

The essence of the notation is to abbreviate the name of the protocol header or payload and put the interesting fields and their values within square brackets. The headers and payload are separated by vertical bars. Also, the outermost (lowest-layer) header is on the left and the upper-layer headers and data are on the right. Finally, we use italics to denote encrypted fields and underlining to denote authenticated fields. The abbreviations used are as follows:

IP	Internet Protocol
AH	Authentication Header
ESP	Encapsulating Security Payload
TCP	Transmission Control Protocol
UDP	User Datagram Protocol
HTTP	HyperText Transfer Protocol
src	IP Source Address or UDP Source Port field
dst	IP Destination Address or UDP Destination Port field
MN	mobile node's home address
COA	care-of address
HA	home agent's address
CN	correspondent node's address
FW	firewall's address
dkeyid	Destination Master Key-ID field

Some examples will help to illustrate this notation:

IP[src=A,dst=B] denotes an IP packet sent from host A to host B (one whose contents are not relevant).

IP[src=MN,dst=HA] | UDP[dst=434] | RegRqst[lifetime=0] denotes a *(de)Registration Request* sent from a mobile node to its home agent.

IP[src=HA,dst=COA] | IP[src=CN,dst=MN] | TCP denotes a packet tunneled by a home agent to a mobile node's care-of address. The inner packet, sent from a correspondent node to the mobile node's home address, carries a TCP header and presumably some application-layer data.

IP | SKIP | AH | ESP | *IP* | *UDP* | *RegRqst* denotes the securely tunneled *Registration Request* that appears in Figure 9-5. Note that the entire packet is authenticated but only the "original" *Registration Request* is encrypted.[†]

Registration Revisited Using Shorthand Notation

Using this notation, let us reexamine the *Registration Request* and *Replies* as they appear at various places in the network:

1. the securely tunneled *Registration Request* as it looks in the public network between the mobile node and the firewall—the "original" request is

---

[†] Well, yes, there is a single field within the SKIP header which is encrypted, but we ignore this inconvenient fact for simplicity.

encrypted and the entire packet is authenticated:
IP[src=COA,dst=FW] | SKIP | AH | ESP | *IP* **|** *UDP* **|** *RegRqst*.

2. the de-tunneled and the re-tunneled *Registration Request* as it looks on the private network between the firewall and the home agent—the firewall strips off the outer IP, SKIP, AH, and ESP headers but tunnels the decrypted packet to the home agent (because the inner IP Source Address is an external address which must be hidden from the routers in the private network):
IP[src=FW,dst=HA] | IP[src=COA,dst=HA] | UDP | <u>**RegRqst**</u>.

3. the *Registration Reply* as it looks on the private network between the home agent and the firewall—it must be tunneled to hide the IP Destination Address from intervening routers and to direct the message to the right firewall (in case there are many):
IP[src=HA,dst=FW] | IP[src=HA,dst=COA] | UDP | <u>**RegReply**</u>.

4. the *Registration Reply* as it looks between the firewall and the mobile node on the public portion of the Internet—the firewall securely tunnels the reply to the mobile node setting the Destination Master Key-ID field to indicate that the identity of the destination is the mobile node's home address (as opposed to its care-of address):
IP[src=FW,dst=COA] | SKIP[dkeyid=MN] | AH | ESP | *IP* **|** *UDP* **|** *RegReply*.

Data Flow

The previous section described how the mobile node registers with its home agent in the presence of secure tunneling firewalls. In this section we describe how data flows between a mobile node and a correspondent node, once the mobile node has registered. We use the shorthand notation described previously.

Figure 9-6 provides an illustration of the packet flow between a mobile node and its correspondent. We now explain the maze of tunnels shown in the figure. A mobile node sends a packet to a correspondent node as follows (see the top half of Figure 9-6):

1. The mobile node generates an IP packet containing header and data. For example, if the mobile node is accessing a Web page on the correspondent node, the packet would contain:
IP[src=MN,dst=CN] | TCP | HTTP.

2. The mobile node securely tunnels the above packet to the firewall, just as it did with its *Registration Request*: **IP[src=COA,dst=FW] | SKIP | AH | ESP |** *IP* **|** *TCP* **|** *HTTP*.

3. The firewall verifies the authenticator and decrypts the packet; strips off the outer IP header, the SKIP header, the *Authentication Header*, and the *Encapsulating Security Payload* header, revealing the packet of step number 1; and forwards it toward the correspondent node: **IP | TCP | HTTP.**

The reply packet sent from correspondent node to the mobile node is routed through the home agent as follows:

1. The correspondent node builds a packet to send to the mobile node and forwards it toward the mobile node's home link:
   IP[src=CN,dst=MN] | TCP | HTTP.
2. The home agent intercepts this packet and tunnels to the mobile node's care-of address. The home agent recognizes the care-of address as an external address and must add an additional layer of tunneling to the firewall in order to shield this address from routers in the private network:
   IP[src=HA,dst=FW] | IP[src=HA,dst=COA] | IP | TCP | HTTP.
3. The firewall consumes the outermost IP header and sees a packet destined to the mobile node's care-of address. The firewall securely tunnels the packet to the mobile node: **IP[src=FW,dst=COA] | SKIP | AH | ESP | IP[src=HA,dst=COA] | IP | TCP | HTTP**.
4. The mobile node verifies the authenticator and decrypts the packet. The mobile node then consumes the outer IP header, the SKIP header, the *Authentication Header*, and the *Encapsulating Security Payload* header, revealing the following packet:
   IP[src=HA,dst=COA] | IP[src=CN,dst=MN] | TCP | HTTP.
   This packet looks just like any other packet a mobile node with a collocated care-of address would receive via a tunnel from its home agent. The mobile

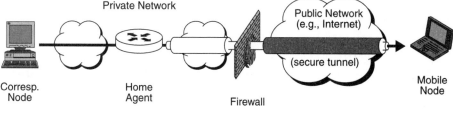

1. Data packets sent from a mobile node to a correspondent node:

Private Network

Public Network
(e.g., Internet)

(secure tunnel)

Corresp.
Node

Router

Firewall

Mobile
Node

2. Data packets sent from a correspondent node to a mobile node:

Private Network

Public Network
(e.g., Internet)

(secure tunnel)

Corresp.
Node

Home
Agent

Firewall

Mobile
Node

Legend:

Encrypted/Authenticated Tunnel
Unencrypted, Mobile IP Tunnel
Plaintext Data Packets

Figure 9-6 Data Packets Sent Between a Mobile Node and a Correspondent Node.

node de-tunnels to reveal the original packet:

IP[src=CN,dst=MN] | TCP | HTTP.

The mobile node then passes the TCP and application-layer data up the stack to the higher-layer protocol.

Analysis

In this section we analyze the SKIP firewall-traversal mechanism from the standpoint of overhead and performance. The following points characterize the SKIP-based solution:

- Despite the complexity of the previous sections, we note here that SKIP is *relatively* easy to comprehend and implement (as compared to ISAKMP/Oakley). Its simplicity makes it desirable from the standpoint of mobile nodes which might be computers with limited processing power.

- The mobile node and the firewall need not negotiate security parameters or perform key management exchanges *before* data (or registrations) may be sent. SKIP's support for so-called inline-keying is highly desirable for mobile nodes, which may change their locations relatively rapidly.

- A disadvantage of this method is the presence of the SKIP header in every securely tunneled packet between the mobile node and the firewall. This adds an extra 20-or-more bytes that technically need not be sent in every packet. SKIP could benefit from a "lightweight" header, which when present would inform the receiver that the current packet has been transformed in exactly the same way as the previous packet.

- According to some cryptographers, it is undesirable to disclose to a potential Bad Guy the identity of the encryption or authentication algorithms being used because this just simplifies his job. We note that the SKIP header contains an explicit identification of these respective algorithms.

- Additionally, we also note that the "winner" in the battle for Internet-wide key management protocols is likely to be ISAKMP/Oakley, based upon consensus within the working group of the Internet Engineering Task Force that is defining this protocol. It is therefore desirable to devise a mechanism that works with the Internet-standard key management protocol.

Summary

In this section we have shown how a mobile node can securely traverse a firewall using SKIP and the other IP security protocols. The solution involves establishing an encrypted and authenticated tunnel between the mobile node and the firewall. We assumed that the firewall required no knowledge of Mobile IP. At this point we move on to describe a similar method for traversing a firewall which implements ISAKMP/Oakley instead of SKIP for key management.

9.4.3 Firewall Traversal Using ISAKMP/Oakley

In the previous section we went into considerable detail describing how mobile nodes can securely traverse a firewall using SKIP. In this section we describe a similar mechanism using ISAKMP/Oakley for key management. As of this writing, such a mechanism is currently "work in progress" within the Mobile IP working group. In addition, there is little to be gained by going through a very detailed discussion such as that found in the previous section, simply replacing any appearance of "SKIP" with "ISAKMP/Oakley."

For both of these reasons, this section will simply outline the similarities and the differences between an ISAKMP/Oakley solution and the one we saw in the previous section. Also, we note that support for inline-keying within the ISAKMP/Oakley framework is also "work in progress," as is the protocol itself. See [draft-ietf-ipsec-inline-isakmp-01.txt] for further details.

Similarities

The following items are common between a solution using SKIP versus one using ISAKMP/Oakley:

- All of the assumptions and requirements listed in *What Are the Assumptions and Requirements for Firewall Traversal?* on page 181 are the same as before. Obviously, though, we assume that the firewall implements ISAKMP/Oakley for key management instead of SKIP.

- All of the items listed in *Administrative Considerations* on page 184 apply here as well. However, there is no need to configure the mobile node and the firewall with each other's Diffie-Hellman public values. Instead, we configure the mobile node and the firewall with each other's RSA public keys. (Equivalently, with the respective public-key certificates.)

Differences

The following items outline the differences between the two approaches:

- The mobile node and firewall use each other's public keys in conjunction with some public-key encryption algorithm to protect the fields within their ISAKMP/Oakley parameter negotiation and session-key derivation.

- The mobile node and the firewall would likely require at least one round-trip of ISAKMP/Oakley negotiation before any packets could actually traverse the firewall. We assume that this would occur when the mobile node first travels outside the firewall. This negotiation would likely create two Security Associations, one used for authentication and one used for encryption. Alternatively, a single security association that integrates both authentication and encryption could be created instead. (This option applies to the SKIP case as well.)

- The mobile node should negotiate a "wildcard" source address as part of these Security Associations which would allow the mobile node to change its care-of address without renegotiating the associations. Otherwise, the mobile node would have to renegotiate these parameters every time it changed location.

- Packets sent between the mobile node and the firewall would not contain a key management header as in the SKIP case. The packet headers would instead look as follows: **IP | AH | ESP | *IP* | *IP* | *TCP* | *DATA***. Furthermore, we note that a Bad Guy has no knowledge of which algorithms are being used for encryption and authentication, unlike in the SKIP case.

Summary

In this section we highlighted a few differences between the SKIP and ISAKMP/Oakley protocols and their impact on firewall traversal for mobile nodes. We noted that without support for inline-keying, the ISAKMP/Oakley approach might require more exchanges between the mobile node and its firewall, but subsequent securely tunneled data exchanges would contain fewer bytes of overhead. Finally, we noted that this discussion is necessarily brief because ISAKMP/Oakley, inline-keying for same, and the use of this technology by mobile nodes to securely traverse firewalls is all "work in progress" within various working groups of the Internet Engineering Task Force.

9.5 Summary/Conclusions

In this chapter we described a more complicated deployment of Mobile IP on an individual corporate campus, as compared to the simple example of the previous chapter. This more complicated deployment was characterized by placing all publicly accessible network jacks outside of the corporation's firewall.

Placing some foreign agents and links outside the firewall provided solid protection for the private network from unauthorized parties. It also allowed visitors to the campus to plug into the network and access their own networks, all without compromising the private network's security. However, this necessitated a method by which authorized mobile nodes—those owned by employees of the enterprise—could traverse the firewall without exposing the mobile nodes or the private network to additional security threats.

We described in detail a solution for firewall traversal based upon SKIP that has been implemented by engineers at SUN Microsystems. We saw how encrypted and authenticated tunnels between the mobile node and the firewall protect both the private network and the mobile node from unauthorized access. Finally, we highlighted the similarities and differences between this SKIP approach and one using ISAKMP/Oakley for key management. The latter was mentioned as "work in progress" within the Internet Engineering Task Force.

At this point we move beyond the security considerations of corporate networks and mobile nodes and begin to look at Mobile IP from the standpoint of service providers. In the next chapter we examine how a service provide might make Mobile IP functionality available to his customers. There we consider the security threats from the perspective of the service provider rather than from the standpoint of the user of the mobile node and his private network.

CHAPTER 10

Applying Mobile IP: A Service-Provider Perspective

This chapter describes an application of Mobile IP from a service provider's perspective. Here we show how a service provider might deploy Mobile IP in order to provide foreign agent and possibly home agent functionality to its customers.

We also describe two security threats commonly faced by service providers: theft-of-service and denial-of-service. Though these threats are not specific to Mobile IP, they are of great concern to commercial service providers. Therefore, we examine solutions to these threats and assess their impact, if any, on Mobile IP.

Finally, we conclude with a case study of Motorola's Integrated Digital Enhanced Network (iDEN) as an example of a commercial, wireless, data service based on Mobile IP.

10.1 What Is the Model for Commercial, Mobile IP Service?

In this section we describe a business model by which a commercial Internet Service Provider (ISP) would support Mobile IP functionality on behalf of its customers. We describe the model in terms of who owns the mobile nodes, foreign agents, and home agents, and the position of these devices with respect to the

Internet and various private networks. Finally we introduce the security threats
that will be dealt with in subsequent sections.

The reference model for this chapter is shown in Figure 10-1. Our model is
characterized by the following assumptions:

- The *Point-to-Point Protocol (PPP)* is the most common link-layer protocol by
  which individuals connect to the Internet via their service providers. Thus,
  in our model, the ISP provides dial-up access to foreign agents via PPP.

- Some mobile nodes will belong to corporate customers of the ISP that have
  a private network which is hooked to the Internet and which has Mobile IP
  functionality deployed throughout. These mobile nodes are assumed to have
  home agents on those private networks. Unless otherwise specified, the
  model in *Chapter 9, Internet-Wide Mobility: A More Complicated Application*, is assumed in which the private network is separated from the rest of
  the Internet by a secure tunneling firewall.

- Other mobile nodes will belong to individual customers of the ISP that have
  no such network. The ISP will provide home agent functionality for these
  mobile nodes.

Note that the second item implies that the home agent is not necessarily
under the control of the service provider, which will have some impact on the
security model we develop in the next few sections. However, we assume that the
foreign agents—at least those that the service provider cares about—are indeed
under the control of the service provider.

We now examine the threats that are faced by service providers and how we
might provide protection against these threats. We note that the threats
described below—theft-of-service and denial-of-service—are threats faced by any
service provider, not necessarily related to Mobile IP. In any case, we analyze the
effect Mobile IP might have on these threats and devise solutions to any new
problems that arise.

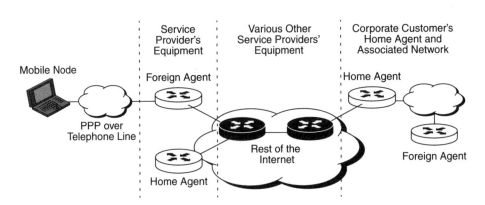

Figure 10-1 Mobile IP/PPP Reference Model

10.2 What Is Theft-Of-Service?

For the purposes of our discussion, theft-of-service occurs when a Bad Guy is able to use a communications resource without paying for it. The most wide-spread example of this occurs in the analog, cellular telephone systems of North America. In this section we examine this cellular system to understand the nature of theft-of-service attacks. Then we will see what might be done differently in order to devise a secure service based upon Mobile IP.

10.2.1 What is Cellular "Cloning" Fraud?

According to Phillip Redman, senior analyst with The Yankee Group, cellular fraud cost the industry approximately $1.1 billion in 1996 in North America [Redman97]. Most of this fraud is perpetrated through a relatively simple theft-of-service attack known as *cloning*. The cloning attack is possible because analog cellular in North America uses you-are-kidding-yourself authentication instead of cryptographically strong authentication.

The attack works as follows (see Figure 10-2). When a user of a cellphone places a call, the system requires the phone to transmit two numbers over the air (wireless link) in order to "authenticate" itself. These two numbers are its Mobile Identification Number (MIN)—a number assigned to the customer by the service provider—and its Electronic Serial Number (ESN)—a number programmed into the phone by the manufacturer.

However, these two values are sent as plaintext, making it possible for a Bad Guy with a radio scanner to eavesdrop on the transmission and discover the MIN and ESN. The Bad Guy can then program his own phone to use the discovered values of MIN and ESN during the "authentication" phase. Programming a phone in this way is referred to as cloning. Any subsequent phone calls placed by the Bad Guy with his cloned phone will be billed to the legitimate owner of the phone, as determined by the MIN.

Of course, when the bill comes to the legitimate owner of the phone, he will refuse to pay for phone calls that he did not make. The service provider then finds himself with millions of dollars worth of calls that cannot be billed to any-

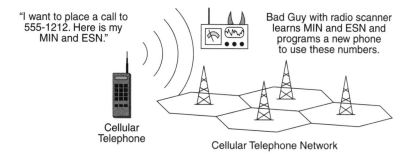

Figure 10-2 Cloning to Commit Cellular Fraud

one—i.e., to anyone who is willing to pay for them. This represents a significant financial cost that the service provider must absorb. The more likely scenario, however, is for the service provider to pass this cost along to all of its customers in the form of higher service fees.

Thus, the true cost of cellular fraud is absorbed by both the customers and the service providers to the tune of millions of dollars per year. See what happens when a system tries to get away with you-are-kidding-yourself authentication!?! It is worth noting that the cellular industry is well aware of these problems and is attempting to address them. See [Redman97] for a discussion of the solutions being proposed and implemented in an effort to combat cellular fraud.

It is also worth noting that the so-called "second-generation" cellular telephone systems, most of them digital as opposed to analog, have cryptographically strong authentication built into them in order to prevent these trivial cloning attacks. Examples of such systems include GSM in Europe, iDEN in North America, and many systems based upon CDMA technology. We discuss one such system in *Motorola's iDEN™: A Case Study* on page 213, but a complete treatment of cellular telephony is beyond the scope of this book (see [Lee95] or [GarWil95] for such a discussion).

10.2.2 How Might an Internet Service Provider Prevent Theft-of-Service with Mobile IP?

In this section we will show how an Internet Service Provider (ISP) that provides foreign agents as described in *What Is the Model for Commercial, Mobile IP Service?* on page 199 might prevent theft-of-service attacks like those that plague the cellular phone industry. In order to give this topic the thorough treatment it deserves, we must first describe how current customers of an ISP access the Internet via PPP. Then we describe two alternatives for protecting against theft-of-service attacks in the context of Mobile IP.

How Does a Person Connect to Internet via PPP But without Mobile IP?

Let us assume that our friend Dominique wishes to access the Internet from her home. To do so, she requires the following items:

*   a personal computer (PC) of some sort;
*   software running on the PC that implements TCP/IP and the *Point-to-Point Protocol (PPP)*;
*   a modem, along with the software provided with the modem, and a telephone line; and
*   an account (service agreement) with an Internet Service Provider.

With her PC and modem, Dominique uses the telephone system to dial into her Internet Service Provider as shown in Figure 10-3. Since our concern is with connectivity and routing, and not necessarily with applications, the figure shows only the lower layers of the protocol stack. Here is how the link is established between her computer and the service provider's router:

1. Her modem dials the telephone number specified by her service provider and establishes a connection with the provider's modem within a device known as a *dial-up server*. For our purposes, we will define a dial-up server to be a network device containing at least one modem, a PPP implementation, and an IP router. In practice, though, these functions are usually implemented in many separate but cooperating devices. The "V.n" in Figure 10-3 refers to the "V" series of modem standards produced by the Consultative Committee on International Telephony and Telegraphy (CCITT)—the specifics of these standards do not concern us here. Furthermore, RS-232 is a physical-layer protocol often used to connect computers to external modems.

2. Once the modem connection is made, PPP begins the link-establishment phase. Here, the PPP *Link Control Protocol (LCP)* [RFC 1661] is used by both ends to determine the link quality, negotiate the use of compression and the size of packets that can be transmitted, etc. Also in this phase, the two PPP peers negotiate which if any authentication protocol will be executed in the authentication phase.

3. Once the link is established, PPP begins the authentication phase. These days, most service providers support only the PPP *Password Authentication Protocol (PAP)* [RFC 1334]. Unfortunately, PAP is based upon plaintext username/passwords—i.e., upon you-are-kidding-yourself authentication. Some service providers are beginning to support the *Challenge Handshake Authentication Protocol (CHAP)* [RFC 1994]. We describe CHAP in more detail below, but for now we note that it provides cryptographically strong authentication.

4. Once Dominique is authenticated to her service provider, PPP begins the *Network Control Protocol (NCP)* phase in which the two ends negotiate

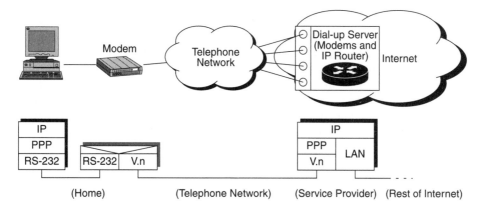

Figure 10-3 Residential Internet Access via PPP, Modem, and Telephone Line

parameters that are needed by each respective network-layer protocol that they will use to communicate. Since Dominique is connecting to the Internet, the only network-layer protocol of interest is IP. Thus, PPP enters the *Internet Protocol Control Protocol (IPCP)* [RFC 1332] phase, which negotiates parameters needed by IP. Such parameters include the use (or not) of TCP/IP Header Compression [RFC 1144], the address of Domain Name Servers [RFC 1877], and IP addresses [RFC 1332]. If Dominique's PC is not a Mobile IP mobile node, then her PC will be assigned an IP address during this phase to use while she is connected to the dial-up server.

5. Once the network-layer protocol phase is complete, Dominique's PC may begin sending IP packets over the PPP link to the Internet. These packets are generated by the protocol software in her PC at the behest of application programs (e.g., a Web browser).

With this basic understanding of PPP, we explore its preferred authentication protocol in the next section.

How Does CHAP Work?

In step 3 of the previous section, Dominique was authenticated to her service provider via PPP's *Challenge Handshake Authentication Protocol (CHAP)* [RFC 1994]. Here we explore CHAP-based authentication in more detail. CHAP authentication is based upon message digests and shared, secret keys in a similar fashion to what we saw in *Authentication and Integrity Checking via Secret Keys and Message Digests* on page 134.

When Dominique obtains an account with an Internet Service Provider, she and the provider agree on several parameters as part of the service agreement. First, they agree on a name string that will be used to identify Dominique. A commonly used name string is her E-mail address, which encodes both her login name and the service provider (e.g., "dominique@isp.net"). Also, at this time, she and the service provider agree on a shared, secret key, K_{DS} (here we use the subscripts "D" for Dominique and "S" for Service provider). Of course, this "manual" key distribution should be accomplished by some secure means so that a Bad Guy cannot discover the key. Usually the key distribution is done by an insecure telephone conversation, because, for some strange reason, people think the telephone system is secure against eavesdropping.

Once this service agreement is in place, Dominique can connect to the Internet via her service provider as described in *How Does a Person Connect to Internet via PPP But without Mobile IP?* on page 202. The authentication phase in step 3 is accomplished via CHAP, in which the message-digest algorithm cur-

rently defined is Keyed MD5. The "handshake" that comprises CHAP is illustrated in the following figure:

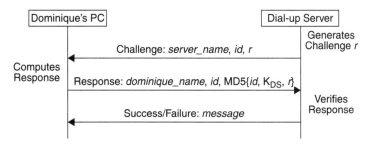

The handshake works as follows:

1. The provider's dial-up server sends a *CHAP Challenge* message to Dominique which includes an ASCII string that identifies the service provider
   (e.g., "Some Company Inc."), a random challenge r, and an *id* (used to match
   this *Challenge* with the ensuing *Response*).

2. Dominique's PC computes an MD5 message digest over the *id*, the secret
   key she shares with the service provider (K_{DS}), and the challenge r. Dominique's PC sends a *CHAP Response* to the dial-up server that includes her
   name string (e.g., "dominique@isp.net"), the *id* copied from the *Challenge* message, and the computed message digest: MD5{*id*, K_{DS}, r}.

3. The dial-up server computes its own value of the message digest and compares it with the value received in the *CHAP Response*. If they are equal,
   then the service provide knows that it is talking to Dominique; i.e,. Dominique has been authenticated. In this case, the dial-up server sends a *CHAP
   Success* message to Dominique's PC thus ending the authentication phase
   of PPP. Otherwise, the dial-up server sends a *CHAP Failure* message and
   usually terminates the PPP link (i.e., it hangs up the phone).

Thus CHAP provides cryptographically strong authentication as well as
replay prevention, because of the presence of the challenge and the *id* (identification) field. A Bad Guy that is able to eavesdrop somehow on the CHAP message
exchange does not learn any information that will be useful to him in connecting
to the service provider at a later time.

How Do Mobile IP and PPP Interact?

This section describes the nuances that come into play between Mobile IP
on the one hand and PPP's *Internet Protocol Control Protocol (IPCP)* on the other.
The material in this section is derived from [draft-ietf-pppext-ipcp-mip-01.txt].
The source of the difficulty is that IPCP, as defined in [RFC 1332], provides no
mechanism for either end of the PPP link to inform the other end that it supports
Mobile IP. While far from being a catastrophe, this does have some unfortunate
consequences, as we will see in this section.

How Does IPCP Negotiate IP Addresses?

One of the goals of IP address negotiation within IPCP is to ensure that the IP addresses being used at both ends of the link are *topologically correct*. By topologically correct we mean that the address can be reached by normal IP routing mechanisms. This generally implies that the network-prefix of the address—particularly that of a nomadic or mobile computer connecting to the Internet via PPP—is consistent with the addresses at the other end of the PPP link and throughout the Internet.

When an individual dials a service provider using PPP, his PC can propose an address to use for the duration of the connection. However, the dial-up server will disallow this address if it determines that the address is not topologically correct and, therefore, that the PC is unlikely to be able to communicate using this address. In the process of disallowing the address, the dial-up server will allocate and assign a topologically correct address for the PC to use while it is connected. The PC either accepts this address or hangs up and tries connecting to some other dial-up server.

What about Mobile Nodes and Foreign Agents?

Consider the case of a mobile node connecting via PPP to a dial-up server that is also a foreign agent. Such a mobile node should be able to propose its IP home address and have that address accepted by the foreign agent. Then, when IPCP completes, the mobile node could listen for an *Agent Advertisement* and then register via the foreign agent.

However, the dial-up server has no way of knowing whether the device at the other end of the link is a mobile node proposing its home address or a conventional node proposing some non-topologically-correct address. Thus, the dial-up server must be conservative, disallow the home address, and assign a topologically correct address to the mystery guest at the other end of the PPP link.

The mobile node can now use this topologically correct address as a collocated care-of address, but note how this defeats one of the main purposes of foreign agents. Specifically, foreign agents were designed to provide a single care-of address that can be shared by many mobile nodes simultaneously, thus placing less of a strain on the availability of IPv4 addresses. The IPCP negotiation described above results in a unique address being assigned to the mobile node, even when the dial-up server is a foreign agent and no such address is actually needed.

The Mobile-IPv4 Configuration Option for IPCP

The problem with the IPCP negotiation as described is that there is no mechanism available for the mobile node and the foreign agent to inform each other that they support Mobile IP until IPCP has already completed and a unique address has already been assigned to the mobile node. The *Mobile-IPv4 Configuration Option for PPP IPCP*, as defined in [draft-ietf-pppext-ipcp-mip-01.txt], provides such a mechanism and also provides the following benefits:

- No unique IP address is assigned to a mobile node unless it absolutely wants one or requires one. Specifically, if the mobile node is content to use a foreign agent care-of address, or if the mobile node connects to its home link, no such address is assigned. However, if the mobile node requires a collocated care-of address (e.g., for firewall traversal as described in *Firewall Traversal Using SKIP* on page 183), then the mobile node can request that such an address be assigned.

- A foreign agent can be deployed by a service provider without the need for a pool of addresses for assignment to dial-up customers. If the service provider wishes to provide only Mobile IP service, rather than conventional IP service, the service provider need not obtain a block from which to allocate addresses to dial-up customers. Instead, the service provider can rely on customers' mobile nodes having their own IP home addresses and he can further rely on Mobile IP to route packets to these topologically incorrect addresses.

Thus, the configuration option defined in [draft-ietf-pppext-ipcp-mip-01.txt] solves the problem of interaction between Mobile IP and PPP's IPCP. With this detailed understanding of Mobile IP and PPP, we now describe how a service provider can protect himself against theft-of-service attacks.

How Do We Prevent Theft-of-Service?

In this section we explore two ways in which an Internet Service Provider can prevent theft-of-service attacks within the framework of Mobile IP and PPP. Once again, we assume that the ISP provides dial-up access to foreign agents, as described in *What Is the Model for Commercial, Mobile IP Service?* on page 199.

A Link-Layer (PPP/CHAP) Solution

The first way to ensure that service is provided only to authorized mobile nodes is simply to use the same CHAP-based authentication we described in *How Does CHAP Work?* on page 204. The owner of the mobile node would need a service agreement with the service provider, and the two would have to agree on a shared, secret key. When the mobile node dialed into the service provider, it would be authenticated via CHAP. Whatever happened "above" PPP, including all of the Mobile IP agent discovery, registration, etc., would be irrelevant to the provider's main concern—getting paid for the mobile node's use of his service.

This solution is attractive in that it requires no new inventions and is a simple application of authentication technology already deployed by many Internet Service Providers. It has some drawbacks, however. First, it requires a unique service agreement between the service provider and each mobile node. For a large corporation, this might be an extremely large number. Second, like all link-layer solutions, it works only with a single data link layer; namely, PPP. This tends to limit this solution to being applicable only in dial-up situations. In contrast, we speculate that service providers and other entities might want to make foreign agents available everywhere, such as in coffee shops, airports, etc., and not just at the end of telephone lines.

A Mobile IP Solution

Another way to authenticate mobile nodes to a service provider is using the Mobile IP authentication extensions within registration messages. The Mobile-Home Authentication Extension is not sufficient, however, because the home agent might not be within the control of the service provider. In this case, a mobile node could conspire with a home agent—which could be located anywhere—to return valid *Registration Replies* to the service provider's foreign agents and ultimately to the mobile node. This accomplishes absolutely nothing from the service provider's standpoint. Here again, we assume that the service provider owns minimally the foreign agent and, therefore, we need to find a way of authenticating *something* to the foreign agent.

Fortunately, Mobile IP also defines extensions for authenticating mobile nodes to foreign agents, foreign agents to home agents, and vice versa. There are a number of methods of providing suitable authentication which we will now examine. Some of these are based on secret-key technology and some are based on public-key technology.

The secret-key solutions, not surprisingly, have scalability problems from the standpoint of key distribution. For instance, if mobile nodes are required to authenticate themselves to service providers' foreign agents, then there needs to be a unique secret key shared between each mobile node and foreign agent taken pairwise. Even if we optimize this somewhat, by limiting the number of keys to be between each mobile node and each set of foreign agents owned by a single service provider, this is still a very large number of keys. Thus, mobile-node-to-foreign-agent authentication based upon secret-key technology scales poorly.

Another type of secret-key solution is one which requires home-agent-to-foreign-agent authentication. Here we assume that there is a many-to-1 relationship between mobile nodes and home agents and, therefore, that the number of keys required is considerably less than in the previous example. In this method, a *Registration Reply* from a home agent to a foreign agent that contains a valid authenticator in the Foreign-Home Authentication Extension authorizes the service provider to bill the owner of the home agent for the resources consumed by the indicated mobile node. As before, we optimize this slightly by requiring a single unique key between the set of all home agents owned by a corporation on the one hand and all foreign agents owned by a service provider on the other hand. Still, this is a difficult key-management problem and it does not scale well.

The alternative to the secret-key solutions is public-key technology. Public-key technology can be applied in roughly the same manner as the secret-key solutions just described. For example, a service provider might be willing to provide service to a mobile node if in its *Registration Requests* it places a valid digital signature within the Authenticator field of the Mobile-Foreign Authentication Extension. Alternatively, a *Registration Reply* from a home agent to a foreign agent that contains a valid digital signature in the Foreign-Home Authentication Extension authorizes the service provider to bill the owner of the home agent for the resources consumed by the indicated mobile node. This second approach transfers the computing-intensive calculations involved in public-key algorithms from the mobile nodes to the foreign agents and home agents.

What about Session Stealing?

For completeness, we note that authenticating a mobile node as a precondition of providing service is a good idea but often is not sufficient. There is a vulnerability that happens whenever a mobile node connects to a foreign link that is built from a shared medium such as Ethernet, as opposed to a point-to-point medium typical of telephone lines. In the shared case, a Bad Guy that is also connected to the foreign link can wait for a legitimate mobile node to register and then "steal" or "take over" the mobile node's session. It does this by programming its network interface to use the mobile node's home address as the IP Source Address of its packets and by listening to all packets on the link, not just those destined to the Bad Guy's address.

This session-stealing or takeover attack is a serious problem in many parts of the Internet and suggests that authenticating a node at the beginning of a session is not enough. The designers of PPP's *Challenge Handshake Authentication Protocol (CHAP)* realized this and [RFC 1994] specifically requires implementations to respond to a *CHAP Challenge* at any time while the PPP link is established. Similarly, foreign agents in Mobile IP can force mobile nodes to authenticate themselves frequently by advertising a small Registration Lifetime in their *Agent Advertisements* which in turn causes mobile nodes to send frequent *Registration Requests*.

While frequent re-authentications are helpful, they still leave the mobile node vulnerable to a session-stealing attack between authentication intervals The real solution, of course, it to require authentication and possibly encryption on all data that passes between a mobile node and the trusted portion of its home network, of which its home agent and home link might be only a small portion. Such a solution was described in detail in *Mobile Nodes as a Special Case of VPNs* on page 179.

10.3 Denial-of-Service Revisited

In *How Does Mobile IP Prevent This Denial-of-Service Attack?* on page 161 we described how strong authentication in the Mobile IP registration messages provides protection against a trivial type of denial-of-service attack. Specifically, strong authentication prevents a Bad Guy from registering some bogus care-of address with a mobile node's home agent in an effort to cut off the packet flow to the mobile node.

Another type of denial-of-service attack has become common in recent days on the Internet and is known as "TCP SYN Flooding and IP Spoofing Attacks" as described in [CA9621]. These attacks are waged by jerks with nothing better to do than prevent useful data from being exchanged between a TCP-based application server and its clients. In this section we describe the nature of these attacks, what service providers are being advised to do in order to minimize the effectiveness of such attacks, and the negative consequences of this response on Mobile IP. Then we describe a solution to this problem being developed by the Mobile IP working group within the Internet Engineering Task Force.

10.3.1 How Does the Flooding Attack Work?

The TCP SYN Flooding attack can be waged against any network computer that provides application services via TCP. The attack involves bombarding the server with TCP connection setup requests. The server, which must process these connection requests and must allocate a certain amount of memory for the connection attempts, can be quickly overwhelmed by these requests. Some server machines actually crash in the presence of this attack. Others are just rendered useless because all of their available connections are being occupied by these bogus connection requests.

To make matters worse, the bombardment mentioned above is usually done with IP packets in which the Source Address is "spoofed"; i.e., the sender sets the IP Source Address field to either a nonexistent address or to some address that is legitimately owned by some other party. What makes spoofing possible is the fact that IP unicast packet routing does not necessarily depend upon the Source Address field. Rather, unicast packet routing depends only on the Destination Address. This allows the attacker to spoof the Source Address while still being able to bombard the server with connection requests.

10.3.2 What Are Service Providers Doing about This Attack?

As [CA9621] describes, there is no good solution to this problem, but there are ways it can be mitigated. The fundamental problem is that it can be difficult or impossible to track down a perpetrator who uses spoofed addresses. Thus, [CA9621] recommends that service providers begin filtering IP packets in their routers to make sure that the IP Source Address of a packet is legitimate before it is forwarded. Here we describe what this means and how it is done.

Recall that dynamic routing protocols provide a mechanism by which routers can learn the destinations in a network and the routes to those destinations. If a packet with a certain Source Address enters a router through an interface that the router would not normally use to forward packets destined to that address, then the router discards the packet, suspecting that the Source Address of the packet has been spoofed.

Note that while such filtering, referred to as *ingress filtering*, can mitigate these attacks, it cannot solve them altogether. This is because the flooding attack can still be waged from spoofed IP addresses, so long as those IP addresses appear to emanate from the appropriate point in the network. The value in performing ingress filtering is that it allows the source of the attack to be traced more accurately than without it. If all ISPs were performing such filters, then it would be possible to isolate the source of a flooding attack to the network in which it originated.

10.3.3 How Does Ingress Filtering Affect Mobile IP?

An ingress filtering router, one that drops packets that appear to have arrived from the "wrong" place, invalidates the Mobile IP assumption that an IP unicast packet is routed without regard to its Source Address. Such a router, by definition, will drop all packets sent by a mobile node when the mobile node is connected to a foreign link, assuming that the IP Source Address in the packet is the mobile node's home address. This is because the mobile node's IP home address is, by definition, "supposed" to be connected to its home link.

Thus, ingress filtering severely impacts Mobile IP for packets generated by mobile nodes on foreign links. Note, however, that packets sent to mobile nodes are not affected by ingress filtering. This is because the tunneling (outer) IP header contains a topologically correct Source Address and Destination Address, namely the home agent's IP address and the care-of address, respectively.

10.3.4 What Does Mobile IP Do about Ingress Filtering?

In order to deal with the presence of ingress-filtering routers, a mobile node connected to a foreign link can tunnel packets to its home agent using a topologically correct reverse tunnel. This procedure, described in [draft-ietf-mobileip-tunnel-reverse-02.txt], provides a method for the mobile node to request such a tunnel from its foreign agent and its home agent when it registers. We now describe the components of this procedure in detail.

Extensions to Agent Discovery

Foreign agents indicate their support for reverse tunneling by setting the T bit within the Mobility Agent Advertisement Extension of their periodically transmitted *Agent Advertisements*. The T bit is allocated from the leftmost reserved bit of the extension shown in Figure 5-2 on page 66. A mobile node that desires a reverse tunnel can shop around for foreign agents that have this bit set in their *Agent Advertisements*.

Extensions to Registration

A mobile node that desires a reverse tunnel to its home agent sets the newly defined T bit within the fixed-length portion of its Registration Request. This T bit is allocated from the leftmost reserved bit of the *Registration Request* shown in Figure 5-4 on page 75. The registration is processed by the foreign agent (if applicable) and the home agent as normal. If either is incapable of supporting a reverse tunnel, they can reject the registration with a Code indicating this fact.

Alternatively, if the foreign agent or home agent requires a reverse tunnel and the mobile node has not requested one, then the foreign agent or home agent can likewise reject the request with a suitable error Code. An foreign agent might insist on a reverse tunnel in situations where the service provider which makes that foreign agent available is himself performing ingress filtering.

In addition to the T bit, a new Type-Length-Data encoded extension is defined in [draft-ietf-mobileip-tunnel-reverse-02.txt] for mobile nodes using a foreign agent care-of address, to specify how mobile nodes wish to deliver packets over the foreign link to the foreign agent. One method involves sending them directly and the other involves tunneling. We will defer a description of the specific mechanisms to the next section.

Routing in the Presence of Reverse Tunnels

When a reverse tunnel is requested and established via the Mobile IP registration procedure, packets sent by mobile nodes are routed differently than before. A mobile node with a collocated care-of address simply tunnels its packets to its home agent, using the care-of address as the Source Address of the outer packet and the home agent's address as the Destination Address.

A mobile node with a foreign agent care-of address, on the other hand, has two options for how it sends packets while connected to a foreign link. The first method involves sending the packets exactly as before, using the foreign agent as the default router. The foreign agent examines the IP Source Address and notices the packet came from a mobile node that requested reverse tunneling service. In such a case, the foreign agent tunnels the packet to the mobile node's home agent, the address of which the foreign agent learned during registration. While this method is easy to implement on the mobile node, it does not allow the mobile node the ability to prevent certain classes of packets from being tunneled to its home agent, assuming that such a feature is actually useful.

To get around this lack of flexibility, a mobile node with a foreign agent care-of address has an alternative way of sending packets on the foreign link. In the so-called "tunneling style of delivery," a mobile node tunnels packets to the foreign agent that the foreign agent is supposed to de-tunnel and then re-tunnel to the home agent. Alternatively, a mobile node designates packets that must not be reverse tunneled by sending them directly to the foreign agent without any encapsulation.

Finally, there has been some recent discussion suggesting that a Bad Guy might be able to "hijack" a reverse tunnel by sending a bogus *Registration Request* (and *Reply*) to a mobile node's foreign agent that tricks the foreign agent into tunneling to a bogus home agent address. The Mobile IP working group is in the process of analyzing this problem and devising appropriate solutions.

Summary

Thus, reverse tunneling can solve the problem introduced to Mobile IP by ingress filtering. A reverse tunnel is requested by a mobile node when it registers and results in traffic generated by the mobile node being tunneled, either by a foreign agent or the mobile node itself, to the mobile node's home agent. The tunneling (outer) headers of such packets have IP Source and Destination Addresses that are topologically correct, preventing these packets from being discarded by ingress-filtering routers.

10.4 Motorola's iDEN™: A Case Study

We conclude this chapter with a description of Mobile IP as the basis of a high-performance, commercial, wireless data service to be offered on Motorola's Integrated Digital Enhanced Network (iDEN). iDEN is a shared communication system that operates in the 800-MHz, 900-MHz, and 1.5-GHz frequency bands in various parts of the world. Figure 10-4 shows iDEN activity throughout the world. The remainder of this section provides a brief introduction to iDEN and then describes how Mobile IP provides part of the mobility solution for iDEN's packet data service.

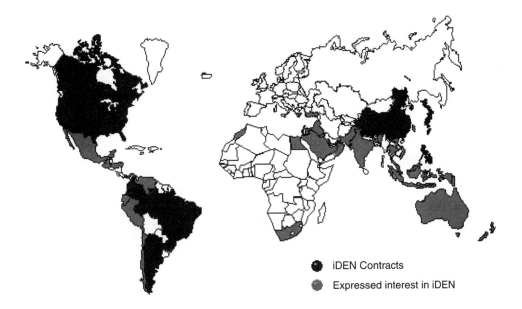

● iDEN Contracts

● Expressed interest in iDEN

Figure 10-4 Worldwide iDEN Activity

10.4.1 What Services Does iDEN Provide?

A user of the iDEN system, assuming that he has purchased service from an iDEN service provider, has access to all of the following services from his iDEN radio unit:

- Telephone Interconnect, which provides digital, high-fidelity, cellularlike telephone calls;

- Digital Dispatch, also known as "fleet" communications, which provides very fast setup, one-to-many, group-oriented communications (such as those used by taxi companies, utilities, construction firms, etc.);

- Messaging Service, which provides two-way, alphanumeric messaging similar to that available in advanced paging systems;

- Circuit-Switched Data and FAX Service, which provides modemlike communications on behalf of an attached computer or FAX machine; and

- Packet Data, a future offering, which will provide connectionless, Mobile IP-based data service to mobile nodes.

The circuit-switched data service is similar to circuit-switched cellular data, in that a user places the equivalent of a phone call and has sole access to the data channel for the duration of the call. Recall that the billing models for such services tend to be based upon the duration of connection rather than the amount of data transferred.

In contrast to circuit-switched data, iDEN packet data is characterized by a data channel that is shared by multiple, simultaneous users whose radios compete for access to the channel when they have a frame to transmit, much like nodes on an Ethernet. Because a user consumes very little of the system's resources when he is not actively transmitting or receiving data, the billing models for packet-oriented data services tend to be based upon the amount of data transferred.

10.4.2 What Is iDEN Packet Data?

The architecture of the iDEN system as it pertains to packet data is shown in Figure 10-5. Geographically, an iDEN Metro-Area Network corresponds roughly with a reasonably large metropolitan area or city. A Metro-Area Network contains numerous Enhanced Base Transceiver Sites, each consisting of one or more packet data channels. The base sites are connected to a bank of foreign agents, the latter of which are interconnected through a wide-area IP routing network.

Customers connect their private networks to the iDEN packet data system the same way they connect to the Internet—namely, through a suitable wide-area network link such as Frame Relay, Asynchronous Transfer Mode, private T1 lines, etc., which terminates at one of the routers in the IP network. From the standpoint of Mobile IP, the iDEN architecture allows customers with existing networks to use their own home agents if they so desire. The architecture also allows service providers to own and operate home agents on behalf of those customers that have no such network or who choose not to operate home agents.

10.4.3 How Does iDEN Packet Data Work?

The iDEN packet data service consists of the components introduced in the previous section. Here we provide more detail on how they work together to realize Mobile IP service to the end-user's mobile node.

The iDEN Airlink

The iDEN airlink uses an adaptive modulation technique to maximize the throughput of the channel. As is common in radio systems, each data channel consists of a pair of frequencies: one for *inbound* transmissions from radio units to the base site and one for *outbound* transmission from the base site to the radio units. Access to the shared data channels is arbitrated through the use of a technique known as *Queued Contiguous Reservation Aloha (QCRA)* [NeCr95], which works roughly as follows:

- when a user has a packet to transmit, his radio unit sends a very short reservation request message to the base site on the inbound frequency—likewise for other users who might have packets of their own to transmit;

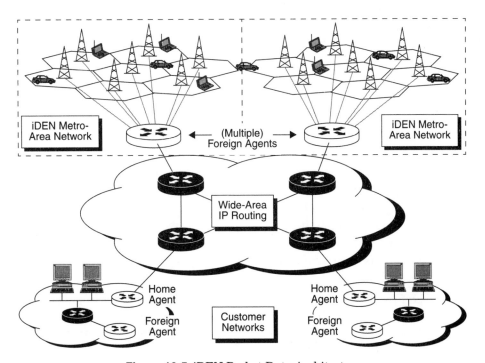

Figure 10-5 iDEN Packet Data Architecture

- equipment at the base site, using a fair scheduling policy, determines which radio unit is allowed to transmit next on the inbound frequency, and transmits the link-layer address of that radio over the outbound frequency where it can be received by all units;

- the requesting radio unit notices that it has been granted access to the inbound frequency, transmits its packet, and then the process repeats.

In the opposite direction, since the base equipment is the only thing that transmits on the outbound frequency, the base equipment is completely in charge of scheduling outbound transmissions. Reliability of data in both directions is guaranteed through the use of error-correction techniques and many of the mechanisms used by higher-layer protocols, such as those described in *How Does TCP work?* on page 274.

The iDEN system has link-layer authentication and encryption mechanisms. The former is a cryptographically strong authentication mechanism that protects the service providers and their customers against the cloning attacks we described in *What Is Theft-Of-Service?* on page 201. Link-layer encryption can protect against trivial theft-of-information and session-stealing attacks but, as always, those who are serious about protecting their data should use strong, end-to-end encryption.

The iDEN airlink is designed to provide reliable transmission of IP packets between radio units and the base-site equipment. Link-layer handoff mechanisms, involving protocols below and invisible to IP, allow radio units to move from one cell to another cell within the same iDEN Metro-Area Network. These mechanisms make the entire collection of media and link-layer switching devices appear to be a single link from the standpoint of the *Internet Protocol (IP)*. Thus, a mobile node and an iDEN foreign agent are exactly one network-layer "hop" away from each other, as required by Mobile IP.

Radio Devices

A mobile node gains access to the iDEN packet data service through an iDEN radio device. The radio performs the following functions:

- exchanges IP packets with the mobile node over a PPP or SLIP interface;

- implements the iDEN physical and link-layer protocols in order to relay IP packets between the mobile node and the base equipment; and

- continuously monitors the signal quality of the current and neighboring cells and performs a handoff when the signal quality of a neighboring cell exceeds that of the current cell.

At least two categories of configurations are envisioned for these radio devices. The first is a PC card (similar in form to a network interface or modem card) which plugs into the PC slots of a notebook or other type of computer. This would be intended for users who require very small devices and only require data services. The second type is a fully functional, multiservice radio telephone which connects to a notebook or other type of computer through a serial interface (like those used to connect computers to external modems). This latter configuration allows users to access all of iDEN's voice and data services from a single integrated handset.

Mobile IP

At a higher layer, Mobile IP allows mobile nodes to move between the various iDEN Metro-Area Networks. Mobile nodes that move from one Metro-Area Network to another will discover and register with a new foreign agent at the new location. Thus, a combination of Mobile IP and link-layer handoff mechanisms allows a mobile node and its attached iDEN radio unit to move anywhere in the world where iDEN packet data service is available. By adopting Mobile IP in this way, iDEN packet data can provide a tremendous range of mobility to a mobile worker that also has the advantage of integrating with the mobility infrastructure in place on his private network.

Specifically, a corporate user of iDEN packet data could:

- connect his mobile node to his home link while at his desk;
- move to a conference room where he registers with a foreign agent on his private network;
- take a train to visit a client, using an iDEN foreign agent while in transit;
- and return home and plug back into his home link

—all without ever needing to restart any of his applications, change the configuration of his machine in any way, or disrupt any ongoing communications.

In other words, iDEN packet data can be part of a worldwide mobility solution that provides mobile nodes with wireless access to foreign agents in those locations where a wired network connection is unavailable. With all due respect to the claims made in [TaWaBa97], *this* is the ultimate in anywhere, anytime communications capability—no other technology even comes close!

10.5 Chapter Summary

In this chapter we described a business model for Mobile IP by which Internet Service Providers could make foreign agent and possibly home agent functionality available to their customers. The model we developed was based upon dial-up PPP connections, which is currently the most common link by which individuals connect to the Internet via their ISP.

With this model in place, we examined two security threats which concern most service providers. The first is theft-of-service in which the lack of strong authentication can allow a Bad Guy to get service without paying for it. We proposed two mechanisms for this authentication, one within PPP and one within the framework of Mobile IP's authentication extensions.

Next we examined the TCP SYN Flooding attacks currently being waged on the Internet and saw how such attacks can be mitigated, but not eliminated, by ingress filtering. We also saw how ingress filtering invalidates one of Mobile IP's central assumptions and how such filtering can severely impede a mobile node's ability to send packets when connected to a foreign link. Then we showed how reverse tunneling solves this problem by creating a topologically correct reverse tunnel from the care-of address to the home agent.

We concluded this chapter with a case study of Mobile IP as the basis for commercial, wireless data service on Motorola's Integrated Digital Enhanced Network (iDEN). iDEN packet data uses Mobile IP to allow mobile nodes to move between metropolitan-area networks while using link-layer handoff techniques to allow the mobile nodes to move from cell to cell within a single Metro-Area Network. Such a service provides a level of mobility unmatched by existing technologies.

CHAPTER 11

Other Applications for Mobile IP

This chapter discusses some additional applications and capabilities of Mobile IP. First, we describe how Mobile IP can provide routing of network-layer protocols other than IP to mobile nodes that connect to their network over an infrastructure that routes only IP packets. Then we look at how Mobile IP can support mobile networks—entire collections of hosts and routers which are mobile, as a unit, with respect to the rest of the Internet.

Finally we look at an application of Mobile IP that is hidden to the ultimate user of the network but nonetheless provides a useful service to those users—namely, secure and efficient remote dial-up. This architecture, embodied in the *Virtual Tunneling Protocol*, is then compared to the *Layer 2 Tunneling Protocol* which is currently working its way through the Internet standards process.

11.1 Support for Other Protocols within the Mobile IP Framework

In this section we examine the ability of Mobile IP to provide routing for protocols other than the *Internet Protocol (IP)*. Using the mechanisms defined in this section, a mobile node which supports protocol suites other than TCP/IP will be able to continue communicating via those protocols while away from its home link.

As in *Firewall Traversal Using SKIP* on page 183, the protocols described here are not science fiction. Bob Geiger and I[†] have implemented the mechanisms described in this section for the AppleTalk [SiAnOp90] suite of protocols on a MacIntosh PowerBook. Owing to our experience gained by this implementation, AppleTalk will be used as an example throughout this section.

11.1.1 Why Support Other Protocols?

While the Internet and the TCP/IP protocols get all of the headlines, there are still an enormous number of organizations that run *other* protocol suites throughout their networks. Some examples of these suites include Novell Netware, AppleTalk, ISO, SNA, and DECNET.

Mobile workers frequently require access to data that can be remotely accessed using applications that run only over these other protocols. For example, a user's files that are stored on an AppleShare file server—one that does not also support TCP/IP access via the *Network File System (NFS)* [RFC 1813] or the *File Transfer Protocol (FTP)* [RFC 959]—currently can be accessed only by the AppleTalk suite of protocols.

Therefore, in many situations it is just as important to route network-layer packets of other protocol suites to mobile nodes that are away from their home link as it is to route IP packets to these mobile nodes. In the next few sections we describe how an extension to Mobile IP can provide this packet-routing service for protocols other than IP.

11.1.2 What Do We Mean by *Other Protocols*?

In this section we use the term *other protocol* to refer to any network-layer protocol other than IP. Similarly, *other protocol suite* refers to any protocol suite other than the TCP/IP Suite of Protocols.

Without going into detail, we note that most of these other protocol suites are layered similarly to the TCP/IP suite. Specifically, these other protocol suites typically contain a network-layer protocol which, like IP, provides end-to-end packet delivery between the original source and the ultimate destination. These network-layer protocols also define addresses which provide logical addressing of the nodes in the network. Furthermore, these logical addresses are typically comprised of a network-prefix portion and a host portion, just like IP addresses.

A node that forwards packets of some other protocol is said to be a router of that other protocol. Many commercial routers are so-called *multiprotocol routers,* meaning that they are capable of forwarding network-layer packets of many protocol suites simultaneously. A node that sends and receives packets of some other protocol, but does not forward them, is said to be a host supporting that other protocol.

[†] Bob did all of the cool, difficult, and interesting parts of the implementation.

11.1.3 Requirements and Assumptions

Throughout the remainder of this section we assume that:

- a mobile node supports at least one protocol other than IP; and
- the mobile node's home agent is a multiprotocol router that is capable of routing packets of this "other protocol" or protocols.

Our solution must allow the mobile node to communicate using this other protocol regardless of its current location. We also require that such communication not force all organizations to have unique addresses assigned to their nodes that implement these other protocols.

The next section describes the Integrated Mobility Extension, which provides a method for mobile nodes to communicate their support for other protocols to their home agents. Then, in subsequent sections we describe how this extension is used and how packets of other protocols are actually routed to mobile nodes when they are connected to a foreign link.

11.1.4 The Integrated Mobility Extension

Tony Li, then of Cisco Systems and former co-chair of the Mobile IP working group, along with Yakov Rekhter of Cisco Systems, submitted an Internet-Draft called the Integrated Mobility Extension [draft-ietf-mobileip-integrated-00.txt], which broadly describes a mechanism for supporting other protocols within the Mobile IP framework. The word *integrated* here refers to simultaneous support for many protocols.

Figure 11-1 illustrates the general form of the Integrated Mobility Extension. A mobile node uses this extension to indicate its support for other protocol suites to its home agent. The processing of the extension is described in *Registration with Other Protocols* on page 222. The fields of the extension are as follows. As always, the Type and Length fields indicate the identity and the size of the extension respectively. The Protocol Suite field indicates *to which* network-layer protocol the Protocol Address field belongs (e.g., AppleTalk versus Netware, etc.). The values for the Protocol Suite field are defined in *Generic Routing Encapsulation (GRE)* [RFC 1701], which ultimately derives from the Type field within Ethernet, as listed in [RFC 1700].

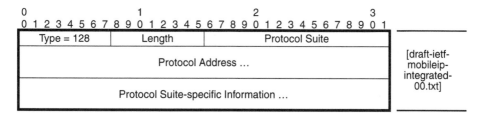

Figure 11-1 Integrated Mobility Extension: Generic Form

The rest of the fields are specific to the individual protocol suite. In most cases, a Protocol Address field is present in which a mobile node places its network-layer address for the corresponding protocol suite. A mobile node can set the Protocol Address field to zero to ask its home agent to assign a suitable address. Other fields might be present within the Integrated Mobility Extension, depending upon the particular Protocol Suite.

For example, Figure 11-2 illustrates the Integrated Mobility Extension for the specific case of AppleTalk. In this case the Protocol Suite field contains 809B (hex), which indicates that this extension is providing information for AppleTalk. The mobile node places its AppleTalk *Datagram Delivery Protocol (DDP)* address in the Protocol Address field or sets it to zero to request that an address be assigned. Our implementation also found it useful for the home agent to return *its* Apple-Talk address to the mobile node, since the mobile node will use this address as its AppleTalk default router. This value is placed in the last field shown in Figure 11-2.

11.1.5 Registration with Other Protocols

This section describes the use of the Integrated Mobility Extension within the Mobile IP registration procedure. The mobile node includes within its *Registration Requests* one Integrated Mobility Extension for each other protocol it supports. In each such extension it places its network-layer address for the corresponding protocol suite. When the home agent receives the *Registration Request*, it parses the extensions to see if it can route packets of the named protocol suite to the mobile node.

For each protocol suite for which the home agent *is* able to provide packet-delivery, it copies the corresponding Integrated Mobility Extension into the *Registration Reply* that it sends back to the mobile node. The home agent fills in the appropriate fields in these extensions before sending the reply. For example, the home agent assigns network-layer addresses for those extensions in which the mobile node specified an address of zero.

For each protocol suite for which the home agent *is not* able to provide packet-delivery, it does not copy the corresponding extension into the reply. Upon receiving the reply, the mobile node inspects the extensions to determine which packets of the requested protocol suites, if any, will be routed by the home agent.

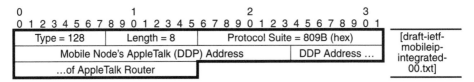

Figure 11-2 Integrated Mobility Extension for AppleTalk (DDP)

For example, consider our mobile node implementation on a MacIntosh PowerBook that supports both the TCP/IP and AppleTalk protocol suites. The mobile node includes exactly one Integrated Mobility Extension in which it places its AppleTalk (DDP) address. If the mobile node has no such address, then it sets the corresponding field to zero, asking the home agent to assign it a DDP address. If the home agent that receives a *Registration Request* containing such an extension is also an AppleTalk router, then it provides its own AppleTalk address in the corresponding field before sending a reply to the mobile node.

11.1.6 Routing Packets of Other Protocols to Mobile Nodes

This section describes how packets of other protocol suites are routed to mobile nodes that are connected to a foreign link. Here we assume that a mobile node has registered an address of some other protocol with its home agent using the mechanism described in *Registration with Other Protocols* on page 222.

The basic mechanism by which packets of other protocol suites are routed to mobile nodes is, not surprisingly, tunneling. The requirements for the home agent are largely the same as before. Namely, the home agent must be capable of intercepting packets that are destined to the mobile node's other-protocol-address and tunneling them to the mobile node.

Figure 11-3 shows packets of some other protocol suite, specifically Apple-Talk, being tunneled to and from a mobile on a foreign link. The exact form of the tunnel depends upon whether the mobile node is using a foreign agent care-of address or a collocated care-of address. Note that *all* care-of addresses are IP addresses, as opposed to addresses of this other protocol suite. We now describe the two cases.

Foreign Agent Care-of Address

If the mobile node is using a foreign agent care-of address, then the home agent tunnels the packet as follows (see the first panel of Figure 11-3):

- a GRE header is prepended to the original packet;
- the resulting packet is encapsulated (tunneled) within a first (inner) IP packet whose Source Address is the home agent and whose Destination Address is the mobile node's (IP) home address;
- the resulting packet is encapsulated (tunneled) within a second (outer) IP packet whose Source Address is the home agent and the Destination Address is the mobile node's (IP) care-of address.

The purpose of the nested encapsulation is similar to that we discussed in *Receiving Broadcasts with a Foreign Agent Care-of Address* on page 103. Specifically, it prevents foreign agents from having to implement any protocols other than IP. That is, the only place where the other-protocol packet is seen is at the mobile node and the home agent. The foreign agent, upon decapsulating the outer IP packet, sees merely an inner IP packet destined to the mobile node's home address—just as with any other IP packet tunneled by the home agent.

In the reverse direction, packets of other protocols generated by the mobile node are tunneled to the home agent. Minimally, this involves the mobile node:

- prepending a GRE header to the original packet; and

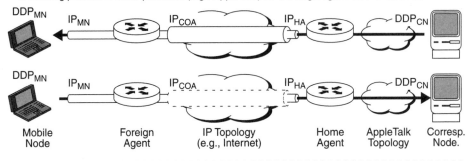

1. Routing packets of other protocols (e.g., AppleTalk) for a foreign agent care-of address:

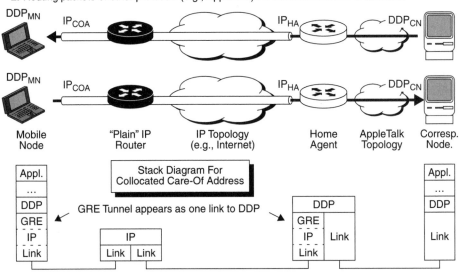

2. Routing packets of other protocols (e.g., AppleTalk) for a collocated care-of address:

Legend:	
▬▬▬▬ AppleTalk Packet	IP_{MN} = Mobile Node's IP Home Address
⬭ IP / GRE Tunnel	IP_{COA} = Mobile Node's IP Care-of Address
⬭ Optional Reverse Tunnel	IP_{HA} = Home Agent's IP Address
DDP_{MN}, DDP_{CN} = Mobile Node's, Correspondent Node's AppleTalk Addresses	
DDP = Datagram Delivery Protocol (AppleTalk Network-Layer Protocol)	

Figure 11-3 Other Protocol (e.g., AppleTalk) Routing for Mobile Nodes

- encapsulating the resulting packet within an IP packet whose Source Address is the mobile node's home address and Destination Address is the IP address of the home agent.

Note that if the mobile node is concerned about its packets being dropped due to ingress filtering (see *What Does Mobile IP Do about Ingress Filtering?* on page 211), then the mobile node should request a reverse tunnel from its foreign agent. In this case, the composite packet which leaves the foreign agent will contain an additional IP header whose Source Address is the foreign agent's address and Destination Address is the home agent's IP address. Such packets, because of their topologically correct source and destination addresses, will not be discarded by ingress-filtering routers.

Collocated Care-of Address

On the other hand, if the mobile node is using a collocated care-of address, then the home agent tunnels the original packet within a single IP packet as follows:

- a GRE header is prepended to the original packet; and
- the resulting packet is encapsulated (tunneled) within a single IP packet whose Source Address is the home agent's IP address and Destination Address is the mobile node's (IP) care-of address.

Here the original packet requires only one level of encapsulation because the mobile node itself is the exit-point of the tunnel. Similarly, in the reverse direction, the mobile node simply encapsulates packets of other protocols within a single IP packet whose Source Address is the care-of address and Destination Address is the home agent's IP address.

Note that this encapsulating packet, because of the topological correctness of both the Source and Destination Addresses, will not be discarded by packet filtering routers. This, along with the fact that only a single level of encapsulation is required, makes collocated care-of addresses preferable to foreign agent care-of addresses for those mobile nodes that require support for protocols other than IP.

11.1.7 Why Use GRE?

In the previous sections we noted that packets of other protocols are encapsulated within GRE before being encapsulated within IP. In this section we examine why GRE was selected for this purpose. Then we examine how this decision interacts with the G bit in the *Registration Request* message which requests GRE encapsulation rather than *IP in IP Encapsulation* for *IP* packets. (See *Registration Message Formats* on page 75 for an explanation of the fields within the *Registration Request* message.)

As described in *What Is Generic Routing Encapsulation (GRE)?* on page 121, GRE is specifically designed for encapsulating packets of different protocol suites within each other. Thus, it is a natural choice for multiprotocol support in Mobile IP. In addition, GRE has an explicit mechanism to guard against recursive encapsulation, as we saw in *Preventing Recursive Encapsulation* on page 122.

As for interaction between the Integrated Mobility Extension and the G bit in a *Registration Request* message, the rules for encapsulating packets by the home agent are as follows:

- Packets of *other* protocols are *always* encapsulated within GRE/IP. If the resulting IP packet must be further tunneled to a foreign agent care-of address, then that further encapsulation may use GRE only if the G bit is set by the mobile node in its *Registration Request*. Otherwise, *IP in IP Encapsulation* must be used.

- *IP packets* destined to the mobile node's home address are treated as before. If the mobile node set the G bit in its *Registration Request*, then the home agent may use GRE to tunnel such packets to the mobile node's care-of address; otherwise, *IP in IP Encapsulation* must be used.

11.1.8 Why Use Tunneling?

There are two main reasons that tunneling is used to deliver packets of other protocols to mobile nodes in the manner described above:

1. We assume that the Internet is now or soon will be available everywhere and that it only provides IP routing. While there might be "islands" of topology within the Internet which route packets of other protocols (e.g., Apple-Talk), such routing is not available everywhere that IP routing is available. Thus, IP tunneling allows packets of the other protocols to be delivered to a mobile node wherever IP routing is available.

2. The second reason is that many protocols have no global address authority which delegates specific addresses for use by various organizations and individuals. In such a case, there is no way to guarantee that one organization is not using the same exact network-layer addresses (e.g., AppleTalk DDP addresses) as some other organization. The IP tunnel allows mobile nodes of two such organizations to communicate via the other protocol with nodes on their private networks, respectively, even though the IP infrastructure (e.g., the Internet) is shared by them. Obviously, however, this mechanism does not allow interorganization communication using these other protocols unless their other-protocol-addresses are unique.

11.1.9 Summary

In this section we described how tunneling can be used to deliver packets of protocol suites other than TCP/IP to mobile nodes that are away from their home link. Mobile nodes indicate their support for such protocols by including the Integrated Mobility Extension within their *Registration Requests*. In this extension, the mobile node places its address for the specified protocol suite.

The home agent, if it is a multiprotocol router that supports the other protocol, returns the Integrated Mobility Extension to the mobile node as an indication of such support. The home agent intercepts packets sent to the mobile node's other-protocol-address and tunnels them to the mobile node.

A GRE tunnel is used to encapsulate these other protocols within IP. The exact form of the tunnel depends upon whether the mobile node has a collocated care-of address or a foreign agent care-of address. We saw how tunneling allows connectivity for mobile nodes anywhere it can gain IP routing services and how tunneling also allows different organizations to communicate with their own respective private networks even if their addresses are not unique.

11.2 Mobile *Networks* (as Opposed to Mobile *Hosts*)

By now you might be wondering why we use the term mobile *node* if the whole point behind Mobile IP is to allow mobile *hosts* (i.e., notebook computers) to communicate regardless of their current location. As you might have guessed, Mobile IP can provide connectivity not only for single mobile hosts but also for entire *mobile networks*. A mobile network is a network whose hosts and routers are usually static (i.e., nonmobile) with respect to each other, but are collectively—as a unit—mobile with respect to the rest of the (fixed) Internet. A mobile network might be found in an airplane, a ship, or a train.

Figure 11-4 shows an example of a mobile network where a mobile node—specifically, a mobile router—maintains connectivity for all the nodes on the SHANK (SHip Area NetworK). The nodes within the ship itself are fixed with respect to each other, but the whole network moves with respect to the fixed portion of the Internet. As suggested by the figure, the mobile router communicates

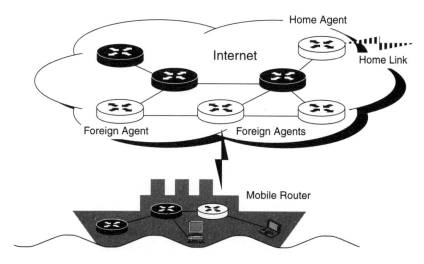

Figure 11-4 Mobile Router Maintains Connectivity for Entire Mobile Network

wirelessly with foreign agents, depending upon its current location. The mobile router's home agent is shown along with the mobile router's home link.

How does Mobile IP work in this case? First of all, the mobile router has a home address just like any mobile node. The network-prefix of the mobile router's home address likewise equals the network-prefix assigned to its home link. When connected to its home link, the mobile router and the home agent are simply neighboring routers which, presumably, exchange routing updates according to some dynamic routing protocol. When the mobile router is connected to a foreign link, the routers still send routing updates to each other, but this time through a bidirectional tunnel.

11.2.1 Mobile Router on Its Home Link

Figure 11-5 shows an example of a mobile network containing a single link whose network-prefix is 7.7.7. One host connected to that link has an IP address of 7.7.7.1. The mobile router's home address is 6.6.6.1 and its home agent's IP address is 6.6.6.2. The mobile router and the home agent participate in some dynamic routing protocol (e.g., OSPF). The mobile router advertises reachability to 7.7.7; the home agent advertises reachability to everything else.

The top portion of Figure 11-5 shows the mobile router, and hence the mobile network, connected to its home link. In this case, the mobile router works just like any other (fixed) router. Specifically, the mobile router and the home agent are neighboring routers which forward appropriate packets between each other and exchange routing updates. The top portion of Figure 11-5 also shows a packet being sent from a host on the fixed portion of the Internet to a host on a mobile network. When the mobile router is connected to its home link, such packets are simply forwarded between the home agent and mobile router without any need for tunneling—as we would expect for nonmobile (fixed) routers.

11.2.2 Mobile Routers on a Visited Link

When the mobile router is connected to a foreign link, as shown in the bottom portion of Figure 11-5, then the mobile router and the home agent still exchange routing updates and forward packets, but this time through a bidirectional tunnel. In this case, packets destined for hosts on the mobile network are tunneled to the mobile router's care-of address, where they are extracted from the tunnel and forwarded to the hosts on the mobile network. The bottom portion of Figure 11-5 illustrates this tunnel by tracing a packet from a host on the fixed portion of the Internet to a host on the mobile network.

Figure 11-5 shows the case of a mobile router using a collocated care-of address. Nothing prevents a mobile router from using a foreign agent care-of address, but this would require the home agent to use nested encapsulation, as was illustrated in the top half of Figure 11-3. In the reverse direction, the mobile router may use the foreign agent as a default router for packets generated by hosts on the mobile network. However, in the presence of ingress-filtering routers (see *What Does Mobile IP Do about Ingress Filtering?* on page 211), the mobile router should tunnel such packets to its home agent. In all cases, the mobile router and the home agent continue to exchange routing updates. These updates must be tunneled to each other to avoid confusing routers along the path from the home agent to the mobile router.

11.2.3 Routing Tables for Mobile Networks

In this section we examine the routing-table entries of a home agent and a mobile router when the mobile router is connected to a foreign link. Virtual interfaces along the lines described in *Routing Table Integration via Virtual Interfaces* on page 92 provide a convenient mechanism for mobile routers as well

1. Home Link: Packets are routed using conventional IP routing.

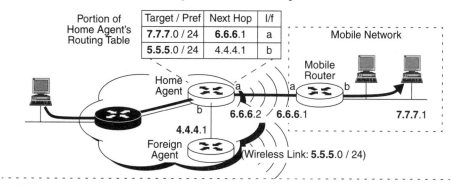

2. Foreign link: Packets are tunneled between home agent and mobile router's care-of address.

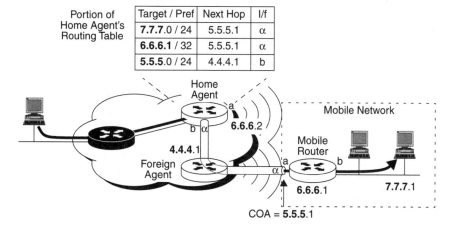

Figure 11-5 Routing Packets to Nodes on a Mobile Network

as for mobile hosts. Figure 11-5 shows an excerpt of the home agent's routing table, both before and after the mobile router registers on a foreign link. The next few sections examine in detail the entries in this table and in that of the mobile router.

Routing-Table Entries When Mobile Router Is at Home

As we would expect, the entries in the home agent's routing table are straightforward when the mobile router is connected to its home link. Table 11-1 reproduces three of the home agent's routing-table entries:

- a direct route to all nodes on the home link through its physical, albeit wireless, interface "a";
- a route to all nodes on the mobile network (**7.7.7**.0/24) via the mobile router (6.6.6.1) through its wireless interface "a"; and
- a route to all nodes on the foreign agent's wireless link (**5.5.5**.0/24) via the foreign agent (4.4.4.1) through another physical interface "b."

Target / Prefix-Length	Next Hop	Interface
6.6.6.0 / 24 (all nodes on the home link)	"directly"	a (wireless interface)
7.7.7.0 / 24 (all nodes on the mobile network)	6.6.6.1 (mobile router)	a (wireless interface)
5.5.5.0 / 24 (the foreign agent's wireless link)	4.4.4.1 (foreign agent)	b (wired interface)

Table 11-1 Home Agent's Routing Table When the Mobile Router Is at Home

Similarly, the mobile router's routing table has direct, network-prefix routes to nodes on the home link and on the mobile network. The mobile router also has a default route to all other nodes via the home agent. These entries are shown in Table 11-2.

Target / Prefix-Length	Next Hop	Interface
6.6.6.0 / 24 (all nodes on the home link)	"directly"	a (wireless interface)
7.7.7.0 / 24 (all nodes on the mobile network)	"directly"	b (e.g., Ethernet interface)
0.0.0.0 / 0 (everything else)	6.6.6.2 (home agent)	a (wireless interface)

Table 11-2 Mobile Router's Routing Table When the Mobile Router Is at Home

Consider a packet that arrives at the home agent which is destined to 7.7.7.1—a node on the mobile network. The home agent finds a matching routing-table entry in the second row of Table 11-1 and forwards the packet to the mobile router over the wireless, home link. The mobile router receives the packet and finds a matching routing-table entry in the second row of Table 11-2, and delivers the packet over its physical interface "b" to the destination host.

In the reverse direction, packets generated by hosts on the mobile network and destined for nodes not on the mobile network will be forwarded to the mobile router. Depending on the specific destination, the mobile router will use either its network-prefix route to nodes on the home link or its default route via the home agent to forward the packet toward its ultimate destination.

Routing-Table Entries When Mobile Router Is Away from Home

Things get more complicated when the mobile router connects to a foreign link, as shown in the lower panel of Figure 11-5. Here we assume that the mobile router registers the IP address 5.5.5.1 as a collocated care-of address with its home agent. When the registration is successful, the home agent and the mobile router must modify their routing tables to perform bidirectional tunneling as described in *Mobile Routers on a Visited Link* on page 228.

As in the case of mobile hosts, the home agent adds a host-specific route to the mobile router via the care-of address and through a virtual interface, as shown in Table 11-3. Additionally, the home agent must modify any routes which specify a Next Hop of the mobile router to likewise point to the mobile router's care-of address and the virtual interface. The network-prefix route to the mobile network (**7.7.7**.0/24) is one such route. The new or modified routes are shown in gray in Table 11-3.

Target / Prefix-Length	Next Hop	Interface
6.6.6.0 / 24 (*most* nodes on the home link)	"directly"	a (wireless interface)
6.6.6.1 / 32 (mobile router)	5.5.5.1 (care-of address)	α ("tunnel" virtual interface)
7.7.7.0 / 24 (all nodes on the mobile network)	5.5.5.1 (care-of address)	α ("tunnel" virtual interface)
5.5.5.0 / 24 (the foreign agent's wireless link)	4.4.4.1 (foreign agent)	b (wired interface)

Table 11-3 Home Agent's Routing Table When the Mobile Router Is Away from Home

Similarly, the mobile router must modify some of its routing-table entries when connected to the foreign link. The mobile router changes all routes which formerly pointed to the home link to be via a tunnel to its home agent. Also, the mobile router must add a host-specific route to its home agent to be via the foreign agent through its physical interface on the foreign link (the reason for this will become clear later). The result is shown in Table 11-4. Note that the first entry in Table 11-4 is no longer needed, because the Target is a subset of the Target in the fourth entry and both of these entries now have the same Next Hop and Interface.

Target / Prefix-Length	Next Hop	Interface
6.6.6.0 / 24 (all nodes on the home link)	6.6.6.2 (home agent)	α ("tunnel" virtual interface)
6.6.6.2 / 32 (home agent)	5.5.5.2 (foreign agent)	a (wireless interface)
7.7.7.0 / 24 (all nodes on the mobile network)	"directly"	b (e.g., Ethernet interface)
0.0.0.0 / 0 (everything else)	6.6.6.2 (home agent)	α ("tunnel" virtual interface)

Table 11-4 Mobile Router's Routing Table When the Mobile Router Is Away from Home

Now consider a packet that arrives at the home agent which is destined to 7.7.7.1—a node on the mobile network. The steps are as follows:

- The home agent finds a matching routing table entry in the third row of Table 11-3 and encapsulates the packet for delivery to the mobile router's care-of address. The home agent then uses the fourth entry in Table 11-3 to forward the encapsulating packet, whose (outer) IP Destination Address is 5.5.5.1, to the mobile router's foreign agent.

- The foreign agent sees a packet destined to 5.5.5.1, an address on the foreign link, and simply forwards it to the mobile router. The foreign agent does not know or care that the packet contains an encapsulated IP packet.

- The encapsulating packet arrives at the mobile router over the wireless foreign link, where it is decapsulated. The mobile router examines the (inner) IP Destination Address and uses the routing table entry in the third row of Table 11-4 to deliver the packet to the destination host.

In the reverse direction, packets generated by hosts on the mobile network that are destined for nodes not on the mobile network will again be forwarded to the mobile router. Assuming the packet is not destined to the home agent itself, the mobile router will use either the first or fourth entry in its routing table to forward the packet. In such a case, Table 11-4 specifies that the mobile router should encapsulate the packet in a new packet whose IP Destination Address is that of its home agent. Then the mobile router uses the host-specific route in the second row of Table 11-4 to forward the encapsulating packet to its foreign agent over the foreign link. The foreign agent forwards the encapsulated packet to the home agent where it is decapsulated and routed to its ultimate destination.

Note how the host-specific route to the home agent provides a physical interface for the mobile router to forward packets which have been tunneled to the home agent. However, some packets generated by the mobile router itself that are destined to the home agent will also match this host-specific route, preventing them from being tunneled to the home agent. Examples include routing updates, which are required to be tunneled to the home agent, as discussed in *Mobile Routers on a Visited Link* on page 228. Such routing updates would be placed within IP packets whose Source Address is the mobile router and whose Destination Address is the home agent and would be forwarded to the foreign agent without being tunneled.

Thus, a mobile router must take special care when forwarding packets that are destined to its home agent, whether received from nodes on the mobile network or generated by the mobile router itself. Such packets that have not already been tunneled require exactly one encapsulating IP header. Those which have already been encapsulated must not be further encapsulated and should be forwarded over the foreign link to the foreign agent or whatever router is at the other end of that link.

11.2.4 What's the Deal with Section 4.5 of RFC 2002?

In the previous sections we considered a mobile router which provided connectivity on behalf of other hosts and routers on a mobile network. Our examples assumed that these other hosts and routers were fixed with respect to each other and with respect to the mobile router, but that the whole network moved as a unit with respect to the Internet.

Section 4.5 of [RFC 2002] examines a more complicated situation in which the hosts and routers on the mobile network might themselves be mobile with respect to the mobile network. An example is a passenger who brings a notebook computer onto a ship or an airplane. Here the notebook computer is mobile with respect to the ship's or the airplane's (mutually fixed) hosts and routers and the entire ship or airplane moves with respect to the rest of the Internet.

Such a situation is illustrated in Figure 11-6, in which we assume:

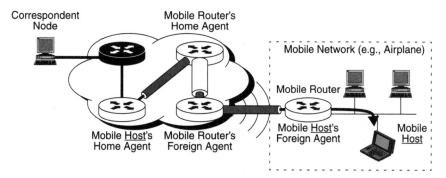

Figure 11-6 A Mobile Router That Also Provides Foreign Agent Functionality

- the mobile host has a home agent somewhere on the fixed portion of the Internet;
- the mobile router has a home agent somewhere (else) on the fixed portion of the Internet, as in the previous examples of this section;
- the mobile router provides foreign agent functionality on behalf of the mobile hosts that are connected to the mobile network link; and
- the mobile host and the mobile router have respectively discovered and registered foreign agent care-of addresses with their home agents.

Now we trace a packet from the correspondent node to the mobile host shown in Figure 11-6:

1. The packet transmitted by the correspondent node is routed to the mobile host's home agent.

2. The mobile host's home agent tunnels the packet to the mobile host's care-of address. Note that the care-of address of the mobile host *is* the IP home address of the mobile router.

3. The tunneled packet is routed to the mobile router's home agent, because, as always, the mobile router's home agent or some other router on its home link advertises reachability to the mobile router's home address.

4. The mobile router's home agent intercepts the tunneled packet and further tunnels it to the mobile router's care-of address. Note that this latter care-of address is that of the foreign agent on the fixed portion of the Internet.

5. When the double-tunneled packet arrives at the mobile router's foreign agent, the outermost tunneling header is removed, revealing a tunneled packet destined to the mobile router. The foreign agent forwards this packet across the wireless link to the mobile router.

6. When the mobile router receives the single-tunneled packet, it removes the remaining tunneling header and sees a packet destined to the mobile host. Because the mobile host is registered with the mobile-router-serving-as-foreign-agent, the mobile router sends the original packet over the mobile network link to the mobile host.

Congratulations are in order to anyone who is able to follow this discussion. Seriously, though, Figure 11-6 does illustrate Mobile IP's ability to accommodate some very complicated topologies. It also illustrates how some nodes, such as the mobile router, might in practice implement all three Mobile IP entities—mobile node, foreign agent, and home agent—simultaneously.

11.2.5 Summary

In this section we examined how Mobile IP can provide connectivity for mobile networks in addition to mobile hosts. We defined a mobile network as a collection of hosts and routers which are fixed with respect to each other but are mobile, as a unit, with respect to the rest of the Internet.

We introduced a mobile router, which is a mobile node which provides connectivity for the mobile network. We assumed that the mobile router and its home agent exchange routing updates, using some dynamic routing protocol and that when the mobile router is connected to a foreign link, this exchange is carried over a bidirectional tunnel. In addition, we saw how the home agent and mobile router must modify their respective routing tables when the mobile router registers a care-of address on a foreign link.

11.3 Mobile IP as a Layer-2, Tunnel-Establishment Protocol

Many corporations have deployed network infrastructure that allows their mobile workforce to dial into the network via PPP or other remote-access protocols. For many companies, the cost of the modems, phone lines, remote-access servers and the administrative costs of this infrastructure have become quite large. Recently, there has been a flurry of activity within the Internet Engineering Task Force to define protocols that allow companies to provide this dial-up access cheaply, efficiently, and securely via the Internet.

Here we describe one such proposal, the *Virtual Tunneling Protocol (VTP)* [draft-calhoun-vtp-protocol-00.txt], an updated version of which Bay Networks has built into their BayStream Dial VPN Service. VTP uses Mobile IP to dynamically establish bi-directional tunnels through the Internet, allowing corporations to outsource their dial-up access equipment and operations. We also describe one of the other proposals for remote dial-in service.

The protocol described here is very similar to various other proposals being considered by the Internet Engineering Task Force. These include:

- *Ascend Tunnel Management Protocol (ATMP)* [RFC 2107];
- *Point-to-Point Tunneling Protocol (PPTP)* [draft-ietf-pppext-pptp-00.txt];
- *Layer Two Forwarding (L2F)* [draft-ietf-pppext-l2f-03.txt]; and
- *Layer Two Tunneling Protocol (L2TP)*—the confluence of L2F and PPTP which is likely to become the ultimate Internet standard for layer-2 tunneling [draft-ietf-pppext-l2tp-03.txt]. We describe the *Layer Two Tunneling Protocol* in more detail in *How Does L2TP Differ from VTP?* on page 242.

In this section we focus on the *Virtual Tunneling Protocol* because it uses Mobile IP explicitly to realize its service. Interestingly, Mobile IP is used in such as way as to keep it hidden from the ultimate user of a network employing the *Virtual Tunneling Protocol*. Equivalently stated, Mobile IP software need not be present on a mobile user's computer in order to use such a network. This further implies that a mobile user that connects to his private network using the *Virtual Tunneling Protocol* is unable to retain his IP address, connect over any possible link or medium, etc., as would a mobile user that has Mobile IP's mobile node software installed on his computer. Thus, the *Virtual Tunneling*

Protocol provides nomadicity rather than mobility. This will become more clear in the next few sections.

11.3.1 What Is Remote Dial-in?

Many organizations have an increasingly mobile workforce. This includes telecommuters as well as "road-warrior" salesforces and other highly mobile workers. These employees frequently require access to information stored on their organization's network and on the Internet. As a result, many organizations have deployed network infrastructure that allows these mobile workers to connect to the network via link-layer protocols such as PPP, most frequently over telephone lines.

The way in which mobile workers connect to their networks via PPP is similar to the Internet Service Provider example we described in *How Does a Person Connect to Internet via PPP But without Mobile IP?* on page 202. Here, instead of dialing into the remote-access equipment operated by an Internet Service Provider, the worker dials into remote-access equipment owned by, and located on, the premises of his corporation's facility or campus.

Why Dial into the Private Network Directly?

The assumption here is that a telephone connection from the remote worker's computer to his private network is more secure than a connection that crosses over the public portion of the Internet. Specifically, it is considered to be more difficult to passively eavesdrop or to wage an active takeover attack on the traffic traversing a telephone line than it is to wage similar attacks on information flowing over the Internet.

Assuming these security stipulations to be true, then no firewall need be erected between the dial-in equipment and the rest of the private network. Of course, this requires the remote-access equipment to be able to authenticate users and to prevent them from accessing the network if they are not authorized to do so.

So What Is the Problem?

To provide remote dial-in service to its remote users, a corporation must purchase and maintain network infrastructure similar to that of Internet Service Providers, including:

- numerous phone lines, one for each simultaneous user;
- banks of modems for terminating these phone lines;
- remote-access servers that terminate the PPP link-layer protocol and perhaps perform network-layer functionality as well;

- authentication servers which the remote-access servers use to authenticate dial-up users before allowing them to access the network; and

- an administrative staff to make sure that this equipment is functional 24 hours a day, 7 days a week.

In addition, because remote users generally connect via phone lines, it is highly desirable for organizations to provide dial-in infrastructure in many geographic areas—otherwise, many of the phone calls will be long-distance ones with correspondingly high per-minute charges. The costs of these phone calls and of maintaining all of the equipment and staff mentioned above can be enormous for many organizations.

For this reason, many organizations are looking toward using the Internet—as opposed to the phone system—to provide remote users with access to their private networks. The idea is to allow a remote user to dial into the equipment of a local Internet Service Provider, using a local telephone call, and to route the traffic back to a device on the private network—all the while making it look as if the user dialed into the private network directly.

This allows the organization to outsource the costs of owning and maintaining this large dial-in infrastructure as well as lowering telephone charges. Additionally, it prevents an organization from worrying about the speed with which such equipment becomes obsolete.

In this section we will see how the *Virtual Tunneling Protocol* can be used to provide this service to remote users. We will also see how the *Virtual Tunneling Protocol* makes use of Mobile IP's registration protocol to dynamically create tunnels on behalf of dial-up users. The main difference between this solution and the one we saw in *How Can Mobile Nodes Traverse the Firewall without Compromising the Corporate Network?* on page 180 is that the *Virtual Tunneling Protocol* need only be implemented in certain service-provider and other infrastructure equipment and not on the mobile computers (i.e., the mobile nodes) themselves. For completeness, however, we note that the solution of *How Can Mobile Nodes Traverse the Firewall without Compromising the Corporate Network?* on page 180 is at least as secure and quite likely more so than the solution described here.

11.3.2 How Does the Virtual Tunneling Protocol Work?

In this section we describe how the *Virtual Tunneling Protocol* uses Mobile IP to dynamically set up and tear down tunnels on behalf of remote users. While the *Virtual Tunneling Protocol* also allows organizations to create VPNs across the Internet, our focus here will be on remote dial-up access for individual users. We will also focus on dial-up via PPP and ignore other point-to-point link-layer protocols such as *Serial Line IP (SLIP)* [RFC 1055].

What Is the Virtual Tunneling Protocol Architecture?

Figure 11-7 is the reference diagram for the *Virtual Tunneling Protocol*. The figure shows a mobile user using a computer to dial into a Network Access Server operated by an Internet Service Provider. The Network Access Server, in addition to terminating the telephone line and the PPP link, also contains a Mobile IP mobile-node function.

The Network Access Server connects via the Internet to a gateway which can be located on the service provider's premise or on the customer's private network. The latter case is shown in Figure 11-7. The gateway looks like a multiprotocol router to the private network. It also implements the *Virtual Tunneling Protocol* as well as the Mobile IP home agent function. Because the Network Access Server always uses a collocated care-of address, there is no requirement for foreign agents in the *Virtual Tunneling Protocol* architecture.

Figure 11-7 also shows two *Remote Authentication Dial In User Service (RADIUS)* servers—one owned by the service provider and one owned by the private network. RADIUS [RFC 2058] is a protocol used between Network Access Servers and authentication servers to authenticate dial-in users, allowing these two functions to be placed in separate network devices.

Virtual Tunneling Protocol Walkthrough

The process by which a mobile user connects to his private network, as implemented by the *Virtual Tunneling Protocol*, is now described. Those unfamiliar with PPP might wish to read *How Does a Person Connect to Internet via PPP*

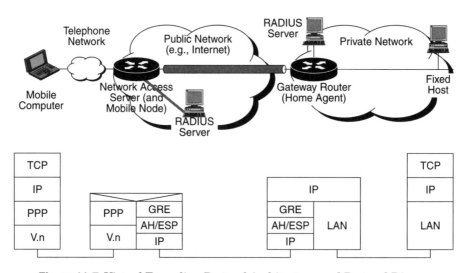

Figure 11-7 Virtual Tunneling Protocol Architecture and Protocol Diagram

But without Mobile IP? on page 202 before proceeding. The steps for connecting are as follows:

1. The mobile user places a local telephone call via his modem to the service provider's Network Access Server.

2. The PPP client in the user's computer and the Network Access Server begin negotiating link parameters in PPP's *Link Control Protocol (LCP)* phase. Among the parameters negotiated are which authentication protocol will be used in the authentication phase of PPP. We assume that this negotiation settles on the *Challenge Handshake Authentication Protocol (CHAP)* for authentication.

3. In the authentication phase, the Network Access Server generates a *CHAP Challenge* to the PPP client in the user's computer.

4. The client responds with the mobile user's username and message digest in a *CHAP Response*.

5. The Network Access Server passes the username and message digest to the local RADIUS server which looks at the username to determine the address of a remote RADIUS server which can actually authenticate and authorize the user.

6. The local RADIUS server recomputes the message digest using a key it shares with the remote RADIUS server, presumably located on the private network, and passes the username and message digest along to the remote RADIUS server.

7. The remote RADIUS server verifies the message digest and returns to the local RADIUS server a message authorizing the user. Additionally, the remote RADIUS server includes information such as the gateway's IP address (for tunnel establishment) and various other *Virtual Tunneling Protocol*-related parameters.

8. The local RADIUS server attaches more tunnel-establishment information to the message from the remote RADIUS server and sends it to the Network Access Server.

9. Assuming that the user has been authorized, the Network Access Server sends a *CHAP Success* message back to the PPP client to complete the authentication phase of PPP.

10. Upon the completion of the authentication phase, the PPP client and the Network Access Server begin the *Network Control Protocol (NCP)* phase where the two negotiate the parameters needed to configure the various network-layer protocols that the mobile computer wishes to use to communicate with the private network.

11. Once the NCP phase completes—i.e., after the mobile computer has acquired an IP address to use within the *Internet Protocol Control Protocol*

(IPCP)—the Network Access Server (mobile node) uses Mobile IP to register with the gateway (the home agent):

a. the *Registration Request* indicates a desire on the part of the Network Access Server to create a tunnel to the gateway on behalf of the mobile computer;

b. the Network Access Server uses its own address as the (collocated) care-of address;

c. the mobile computer's IP address (e.g., the one negotiated in IPCP) is used as the Mobile Node's Home Address in the *Registration Request*;

d. the gateway's IP address is used as the Home Agent Address;

e. a Tunnel Identifier is included as a Mobile IP extension, which is used to distinguish the new tunnel from all others that have this Network Access Server and this gateway as the end-points.

12. The gateway processes the *Registration Request*, verifies the authentication contained therein, and returns a *Registration Reply* to the Network Access Server. Among other things, the request and replies contain information specific to setup and configuration of the tunnel over which the user's data will ultimately flow. The reply can specify codes which indicate whether the IP address of the mobile computer is already in use by some other node. (Note that the IP address of the mobile computer was originally negotiated by the Network Access Server, which has no idea if some other node connected to some other Network Access Server had been assigned the same address.)

13. A *Registration Reply* with a Code indicating that the registration was successful is interpreted to mean that the formation of the tunnel was successful and that the mobile computer's IP address is valid.

From this point on, IP packets generated by the mobile computer are tunneled by the Network Access Server within GRE to the gateway. The gateway strips off the outer IP and GRE headers, and routes the inner packet to its ultimate destination. When the mobile computer disconnects, a Mobile IP deregistration (i.e., a *Registration Request* with the Lifetime field set to zero) is sent from the Network Access Server to the gateway to bring down the tunnel.

The *Virtual Tunneling Protocol* architecture also allows layer-2 frames (i.e., PPP frames carrying IP packets) to be tunneled from the Network Access Server to the gateway [draft-calhoun-vtp-ext-l2-00.txt]. This allows the architecture to accommodate layer-2 tunneling as defined in L2TP, which we describe in *How Does L2TP Differ from VTP?* on page 242.

11.3.3 What Are the Security Considerations of the Virtual Tunneling Protocol?

The *Virtual Tunneling Protocol* explicitly addresses the following threats:

- Users are authenticated by PPP CHAP or other authentication mechanisms, preventing unauthorized users from accessing the private network or stealing service from the service provider.

- The authentication extensions within the Mobile IP registration protocol prevent unauthorized Network Access Servers from establishing tunnels to the gateway on a private network.

- The tunnel itself can be encrypted or authenticated by the use of the IP security protocols—the *Encapsulating Security Payload* and the *Authentication Header*, respectively. If applied properly, these protocols can prevent passive eavesdropping and active session-stealing attacks along the path between the Network Access Server and the gateway.

This leaves the PPP link over the telephone network, between the mobile computer and the Network Access Server, as the only point of vulnerability. If one believes that passive eavesdropping and active session-stealing attacks are difficult to perform on the telephone network (compared to Internet), then this might represent a satisfactory security risk.

The telephone system, however, is not nearly as secure as many people believe. James M. Atkinson of the Granite Island Group, an engineer specializing in communications security, indicates that a telephone line can be tapped by an amateur in about 10 seconds [Atki96]! Also, Kevin Murray of Murray & Associates, a counterespionage consultant, has identified over 16 types of attacks that can be waged against a telephone, involving bugs, taps, and other compromises [Murr97b]. Finally, Bruce Sterling, in *The Hacker Crackdown*, notes that sophisticated attacks can be waged against the private branch-exchange (PBX) telephone switches within large corporations, simply by placing a local phone call [Ster92].

The claim that phone lines are secure while the Internet is trivial to attack is somewhat naive. As mentioned previously, those with sensitive information to protect should encrypt it across phone lines and across the general Internet, preferably on an end-to-end basis.

11.3.4 Why Not Just Use Mobile IP?

The *Virtual Tunneling Protocol* does have a number of potential advantages over Mobile IP. First of all, it requires only TCP/IP and PPP software on the mobile computers—something we assume to exist already on most new computers. Specifically, the mobile computer need not contain software that implements Mobile IP's mobile-node function. As of this writing, that is a big advantage because Mobile IP software does not come loaded on most new computers. We expect this situation to change, however, in the coming months and years.

Another supposed benefit is that the *Virtual Tunneling Protocol* can provide support for protocols other than IP and can allow organizations that use private IP addresses to use those addresses over a public infrastructure. However, in *How Can Mobile Nodes Traverse the Firewall without Compromising the Corporate Network?* on page 180 and in *Support for Other Protocols within the Mobile IP Framework* on page 219 we described a mechanism by which Mobile IP can provide the same functionality for organizations and users that require it. We acknowledge that such functionality is in the process of being defined in the Mobile IP working group and is not yet standardized.

Of course, if one does not buy into the claim that the telephone system is sufficiently more secure than the Internet, then both of these "advantages" seem somewhat less so. Specifically, to protect the confidentiality of data sent over the PPP link, encryption software needs to be installed on the mobile computers. This might or might not be preferable to installing Mobile IP with firewall-traversal enhancements of the kind we described in *How Can Mobile Nodes Traverse the Firewall without Compromising the Corporate Network?* on page 180. The latter allows mobile computers to connect securely over any type of medium or link—such as an Ethernet at a conference, trade show, or customer or vendor premise—rather than only by PPP links and telephone lines.

11.3.5 How Does L2TP Differ from VTP?

In this section we describe the *Layer Two Tunneling Protocol (L2TP)* architecture and compare it with that of the *Virtual Tunneling Protocol*. The term *layer-2 tunneling* refers to the fact that PPP frames—as opposed to network-layer packets—are tunneled across a public infrastructure such as the Internet. In the previous sections, network-layer packets (e.g., IP packets) were taken out of the PPP frames before being tunneled.

Layer Two Tunneling Protocol Architecture

Figure 11-8 shows the architecture of networks employing the *Layer Two Tunneling Protocol*. An L2TP Access Concentrator performs similar functions to the Network Access Server in the *Virtual Tunneling Protocol* architecture. Specifically, the L2TP Access Concentrator terminates the phone and modem connection to the mobile computer. The L2TP Network Server is similar to the gateway in the *Virtual Tunneling Protocol* architecture. The L2TP Network Server terminates the PPP link and looks like a multiprotocol router to the rest of the private network.

The L2TP Access Concentrator and the L2TP Network Server form the two end-points of the layer-2 tunnel. Not shown in Figure 11-8 are the RADIUS servers or other servers that might be used to authenticate dial-in users.

Layer Two Tunneling Protocol Walkthrough

A mobile worker connects to his private network over a public network that employs the *Layer Two Tunneling Protocol* as follows:

1. The remote user places a local phone call and initiates a PPP connection to an Internet Service Provider's L2TP Access Concentrator.

2. The L2TP Access Concentrator gathers enough information from the mobile computer to be able to look up the type of service to provide—standard Internet service or a layer-2 tunnel to an L2TP Network Server. The concentrator can use the caller or dialed phone number, if provided by the telephone network, to perform this lookup. Otherwise, the concentrator might have to negotiate much of PPP's link and authentication phases in order to obtain a username (such as that provided in PAP or CHAP) to look up the user. If the lookup determines that the user requires *Layer Two Tunneling Protocol* service, then the lookup also provides the address of the user's L2TP Network Server.

3. The L2TP Access Concentrator sets up a tunnel to the L2TP Network Server determined in the previous step, assuming no such tunnel already exists. Whereas Figure 11-8 shows the tunnel medium being UDP/IP over the Internet, the *Layer Two Tunneling Protocol* architecture can support almost any type of public or private switched network, including Frame Relay, X.25, or dedicated lines.

4. Once the tunnel exists, a Call ID is allocated and a connect indication is sent from the L2TP Access Concentrator to the L2TP Network Server. This indication can contain any of the PPP parameters already negotiated by the concentrator with the mobile computer. For example, if the concentrator negotiated LCP and CHAP with the mobile computer, in order to determine the username and to look up the address of the server, then the concentra-

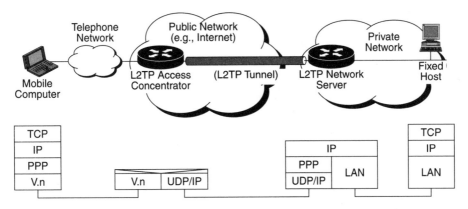

Figure 11-8 Layer Two Tunneling Protocol (L2TP) Architecture

tor can pass the negotiated LCP parameters and the CHAP challenge, user-name, and message digest along to the server in the connect indication.

5. The server uses the parameters in the connect indication to authenticate the user (e.g., by verifying the CHAP message digest). Assuming that the user is legitimate, the server creates a PPP "virtual interface," which is functionally identical to the interface it would create if the modem and tele-phone link were terminated there as well.

6. The server sends an acceptance message to the concentrator which com-pletes the call setup process.

At this point, PPP frames can be sent all the way from the mobile computer to the L2TP Network Server as if the telephone call were placed between these two elements. Such frames are sent by the mobile computer over the phone line to the L2TP Access Concentrator, where they are stripped of any framing and transparency bytes and tunneled to the L2TP Network Server. The L2TP Net-work Server strips off the tunneling headers and treats the resulting PPP frames as if they had arrived through a direct modem/phone line. The latter generally involves removing the enclosed network-layer packets from the PPP frames and forwarding them toward their ultimate destination.

Security Considerations

The *Layer Two Tunneling Protocol* explicitly addresses the following threats:

- The L2TP Network Server can require authentication to prevent unautho-rized concentrators or other parties from establishing tunnels.

- Users are authenticated at the L2TP Network Server via PAP, CHAP, or any other authentication mechanism that is used in the context of remote dial-in via PPP. The L2TP Access Concentrator passes enough information to the L2TP Network Server to allow it to authenticate the user in this way.

- The tunnel itself can be encrypted or authenticated by the use of the IP security protocols—the *Encapsulating Security Payload* and the *Authenti-cation Header*, respectively. If applied properly, these protocols can prevent passive eavesdropping or active session-stealing attacks along the path between the concentrator and the server.

Without link encryption, the path between the mobile computer and the L2TP Access Concentrator is vulnerable to wiretapping and monitoring. Note, however, that PPP-based encryption can protect the user's data against passive eavesdropping and session-stealing attacks all the way from the mobile com-puter to the L2TP Network Server. This provides a level of protection equivalent to the secure tunnel used between mobile nodes and their firewalls in Mobile IP.

As before, Mobile IP has the advantage of not being tied to any specific link-layer (i.e., PPP) and provides the user with all of the mobility advantages we dis-cussed in *Chapter 3, The Need for Mobile IP.*

11.3.6 Summary

In this section we described the *Virtual Tunneling Protocol* architecture, which uses Mobile IP to dynamically create tunnels on behalf of remote dial-up users. This architecture applied Mobile IP in such a way as to keep it hidden from the ultimate user. In addition, we looked at the *Layer Two Tunneling Protocol,* which has a similar architecture and provides a similar service but tunnels layer-2 (i.e., PPP) frames—as opposed to network-layer packets—over the public infrastructure.

11.4 Chapter Summary

In this chapter we described three additional applications and capabilities of Mobile IP. We began with a description of the Integrated Mobility Extension, which provides multiprotocol support within the Mobile IP framework. A mobile node uses this extension to inform its home agent of any network-layer protocols the mobile node supports in addition to IP. The home agent and the mobile node then use *Generic Routing Encapsulation (GRE)* to exchange packets of these "other" protocols through a bidirectional IP tunnel. This solution allows mobile nodes to communicate with correspondents that do not implement TCP/IP when the mobile nodes are away from their home links.

Next we described how Mobile IP can be used to support mobile *networks*—hosts and routers that are fixed with respect to each other but are mobile, as a unit, with respect to the rest of the Internet—in addition to mobile *hosts*. Examples of mobile networks include the hosts and routers on a ship, an airplane, and a train. A mobile router maintains connectivity for a mobile network by using Mobile IP to acquire and register a care-of address at its current link and by exchanging routing updates with its home agent over a bidirectional tunnel.

Finally we looked at the *Virtual Tunneling Protocol,* an application of Mobile IP that is invisible to the end-user of the network but nonetheless provides a useful service to nomadic computers. The *Virtual Tunneling Protocol* allows organizations to outsource secure, remote dial-in to a service provider rather than owning and maintaining their own dial-in infrastructure. The *Virtual Tunneling Protocol* uses Mobile IP to dynamically create tunnels from a Network Access Server to a device on the private network, giving the illusion of local dial-in and letting the mobile user place a local telephone call. We described a similar system, the *Layer Two Tunneling Protocol (L2TP),* which tunnels PPP frames between a local dial-in device and a device on a private network.

4

FUTURE TOPICS

C H A P T E R **12**

Mobility for IP Version 6

This chapter discusses mobility support for the *Internet Protocol Version 6 (IPv6)*. IPv6 is the "next generation" of the Internet Protocol, which will ultimately replace IPv4 as the primary network-layer protocol of the Internet. We begin our discussion with a primer on IPv6, describing its new features and comparing it with IPv4. Then we examine the current proposal for Mobile IPv6 and show how some of the new features in IPv6 make it more accommodative of mobility than IPv4.

It is important to note that this chapter describes "work in progress." As of this writing, Mobile IPv6 is one of the important work items on the agenda of the Mobile IP working group of the Internet Engineering Task Force. As such, the Mobile IPv6 specification document is evolving quite rapidly, and the discussion in this chapter is simply a snapshot. Our discussion is based primarily on version 02 of the Mobile IPv6 document [draft-ietf-mobileip-ipv6-02.txt].

12.1 How Does IPv6 Differ from IPv4?

IP version 6 differs in some very important ways from IP version 4. This section
will highlight these differences, thereby laying the groundwork for an investiga-
tion of Mobile IPv6. The two biggest differences between IPv4 and IPv6 are the
size of the addresses—128 bits in IPv6 versus 32 bits in IPv4—and the fact that
many of the less frequently used fields in IPv4 have been moved out of the IPv6
header and into optional, extension headers. Also, IPv6 options are more rigorously defined and are therefore more useful than IPv4 options.

12.1.1 IPv6 Base Header

As with IPv4, we begin our exploration of IPv6 by examining the fixed-
length (base) portion of the IPv6 header, which is shown in Figure 12-1. The first
thing we notice is that IPv6 addresses are four times as big (16 bytes versus
4 bytes) as IPv4 addresses. There are several benefits of such large addresses:

- First of all, there is no real chance of running out of addresses during the
  lifetime of IPv6.

- Second, and more importantly, large addresses allow aggregation of many
  network-prefix routes into a single network-prefix route (with a longer network-prefix) which solves the "routing table explosion" problem we discussed in *Why is Routing Based on Network-Prefix?* on page 29. For more
  information on route aggregation and hierarchical routing, see [Huitema95].

- Finally, large addresses allow nodes to autoconfigure using very simple
  mechanisms, which we will describe in *What Is Stateless Address Autoconfiguration?* on page 260.

The other fields in the fixed-length portion of the IPv6 header are described
briefly as follows. The Version field performs the same purpose as the correspond-

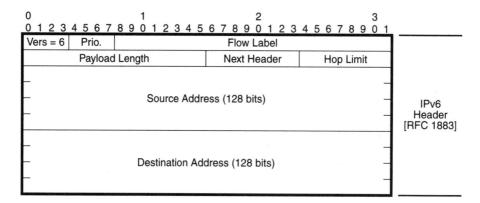

Figure 12-1 Fixed-Length (Base) Portion of IPv6 Header

ing field in IPv4 and equals 6 for IPv6. The Priority field allows the sender to attach a *relative* priority to a given packet with respect to other packets sent by that same sender. Uses for the Flow Label field are currently not well understood, though some have suggested that real-time traffic such as audio and video might find applications for this field. (Real-time traffic is discussed in *RSVP and Real-Time Traffic* on page 282.)

The Payload Length gives the length of the "rest" of the IPv6 packet (i.e., not including the header itself), measured in bytes. The Next Header field is similar to the Protocol field in IPv4. The Next Header field tells the receiver the "type" of header which follows the current header—either an IPv6 Extension Header (described in the next section) or a header of some higher-layer protocol (e.g., TCP or UDP). Finally, the Hop Limit field provides the same functionality as the IPv4 Time to Live field; namely, it is decremented each time a packet is forwarded, and the packet is discarded when the Hop Limit is decremented to zero.

12.1.2 IPv6 Extension Headers

Recall that in IPv4, options are carried in the "base" portion of the IPv4 header and the IPv4 Protocol field always points to a higher-layer protocol (or IPv4 itself in the case of a tunnel). In IPv6, however, options are carried in "extension headers." These extension headers form a chain that leads from the base IPv6 header (as described in *IPv6 Base Header* on page 248) to the actual higher-layer protocol header, as shown in Figure 12-2. Many such extension

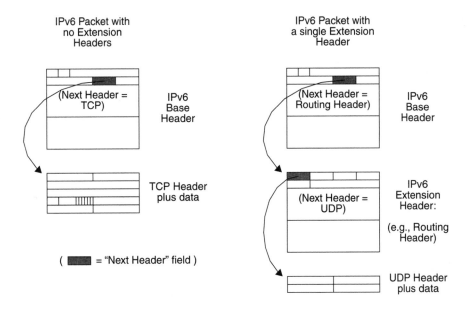

Figure 12-2 IPv6 Extension Headers

headers can appear in a single IPv6 packet. The currently defined extension headers are as follows:

- *Hop-by-Hop Options Header*, which, as the name implies, contains options that must be examined by every router along the path from the original source to the ultimate destination;

- *Destination Options Header*, which contains options which are examined only by the ultimate destination (and by intermediate destinations explicitly listed in a *Routing Header*, if present);

- *Routing Header*, which is similar to a combination of the IPv4 Loose/Strict Source and Record Route Option (see *What Is Source Routing?* on page 99);

- *Fragment Header*, which is used by a source node to send a packet that is larger than the path MTU—the Maximum Transfer Unit that can be accommodated by the links comprising the path from that source to the ultimate destination;

- *IP Authentication Header* [RFC 1826], which provides authentication and possibly replay protection, integrity checking, and non-repudiation of the payload (see *What Do We Mean by Authentication, Integrity Checking, and Non-Repudiation?* on page 132);

- *IP Encapsulating Security Payload (Header)* [RFC 1827], which provides confidentiality and possibly authentication of the entire packet's payload;

- *Upper-Layer Header*, which is the transport- or application-layer header, or an IPv6 or IPv4 Header in the case of a tunnel.

The *Hop-by-Hop Options Header* and the *Destination Options Header* are actually "wrappers" that contain one or more Type-Length-Data-encoded options. One such option is the Jumbo Payload Option, which allows IPv6 packets to be sent which are longer than 65536 bytes. As we will see in *Which of These Differences Is Relevant to the Design of Mobile IPv6?* on page 252, the extension headers of particular interest to Mobile IPv6 are the *Destination Options Header*, the *Authentication Header*, and the *Routing Header*.

12.1.3 IPv6 Address Types

The IPv6 Addressing Architecture [RFC 1884] defines three primary types of addresses:

1. A packet sent to a *Unicast Address* is called a unicast packet. As in IPv4, a unicast packet is delivered to exactly one node—the node which has the unicast address assigned to one of its interfaces.

2. A packet sent to a *Multicast Address* is called a multicast packet. As in IPv4, a copy of the multicast packet is delivered to each and every node that is a member of the group identified by the multicast address.

3. A packet sent to an *Anycast Address* is called an anycast packet. Unlike unicast and multicast, IPv4 has no equivalent of the IPv6 anycast address. An anycast packet is delivered to "any" one of several possible nodes that are identified by that address, typically the node that is closest to the sender of the packet. (It might help to think of an anycast packet as being similar to a multicast packet, except that the anycast packet is delivered to only one of the group members, not to all of them. However, the syntax of an anycast address makes it closer to a unicast address than a multicast address.)

Notably missing from this list is a broadcast address. IPv6 treats broadcast as a special case of multicast and therefore does not distinguish broadcast as a primary address type.

Special IPv6 addresses have been reserved to provide compatibility with IPv4 nodes and to embed the network-layer addresses of various other protocols. IPv6 also defines special "local-use" addresses which we now describe. As defined in [RFC 1884], there are three subcategories of unicast addresses:

- *Link-Local Addresses* are designed to be used on a single link for the purposes of address autoconfiguration and neighbor discovery, and for communication between hosts when no routers are present on the link. (We will describe address autoconfiguration and neighbor discovery throughout this chapter.) As the name suggests, packets containing link-local addresses, must never be forwarded by routers.

- *Site-Local Addresses* may be used by a site (organization) that is not connected to the global Internet. If the organization later connects to the Internet, then it must obtain globally routable addresses (described next). Similarly, packets containing site-local addresses must never be forwarded by routers outside of the site in which those addresses are being used.

- *Globally Routable Addresses*[†] must be used by nodes which wish to communicate with other nodes both outside of their own link and outside of their own site. As the name suggests, a packet destined to a globally routable address may be forwarded by routers and may be sent from anywhere (notwithstanding administrative policies which forbid such things).

In this chapter we deal almost exclusively with globally routable (unicast) addresses. The exception is when a mobile node has a link-local address that it uses on its home link in addition to its globally routable home address. We draw the distinction between link-local addresses and globally routable addresses as the need arises.

[†] The term "globally routable address" does not appear in [RFC 1884], which uses the slightly less descriptive term "global address."

12.2 Which of These Differences Is Relevant to the Design of Mobile IPv6?

In this section we highlight the differences between IPv4 and IPv6 which influence the design of Mobile IPv6. Specifically, we recount the limitations of IPv4 that drove the design of Mobile IPv4 and see how the lack of such limitations in IPv6 drive the design of Mobile IPv6.

12.2.1 How Do Larger Addresses Help?

Recall that one of the virtues of foreign agents in IPv4 was that they provide a care-of address that can be shared by very many mobile nodes. Specifically, foreign agents eliminate the need to assign a unique, co-located care-of address to each and every mobile node. In IPv6, however, the availability of addresses is not a problem—IPv6 allows up to 2^{128} = 3.4028237 × 10^{38} addressable nodes (note that 10^{12} equals one trillion!).

Also, this enormous address space allows very simple autoconfiguration of addresses as we will see in *What Is Stateless Address Autoconfiguration?* on page 260. This allows a mobile node to acquire a collocated care-of address on any foreign link quickly and easily. As a result, the foreign agent function is gone from Mobile IPv6, as is the foreign agent variant of the care-of address. This further implies that the only type of care-of address in Mobile IPv6 is the collocated care-of address.

12.2.2 How Does the New Routing Header Help?

Recall the many undesirable aspects of the IPv4 Loose Source and Record Route Option. First of all, nodes that receive a packet containing this option are required to reverse the option when replying to the original source of the packet. This opened the door to trivial denial-of-service attacks, as we discussed in *Why Use Tunneling Instead of Source Routing?* on page 99. The *IPv6 Routing Header*, as defined in [RFC 1883], does not possess this property; namely, a node which receives an IPv6 packet containing a *Routing Header* need not include a *Routing Header* when replying to the original source.

Second, IPv4 packets that contain *any* options must be scrutinized by every router along their path, making the forwarding of such packets relatively inefficient. In contrast, recall that IPv6 explicitly categorizes options into those that must be examined by every router and those that must be examined only by the ultimate destination. Thus, the *IPv6 Routing Header* can be completely ignored by most of the routers along the path (the exceptions are the routers explicitly named as intermediate destinations in the *Routing Header* itself), allowing very fast forwarding decisions in most of these routers.

Finally, the fact that many existing IPv4 nodes do not correctly implement the Loose Source and Record Route Option is not an issue in IPv6. Certainly, though, we hope that the IPv6 implementors will learn from the mistakes of their predecessors and implement the *IPv6 Routing Header* correctly!

As we will see, Mobile IPv6 uses the new-and-improved *IPv6 Routing Header*, along with the *Authentication Header* and other pieces of IPv6 functionality, to simplify routing to mobile nodes and to perform route optimization in a secure fashion.

12.2.3 How Does the Authentication Header Help?

Mobile IPv4 devised its own authentication mechanism for two reasons. First of all, the documents specifying the *IP Authentication Header* were not quite ripe by the time Mobile IPv4 needed to choose an authentication mechanism. Second, the *IP Authentication Header* does not support the idea of an application-layer relay—at least not gracefully. This assertion requires further clarification.

Recall that when a mobile node registers via a foreign agent, the IP packet which carries its *Registration Request* has an IP Destination Address of the foreign agent. Although the foreign agent ultimately relays the UDP Payload (i.e., the *Registration Request*) portion of the packet to the home agent, it is important to note that the foreign agent is indeed the destination of the IP packet. A node which is the destination of an IP packet assumes that any *IP Authentication Header* contained therein is meant for itself—in our case, for the foreign agent. This is clearly not desirable, since the authentication included by a mobile node is meant for its home agent, not for the foreign agent.

Unfortunately, there is no graceful way to use the *IP Authentication Header* with application-layer relays, at least as of the time Mobile IPv4 required an authentication mechanism. This and the fact that the *IP Authentication Header* was not quite finished were the primary reasons that Mobile IPv4 decided to use its own authentication mechanism. Note, however, that both of these reasons no longer apply in the case of Mobile IPv6—the *IP Authentication Header* specification is reasonably stable and there is no such thing as a foreign agent in Mobile IPv6.

Furthermore, implementation of the *IP Authentication Header* is mandatory for IPv6 nodes. This might provide a mechanism for wide-scale adoption of route-optimization techniques. The case to be made in this regard is not a very strong one, however, as we will now explain.

Recall that route optimization, in the context of Mobile IP, requires a mobile node to report its current care-of address to its correspondents, for largely the same reason that the mobile node is required to register its care-of address with its home agent—namely, to inform these nodes of the exit-point of a tunnel that must be used to send packets to the mobile node. Because a Bad Guy can lie to a mobile node's correspondents just as easily as he can lie to a mobile node's home agent, this reporting of care-of address must be done securely (i.e., using strong authentication) in order to guard against trivial denial-of-service attacks.

Recall, however, that key distribution is a prerequisite for authentication. That is, a mobile node must share a secret key with a correspondent, or the correspondent must be able to obtain the mobile node's public key in a secure fashion, in order for the correspondent to be able to verify the authentication provided by the mobile node.

As we mentioned in *Why the Triangle Route?* on page 101, it is simply not feasible for some poor soul to manually configure secret keys between a mobile node and its potential correspondents. We acknowledge that such a key could be manually configured between the mobile node and, say, one or two hosts with which it regularly communicates, such as its file server and its mail server. On the other hand, we also note that these two hosts are likely to be close to the mobile node's home agent anyway, in which case the benefit of route optimization is negligible.

Thus, route optimization requires a key management infrastructure to be made widely available on the Internet in order to be useful. As we discussed in *How Can We Manage Keys Securely?* on page 139, this would require not only an infrastructure for certifying public keys but also a mechanism for generating session keys, such as ISAKMP/Oakley. All of this, quite frankly, seems like overkill in comparison with the benefit gained by route optimization. Nonetheless, Mobile IPv6, through its use of the *Authentication Header*, can migrate gracefully to route optimization once a key management infrastructure becomes widely available on the Internet.

12.3 Doesn't Address Autoconfiguration Eliminate the Need for Mobile IPv6?

Simple address autoconfiguration is a very powerful mechanism for nomadic nodes to acquire an address and begin communicating on their current link. However, address autoconfiguration, whether simple or not, does not change the nature of network-prefix routing, or the need to devise special ways to route packets to mobile nodes that move from link to link while retaining any ongoing communications. Thus, IPv6 requires a mobility solution for exactly the same reason that IPv4 requires one—namely, for all of the reasons stated in *Chapter 3, The Need for Mobile IP*.

12.4 How Does Mobile IPv6 Work?

This section provides a high-level overview of the Mobile IPv6 solution. We examine each of the components in more detail throughout the chapter.

Mobile IPv6 borrows many of the concepts and terminology of Mobile IPv4, as shown in Table 12-1. We still have mobile nodes and home agents but there are no foreign agents. The concepts of home address, home link, care-of address,

Mobile IPv4 Concept	Equivalent Mobile IPv6 Concept
Mobile node, home agent, home link, foreign link	*(same)*
Mobile node's home address	Globally routable home address and link-local home address
Foreign agent	A "plain" IPv6 router on the foreign link (foreign agent no longer exists)
Foreign agent care-of address	All care-of addresses are collocated
Collocated care-of address	
Care-of address obtained via Agent Discovery, DHCP, or manually	Care-of address obtained via Stateless Address Autoconfiguration, DHCP, or manually
Agent Discovery	Router Discovery
Authenticated registration with home agent	Authenticated notification of home agent and other correspondents
Routing to mobile nodes via tunneling	Routing to mobile nodes via tunneling and source routing
Route optimization via separate protocol specification.	Integrated support for route optimization.

Table 12-1 Comparison Between IPv6 and IPv4 Mobility

and foreign link are roughly the same as in Mobile IPv4. Mobile IPv6, however, makes use of both tunneling *and* source routing to deliver packets to mobile nodes connected to a foreign link, the former being the only mechanism used in Mobile IPv4. The high-level functions of Mobile IPv6 are the same as in Mobile IPv4 and roughly correspond to the three components of Mobile IPv4: Agent Discovery, Registration, and Routing.

12.4.1 What Are the Mobile IPv6 Components?

The operation of Mobile IPv6 can be summarized as follows:

- a mobile node determines its current location using the IPv6 version of Router Discovery;
- the mobile node acts like any fixed host or router when connected to its home link; otherwise, in the case of a foreign link ...
- a mobile node uses IPv6-defined address autoconfiguration to acquire a (collocated) care-of address on the foreign link;
- the mobile node notifies its home agent of its care-of address;
- the mobile node also reports its care-of address to selected correspondents, assuming it can do so securely;
- packets sent by correspondents that are ignorant of the mobile node's care-of address are routed just as in Mobile IPv4—namely, they are routed to the mobile node's home network, where the home agent tunnels them to the care-of address;

- packets sent by correspondents that know the mobile node's care-of address are sent directly to the mobile node using an *IPv6 Routing Header*, which specifies the mobile node's care-of address as an intermediate destination;

- in the reverse direction, packets sent by a mobile node are routed directly to their destination using no special mechanisms; however, in the presence of ingress filtering, the mobile node can tunnel packets to its home agent using its care-of address as the IP Source Address of the tunnel. (See *What Does Mobile IP Do about Ingress Filtering?* on page 211 for more information about ingress filtering.)

In the remaining sections we describe each of these components in detail. Before doing so, however, we should take a quick look at *IPv6 Neighbor Discovery* [RFC 1970], which defines many of the functions that are used in Mobile IPv6.

12.4.2 What Is IPv6 Neighbor Discovery?

Neighbor Discovery for IP version 6 [RFC 1970] contains a smorgasbord of functions that relate to how nodes discover and interact with neighboring nodes on their current link. Table 12-2 lists these functions along with their closest analogues in IPv4.

IPv6 Neighbor Discovery Functions	Similar IPv4 Functionality	Description
Router Discovery	ICMP Router Discovery [RFC 1256]	How nodes locate routers on their link.
Prefix Discovery	DHCP [RFC 2131] or Manual Configuration	How nodes determine the network-prefix(es) assigned to the current link.
Parameter Discovery	Manual Configuration	How nodes learn such things as the link MTU and a reasonable value to put in the Hop Limit (Time to Live) field.
Address Autoconfiguration	DHCP [RFC 2131]	How nodes automatically obtain an IP address for use on an interface.
Address Resolution	ARP [RFC 826]	How nodes determine the link-layer address of a neighbor whose IP address is known.
Next-Hop Determination	Routing Table Searches	How nodes choose a Next Hop for any outgoing packets.
Neighbor Unreachability Detection	(No standard mechanism)	How nodes determine that a neighbor is no longer reachable.
Duplicate Address Detection	(No standard mechanism)	How nodes determine that their respective addresses are unique.
Redirect	ICMP Redirect [RFC 792]	How routers inform nodes of a better choice for a Next Hop to a destination.

Table 12-2 Neighbor Discovery Functions

We explain each of these functions in detail within the specific section where we show how they are used in Mobile IPv6.

12.5 How Does a Mobile Node Determine Its Location?

This section describes Mobile IPv6 Agent Discovery, the process by which a mobile node:

- determines whether it is currently connected to its home link or a foreign link;
- detects whether it has moved from one link to another; and
- obtains a care-of address when connected to a foreign link.

The rest of this section describes how mobile nodes, routers, and home agents cooperate to accomplish these functions.

12.5.1 What Is ICMPv6 Router Discovery?

ICMPv6 Router Discovery is very similar to Mobile IPv4 Agent Discovery as described in *What Is Agent Discovery?* on page 65. Router Discovery, as defined in the *IPv6 Neighbor Discovery* document [RFC 1970], consists of two messages: *Router Solicitations* and *Router Advertisements*. As before, *Router Advertisements* are periodically transmitted as broadcasts by routers and home agents on each of their attached links. *Router Solicitations* are sent by mobile nodes that are too impatient to wait for the next periodically transmitted *Router Advertisement*. As in Mobile IPv4, Router Discovery messages are not required to be authenticated.

Router Discovery Message Formats

An *ICMPv6 Router Solicitation* message is shown in Figure 12-3. Once again, there's not much to say about this message: a router or home agent that receives one from a mobile node should immediately respond by sending a *Router Advertisement*. Assuming that no IPv6 extension headers are present, the IPv6 Next Hop field is set to 58 (ICMPv6) and the ICMPv6 Type field is set to 133 to identify the message as a *Router Solicitation*.

An *ICMPv6 Router Advertisement* message is shown in Figure 12-4. Rather than get mired in the details of IPv6, we will describe only the fields of the *Router Advertisement* which are relevant to Mobile IPv6.

If the Router Lifetime field is nonzero, then the router sending the advertisement, as identified by the IPv6 Source Address field, may be used by the mobile node as a default router. If the advertisement contains one or more Prefix Identification Options, then the mobile node can use the listed Prefixes both to perform move detection and to determine if it is connected to its home link, as described in the next two paragraphs.

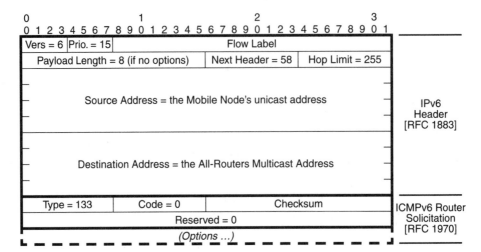

Figure 12-3 ICMPv6 Router Solicitation

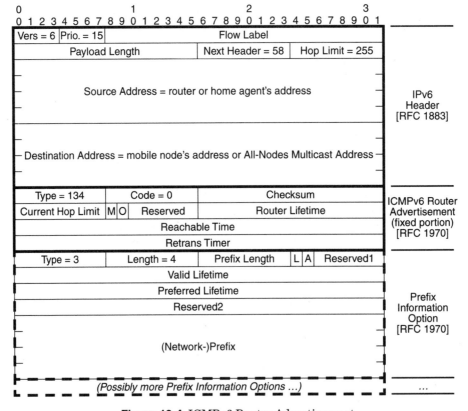

Figure 12-4 ICMPv6 Router Advertisement

Location and Movement Detection

First of all, the mobile node examines the network-prefixes contained in a received advertisement. If any of these prefixes match the network-prefix of the mobile node's home address, then the mobile node is connected to its home link. At this point, the mobile node should inform its home agent that it has returned home, as described in *What Is Notification?* on page 261.

Otherwise, if none of the prefixes matches the network-prefix of the mobile node's home address, then the mobile node is connected to a foreign link. At this point, the mobile node compares the prefixes in the most recently received advertisement with those of previous advertisements to see if it has moved. This procedure is the same as for IPv4 (see *Move Detection Using Network-Prefixes* on page 69).

If the mobile node has moved, then it should acquire a care-of address on the new link by one of the two methods described in the next section. The M bit informs the mobile node which of these two methods it should use. Once the mobile node obtains a care-of address, it should inform both its home agent and an appropriate set of correspondents of its new care-of address, as described in *What Is Notification?* on page 261.

12.5.2 How Does a Mobile Node Obtain a Care-of Address?

This section describes the two methods by which a mobile node can acquire a care-of address, once it determines that it is connected to a foreign link. Recall that there is no such thing as a foreign agent in Mobile IPv6, so the only type of care-of address in Mobile IPv6 is the collocated care-of address. A mobile node uses the M bit in any received *Router Advertisements* to determine which method should be used. If the M bit is equal to 1, then the mobile node uses Stateful Address Autoconfiguration, otherwise the mobile node uses Stateless Address Autoconfiguration. These methods are described in the next two sections.

What Is Stateful Address Autoconfiguration?

Mobile nodes can acquire a care-of address by "Stateful Address Autoconfiguration," which is a fancy way of saying, "from a server that remembers what address it handed out to whom." In this method, the mobile node simply asks a server for an address and uses that address as a care-of address. As in IPv4, one protocol for "stateful" address assignment is the *Dynamic Host Configuration Protocol for IPv6 (DHCPv6)* [draft-ietf-dhc-dhcpv6-10.txt]. DHCPv6 is very similar to DHCP for IPv4 which we described in *How Does a Node Obtain an IP Address?* on page 20. Also, PPP's *IPv6 Configuration Protocol* [RFC 2023] provides a method by which a server can provide a mobile node with a care-of address.

What Is Stateless Address Autoconfiguration?

Mobile nodes can also acquire a care-of address by "Stateless Address Auto-configuration," which is a fancy way of saying "automatically." Stateless Address Autoconfiguration [RFC 1971] is new to IPv6, meaning that there is no similar functionality defined in IPv4. Simplifying greatly, Stateless Address Autoconfiguration works as follows:

- The mobile node first forms an *interface token*, a link-dependent identifier for the interface by which it connects to the foreign link. The interface token is typically the node's link-layer address on that interface. For example, on Ethernet, the interface token would be the mobile node's 48-bit Ethernet address as described in [RFC 1972].

- The mobile node examines the Prefix Information Options that are contained within *Router Advertisements* to determine the valid network-prefixes on the current link.

- The mobile node forms a care-of address by concatenating one of the valid network-prefixes with the interface token.

Address Autoconfiguration, both stateful as described in the previous section and stateless as described in the current section, contains mechanisms by which a node can determine whether the address it has acquired is identical to an address being used by any other node on the link. If there is such a duplicate address, then the autoconfiguration protocols define ways in which a unique address can be acquired by the node.

12.6 How Does a Mobile Node Inform Other Nodes of Its Care-of Address?

This section will describe the Mobile IPv6 equivalent of Mobile IPv4 Registration, which is used by mobile nodes to inform their home agent and various other nodes of their current care-of address. Unfortunately, no term is given for this function in the latest Mobile IPv6 document [draft-ietf-mobileip-ipv6-02.txt]. We will use the term *Notification,* which is reasonably descriptive and also has the virtue of being different from the term *Registration,* because, as we will see, Mobile IPv6 Notification is very different from Mobile IPv4 Registration.

In Mobile IPv4, mobile nodes inform their home agent of their care-of address through registration messages carried within UDP/IP packets. In contrast, mobile nodes in Mobile IPv6 use *Destination Options* to inform various other nodes of their care-of address. This section explores these operations in detail.

12.6.1 What Is Notification?

Mobile IPv6 Notification is the method by which a mobile node informs both its home agent and various correspondent nodes of its current care-of address. The home agent uses the care-of address as the exit-point of a tunnel to get packets to the mobile node when it is connected to a foreign link, as in Mobile IPv4. In addition, correspondent nodes use the care-of address to route packets directly to the mobile node, without requiring the packet to be routed first to the mobile node's home agent. Thus, Mobile IPv6 has built-in support for route optimization. Mobile nodes must also notify their home agents when they return to their home link.

Like Mobile IPv4 Registration, Notification consists of a simple exchange of messages. However, Mobile IPv6 Notification uses an extension to the IPv6 packet header to realize its exchange, whereas Mobile IPv4 uses messages within the payload of UDP/IP packets. We will see this in more detail in the next section.

12.6.2 What Are the Common Notification Scenarios?

Mobile IPv6 Notification consists of an exchange of a *Binding Update* and a *Binding Acknowledgment* between a mobile node and a home agent or correspondent node, possibly prompted by the mobile node receiving a *Binding Request*. The message exchange for common scenarios is as follows:

1. A mobile node connects to a foreign link and informs its home agent of its new care-of address:

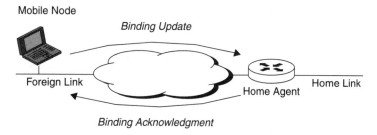

2. A mobile node connects to a foreign link and informs a correspondent node of its new care-of address:

3. A mobile node returns to its home link and informs its home agent that it is no longer attached to a foreign link:

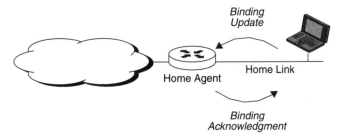

12.6.3 What Is the Notification Protocol?

In some cases, a correspondent node initiates the notification process by sending a *Binding Request* to a mobile node. Otherwise, the mobile node initiates the process by sending a *Binding Update* (unprompted by any *Binding Request*). In both cases, the mobile node sends a *Binding Update* to its home agent or a correspondent node to inform them of its current care-of address. The mobile node can specify within a *Binding Update* whether or not the receiver should respond by sending a *Binding Acknowledgment* to the mobile node. The *Binding Acknowledgment* tells the mobile node first that the original *Binding Update* was received and second whether it was accepted or rejected.

12.6.4 What Messages Are Used in Notification?

The three messages defined for Mobile IPv6 Notification are *Binding Updates, Binding Acknowledgments*, and *Binding Requests*. All of these messages are encoded as options to be carried within a *Destination Options Header* (i.e., an IPv6 extension header). This means that the options are examined only by the ultimate destination and not by any of the routers along the path. These options are now examined in detail.

Binding Update

An IPv6 packet containing a Binding Update Option is shown in Figure 12-5. Note that the figure depicts the Binding Update Option the way it *should* be and not necessarily the way it is defined in the latest Mobile IPv6 document. A *Binding Update* is sent by a mobile node to its home agent or to a correspondent node to inform them of its current care-of address.

As the figure suggests, a Binding Update Option either can be sent within a stand-alone IPv6 packet (i.e., one containing no user data) or can be "piggybacked" on an existing IPv6 packet (i.e., one containing user data). To simplify the discussion, we will define a *Binding Update* to be any IPv6 packet that contains a Binding Update Option, whether piggybacked or not. The minimum length of a *Binding Update* is 112 bytes, approximately 50% larger than a Mobile IPv4 *Registration Request* (including UDP/IP headers). Such is the cost of 16-byte IPv6 addresses!

As with IPv4 registration messages, *Binding Updates* are required to be authenticated. Mobile IPv6 uses the *IP Authentication Header* [RFC 1826] to carry the authentication data. Once again, Keyed-MD5 authentication with manual key distribution must be supported by any Mobile IPv6 implementation.

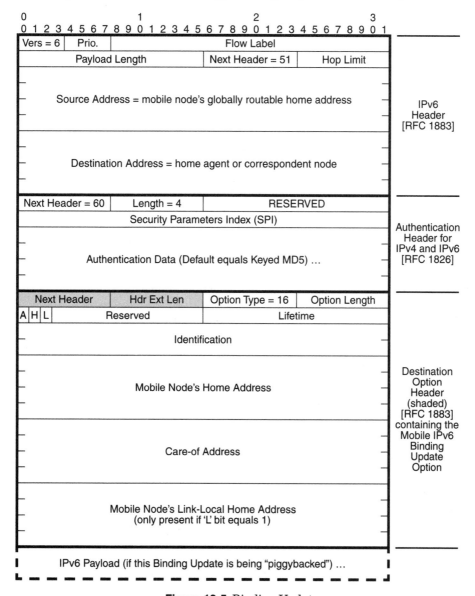

Figure 12-5 Binding Update

As before, an implementation may support any other authentication algorithms and key distribution mechanisms it desires.

The fields within the Binding Update Option itself are specified as follows. As always, the Option Type and Option Length fields identify the kind and the size of the option, respectively. The A bit is set by the mobile node to request that the receiver of the option send a *Binding Acknowledgment*, which allows the mobile node to determine if the *Binding Update* actually made it to the intended recipient. The H bit is set by the mobile node to inform the recipient that the mobile node wishes it to serve as a home agent.

The Lifetime, Identification, Mobile Node's Home Address, and Care-of Address fields are identical to the corresponding fields in the Mobile IPv4 *Registration Request*. Note that both the Mobile Node's Home Address and the Care-of Address fields must contain globally routable unicast addresses.

The L bit may be set by the mobile node if it wishes to receive packets destined not only to its globally routable home address but also to its link-local home address. (See *IPv6 Address Types* on page 250 for a discussion of these different types of addresses.) If so, the mobile node includes this address in the Mobile Node's Link-Local Home Address field, which may be present only if the L bit is set to 1.

Binding Acknowledgment

An IPv6 packet containing a Binding Acknowledgment Option is shown in Figure 12-6. Once again, this figure depicts the *Binding Acknowledgment* as it *should* be and not necessarily as it is defined in the latest draft. A *Binding Acknowledgment* is sent to a mobile node by a home agent or any other correspondent node to indicate that it has successfully received the mobile node's *Binding Update*. The A bit in the received *Binding Update* indicates whether an acknowledgment should be sent.

As with the *Binding Update*, a *Binding Acknowledgment* can be sent within a stand-alone IPv6 packet or can be "piggybacked" on an IPv6 packet that contains user data. A *Binding Acknowledgment* is sent to a mobile node in the same way that a node would send any other packet to the mobile node, as we will see in *How Are Packets Routed to and from Mobile Nodes?* on page 270. For now we note that the sender might be required to include a *Routing Header* in order for the packet to be delivered to the mobile node.

The minimum length of a *Binding Acknowledgment* is 96 bytes, compared to the 70-byte *Registration Reply* in Mobile IPv4. *Binding Acknowledgments* have the same authentication requirements as *Binding Updates* (see *Binding Update* on page 262).

The fields within the Binding Acknowledgment Option itself are specified as follows. As always, the Option Type and Option Length fields identify the kind and the size of the option, respectively. The Status field is equivalent to the Code field in a Mobile IPv4 *Registration Reply*—it tells the mobile node whether the *Binding Update* was accepted or rejected (and why). The Refresh field tells the mobile node how long the sender of the *Binding Acknowledgment* is willing to store the mobile node's current care-of address in its memory and, therefore, how often the mobile node should send *Binding Updates* to that node. The Lifetime, Identification, and Mobile Node's Home Address fields are simply copied from the corresponding fields in the *Binding Update*.

Binding Request

An IPv6 packet containing a Binding Request Option is shown in Figure 12-7. A *Binding Request* is sent to a mobile node by a correspondent node to request that the mobile node send it a *Binding Update*. That is, a *Binding Request* indicates that the correspondent would like to know the mobile node's care-of address. This is useful when the Lifetime in an original *Binding Update* is near expiration and the correspondent node has reason to believe that it will continue to send packets to the mobile node.

A *Binding Request* should be "piggybacked" on an IPv6 packet containing user data—after all, if there is no data transfer occurring between the sending

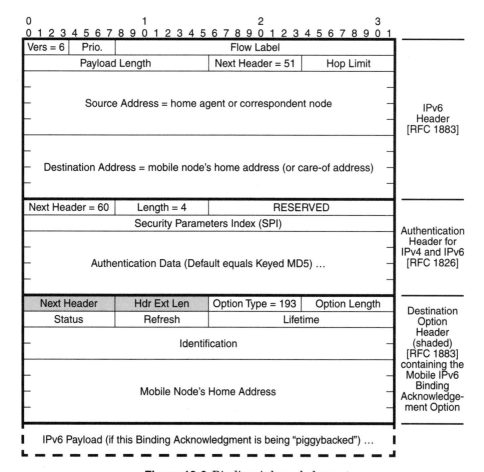

Figure 12-6 Binding Acknowledgment

node and a mobile node then the correspondent does not need to know the mobile node's care-of address. The *Binding Request* can be encoded in very few bytes, as shown in Figure 12-7. *Binding Requests* need not be authenticated, because they are only advisory in nature—a mobile node should (but need not) respond by sending a *Binding Update* to the requesting node.

12.6.5 How Does the Mobile Node Know the Address of Its Home Agent?

Frequently, mobile nodes in IPv6 will be configured manually with the IPv6 address of their home agent. The methods by which a mobile node dynamically ascertains its home agent's IPv6 address are currently under study. However, one promising method, based upon the Mobile IPv4 mechanism, is described in this section.

Recall that Mobile IPv4 allows mobile nodes to discover home agents by setting the Home Agent field of its *Registration Request* to the prefix-directed broadcast address of its home link. The registration is then received by all home agents on the link, which reject the registration but supply the mobile node with their unicast address in the reply. In a subsequent *Registration Request*, the mobile node can use the unicast address of one of these home agents.

In IPv6, however, there is no such thing as a broadcast address per se, and there is no easy way to create a multicast address for every possible link which could potentially serve as some mobile node's home link. However, the *IPv6 Addressing Architecture* [RFC 1884] does define a *Subnet-Router Anycast*

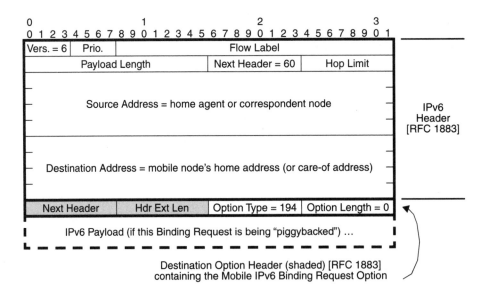

Figure 12-7 Binding Request

Address. Packets sent to this address are delivered to exactly one router on the link whose network-prefix is present in the address. However, this is not exactly what we want—for two reasons:

1. IPv6 routers are not required to be home agents. Therefore, a packet containing a subnet-router anycast address might be delivered to a router that does not implement home agent functionality. In this case, the mobile node would ascertain the address of a router which specifically *cannot* serve as its home agent! This is not entirely useful.

2. Even if the router that receives the anycast is a home agent for some nodes, it might not be *the* home agent for the specific mobile node that sent the anycast packet. (This might be the case if there are so many mobile nodes that a single home agent could not possibly handle all of their combined traffic.) Thus, we want the mobile node's packet to be delivered to *all* of the home agents on the home link, not just one of the home agents.

The way we can solve this problem is to have the mobile node tunnel *something* to the subnet-router anycast address, where *something* is a packet that will be sent to all home agents on the mobile node's home link. The closest thing currently defined in IPv6 is the "all routers on this link" multicast address. Since all home agents are required to be routers (recall the discussion in *Zombie Alert!* on page 56), this multicast address is sufficient, if not optimal, for our purposes.

Thus a mobile node which wishes to dynamically ascertain the address of a home agent builds an (inner) IPv6 packet in which it places a Binding Update Option within a *Destination Option Header*. The Destination Address of this inner packet is set to the "all routers on this link" multicast address and the Source Address is set to the mobile node's home address. The mobile node then encapsulates this inner packet within an outer packet whose Destination Address is the subnet-router anycast address and forwards the resulting packet over its current link to its default router.

This encapsulated packet will be delivered by IPv6 to "any" router that connects to the mobile node's home link. The router will then decapsulate the packet, revealing the inner packet, which is destined to the "all routers on this link" multicast address. The decapsulating router then multicasts the inner packet on the mobile node's home link (using the Source Address field of the inner packet to select the appropriate Interface), where it will be received by all home agents on that link. (Of course, it will also be received by routers that are not home agents, but they will ignore it.)

Home agents that receive these *Binding Updates* perform similar processing as did their counterparts in Mobile IPv4. Namely, all home agents that receive *Binding Updates* within multicast packets are required to reject the *Binding Update* by sending a *Binding Acknowledgment* in which they place their globally routable IPv6 unicast address. The mobile node collects these rejections and then selects one of the home agents to which to send a subsequent *Binding Update*.

12.6.6 When Should Mobile Nodes Send Binding Updates?

This section will explore the conditions under which a mobile node should send *Binding Updates* to its home agent and to various correspondent nodes. Also, we will determine which correspondent nodes should receive *Binding Updates* and which should not.

When Does a Mobile Node Send Binding Updates to Its Home Agent?

A mobile node that moves to a new link acquires a care-of address on that link (as described in *How Does a Mobile Node Obtain a Care-of Address?* on page 259) and then immediately sends a *Binding Update* to its home agent. The *Binding Update* has the H bit set to 1 to indicate that the mobile node expects the receiving node to act as its home agent. Also the A bit is set to 1 to request that the home agent send a *Binding Acknowledgment* upon receiving the *Binding Update*. As in Mobile IPv4, the *Binding Update* is retransmitted by the mobile node until it receives a *Binding Acknowledgment*.

When Does a Mobile Node Send Binding Updates to Correspondent Nodes?

As we will see in *How Do Correspondents That Know the Care-of Address Send Packets to a Mobile Node?* on page 270, correspondent nodes that have received a *Binding Update* from a mobile node can send packets directly to that mobile node without the packets being routed first to the mobile node's home link. Thus, it is desirable for a mobile node to send *Binding Updates* to correspondent nodes with which it will be communicating while connected to a given link. This section will explore the ramifications of certain policies that a mobile node might use to decide whether or not it should send a *Binding Update* to a given correspondent node.

The Correspondent Node and the Mobile Node Must Share a Security Association

Because all packets containing *Binding Updates* must also include an *IP Authentication Header*, a mobile node may send *Binding Updates* only to those correspondents with which it can develop a security association. In the absence of an Internet-wide key management infrastructure, developing such a security association can be extraordinarily difficult—manual configuration of authentication keys is frequently the only alternative. The question we wish to answer, therefore, is this: Assuming that the mobile node can develop a security association with a correspondent node, should the mobile node send it a *Binding Update,* and, if so, when and how often?

The Correspondent Node Must Understand the Binding Update

We can go a step further by ruling out those correspondent nodes which do not understand the Binding Update Option. Fortunately, IPv6 options are encoded in such a way that when a node receives an option it does not understand, the node knows whether to ignore the option or to send an ICMPv6 error message to the sender. The Binding Update Option takes the latter approach, such that a mobile node can determine whether a correspondent node understands the Binding Update Option. This helps narrow our search a little more, but we still do not know to which of the remaining correspondent nodes a mobile node should send *Binding Updates*.

Other Considerations

One goal in developing a policy is not to waste network resources. Since *Binding Updates* are quite large, especially those sent as stand-alone packets, it is desirable for a mobile node to send them only to nodes for which it has user data to send.

Another challenge is to make sure that correspondent nodes do not have *stale* information about a mobile node's care-of address. Stale information is that which is obsolete. For example, a correspondent node that knew the mobile node's care-of address at an old link, but not at the mobile node's current link, would have stale information about the mobile node's care-of address. Such a correspondent node will source-route packets to the old link, making them undeliverable to the mobile node (see *How Do Correspondents That Know the Care-of Address Send Packets to a Mobile Node?* on page 270). Thus, a second goal of this policy is to minimize the stale information in correspondent nodes.

Creating such a policy is very difficult in practice. The Mobile IP working group is in the process of writing such a policy as part of the Mobile IPv6 effort. Below we take a look at a policy which looks promising and is described in the most recent Mobile IPv6 document [draft-ietf-mobileip-ipv6-02.txt].

An Example Policy

The mobile node keeps a list of nodes to whom it has sent a *Binding Update*. When the mobile node moves to a new link, it sends a new *Binding Update* to all nodes on the list whose previous *Binding Updates* have not yet expired (recall the Lifetime field in a Binding Update Option). However, the mobile node does not send these new *Binding Updates* immediately if it has reason to believe that it will soon have an IPv6 packet with user data to send to the correspondent node. In this way the mobile node tries to minimize network overhead by piggybacking as many *Binding Updates* as possible.

12.7 How Are Packets Routed to and from Mobile Nodes?

In this section we examine how packets are routed to and from mobile nodes in Mobile IPv6. Because mobile nodes send and receive packets just like any other (fixed) node when they are connected to their home link, the remainder of this section assumes that a mobile node is connected to a foreign link. Also, we assume that the mobile node has already notified its home agent of its current care-of address, as described in *How Does a Mobile Node Inform Other Nodes of Its Care-of Address?* on page 260.

12.7.1 How Do Correspondents That Know the Care-of Address Send Packets to a Mobile Node?

A correspondent node that knows a mobile node's care-of address sends packets directly to the mobile node using an *IPv6 Routing Header.* These packets do not necessarily pass through the mobile node's home agent; rather, they take an optimal route from the correspondent node to the mobile node. The remainder of this section describes how the *Routing Header* works.

The *IPv6 Routing Header,* as defined in [RFC 1883], contains a list of intermediate destinations that a packet containing the header must visit along its path to the ultimate destination. Note that, especially in Mobile IPv6, a mobile node's care-of address makes a fine choice for such an intermediate destination, since the care-of address is collocated with the mobile node itself. Thus, a correspondent node specifies the mobile node's care-of address as the lone intermediate destination within a *Routing Header* in order to route a packet directly to the mobile node at its current location.

Figure 12-8 shows an IPv6 packet as it would look just after being transmitted by a correspondent node. The correspondent node puts the intermediate destination—the mobile node's care-of address—in the IPv6 Destination Address field, puts the ultimate destination—the mobile node's home address—within the *Routing Header,* and forwards the packet through the network. IPv6 specifies that the *Routing Header* is inspected only by the node whose address appears in the IPv6 Destination Address field and is ignored by any intervening routers.

When the packet gets to the IPv6 Destination Address—the mobile node's care-of address (which is collocated with the mobile node itself)—the mobile node looks within the *Routing Header* and finds its home address as the ultimate destination of the IPv6 packet. Thus, the mobile node "consumes" the packet by sending it to the higher-layer protocol indicated by the Next Header field within the *Routing Header.*

12.7.2 How Do Correspondents That Do Not Know the Care-of Address Send Packets to a Mobile Node?

If a correspondent node does not know a mobile node's care-of address, then it sends packets to the mobile node just as it would send packets to any other (fixed) node. In this case, the correspondent node simply places the mobile node's home address—the only address it knows—in the IPv6 Destination Address field and places its own address in the IPv6 Source Address field. The correspondent node then forwards the packet to a suitable Next Hop, as determined by examining its IPv6 routing table.

A packet sent in this way will be routed toward the mobile node's home link in the same way as in Mobile IPv4. There, the home agent will intercept the packet and tunnel it to the care-of address. The mobile node decapsulates the packet, sees that the inner packet is destined to its home address, and passes the inner packet up to the higher-layer protocol.

So far, what we have described is identical to packet routing in Mobile IPv4. However, in Mobile IPv6, the mobile node interprets the presence of the tunnel to mean that the correspondent node does not know the mobile node's current care-of address. Thus, if the mobile node can develop (or already has) a security association with that correspondent node, then the mobile node might send a *Binding Update* to it, based upon its policy for sending *Binding Updates* (see *When Does a Mobile Node Send Binding Updates to Correspondent Nodes?* on page 268). Once this occurs, the correspondent node can then send packets directly to the mobile node as described in *How Do Correspondents That Know the Care-of Address Send Packets to a Mobile Node?* on page 270.

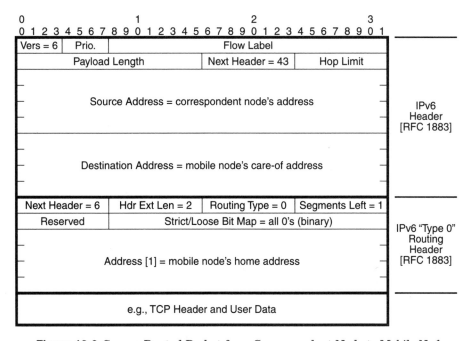

Figure 12-8 Source-Routed Packet from Correspondent Node to Mobile Node

12.7.3 How Do Mobile Nodes Send Packets?

When a mobile node is connected to a foreign link, it must have a way to determine a router that can forward packets generated by the mobile node. This is easier in Mobile IPv6 than it was in Mobile IPv4, because *all* IPv6 routers are required to implement Router Discovery (the same is not true for IPv4 routers). Thus, a mobile node can select any router on the foreign link from which it has received *Router Advertisements*. The mobile node configures its routing table such that all packets it generates are sent to this router.

12.8 Chapter Summary

This chapter began with a description of IPv6, the next version of the Internet Protocol, which is designed to improve upon the shortcomings of the current version (IPv4). IPv6 has much larger addresses and better support for header extensions and options than does IPv4. IPv6 also defines many functions, collectively known as Neighbor Discovery, which can be used directly to provide some of the functions required by Mobile IPv6. For more information on IPv6 itself, see [Huitema97].

Next we examined Mobile IPv6 and showed how this rich functionality of IPv6 provides many convenient features required by any mobility solution, such as Address Autoconfiguration and Router Discovery. We saw how mobile nodes use *Router Advertisements* to determine their current link and use Stateless Address Autoconfiguration to acquire a collocated care-of address on a foreign link. We also saw how foreign agents were no longer required in Mobile IPv6 because of the immensity of the IPv6 address space and the fact that all routers are required to implement Router Discovery.

In Mobile IPv6, a mobile node notifies not only its home agent but also certain correspondent nodes of its current care-of address. This allows correspondents which know the mobile node's care-of address to route packets directly to the mobile node using a *Routing Header*. Packets sent by correspondents that do not know the care-of address are routed just as in Mobile IPv4—namely, they are routed to the home link where the home agent tunnels them to the care-of address. Also as in Mobile IPv4, packets sent by mobile nodes are routed directly to their destination, without the need for any special routing mechanisms.

Open Issues

In this chapter we describe several areas in which further research and standardization efforts are required with respect to mobility. The first has to do with the performance of reliable transport-layer protocols in the presence of mobility and wireless links. Thus we describe TCP and then investigate the impact that mobility has upon its assumptions and therefore its performance. Then we look at real-time traffic, its support in the Internet via RSVP, and the impact of mobility upon RSVP and real-time traffic. Finally we look at service location, a way in which mobile nodes can discover and make use of resources available on their home or foreign networks.

13.1 TCP Performance and Mobility

In this section we describe the impact of mobility on TCP, the Internet's reliable transport-layer protocol. First we provide an overview of TCP, focusing on the assumptions it makes about the Internet. Then we see how these assumptions affect its performance in the presence of mobile nodes which move before receiving packets sent to their old location. We then provide a summary of the research in this area that attempts to address the resulting performance problems.

We begin by giving a high-level overview of TCP. This introduction is necessarily brief for two reasons. First, TCP is very complicated and it would require doubling the size of this book to give a thorough treatment to the topic. Second, other authors have already provided such treatments and have done so extremely well. One of my favorite references for TCP (and IP, for that matter) is Douglas Comer's *Internetworking with TCP/IP* [Come95]. Also highly recommended is *TCP/IP Illustrated* [Stev94].

13.1.1 What Is TCP?

The *Transmission Control Protocol (TCP)* [RFC 793] is the reliable, transport-layer protocol in the Internet. It is characterized by the following attributes:

- TCP provides a *reliable* service to applications, meaning that TCP guarantees that the application's data is delivered to the ultimate destination sequentially and error-free.
- TCP provides *full-duplex, stream-oriented* communications, meaning that information can flow simultaneously in both directions between two communicating nodes.
- TCP is *connection-oriented*, meaning that it has three distinct phases: connection establishment, data transfer, and connection close.

A transport-layer protocol generally accepts data from the application layer, chops it up into optimally sized chunks, prepends a transport-layer header to those chunks to form *segments*, and transmits each segment as the payload portion of a network-layer packet. In the specific case of TCP, the transport-layer header is a TCP header and the TCP segment is transmitted in the payload of an IP packet, as shown in Figure 13-1.

13.1.2 How Does TCP work?

TCP has many attributes which work together to provide a reliable service to the application layer. Each of these is described briefly in this section.

Error Detection

TCP detects errors in transmission by use of a *checksum*. The sender computes a checksum over contents of the TCP segment (and portions of the IP

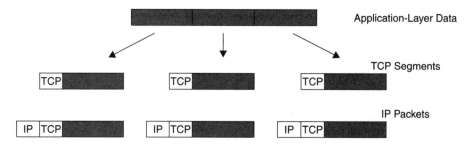

Figure 13-1 Application-Layer Data, TCP Segments, and IP Packets

header), places it in the TCP Checksum field, and transmits the packet to the receiver. At the receiver, the checksum is computed and compared with that in the Checksum field. If they are not identical, then an error has occurred in transmission and the packet is discarded by the receiver.

Error Correction

TCP corrects errors through *acknowledgments* and *retransmissions*. An acknowledgment is a message that informs a sender that its data has been received correctly by the intended recipient. If a sender does not receive an acknowledgment in a "reasonable amount of time," then it assumes that the data (or the acknowledgment, it really doesn't matter which) has been lost and therefore that the data should be retransmitted.

The trick is figuring out how long is "reasonable" in this context. Premature retransmissions waste network bandwidth, while overdue retransmissions slow down the speed with which an application can transfer data. TCP performs an algorithm by which it estimates the *round-trip time*—the time it is supposed to take a packet to go from the source to the destination and for the acknowledgment to make it back to the original source—and how much that round-trip time varies. TCP uses the round-trip time estimate and variance to make an educated guess as to how long to wait before concluding that a packet has been lost.

Because TCP is full-duplex, a first node can acknowledge previously received data at the same time, and within the same packet, that it sends its own data to the second node. Because of the layout of the TCP header, piggybacking an acknowledgment in this way requires zero bytes over-and-above the data being sent to that second node. In contrast, a stand-alone acknowledgment has a minimum length of 40 bytes—20 for the TCP header and 20 for the IP header. For this reason, a receiving node might delay the transmission of an acknowledgment, waiting for opportunities to piggyback the acknowledgment atop a packet containing user data.

Sliding Windows

If a TCP node simply transmitted a segment and waited for an acknowledgment before sending any further segments, then it would spend an awful lot of time waiting for acknowledgments. Instead, TCP allows a node to send many segments before requiring it to wait for some of them to be acknowledged. The maximum number of segments that a node is allowed to send before it must stop and wait for an acknowledgment is defined by a *window*.

As a node receives acknowledgments for the segments it has already transmitted, it can "slide" its window forward and in some cases increase the size of the window. The node is permitted to send more segments when its window slides forward or increases in this way.

Flow Control

A sliding window provides a mechanism for preventing a fast sender from overwhelming a slow receiver with more data than it can handle—a process called *flow control*. Specifically, the fast sender must wait for the slow receiver to send acknowledgments before it may send any additional segments. A first node sets the Window field within the TCP header to inform a second node how many additional segments the first node is currently willing and able to accept.

Congestion Control

Congestion is a condition where the routers of a network are overloaded with packets and are unable to forward them, because of the speed of their connected links or otherwise. In a congested network, some packets are dropped and others experience high delays, while the amount of actual data transferred goes down considerably. TCP is designed to detect congestion and to help alleviate the condition by slowing down the rate at which it transmits (or retransmits) segments.

With respect to congestion, TCP makes a fundamental assumption about the Internet. Specifically, TCP assumes that almost all of the packet loss in the Internet is due to congestion and not due to hardware, transmission, or other errors in transmitting and receiving those packets. (We examine whether or not this is valid in *Are TCP's Assumptions Regarding Congestion Correct?* on page 277.) Thus, when TCP detects a lost segment (e.g., it fails to get an acknowledgment in a reasonable amount of time), it dramatically reduces the number of segments it transmits and waits a longer time before retransmitting segments that have not yet been acknowledged.

Slow Start

When TCP detects that the congestion condition is beginning to alleviate, it begins increasing the number of segments it transmits and adjusts the time for which it waits for acknowledgments. If this increase were to occur too quickly, considering all the hosts on the Internet in aggregate, then a congestion condition might quickly return. For this reason, TCP increases this rate slowly both after a congestion condition has occurred and at the beginning of a new connection. The latter prevents a host from sending too many segments at the beginning of a new connection, wherein the host has no idea whether the Internet is capable of delivering that many segments.

Fast Retransmit

A TCP acknowledgment tells a first node how many bytes, since the start of the connection, have been received correctly *and sequentially* by a second node. In addition, TCP sends an acknowledgment only upon the receipt of a segment; that is, it does not send an acknowledgment just for the heck of it.

For example, if the second node receives segments 1 through 9 without error, then on the receipt of the 9th segment it would acknowledge receipt of all of those segments. Now consider what happens if the 10th segment is lost, but the 11th, 12th, and 13th segments arrive error-free. The second node can *still* only acknowledge the receipt of the 1st through 9th segments. Thus, the arrival of the 11th, 12th, and 13th segments will each prompt an acknowledgment that acknowledges only the receipt of segments 1 through 9.

The first node can examine the acknowledgments, notice the three identical acknowledgments, and conclude that there is a "hole" in the data—i.e., that the 10th segment was lost. The first node further concludes that this 10th segment was not lost because the network was hopelessly congested—otherwise, the other segments and their corresponding acknowledgments would not have made it through the network so easily. Therefore, the first node retransmits that 10th segment immediately, without waiting the "reasonable amount of time" it would ordinarily wait. This immediate retransmission, as described, is called *fast retransmit*.

Summary

TCP combines a number of algorithms to adapt to a variety of combinations of links, network topologies, and computational speeds. Under normal circumstances, TCP can adapt to transfer data reliably between any two hosts at speeds which approach those of the underlying links that comprise the path between those two hosts. TCP also protects the health of the Internet by detecting congestion and quickly reducing the number of packets it will transmit when congestion has occurred.

13.1.3 Are TCP's Assumptions Regarding Congestion Correct?

As mentioned in *How Does TCP work?* on page 274, TCP assumes that the overwhelming majority of lost segments and acknowledgments is due to congestion in the Internet. For most of the operational Internet, this assumption is quite valid, especially considering the optical fiber that comprises so many of its links.

However, for wireless links, this assumption is generally false—most lost packets are due to errors that occur in the transmission of packets over error-prone media such as infrared or radio-frequency links. When these errors occur, TCP mistakenly assumes that the network is congested and dramatically reduces its transmission of old and new segments. This causes the performance of TCP over wireless links to be quite poor in certain circumstances.

Similarly, consider a home agent that tunnels a packet to a mobile node's care-of address the instant before that mobile node moves to a new link. By the time the tunneled packet arrives at the mobile node's old link, the mobile node will no longer be there to receive it. Thus, TCP in the original sender will detect a lost packet, assume that there is congestion, and begin sending packets much more slowly. As we can see, two things common to mobile nodes—mobility itself and the wireless links over which mobile nodes communicate—can severely degrade the performance of TCP.

In the next section we describe some proposed enhancements to TCP which are aimed at improving its performance for wireless and mobile nodes. Before proceeding, however, it is important to note that TCP's assumption regarding congestion—largely true in most of the Internet—is quite possibly the only thing that has prevented the Internet from melting down over the past few years. Those who wish to "solve" this "problem" of TCP in the context of wireless/mobile computing should pause to ponder this for a few moments.

13.1.4 How Can TCP Performance Be Improved for Mobile Nodes?

In this section we provide a survey of ongoing research that is attempting to improve the performance of TCP when used by mobile nodes over wireless links. At this point I would like to thank Mike Pearce of Motorola Inc., who provided the information that was adapted for this section [Pear97]. The possible enhancements to TCP fall into three categories: those which can be applied to link-layer protocols, TCP itself, and application-layer protocols, respectively. The next few sections describe each of these in turn.

Link-Layer Enhancements

Many wireless link-layer protocols contain similar functionality to TCP. These link-layers tend to be tuned to the specific characteristics of the (unreliable) wireless medium over which they run. Such characteristics include the raw speed of the medium, the probability of errors, the changes in signal quality, etc. Owing to the nature of the underlying medium, wireless link-layer protocols often contain windows and error detection and correction mechanisms that are similar to those in TCP.

A problem arises when a packet is undergoing retransmission at the link layer due to errors. If it takes the link-layer many tries to get the packet across the link, there is the possibility that TCP will finish waiting its "reasonable amount of time" and retransmit the segment. When it does, and the first segment has not yet successfully traversed the link, then the link-layer protocol might find itself with two (or, eventually, more than two) copies of the same segment that it is trying to move across the link.

One promising solution is for a link-layer to examine the higher-layer protocol headers of all its frames to determine if multiple copies of the same segment are waiting to traverse the link [BSAK95]. If so, then the link-layer can discard the duplicates and attempt only to move a single copy of the segment. In practice, however, higher-layer encryption can make it impossible for link-layer protocols to "snoop" inside frames to see if segments are duplicated.

TCP Enhancements

In this section we describe four proposed enhancements to TCP itself.

Fast Retransmit for Mobile-Node Movement

Recall that when a mobile node moves to a new link, tunneled packets destined for the old link will be undeliverable, causing timeouts and congestion control to occur in the correspondent node and the mobile node itself. A mobile node knows when it moves, however, by virtue of Agent Discovery and the fact that it had to reregister at its new foreign link. [CacIft95] proposes that TCPs on mobile nodes should go into fast retransmit once they register on a new link.

This causes the mobile node to immediately transmit unacknowledged segments without going into a congestion mode. [CacIft95] also proposes that the mobile node send three duplicate acknowledgments to certain correspondents to force the correspondents to enter fast retransmit as well. Combined with slow start, which prevents the mobile node's new link from being overwhelmed with packets upon the mobile node's arrival, this provides a dramatic increase in TCP performance.

Note that this proposal involves cooperation between the Mobile IP software and the TCP software. Specifically, it requires the mobile-node software to provide an indication to TCP whenever the mobile node moves to a new link. This is an example of how the layers in the protocol stack tend to be slightly more intermingled than the abstract layering models would lead one to conclude.

For completeness we note that if the time it takes a mobile node to move from one link to another is long—specifically, the time it takes the mobile node to register at the new link and for the home agent to begin tunneling to the correct location—then the freezing enhancement we describe in *Transmission and Time-out Freezing* on page 280 can also improve TCP performance in the presence of mobile-node movement.

Connection Segmentation

One goal in devising these enhancements to TCP is to avoid modifications to the TCP software already installed in a tremendous number of nodes on the Internet. Accordingly, it is desirable to change only the software in the nodes that need such changes—namely, the mobile nodes themselves. However, there is a limit to what can be accomplished by changing the mobile node's software, if the TCP software on a correspondent node still behaves in undesirable ways.

Many proposals for dealing with this problem treat the TCP connection between a mobile node and a (presumably fixed) correspondent node as two concatenated connections. Figure 13-2 illustrates this situation, where the first con-

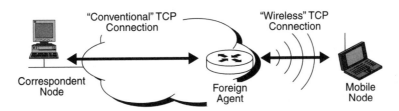

Figure 13-2 Segmented TCP Connections

nection is between a correspondent node and some intermediate node over the wired Internet and the second connection is between the intermediate node and the mobile node over some wireless link. Here, the intermediate node serves as a relay between the two TCP connections.

This approach allows the TCP in mobile nodes to be modified to be more aggressive in the presence of errors, without causing congestion and without diminishing the mobile node's ability to communicate with older TCP implementations in other nodes. Proposals along this line include those described in [BakBad95], [KoRaAl94], and [YavBag94].

Transmission and Timeout Freezing

Nodes on wireless links can experience long, though temporary, periods during which *no* data can be exchanged at all. An example of such a condition is when a mobile node in an automobile or train enters a long tunnel and the wireless signal quality approaches zero. Another example occurs when a wireless link that is shared by telephone users and data users is temporarily allocated to a cellular telephone call, temporarily preempting transmission of any data packets.

Fortunately, the link layers of various wireless systems are often capable of detecting such events. [BKVP96] proposes that such link layers inform TCP upon detecting a temporary disruption in service. In response, the TCP software would not try to send any new packets and would not make any assumptions about the presence of network congestion or about the round-trip time. Then, when service resumes, the link-layer can again signal TCP, causing it to begin transmitting once again [Pear97].

One advantage of this scheme, at least on the mobile side, is that it is unaffected by encryption. The proposed signals from the link layer to TCP are based upon the conditions of the medium and specifically not upon the contents of the data itself.

Selective Acknowledgment

In *Fast Retransmit* on page 276 we described how TCP acknowledgments are cumulative in nature, where a first node effectively tells a second node how many segments have been received both error-free *and sequentially*. While Fast Retransmit can prevent congestion control from occurring when a "hole" in the data is received, it does not always prevent a first node from sending those segments that have already been received, though out of order, by the second node.

[RFC 2018] proposes a "selective acknowledgment" scheme which would allow a node to inform another node of all segments it has received—not just those that have been received sequentially. This has the potential of preventing unnecessary retransmissions when a "hole" appears in the data. This is especially important for mobile nodes that communicate over slow (e.g., wireless) links.

Transaction TCP

Recall that TCP consists of three phases: connection establishment, data transfer, and connection close. Each of the connection-establishment and connection-close phases involves an exchange of at least three messages. For connections over which a lot of data is transferred, these three messages represent a small amount of overhead.

However, for application exchanges that are very small in nature—for example, a simple query followed by a simple response—connection establishment and close presents a rather large overhead. [RFC 1644] defines a transactional version of TCP for just such applications. This works by combining connection establishment and close packets with the packets that contain actual data. This has the potential of lowering the minimum number of packets from 7 or 8 down to 2 or 3—a considerable savings if many such applications are being run over a slow link.

Application-Layer Enhancements

There are numerous things that application developers can do to improve the performance of their applications in mobile and wireless environments. Such things include intelligent caching and distribution of information. For example, at least one vendor, who shall remain nameless, sells an E-mail package that downloads a user's entire address book (regardless of its size) from a server as soon as the application is invoked. Needless to say, such things perform miserably over slow links.

Our focus in this section, however, is on an application-layer protocol enhancement that is directly relevant to TCP and overall performance. The idea is simply to architect application-layer protocols to use a single TCP connection for all data-transfer operations instead of many such connections. An example of an application that uses many connections is the World Wide Web, whose application-layer protocol is the *HyperText Transfer Protocol (HTTP)*.

Version 1.0 of HTTP [RFC 1945] specifies that each element of a Web page—e.g., the main document itself and each image—is downloaded from the Web server to the client browser over a separate TCP connection. The problem with this is that each individual connection, due to Slow Start, spends much of its time with small windows and suboptimal transfer rates—especially when each individual text or image element is small. This also has the undesirable effect of causing the Web server to have more TCP connections open than necessary, each of which consumes memory and other resources.

Fortunately, Version 1.1 of HTTP [RFC 2068] solves this problem by allowing many elements of a Web page to be transferred over a single TCP connection. In many cases, this single connection now transfers enough data to get past the Slow Start phase and begin transferring data at nearly optimal speeds. In addition, a single connection consumes less resources on both the Web server and the client.

13.1.5 Summary

In this section we described TCP, the Internet's reliable transport-layer protocol, in some detail. We saw how TCP's assumption that lost segments are due to congestion is generally valid on much of the Internet but is not necessarily valid in wireless and mobile environments. We also saw how this assumption on the part of TCP makes it perform poorly in these latter environments.

With this background, we described several enhancements to TCP that have been proposed as part of various research projects. Many of these enhancements involved cooperation between many layers of the protocol stack—the link layer, the network layer, TCP itself, and the application layer—in order to maximize performance. Thus, this entire section illustrates that there is more to mobility than providing a way of routing packets to mobile nodes. While Mobile IP provides this packet-routing capability, it does not address these other enhancements that provide a more complete mobility solution.

13.2 RSVP and Real-Time Traffic

In this section we distinguish real-time applications and their associated traffic from other types of applications. Then we introduce RSVP as a protocol used to accommodate real-time traffic in the Internet. Finally, we discuss several issues regarding Mobile IP, specifically those relating to mobile nodes as senders and receivers of real-time traffic.

13.2.1 What Is Real-Time Traffic?

In this section we describe the distinguishing characteristic of real-time traffic and then define real-time vs. non-real-time applications.

An example

To introduce the concept of *real-time* traffic, consider an application that sends "live" audio performances over the Internet. For simplicity we assume that the sender portion of the application works as follows:

- the audio is converted continuously into a digital format (such as that found on audio Compact Discs);

- when a segment (e.g., a few tenths of a second) of audio has been collected, the sender immediately transmits the digitized audio segment within the payload portion of an IP packet;

- when the next segment of audio has been collected, it is immediately transmitted within the payload of an IP packet, etc.

Also for simplicity, we assume that there is only one receiver—i.e., that the audio is carried in unicast IP packets. The receiver performs the opposite processing, converting the digital segments as they arrive back into audio and presumably playing the recovered audio through a speaker.

For such an application to work well, the following requirements must all be fulfilled:

- most (preferably all) of the packets must arrive at the receiver;

- most (preferably all) of those packets that arrive must contain few or no errors; and

- an individual packet must arrive in a *timely enough fashion* to be pieced back into the recovered audio signal, in time for it to be played back through the speaker—otherwise, the resulting audio will contain holes, misordered passages, or other severe degradations in audio quality.

The first two requirements can be fulfilled by using TCP to perform error detection and correction. Doing so could ensure that the audio arrives at the receiver completely error-free. The third requirement—a constraint on the timing of arrival of *individual* packets at the receiver—is the distinguishing characteristic of real-time traffic.

Categories of Internet Applications

Based upon the preceding discussion, we identify two broad categories of Internet applications:

1. *Non-real-time* applications are those which place no restrictions on the time it takes any *individual* packet to arrive at the destination(s) or the time between arrival of successive packets. Examples include file-transfer applications, E-mail, remote login, and the World Wide Web. Users of these applications simply want their files, Web pages, or keystrokes—as a unit—to be transferred quickly and reliably.

2. *Real-time* applications are those which have very strict requirements for interarrival time between successive packets. Examples include audio, video, and some types of computerized games. For some real-time applications, it is more important that an individual packet arrive on time than it is that the packet arrive without error. For example, an audio application might be able to tolerate a few uncorrected bit-errors in the received, digitized audio, which might sound like background noise in the recovered audio signal. However, the audio application might be extremely intolerant of delay.

We now analyze the Internet's and IP's ability to support real-time applications.

13.2.2 Why is IP Not Well Suited to Real-Time Traffic?

Connectionless Protocols

IP is a *connectionless* protocol, meaning that if a host has a packet of data to send to a destination, then it simply sends it without having to first set up a connection or circuit to that destination. In contrast, a *connection-oriented* protocol requires a circuit to be set up between the source and the destination before any data can be exchanged. A telephone call is an example of a connection-oriented protocol.

In addition, recall the service provided by IP. IP routes packets from an original source to an ultimate destination, making no guarantees as to if, when, or how many packets might actually arrive at that destination. IP can make no such guarantees because—due to IP's connectionless nature—it is impossible for routers to predict how many packets they will need to forward at any given moment. During periods of high traffic, packets wait longer in the memory of routers before being forwarded or might even be discarded if the level of traffic is high enough.

Delay Variance

Thus, successive packets sent from the same host across the Internet to the same destination can experience widely varying amounts of delay. For many real-time applications, this delay variance—and large average delays, for that matter—make IP ill suited to real-time applications. (See *Buffering Techniques* on page 285 for techniques by which *some* real-time applications can accommodate these delay properties.)

Note that TCP can make matters worse for an application. If an IP packet containing a TCP segment arrives in error, then TCP will wait for some period of time and retransmit the segment. By the time the segment finally arrives at the receiver error-free, it will have taken at least twice as long to reach the destination. Thus, the TCP timeout-and-retransmission mechanism adds increased average delay and delay variance to an application over that experienced by IP itself.

The properties of the Internet in general, and IP in particular, which make them ill suited to real-time traffic can therefore be stated as follows:

1. Because IP is connectionless, routers have no way of reserving the CPU and memory resources required to forward with small and predictable amounts of delay those packets containing real-time, application data.

2. Many links over which IP runs similarly have no way to reserve access to the medium or bandwidth, causing unpredictable and often large delay to packets containing real-time data.

Equivalently stated, IP provides a very basic Quality of Service to higher-layer protocols. *Quality of Service* is a guaranteed level of performance that a protocol is capable of delivering to a higher-layer protocol. Here performance refers to such underlying network characteristics as bandwidth, delay, delay variance, and error rate. For example, TCP's Quality of Service guarantees error-free delivery but makes no guarantees with respect to bandwidth and delay. IP's Quality of Service guarantees none of these characteristics.

Buffering Techniques

One way an application can account for delay variance is to store a significant amount of data (e.g., audio) before playing it back to the user. At one extreme, an application can buffer no data, and any variance in delay will result in holes in the recovered audio. At the other extreme, an application can buffer *all* of the data before playing it back, guaranteeing that all individual packets have arrived before they are needed. Somewhere between these two extremes lies a compromise in which most of the packets arrive in time and only a handful of holes occur in the recovered data. This method of storing data for future use is called *buffering*.

Buffering can be sufficient for some real-time applications, most notably those which are one-way in nature. For example, someone listening to a live musical performance usually does not care if a few seconds or even a few minutes of delay are introduced by a buffering scheme.

However, buffering techniques are less attractive for interactive, two-way applications. For example, a few seconds of delay can make a conversation between two individuals extremely awkward and cumbersome, as anyone who has placed an intercontinental telephone call can attest. In the next section, we describe a general-purpose framework for supporting real-time applications in the Internet which does not suffer from the delays introduced by buffering.

13.2.3   What Is RSVP?

The *Resource reSerVation Protocol (RSVP)* [draft-ietf-rsvp-spec-16.txt] is used by a host on behalf of an application to request a given Quality of Service from the network. The RSVP working group of the Internet Engineering Task Force is chartered with defining this protocol for use in the Internet.

At a high level, a real-time application operates in two phases. In the first phase, the application uses RSVP to reserve resources in the routers along the path between the sender and the receiver. Then, the application makes use of these reservations to send real-time traffic along this same path.

How Does RSVP Work?

Figure 13-3 shows an example network in which RSVP might be used on behalf of an application. For simplicity, we focus on unicast applications while noting that RSVP scales to handle multicast applications with both many senders and many receivers.

First, the applications running in the sender and the receiver exchange messages to agree on what type of traffic will be sent and whether the receiver can accept that type of traffic. Since this exchange is not *itself* real-time traffic, these messages can be carried by UDP or TCP without any need to reserve resources. Once this agreement occurs, then the RSVP process begins as follows (see Figure 13-3):

1. In order to determine and record the path through which the application's data will ultimately traverse, the sender transmits an *RSVP Path* message to the receiver which contains:

    a. the IP address of the node sending (or forwarding) the message;

    b. the Quality of Service being requested; and

    c. a *flow* that defines *which* packets are to receive the specified Quality of Service.

The flow is specified as a set of protocol header fields that can be used by a node to distinguish the application's data packets from all others. For example, a flow can be specified by the IP Source Address, Destination Address, and Protocol fields (the latter specifying the transport-layer protocol), and optionally a transport-layer Source and/or Destination Port.

Any RSVP-aware node receiving a *Path* message swaps its own IP address with that in the sender field of item 'a' above, and forwards the message to the Next Hop along the path to the ultimate receiver.

Note that a *Path* message has an IP Destination Address of the ultimate receiver, which implies that routers along the path would normally forward them without necessarily inspecting their contents. Thus, *Path* messages must contain the IP Router Alert Option [RFC 2113], which is used to inform a router that an IP packet must be processed in a special way.

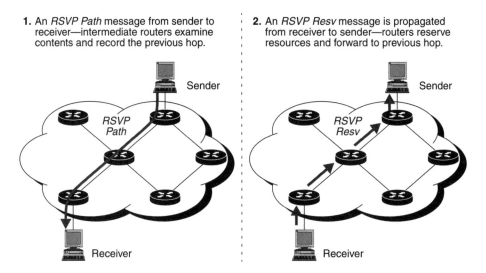

1. An *RSVP Path* message from sender to receiver—intermediate routers examine contents and record the previous hop.

2. An *RSVP Resv* message is propagated from receiver to sender—routers reserve resources and forward to previous hop.

Figure 13-3 A Simple RSVP Reservation for a Unicast, Unidirectional Flow

Ultimately, the *Path* message will arrive at the receiver.

2. In order to actually reserve resources along the path from sender to receiver, the receiver sends an *RSVP Resv* message to the node from which it received the *Path* message. A *Resv* message contains much the same information as a *Path* message:

   a. the IP address of the node sending the *Resv* message;

   b. the Quality of Service being requested; and

   c. a *flow* that defines *which* packets are to receive the specified Quality of Service.

A node receiving a *Resv* message examines the Quality of Service to determine if it has sufficient resources to fulfill the request. If so, it reserves the necessary resources (e.g., link bandwidth, CPU, memory, etc.) and sends a (possibly modified) *Resv* message to the node from which *it* received a *Path* message (which it recorded in step 1 above).

Since the IP Source and Destination Addresses of a *Resv* message are those of the node sending and receiving the *Resv* message, respectively, no IP Router Alert Option need be present in such messages.

Assuming that all routers along the path are able to fulfill the requested Quality of Service, the *Resv* message eventually arrives at the original sender.

Once resources have been reserved along the entire path, the application program within the sender begins transmitting real-time data along the path through which resources were reserved in step 2 above. An application may use a variety of transport-layer protocols (summarized in the next section) to send the actual data. These transport-layer protocols are outside the scope of RSVP.

Finally, RSVP makes reservations for a specific lifetime (not unlike Mobile IP registrations). Thus steps 1 and 2 above must be repeated periodically in order to sustain an application which lasts longer than the reservation lifetime. This further implies that the lack of such messages provide a passive way to delete reservations, though RSVP also defines messages that can be used to delete reservations actively. This periodic refreshing along with automatic timeout also provides opportunities to accommodate routing changes which alter the path between sender and receiver.

RSVP Summary

The following list summarizes the key elements of RSVP, some of which were described in previous sections:

* A host uses RSVP to request a specific Quality of Service from the network on behalf of a particular application-layer data stream or flow.

- An RSVP reservation is unidirectional. Bidirectional real-time flows require two reservations—one initiated by each of the respective receivers.

- Reservations are initiated by the receiver (once the path from the sender has been established). This allows RSVP to accommodate multicast groups with large and/or changing group membership.

- RSVP messages are carried "directly" within IP packets, like ICMP and IGMP messages.

- RSVP is not a routing protocol—it does not *select* a route for packets that are part of an application flow. Rather, it uses information provided by routing protocols to determine the path that flows from a sender would take, in order to request Quality of Service along *that* path.

- RSVP is not a transport protocol—once RSVP has been used to reserve resources along a path, an application uses an appropriate transport-layer protocol to carry the actual real-time data. Such protocols include UDP, the *Real-time Transport Protocol (RTP)* [RFC 1889], and the *Internet Stream Protocol (ST2)* [RFC 1819] among others. TCP is generally not used for the reasons described in *Delay Variance* on page 284.

- Reservations are expensive to the Internet routing infrastructure in that they give preferential treatment to some packets at the expense of others. Presumably, service providers will want to charge for the preferential Quality of Service they deliver to customers. As always, there is a strong link between billing and authentication, in order to ensure that the correct party is billed and to prevent theft-of-service attacks. A proposal for authenticating RSVP messages using Keyed MD5 is described in [draft-ietf-rsvp-md5-03.txt].

With this understanding of RSVP and real-time traffic, we now examine the issues involved in supporting real-time applications in the context of Mobile IP, where mobile nodes may be senders or receivers.

13.2.4 How Does Mobile IP Affect Real-Time Traffic?

In this section we describe the challenges of supporting real-time application flows to and from mobile nodes as they change their location. As of this writing, there is no activity within the Mobile IP working group of the Internet Engineering Task Force that is attempting to deal with these issues. Instead, the working group is addressing higher-priority items—firewall traversal, PPP interaction, reverse tunneling, and IPv6 mobility to name a few.

Thus, this section provides the author's thoughts with respect to Mobile IP and RSVP and simply highlights a few of the important problems that need to be solved in this regard. As always, we can ignore the case where a mobile node is connected to its home link, since it functions just like any fixed host or router when so connected.

Mobile Nodes as Receivers of Real-Time Traffic

The most obvious challenge to real-time traffic introduced by Mobile IP is the fact that mobile nodes change their locations—up to once per second, according to [RFC 2002]. Because RSVP reserves resources only along a specific path, the fact that the path from sender to mobile node can change relatively frequently implies that new reservations will be required every time a mobile node changes link.

In addition, we note that the path from a sender to a mobile node—in the absence of route optimization—involves a tunnel from the mobile node's home agent to its care-of address. Thus, one strategy for accommodating movement is to have the mobile node reserve resources for the (new) tunnel—from its care-of address back to the home agent—each time it moves. The path from the sender to the home agent, assuming a stationary sender, will not change very often—no more quickly than any path between fixed nodes on the Internet. Figure 13-4 illustrates this approach.

Alternatively, if route optimization is used, then the mobile node must re-reserve resources from its care-of address back to the original sender. Whether this presents an improvement depends upon the relative locations of the sender, the home agent, and the mobile node's current link. In some cases there might be rather large opportunities for savings in the number of nodes from which resources must be reserved as the mobile node moves. In other cases, the savings are negligible.

A more subtle complication introduced by Mobile IP is the presence of the tunnel itself. Recall that *RSVP Path* and *Resv* messages contain a description of the flow for which resource reservations are being requested. This flow description contains a list of packet header fields that a router can use to distinguish packets of the real-time flow—those to which the requested Quality of Service must be provided—from all other packets that might pass through the router.

Specifically, the flow description usually contains such information as the sender's and receiver's IP addresses, the IP Protocol field (which identifies the

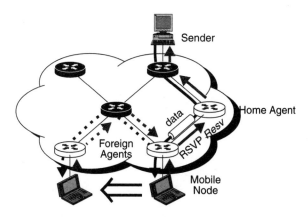

Figure 13-4 Reservations from Care-of Address to Home Agent as Mobile Node Moves

transport-layer protocol), and optionally transport-layer Port numbers. Note that *IP in IP Encapsulation* [RFC 2003] moves all of these fields to a different location within the encapsulating packet.

Thus, some way is needed to inform the intermediate routers that they should "peek within the tunnel" to determine whether the tunneled packets are deserving of special handling, in order to deliver the requested Quality of Service. Of course doing so requires more processing on the part of these intermediate routers and therefore is likely to slow them down, which implies that such a reservation might cost more than one without tunneling. The alternative, suggested in [draft-ietf-rsvp-tunnels-interop-00.txt], is for the tunneling method to include not only an (outer) IP header but also a transport-layer header (e.g., UDP), such that port numbers can be used to classify tunneled packets as well.

Furthermore, IP-level security, such as that used for firewall traversal by mobile nodes, can further complicate matters. On the one hand, the use of the *Authentication Header* simply changes the location of the fields which routers would use to classify packets in a similar way as *IP in IP Encapsulation* described previously. On the other hand, the *Encapsulating Security Payload* can render some of these fields encrypted and therefore unidentifiable to intermediate routers, making packet classification rather difficult. One solution is to introduce an extra protocol layer (e.g., UDP), below the encrypted tunnel but above the outer IP header, as described above. Another method, described in [draft-berger-rsvp-ext-07.txt], involves using the Security Parameters Index field from the *Authentication Header* or the *Encapsulating Security Payload* header as an additional field to perform packet classification.

In summary, mobility itself, the presence of the tunnel, and IP-level security introduce challenges to mobile nodes as receivers of real-time traffic in networks using RSVP. The challenges facing mobile nodes as senders are largely the same conceptually, but vary in some important ways. We describe these issues in the next section.

Mobile Nodes as Senders of Real-Time Traffic

In the previous section we described how changes of location, the presence of the tunnel, and IP-level security affect mobile nodes as receivers of real-time traffic. All of these properties affect mobile nodes as senders of real-time traffic as well. In this section we provide some additional insight into these issues as they affect mobile nodes as senders of real-time traffic.

First of all, the issues related to IP-level security are identical for mobile nodes as senders and receivers. Of course, this assumes that the *Authentication Header* and/or the *Encapsulating Security Payload* is used both for packets sent to and packets generated by the mobile node.

As for the presence of the tunnel, we note that mobile nodes—in the absence of ingress-filtering routers—can send packets directly to the receiver without the need for tunneling. However, this represents the analogous situation of route optimization, described in the previous section, which requires a new set of reservations from the mobile node to the receiver every time the mobile node moves.

Alternatively, a mobile node can reverse tunnel to its home agent, solving the ingress-filtering problem, but requiring new reservations from the mobile node's new location back to its home agent. As before, the advantages of one alternative compared to the other depend upon the relative locations of the receiver, the home agent, and the mobile node's current location. It is also worth noting that packets belonging to flows for which explicit resources have been reserved in intermediate routers (via RSVP) might be exempted from ingress filtering as a matter of policy. There is no way to predict whether this will be the case at this time.

As for mobility itself, the receiver-oriented nature of RSVP presents a problem when the sender is a mobile node but the receiver is a fixed node that has no concept of mobility. RSVP is designed to handle changes in path due to relatively slow variations in topology or congestion conditions. However, to work well with Mobile IP, RSVP would need a mechanism by which a mobile node could provide an explicit indication to a receiver that it has changed location and hence that the receiver should reserve resources along the new path.

Note that Mobile IP registration is exactly the type of explicit notification that a home agent could use to re-reserve resources on behalf of a mobile node as a sender of real-time traffic. Every time the mobile node successfully registers at a new location, the home agent would then perform reservations between itself and the mobile node. This solution requires the mobile node to reverse tunnel its real-time traffic to its home agent.

13.2.5 Summary

In this section we introduced real-time traffic and contrasted it with non-real-time traffic. The distinguishing characteristic of real-time traffic is that the timing of arrival of individual packets—rather than all packets taken in aggregate—is very important, perhaps more important than the fact that all such packets arrive error-free. Then we defined delay variance as a measure of these timing properties.

Next we described connectionless protocols, of which IP is an example, and mentioned their intrinsic properties that make them ill suited to supporting real-time traffic. Specifically, the lack of any connection-establishment procedure makes it impossible for routers to predict whether at any given moment they will have the resources necessary to guarantee a given level of service—most notably an upper bound on delay—to any particular packets.

Further, we noted that many of the links comprising the Internet similarly have no ability to reserve bandwidth, which also introduces delays which are long, unpredictable, or both to real-time traffic. Also, we saw how TCP's timeout-and-retransmission mechanism can only make matters worse.

To address these problems, the Internet Engineering Task Force is in the process of defining mechanisms by which nodes can request a given Quality of

Service from the network. This mechanism, the *Resource reSerVation Protocol
(RSVP)*, is used on behalf of an application to request special handling—to
deliver a specific Quality of Service—on the part of intermediate routers between
a sender and a receiver of real-time traffic. Quality of Service measures such network characteristics as bandwidth, delay, delay variance, and error rate.

Finally, we examined the issues that arise when mobile nodes are either
senders or receivers of real-time traffic wherein those mobile nodes use RSVP to
reserve resources. The three issues we identified related to:

1. mobility itself, and the need for the mobile node or its correspondent(s) to
   re-reserve resources every time the mobile node changes location;
2. the presence of the Mobile IP tunnel, and the fact that the protocol header
   fields that would normally be used to classify packets as belonging to real-
   time flows are now located in a different location within the packet; and
3. IP-level security which might encrypt or likewise change the locations of
   these header fields.

These issues will be addressed eventually by the Mobile IP working group
of the Internet Engineering Task Force, after the group finishes dealing with firewall traversal, IPv6 mobility, and other higher-priority items.

13.3 Service Location

Some protocol suites provide sophisticated mechanisms by which computers can
discover resources that are available on their networks. Examples of these
resources include file servers, Web servers, mail servers, and, most notably,
printers. Two protocol suites providing automated discovery of such resources
include Novell's Netware and Apple Computer's AppleTalk. The Chooser application in AppleTalk provides the user interface for this automated discovery; the
protocols which do all the work are the *Name Binding Protocol* and the *Zone
Information Protocol* [SiAnOp90].

Notably, the TCP/IP protocol suite has no such functionality. Generally, a user
must know the Domain Name System (DNS) name of a host that provides a service
before being able to access that service through some application. The Internet
Engineering Task Force is in the process of defining the *Service Location Protocol*
[RFC 2165] to eliminate this need and to allow a node to locate a service simply by
describing the service itself. In this section we provide an overview of the *Service
Location Protocol* and describe its relevance to mobility.

13.3.1 What Does the Service Location Protocol Accomplish?

The purpose of the *Service Location Protocol* is to allow an application in a
computer to discover the network address (e.g., IP address and TCP port number) of a service without previous knowledge of where that service is located. In

theory, this greatly simplifies network administration, since services can then come and go at will and users can dynamically discover and make use of them.

Consider, for example, the often nightmarish task of configuring hosts to talk to printers (and vice versa). In the absence of service location, someone, usually a grumpy system administrator, has to manually configure each host with a list of printers, their respective capabilities, and the protocols that must be used to access them. Thankfully, the availability and configuration of various printers changes relatively infrequently.

Now imagine a mobile node moving to a foreign link—perhaps one belonging to a completely different organization—where very different printers are available, none of them equivalent to the printers near the home link. Let us also assume that the user has an important document to print. We assume that he wants to print the document locally, since his home might be far away and printing the document there would not be terribly useful. The user must first discover the network address of the printer (or, equivalently, its "name") and then configure his mobile node to print to it. This becomes somewhat difficult if there is no one available to ask about the location and the attributes of the local printers. In addition, many users do not possess enough knowledge about their computers to be able to perform this configuration themselves—at least not without investing unreasonable amounts of time that could better be spent doing useful work.

Service location has the potential to eliminate this problem of discovering local resources and figuring out how to access them. For example, an application which seeks to print a document could invoke the *Service Location Protocol* to dynamically discover the existence of local printers, determine their capabilities, automatically configure itself to use one of them, and then begin printing. This would likely require very little intervention on the part of the user, perhaps only the act of selecting a single printer from a list of those discovered through service location.

13.3.2 How Does the Service Location Protocol Work?

Figure 13-5 shows the architecture of the *Service Location Protocol*. The three architectural elements are as follows:

- A *User Agent* is software running on the user's computer (for simplicity, we call this computer the *client*) which, on behalf of an application, uses the *Service Location Protocol* to discover the location and the attributes of services on the network that are needed by that application.

- A *Service Agent* is software running on a computer that advertises the presence and attributes of services available on that computer (for simplicity, we call this computer the *server*). A Service Agent responds to User Agents from which it has received *Service Requests*.

- A *Directory Agent* is software running on some computer (perhaps not a client or server per se) which can respond to *Service Requests* from User

Agents if the servers do not have Service Agents and therefore cannot respond themselves. Also, Directory Agents can aid the scalability of the *Service Location Protocol*, as described below.

In the next two sections we describe how these agents cooperate to realize service location: first in a small network environment and then in a larger campus environment.

Service Location in a Local Area Network environment

In its simplest form, these agents cooperate to realize service location roughly as follows:

1. A client application asks the User Agent to find a service on its behalf.

2. The User Agent multicasts a *Service Request* which contains a description of the service desired. For example, the request might seek a color printer that supports the PostScript printer language. A *Service Request* therefore identifies "what" is sought.

3. The multicasts arrive at Service Agents which inspect their contents to see if a service matching the request is available on the receiving node. If so, the Service Agent sends a unicast *Service Reply* to the requesting User Agent which contains the network address and the attributes of that ser-

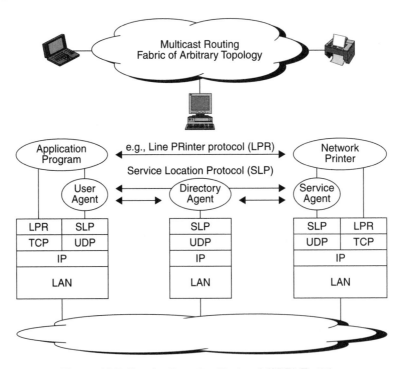

Figure 13-5 Service Location Protocol (SLP) Entities

vice. A *Service Reply* therefore informs the User Agent "where" the requested service can be obtained.

4. The User Agent collects the replies and returns the list of locations and attributes to the original client application. The application then picks one and proceeds to use its service.

This simple example—specifically, one involving no Directory Agents—is intended for very small networks with relatively few clients and servers. In fact, [RFC 2165] recommends service location be deployed in this way only for Local Area Network environments with a single link and no routers. This is because the amount of traffic generated by all of the clients and servers could consume a large amount of the available network bandwidth, if service location were deployed this way in a large network. In the next section we describe Directory Agents and the way in which they can provide a solution that is more appropriate for larger networks.

Service Location in a Routed Campus Environment

For medium-sized networks—those characterized by several links and routers but a limited number of hosts—[RFC 2165] suggests that a single Directory Agent be used to limit the amount of network traffic needed to realize service location. Here the protocol becomes slightly more complicated, in that each service has to "register" its presence with the Directory Agent. In the presence of Directory Agents, service location works roughly as follows:

1. Each Service Agent sends a *Service Registration* message to the Directory Agent in order to inform the Directory Agent of those services—and their attributes—that the server supports. The Service Agent can be manually configured with the address of the Directory Agent, can obtain its address via the *Dynamic Host Configuration Protocol (DHCP)*, or can use the *Service Location Protocol* itself to discover the address of the Directory Agent (by using the procedure described in the previous section).

2. The Directory Agent sends a *Service Acknowledgment* message to the Service Agent upon receipt of the *Service Registration*. This completes the registration process.

3. The User Agent, on behalf of some client application, sends a unicast *Service Request* to the Directory Agent containing identical information as in the multicast case of the previous section. As with Service Agents, User Agents can be manually configured with the address of the Directory Agent or they can dynamically learn the address via DHCP or service location.

4. The Directory Agent responds to the User Agent with a *Service Reply* that contains a list of all services available on the network which fulfill the criteria listed in the *Service Request*.

5. The User Agent presents the list to the client application which selects a suitable server and proceeds to use its service.

6. Later, if a server becomes unavailable, a Service Agent can send a *Service Deregister* message to the Directory Agent, at which time the Directory Agent will cease listing the service in any *Service Replies*. (Sound familiar? Service location uses many of the concepts of—and, in fact, some of the same terminology—as Mobile IP.)

Here we note that a User Agent sends only unicast packets to the Directory Agent, which in turn sends only a single response—containing a list of all matching services—back to the User Agent. This is in contrast to the previous section, where a User Agent sends multicast packets, and each matching server sends a unicast packet back to the User Agent. Thus the use of Directory Agents can lower the amount of traffic needed by service location. However, a single Directory Agent becomes a single point of failure, which is why the *Service Location Protocol* allows for, and in fact recommends, the use of many such Directory Agents for robustness.

To provide even more scalability, [RFC 2165] makes use of a concept known as *multicast scoping*. Here the IP Time to Live field is set to a small value, limiting the number of times that multicast *Service Requests* may be forwarded. The specifics of this are quite complicated, and the interested reader is referred to [RFC 2165] for the details. Scoped multicasts along with multiple Directory Agents allow service location to scale to large networks with many routers, links, and hosts. However, the mechanisms needed to deploy service location on a global scale—i.e., on the entire Internet—are currently being investigated.

13.3.3 Security Considerations of Service Location

Consider a client host that wishes to locate a printer and multicasts a *Service Request*. Now consider a Bad Guy host that responds to the *Service Request* with a *Service Reply*, in which it claims to be a printer with all of the attributes requested by the client host. If the client host selects the Bad Guy as its printer, then the client might subsequently print a document to the Bad Guy, which generally means transferring a file to the Bad Guy over the network in a form which can be printed. In this scenario, the Bad Guy has successfully stolen a copy of a user's document by masquerading as a printer.

What is interesting about service location is that authentication alone is not sufficient to prevent the attack just described. Even if a server authenticates itself—e.g., the server proves that it legitimately "owns" its claimed IP Source Address—this does *not* necessarily mean that the device is *authorized* to provide a specific service. Recall that authentication deals with proving a claimed identity, while authorization deals with determining whether that identity has the permission or privilege to do something. Thus, in the absence of additional security measures, a Bad Guy might indeed be able to authenticate its IP address while still stealing a copy of a document as described above.

It is worth noting that the first attempt to publish the *Service Location Protocol* as an Internet standards-track Request For Comments (RFC) was rejected by the Internet Engineering Steering Group—the body which makes such decision—precisely because of these security concerns. The latest draft [RFC 2165] proposes a number of solutions to these security concerns, one of which is similar to that described below.

One way to solve this problem is to have each *Service Reply* contain a public-key certificate for the replying server, a timestamp, and a digital signature computed over the entire contents. The certificate would include a list of services which that server is authorized to provide, the server's public key, and a digital signature computed over the entire certificate using some third-party certificate authority's private key.

Upon receipt of a reply, a User Agent would verify it as follows:

1. The client checks the validity of the certificate by using the certifying authority's public key. This verifies the server's public key and the list of services that the server has been authorized to provide.

2. If the server's public key is valid, then that key is used to verify the digital signature computed over the entire *Service Reply* message. If the signature is valid, then the timestamp is used to guard against replays.

3. If the *Service Reply* is valid, then the certificate is examined to see if the server has permission to provide the service it claims to support in the *Service Reply*.

4. If the server is authorized to provide the claimed service, then the client knows that it is safe to use that server as part of an application-layer exchange.

In the mechanism described above, a Bad Guy would have no way of transmitting to a User Agent a certificate which included a valid list of permissions—nor would the Bad Guy have a public key signed by the certificate authority. Note that each client need be configured only with the public key of the certifying authority. The clients can use this public key to verify the signatures provided by the various servers.

A security environment such as that described above is not necessarily easy to administer. Each server must generate a public/private-key pair and have its public key, along with a list of authorizations, signed by a certifying authority. A similar security architecture is described in the appendices of [RFC 2165], to which the reader is referred for all the details.

13.3.4 Service Location and Mobility

Service Location is a natural for mobile computing, especially for mobile nodes which visit foreign links and need to discover services available at those networks. In this section we describe some of the issues of service location that are unique to mobility—specifically, to mobile nodes.

A mobile node that uses a collocated care-of address might consider using that address to communicate with servers near the foreign link. This provides optimized routing, eliminates most of the problems of traversing firewalls, and can hide the true identity—as manifest by the mobile node's home address—from the local network devices.

However, a mobile node that does so is in actuality acting as a nomadic node for the purposes of this correspondence. This is because the node must acquire a new care-of address and will not be able to receive packets at the old care-of address if the node were to move. In addition, there is no way for a server to send an unsolicited packet to a nomadic node—one known to the server only by its collocated care-of address—that has changed location and is using a new care-of address. Thus, nodes that might change location before finishing an exchange with a local resource should use their home address and Mobile IP to accommodate such changes.

The security implications of mobility with respect to service location are not as straightforward as suggested in [RFC 2165]. In particular, consider the fact that it might be relatively easy to manually configure a mobile node to contain the public key of its "home" certificate authority, as described in *Security Considerations of Service Location* on page 296. This would allow the mobile node to determine the authenticity and authority of all the servers in its home network.

However, consider what happens when a mobile node visits a foreign link, one owned and operated by some authority other than its home network. Assume that the servers on the foreign network are authenticated and authorized as previously described through some certificate authority on the foreign network. The mobile node might indeed be able to obtain the public key of this foreign certificate authority. [RFC 2165] suggests that the public key could be read from a Web page. However, the mobile node must also:

- verify the authenticity of that public key;
- verify that the foreign certificate authority is indeed the entity vested with authorizing the services on the foreign network; and
- verify that this whole infrastructure, consisting of a foreign certificate authority and the various network services, is not simply conspiring to trick the mobile node into believing that the servers are safe to use.

The first two items—verifying the authority and authenticity of the foreign certificate authority—can be accomplished by having some higher-order certificate authority sign the public key of the foreign certificate authority. Likewise, this higher-order certificate authority might include within the foreign certificate authority's public-key certificate an authorization to further certify the servers on the foreign network.

In this case, mobile nodes would need to be configured with the public key of the higher-order certificate authority and could use this public key to verify the identity and authority of the foreign certificate authority, which in turn could be used to verify the identity and authority of the various services on the foreign link. Of course, this higher-order certificate authority must be operated by someone or some company that is trusted by the mobile node; otherwise, the mobile node would have no reason to believe any certificates the authority produces.

We still have not discussed how the mobile node can trust that the services on the foreign link—e.g., the printers—are not doing something nasty such as storing an electronic copy of all documents that a visiting mobile node might try to print. Thus, the gist of the third item above is really a recognition of a fundamental notion in security which has to do with trust. That is, before a mobile node sends sensitive information to a service on the foreign link, the mobile node must trust the higher-order certificate authority, the foreign certificate authority, and the services on the foreign network.

In summary, there is very little that cryptography, including digital signatures, certifying authorities, etc., can do to solve some of the "trust" problems that arise in the field of computer security. Users of mobile nodes need to be aware of this when deciding to use network services that are operated by administrative authorities that they have no basis for trusting.

13.3.5 Summary

In this section we described the *Service Location Protocol* as an automated way for applications to discover resources available on the network, such as servers and printers. A User Agent running in a client multicasts *Service Requests* on behalf of an application in order to discover services that fulfill the application's needs. Server Agents running in the servers respond to the User Agents upon receipt of *Service Requests* seeking the services they provide. In addition, Directory Agents allow service location to scale to large campus networks.

Then we described the security implications of service location, noting that authenticating servers was not sufficient and that clients need to determine in addition whether a given server is authorized to provide the service it claims to support. We described an infrastructure using a certifying authority, public-key certificates, and digital signatures which can accomplish the necessary authentication and authorization for a secure deployment of service location on an organization's network.

Finally, we discussed how mobility affects service location. We noted how mobile nodes might want to use a collocated care-of address to correspond directly with a local service on a foreign network in order to optimize the routing and avoid firewall issues. However, we also noted the security implications of mobile nodes using services on the foreign network—particularly, the fact that users having no basis for trusting the administration of a foreign network should not send sensitive information to the services on that network.

13.4 Chapter Summary

This chapter examined three areas in which further research and standardization effort is required in order to improve the performance and the nature of services available to mobile nodes.

First we described how the *Transport Control Protocol (TCP)*, as a reliable transport-layer protocol in the Internet, makes an assumption that the reason a packet fails to arrive at its destination is due to congestion. We saw how this assumption is generally true for much of the Internet but not necessarily true for mobile nodes which move rapidly, communicate via unreliable wireless links, or both. For such mobile nodes we described a number of enhancements that could be made to link-layer protocols, TCP itself, and application-layer protocols in order to improve the performance of mobile computing.

Next we described the concept of real-time traffic, whose distinguishing characteristic is strict timing requirements on the arrival of *individual* packets at the destination. We saw how the connectionless nature of both IP and many of the links comprising the Internet make supporting real-time traffic (e.g., audio and video) difficult. Then we described the *Resource reSerVation Protocol (RSVP)* which is used by senders and receivers of real-time traffic to request special handling by intervening routers of the packets that comprise a real-time traffic flow. We then described the way a mobile node must re-reserve resources whenever it moves and the complications that security and tunneling introduces with respect to RSVP and mobility.

Finally we examined the *Service Location Protocol*, a method by which nodes can automatically discover network resources, such as servers and printers. We saw how service location has profound security implications and how sophisticated mechanisms are necessary to prevent a variety of attacks. We also noted that these mechanisms might not necessarily be useful for mobile nodes that visit foreign links, if the owner of the mobile node has no basis for trusting the administration of the foreign network. Nonetheless, service location is potentially very useful for mobile nodes which might need to find local resources, such as printers, upon visiting foreign networks.

These three areas—performance of TCP, real-time traffic, and service location—underscore the claim made throughout this book: namely, that a total mobility solution involves more than simply the ability to route IP packets to mobile computers, the latter being solved by Mobile IP. Specifically, link-layer, transport-layer, and application-layer enhancements are necessary to give users of mobile computers equivalent functionality to what they enjoy when connected to their home link.

CHAPTER **14**

Summary and Final Thoughts

This chapter summarizes the primary points made throughout this book with respect to mobility in general and Mobile IP in particular. Then we conclude with a vision of the future in which Mobile IP is widely deployed and of the communications that will be possible in such a world.

14.1 Mobile IP Summary

The forces motivating mobile computing are: an increasingly mobile workforce, an increased reliance on networked computing and the Internet, and the increased portability and capability of notebook computers. Along with this dramatic increase in mobile computing comes the need for standards to which vendors can build products that interoperate, including the portable computers themselves and the infrastructure over which they communicate. Mobile IP provides this standard for the global Internet as well as for private networks based on the TCP/IP Suite of Protocols.

14.1.1 Background, Context, and Motivation

To understand Mobile IP, we first must understand the layered model of computer communications, and the role that each layer plays in the protocol stack. The network layer, layer 3 in the Open Systems Interconnect model, is responsible for routing packets from their original source to their ultimate destination, traversing an arbitrary topology of links and switching devices, or routers, along the way. Manual configuration, redirects, and dynamic routing protocols are the methods by which hosts and routers learn one or more paths to the various destinations in a network.

The *Internet Protocol (IP)* provides this routing capability in the Internet. IP works by assigning logical addresses, called IP addresses, to all nodes (hosts and routers). A node has one IP address assigned to each one of its respective interfaces, the latter being the hardware and/or software through which a node connects to a link. IP addresses consist of a network-prefix and a host portion, where all nodes on a link generally share a common network-prefix and have unique host portions. This allows IP routing to be based upon the network-prefix portion of the destination's IP address, allowing routers to maintain a single network-prefix route instead of as many individual routes as there are hosts. This turns out to be a key factor in the scalability of the Internet.

Because of network-prefix routing, a node that moves from one link to another and does not change its IP address will not be able to receive packets at the new link. In theory this can be solved with host-specific routing (as opposed to network-prefix routing), where host-specific routes are propagated to an appropriate number of routers every time a node moves. However, this solution suffers from scalability, robustness, and security problems. Alternatively, this problem could be solved at the data link layer. This requires a unique solution for each type of link and, by definition, there are geographic constraints on the range of mobility that link-layer solutions can provide.

Another possible solution is simply to change a node's IP address as it moves from one link to another. However, this would break TCP and higher-layer protocols, which expect a correspondent's IP address to remain fixed throughout the duration of a connection. In addition, there is the difficulty of determining at any point in time the address being used by a nomadic node—one whose IP address changes every time it moves. Even if the nomadic node is able to dynamically update the Domain Name System (notwithstanding the security issues this raises), a correspondent node has no way of knowing if or when the IP address returned will become stale.

14.1.2 Terminology and Operation

Thus, Mobile IP was designed to allow nodes to move from one link to another, without changing their IP address, and without interrupting any ongoing communications. It does so in a way which solves all of the robustness, scalability, security, and media-dependence problems which plague the alternatives discussed above. In addition, the ability of mobile nodes to retain their IP address as they move solves other problems, including those relating to the configuration databases and network-based licensing protocols used by some applications. It also enables mobile nodes to be both clients *and* servers, a property we expect to become increasingly important in the future.

Mobile IP itself is an Internet standards-track protocol which builds upon and enhances the existing functionality of IP. As of this writing, the documents defining Mobile IP are Request For Comments (RFC) numbers 2002-2006. As a network-layer solution to mobility, enhancements to link-layer, TCP, and application-layer protocols that can improve the nature and performance of applications used by mobile nodes are important but are nonetheless outside the scope of Mobile IP. With this background, we now summarize how Mobile IP works.

Mobile IP Entities

Mobile IP defines three new functional entities:

1. A *mobile node* is a host or router that can change its location from one link to another without changing its IP address and without interrupting any ongoing communications.

2. A *home agent* is a router with an interface on a mobile node's home link which intercepts packets destined to the mobile node's home address and tunnels them to the mobile node's most recently reported care-of address(es).

3. A *foreign agent* is a router with an interface on a mobile node's foreign link which assists a mobile node with movement detection and provides routing services on behalf of mobile nodes, including de-tunneling of encapsulated packets when the mobile node uses the foreign agent's care-of address.

Home agents and foreign agents are typically software products that run on conventional routers or in host computers (e.g., PCs and workstations). Mobile nodes are most common in host computers that are highly portable, such as notebook computers and the like. It is common for a single node to be simultaneously a foreign agent for some mobile nodes while being a home agent for other mobile nodes. Nonetheless, all three entities—mobile node, home agent, and foreign agent—can be implemented and simultaneously operating on a single node.

Each mobile node has two addresses associated with it:

- A *home address* is the IP address by which a mobile node is known to its correspondents. The home address remains fixed as a mobile node moves throughout the Internet. The network-prefix of a mobile node's home address is the same as the network-prefix that has been assigned to hosts and routers on the mobile node's home link. A mobile node's home address, home link, and home agent are thus intimately interrelated.

- A *care-of address* is an IP address that is used temporarily by a mobile node as an exit-point of a tunnel from the mobile node's home agent. The care-of address changes as a mobile node moves throughout the Internet. There are two types of care-of addresses: a foreign agent care-of address is an address of a foreign agent that has an interface on the mobile node's visited link, while a collocated care-of address is an address that is temporarily assigned to one of the mobile node's own interfaces. The mobile node's care-of address, foreign link, and foreign agent (if applicable) are thus intimately interrelated.

Mobile IP defines three functions, which occur roughly in the order presented below.

Agent Discovery

Agent Discovery is the process by which a mobile node determines its current location, determines if and when it has moved, and (if applicable) obtains a foreign agent care-of address. In the case where no foreign agent is available on a mobile node's foreign link, the mobile node may obtain a collocated care-of address through such means as manual configuration, the *Point-to-Point Protocol's IP Control Protocol (IPCP)*, or from a *Dynamic Host Configuration Protocol (DHCP)* server.

Agent Discovery is implemented by having home agents and foreign agents periodically transmit *Agent Advertisement* messages which are themselves extensions to *ICMP Router Advertisements*. A mobile node can also send an *Agent Solicitation* to elicit an immediate advertisement from any agents present on its current link.

Registration

Registration is an authenticated procedure by which a mobile node informs its home agent of its current care-of address. It is also the procedure by which a mobile node deregisters such care-of addresses upon returning to its home link. A mobile node can also learn the address of its home agent through the registration procedure.

Registration is implemented as a sequence of messages which are carried by the *User Datagram Protocol (UDP)*. A *Registration Request* message is sent from a mobile node to its home agent, possibly via a foreign agent. The home agent returns a *Registration Reply* to the mobile node, possibly via a foreign agent, to inform the mobile node of the disposition—acceptance or rejection—of its request.

Tunneling

Special procedures for routing packets—specifically those to and from a mobile node currently connected to a foreign link—comprise the third function defined by Mobile IP. A mobile node connected to its home link, on the other hand, functions just like any other (fixed) host or router from the standpoint of packet routing.

Protocol *tunneling* is used to deliver packets to a mobile node connected to a foreign link. Packets destined to the mobile node's home address are first routed toward its home link, a natural consequence of network-prefix routing. At the home link, the home agent intercepts these packets and tunnels them to the mobile node's care-of address, where they are extracted from the tunnel and delivered to the mobile node.

In the opposite direction, packets generated by the mobile node are sourced using its home address and routed directly to their destination. A foreign agent, if present, serves as a mobile node's default router. Mobile IP thus assumes that unicast IP packets—those which have a single destination—are routed without regard to their source address. Figure 4-3 on page 59 illustrates how all of these pieces fit together.

Packets from correspondent nodes to mobile nodes frequently take suboptimal paths, being first routed to the mobile node's home link and then being tunneled to the mobile node at its current location. Solving this problem involves mobile nodes reporting their current care-of address to various correspondent nodes, which, like Mobile IP registration, must be done in an authenticated manner. The difficulty here is distributing keys between these nodes in a secure fashion, without which authentication is impossible, leaving route optimization vulnerable to trivial denial-of-service attacks. Route optimization in Mobile IP is "work in progress."

Additional Capabilities

Mobile IP also defines procedures by which a mobile node can send and receive both multicast and broadcast packets when it is connected to a foreign link. In addition, Mobile IP can provide connectivity for an entire mobile network as well as for a mobile host. A mobile network is one whose component hosts and routers are fixed with respect to each other but are mobile, as a unit, with respect to the rest of the Internet.

Other vendors have found a use for Mobile IP as a method for the dynamic creation of IP tunnels wherein Mobile IP itself is not exposed to the ultimate user of such a network. Finally, there is an effort underway to define procedures by which a mobile nodes can communicate using protocol suites other than TCP/IP while connected to a foreign link, even when the intervening network— e.g., the Internet—supports the routing of only IP packets.

14.1.3 Applying Mobile IP

Deploying Mobile IP on a campus environment is a simple matter of upgrading the existing routers or hosts to serve as home agents and foreign agents, and installing mobile-node software on the portable computers (e.g., notebook computers). Applying Mobile IP in this way introduces no substantially new security threats over and above those faced by any network based on the TCP/IP protocols.

The Mobile IP Management Information Base (MIB) defines a rich set of variables which can be examined and modified by a network manager using version 2 of the *Simple Network Management Protocol (SNMPv2)*. This lets a network administrator configure the agents remotely, monitor their performance, and "twiddle the knobs," so to speak, to turn on and off such functions as broadcast packet delivery, mandatory registration with foreign agents, etc.

Firewalls complicate an Internet-wide deployment of Mobile IP, since they are specifically designed to prevent unauthorized access to private networks from the external portion of the Internet. The Mobile IP working group is in the process of defining procedures by which mobile nodes can send and receive packets through the firewalls protecting their private networks—all without compromising the security of those networks. These procedures use the IP security protocols—the *Authentication Header* and the *Encapsulating Security Payload*—to realize authenticated and encrypted tunnels between a mobile node and its firewall.

Another complication is ingress filtering, a policy which some Internet Service Providers are implementing in order to protect their customers from untraceable denial-of-service attacks. A router performs ingress filtering by examining the Source Address of an arriving IP packet. If that packet appears to arrive from a direction inconsistent with that router's notion of the network topology—i.e., the source address is topologically incorrect—then the packet is discarded. Unfortunately, packets sourced from a mobile node's home address, when that mobile node is connected to a foreign link, are exactly the types of packets that ingress filtering is designed to drop.

To address ingress filtering, the Mobile IP working group is defining the procedures by which a reverse tunnel is created from the mobile node's care-of address to its home agent, for packets generated by the mobile node. Such a tunnel is by definition topologically correct and allows the inner, encapsulated packets which are sourced from the mobile node's home address to pass through ingress-filtering routers.

Mobile IP can also form the basis of commercial services provided by wired or wireless service providers. Such a provider would generally make foreign agents available for its customers wherever they might wish to connect to the Internet and also might make home agents available for those customers without their own home agents. Service providers should heed the painful lessons learned by the analog, cellular telephone operators of North America and use cryptographically strong authentication in order to prevent theft-of-service.

14.1.4 Work in Progress and Open Issues

The Mobile IP working group of the Internet Engineering Task Force (IETF) has a number of items currently on its agenda. In addition to firewall traversal and reverse tunneling, one prominent work item is the definition of mobility support for *Internet Protocol version 6 (IPv6)*, the successor to the current version of IP, written IPv4.

Mobile IPv6 borrows many of the concepts of Mobile IPv4, including mobile nodes, home agents, home addresses, and care-of addresses. Mobile IPv6 has no foreign agents or, by definition, foreign agent care-of addresses. The Address Autoconfiguration procedure defined in IPv6 is used by mobile nodes to acquire a collocated care-of address, the only type of care-of address defined for Mobile IPv6.

In Mobile IPv6, correspondent nodes which know a mobile node's current care-of address can send packets directly to the mobile node by using an *IPv6 Routing Header*. Correspondent nodes not possessing this information send packets without such a header where they are routed to the mobile node's home link, intercepted by the home agent, and tunneled to the mobile node's care-of address as in Mobile IPv4.

Other areas of research and standardization relevant to mobility include the performance of reliable transport-layer protocols, such as TCP, in the presence of unreliable wireless links and nodes which change locations rapidly. More research is also needed to understand the interaction between mobility and the *Resource reSerVation Protocol (RSVP)*, the latter allowing the use of real-time applications such as audio and video over connectionless infrastructures such as the Internet. Finally, the *Service Location Protocol* can make it easier for mobile nodes to discover and use application services available on their visited, foreign link.

14.2 The Future of Mobile IP

With the base specifications having been published in late 1996, numerous free and commercial implementations of Mobile IP are already available. Ultimately, we expect almost all routers to be capable of serving as home agents, foreign agents, or both and all new notebook computers, palmtops, and personal organizers to come preloaded with mobile-node software. Furthermore, we expect Internet Service Providers to adopt this technology as well. What would be possible in such a world?

One lesson that the Internet has taught us over the last several years is that people will find new and fascinating applications for Internet-related technologies and that these applications cannot possibly be predicted in advance. For example, no one predicted the World Wide Web phenomenon back when the TCP/IP protocols were first being designed. Similarly, it would be an exercise in futility to predict the applications that mobile workers will be running on their mobile nodes once Mobile IP is widely deployed. Thus, the focus of this section will be on the connectivity that Mobile IP infrastructure will ultimately provide for mobile users, rather than on the applications they will run.

First and foremost, without high-quality implementations of mobile nodes, foreign agents, and home agents, none of the things we have discussed in this book is possible. Thus the role of the protocol-stack vendors, host vendors, and router vendors cannot be understated in realizing the potential of mobile communications and applications. In addition, while it is important that Mobile IP be adopted on campus networks, such as those owned by corporations and universities, it is likewise important that Internet Service Providers make Mobile IP functionality available to their customers, particularly in the form of foreign agents, in order to assist their customers' mobile nodes with move detection.

At first we expect to see service providers upgrading their dial-in equipment to provide foreign agent functionality, allowing customers to connect via PPP over phone lines. Some service providers will provide wireless access for their customers, allowing them to connect to the Internet wherever they might be, whether or not there is a telephone line available. Such systems will be extremely powerful in the range of applications they enable. They will also have serious security concerns, both for the service providers and for their customers, a topic requiring further comment.

First, the confidentiality of customers' data and access to their private networks must be controlled and made secure. In my opinion, the responsibility for this protection belongs *solely* in the hands of the customers and their networks— not with the service providers. The encrypted tunneling mechanisms described in *Chapter 9, Internet-Wide Mobility: A More Complicated Application*, are both necessary and sufficient to protect customers' information and their networks. We expect serious implementations of Mobile IP to support these protocols in the near future.

For other customers, those who might access the Internet but have no such private networks, link-layer encryption will be more appropriate. This is especially true for wireless links, which are extraordinarily susceptible to eavesdropping. This does not, of course, protect these customers' data over any of the other links in the Internet. As always, end-to-end encryption is the solution of choice for those who are serious about protecting their data.

As for the service providers themselves, they are most concerned about theft of service. Serious authentication mechanisms, of a strength that can protect against theft-of-service attacks, also require secure key distribution. The latter currently has high visibility within the Internet Engineering Task Force, and we expect an Internet-wide key management protocol and supporting infrastructure to be available in the coming months and years. We also call on legislators to repeal restrictions on the use and export of cryptographic systems in order to allow this infrastructure to grow and to flourish.

The current model of contracting for service with a provider, including the provider's setting up billing records and performing manual key distribution (even if this distribution is only in the form of a username/password), is cumbersome at best and unwieldy at worst. A far more desirable solution is one in which a user pays "digital cash" to a service provider for access to the Internet. In this case, a user might not need to establish a relationship with a service provider in advance. A user simply "plugs in" to a link, wireless or otherwise, and pays for service in real time as he uses the network.

One can envision a mobile-node implementation that is integrated with an application that informs the user of the per-minute charges being offered by any service providers of which the node is in range. This billing information could be appended as an extension to *Agent Advertisements* broadcast by the service providers' foreign agents. In this case, the user examines the cost and quality-of-service being offered by the various providers, selects one, and his mobile node registers via the selected foreign agent.

This would certainly open up the possibilities of the locations and media over which Internet service can be provided. A coffee shop or bookstore might have wired or wireless links to the Internet with service provided by one or more competing companies, all paid for by customers of the bookstore via digital cash. Similar scenarios can be envisioned for vacation spots—e.g., wireless service provision at beaches and other resort areas, with digital cash eliminating the need for service arrangements and contracts.

Mobile IP is the integrating technology for this vision. It is unique in its ability to allow a mobile node to connect anyway, anyhow, and anywhere, without requiring applications or any other state of the machine to be modified. No other technology even comes close. As of this writing, many commercial and freeware implementations of Mobile IP are available and many others are in the works. The additional pieces of the puzzle, including the strong encryption needed to protect the confidentiality of users' data; the strong authentication needed to guard against unauthorized access to private networks and to prevent theft-of-service; and the digital cash which will make commercial, mobile networks simple and easy to use, are starting to become widely available as well.

Glossary

acknowledgment—a message that informs a sender that its data has been received correctly by the intended recipient.

ACL (Access Control List)—a set of rules which specify whether a router may forward a given packet or whether the packet must be discarded.

active session-stealing (takeover)—an attack in which a Good Guy authenticates himself and begins communicating only to have a Bad Guy assume his identity (i.e., his IP address) and take over his ongoing communication.

address autoconfiguration—(see stateful/stateless address autoconfiguration).

address resolution—the process of determining the link-layer address of a node whose network-layer address is known (e.g., determining the Ethernet address that corresponds to an IP address—see also ARP).[†]

advertise reachability—the process by which a router sends routing updates in order to announce that the router is a good Next Hop to use to reach a specific destination or set of destinations.

Agent Discovery—the process by which a mobile node determines its current location, determines if it has moved, and acquires a foreign agent care-of address on a foreign link. Agent Discovery is an extension to ICMP Router Discovery.

AH (Authentication Header)—a protocol header which provides authentication, integrity checking, and possibly replay protection and non-repudiation for an entire IP packet.

algorithm—in the context of cryptography, a mathematical function that transforms data, generally using one or more keys, in order to provide confidentiality, authentication, and/or other security properties.

[†] Some texts also use the term *address resolution* to refer to the process of determining the IP address that corresponds to a given hostname (e.g., via the Domain Name System).

application layer—Layer 7 of the OSI Reference Model which is responsible for moving application-oriented data between user applications (e.g., electronic-mail messages, Web pages, files, etc.).

ARP (Address Resolution Protocol)—a standard protocol for performing address resolution between IP addresses and various link-layer addresses. (See also proxy ARP and gratuitous ARP.)

authentication—proving or disproving someone's or something's claimed identity.

authorization—the process of checking to see that an individual has permission to access a resource.

backbone—a high-speed link or links used to interconnect an organization's or service provider's routers.

Bad Guy—an individual who might try to steal information, deny or steal service, or otherwise perform some type of attack on a computer or network.

best-effort—describes a quality of service in which delivery of any given piece of information is not guaranteed by a protocol. For example, IP provides a best-effort service to higher-layer protocols.

binding—an association at the home agent between a mobile node's home address, its current care-of address, and the remaining lifetime of that association.

bit—a binary digit of 0 or 1.

branch point—of the nodes along the path from a mobile node's home link to both its old foreign link and its new foreign link, the node that is furthest from the home link.

bridge—a link-layer device that forwards frames between two or more attached links. A bridge is invisible to the network layer.

broadcast packet—a packet destined to all nodes on a single link or on several such links.

buffering—in the context of real-time traffic, a strategy by which data is accumulated for some period of time, to account for variations in transmission delay, before being played back to the user of an application.

byte—an 8-bit chunk of data (also called an octet or a character).

care-of address—an address used temporarily by a mobile node as a tunnel exit-point when the mobile node is connected to a foreign link.

CCITT (Consultative Committee on International Telephony and Telegraphy)—an organ of the International Telecommunication Union that produces telephone and data-communications standards. (The actual name of the organization is *Comité Consultatif International de Télégraphique et Téléphonique*.)

CDPD (Cellular Digital Packet Data)—a wireless WAN standard for sending IP packets over the unoccupied channels of analog cellular systems in North America.

CHAP (Challenge Handshake Authentication Protocol)—a cryptographically strong authentication protocol used in PPP.

checksum—a value computed from the contents of a protocol header and/or payload used to detect errors in transmission.

ciphertext—the (unreadable) output of an encryption operation.

cloning—a simple form of cellular fraud in which a Bad Guy programs his cellphone to use the Mobile Identification Number and Electronic Serial Number of a legitimate cellphone by eavesdropping on the legitimate phone's call requests.

collocated care-of address—an address temporarily assigned to one of a mobile node's interfaces. (See also care-of address.)

computer networking—the branch of computer science concerned with solving the problems relating to computer communications.

confidentiality—transforming data such that it can be decoded only by authorized parties.

confluence—the coming together of two or more things.

congestion—a condition in which the routers of a network are overloaded with packets and are unable to forward them, because of the speed of their connected links or otherwise.

congestion control—a TCP algorithm which detects congestion and dramatically decreases the amount of data a sender may transmit during periods of congestion.

connectionless—a protocol that has no explicit connection establishment or connection close phases; rather, a node with data to send simply sends it as soon as the data is available.

connection-oriented—a protocol that has three distinct phases: connection establishment, data transfer, and connection close.

consuming—the process by which a receiving protocol hardware or software module removes the protocol header and passes the payload to the higher-layer protocol module.

coverage area—the area over which the signal from a wireless transmitter can be reliably received.

cryptographically strong—a security solution that cannot be defeated by simple eavesdropping or decoding methods.

cryptography—mathematical manipulation of data in seemingly bizarre ways to accomplish surprisingly useful things. (See also encryption, message digests, and digital signatures.)

dial link layer—Layer 2 of the OSI Reference Model which is responsible for reliably transferring frames among nodes on neighboring links.

decapsulation—the process of extracting a first packet, header plus payload, from the payload portion of a second packet.

decrypt—to recover the original data from encrypted ciphertext.

default route—a routing table entry that matches all possible destinations. A default route has a Prefix-Length equal to 0 bits.

denial-of-service—an attack waged by Bad Guys that prevent Good Guys from getting useful work done. Mobile IP is designed to prevent the denial-of-service attack where a Bad Guy tries to send a bogus Registration Request to a Good Guy's home agent.

device driver—software that hides the specific characteristics of network-interface hardware and lower-layer protocols from the network layer.

DHCP (Dynamic Host Configuration Protocol)—a protocol by which a host obtains from a server certain information it needs to communicate, such as an IP address, prefix-length, and DNS server address.

Dial-up Server—a network device (or collection of devices) which includes modems, PPP interfaces, and an IP router.

digital signature—the output of a public-key algorithm which can provide authentication, integrity protection, replay protection, and non-repudiation of a message. A digital signature is computed using an individual's private key.

Directory Agent—as defined by the Service Location Protocol, software on some computer that can respond to requests from User Agents on behalf of Server Agents.

DNS (Domain Name System)—a system in the Internet which maps host-names into IP addresses.

encapsulation—the process of placing a first packet, header plus payload, within the payload portion of a second packet.

encrypt—to transform data such that the original data can be recovered only by those that possess the appropriate key.

encryption—a cryptographic technique used to provide confidentiality.

end-to-end protocols—protocols above the network layer in which the communicating peers are in the original source and ultimate destination.

entry-point—the node performing the encapsulation portion of a tunnel.

ESP (Encapsulating Security Payload)—a protocol header which provides confidentiality and possibly authentication for the higher-layer protocols encapsulated within the payload portion.

Ethernet—a link-layer protocol designed for shared media and typically used over copper wire. Ethernet generally operates at 10 Mbps or 100 Mbps (megabits per second).

exit-point—the node performing the decapsulation portion of a tunnel.

extensibility—the ability of a protocol's features to be extended in the future.

fast retransmit—a TCP algorithm which allows a sender to immediately retransmit a segment if it determines that this segment was lost but other, later segments arrived without error at the receiver.

FDDI (Fiber Distributed Data Interface)—a link-layer protocol designed for shared, fiber-based media that operates at speeds of 100 Mbps (megabits per second).

firewall—a device which protects a private network against intrusion from nodes on a public network.

flow—in the context of RSVP, the specific packets for which the Quality of Service is being requested. A flow is typically specified as a collection of network-layer and transport-layer header fields (e.g., IP Source/Destination Address, UDP Source/Destination Port).

flow control—the process of preventing a fast sender from overwhelming a slow receiver with more data than it can handle.

Foreign Agent—A router with at least one interface on a mobile node's (current) foreign link. When a mobile node uses a foreign agent's care-of address, the foreign agent de-tunnels and delivers packets to the mobile node that were tunneled by the mobile node's home agent. A foreign agent might also serve as a default router for packets sent by a registered mobile node.

foreign agent care-of address—an address of a foreign agent that has at least one interface on a mobile node's current foreign link.

foreign link (foreign network)—any link other than a mobile node's home link; i.e., any link whose network-prefix does not equal the network-prefix of a mobile node's home address.

forwarding—the process by which a router transmits a packet it has received in order to move the packet closer to its ultimate destination.

fragmentation—the process by which a large IP packet is chopped up into smaller pieces (called fragments) in order for the smaller pieces to fit within a link's Maximum Transfer Unit (MTU).

frame—a link-layer header plus payload; e.g., a link-layer header plus a packet.

FTP (File Transfer Protocol)—an application-layer protocol in the Internet used to transfer files between two hosts over a network.

full-duplex—a protocol in which the communicating peers may send information in both directions simultaneously. (See also half-duplex.)

globally routable address—an IPv6 address which is globally unique and therefore can be used by a node to communicate with all nodes on the Internet.

Good Guy—someone who doesn't do any of the things a Bad Guy might try to do; someone doing something that he is properly authorized to do.

gratuitous ARP—an *ARP Reply* message (providing a mapping between the sender's IP address and link-layer address) which is not prompted by any corresponding *ARP Request* message. For example, a mobile node sends several gratuitous ARPs whenever it returns to its home link.

GRE (Generic Routing Encapsulation)—an optional form of tunneling that may be supported by home agents, foreign agents, and mobile nodes. Generic Routing Encapsulation allows a payload packet of any network-layer protocol to be encapsulated within a delivery packet of any other (or same) network-layer protocol.

half-duplex—a protocol in which information may be sent only in one direction at a time. (See also full-duplex).

header—a small piece of data prepended to the data passed down from a higher layer, and sent to the peer protocol entity(s) across a network; e.g., the IP header.

heterogeneous mobility—mobility across different types of links and underlying media. Mobile IP is unique in its ability to provide heterogeneous mobility.

higher layer—a protocol layer immediately above IP. Examples are transport protocols such as TCP and UDP, control protocols such as ICMP, routing protocols such as OSPF, and Internet or lower-layer protocols being "tunneled" over (i.e., encapsulated in) IP, such as IPX, AppleTalk, or IP itself.

home address—a (permanent) address of a mobile node which it uses in correspondence with other nodes regardless of its current location.

Home Agent—A router with at least one interface on a mobile node's home link. A home agent intercepts packets destined to a mobile node's home address and tunnels them to the mobile node's care-of address when the mobile node is connected to a foreign link. A mobile node informs its home agent of its current care-of address through an authenticated registration protocol defined by Mobile IP.

home link (home network)—the link whose network-prefix equals the network-prefix of a mobile node's (permanent) home address.

homogeneous mobility—mobility across a single type of link and underlying medium. CDPD and IEEE 802.11 provide homogeneous mobility, while Mobile IP accommodates both homogeneous and heterogeneous mobility.

hop—the distance between a source and a destination measured in the number of routers that separate them (e.g., neighboring hosts are "zero hops" away; hosts separated by a single router are "one hop" away, etc.).

hop-by-hop protocols—protocols below the network layer in which the communicating peers are in neighboring nodes on each link.

hop-by-hop routing—a system in which each router makes only a "local" decision about the next host or router to which a packet must be forwarded in order to reach its ultimate destination. This is in contrast to systems in which an entire path is established from source to destination before any data flows along that path.

host—any node that is not a router.

host portion—some number of bits "to the right" of the network-prefix portion of an IP address. The host portion must be unique for each node on a link.

host-specific route—a routing table entry that matches exactly one destination. A host-specific route has a Prefix-Length equal to 32 bits.

hostname—a human-readable string of characters used to identify a host or router in the Domain Name System (DNS) (e.g., www.stlblues.com).

HTTP (HyperText Transfer Protocol)—an application-layer protocol in the Internet used to transfer Web pages and other content for the World Wide Web.

IAB (Internet Architecture Board)—a group of individuals who set architectural guidelines for the Internet to which the standards produced by IETF working groups must adhere.

ICMP (Internet Control Message Protocol)—a set of error and diagnostic messages used by hosts and routers to report problems or status information. ICMP must be supported by a node that claims to support IP.

IESG (Internet Engineering Steering Group)—a group that oversees the activities of the IETF and approves working group documents before they may be published as RFCs.

IETF (Internet Engineering Task Force)—a set of working groups each with a specific charter for producing an Internet standard or solving an operational problem of the Internet. The IP Routing for Wireless/Mobile Hosts (mobileip) working group produced Internet RFCs 2002-2006, which define the operation of Mobile IP.

IGMP (Internet Group Management Protocol)—a set of messages used by hosts to join (become members of) multicast groups and by multicast routers to probe for any members on a specific link.

ingress filtering—the process by which a router drops a packet that appears to arrive from a direction inconsistent with that packet's source address.

inline-keying—a feature by which information needed to perform key management is included within the same packets that carry user data.

Integrated Mobility Extension—an extension that a mobile node can append to its Registration Request in order to receive packets of protocols other than IP while it is connected to a foreign link.

integrity checking—ensuring that data cannot be modified without such modification being detectable.

interface—a node's attachment to a link.

interface token—a link-dependent identifier used as the host portion of a node's IPv6 address during Stateless Address Autoconfiguration. For example, a host may use its Ethernet address as an interface token.

Internet—a global network based upon the TCP/IP Suite of Protocols.

Internet Drafts—working documents of the Internet Engineering Task Force (IETF), its areas, and its working groups.

intranet—a private network based upon TCP/IP protocols which is either a portion of the global Internet secured against intrusion by a firewall, or a network which is not connected to the global Internet at all.

IP (Internet Protocol)—the Internet's network-layer protocol. IP provides best-effort, connectionless packet delivery on behalf of transport-layer and higher-layer protocols.

IP address—an IP-layer identifier for an interface or a set of interfaces.

IP in IP Encapsulation—the Internet-standard protocol for tunneling IPv4 packets within IPv4 packets. All foreign agents, all home agents, and those mobile nodes that support operation with collocated care-of addresses must implement IP in IP Encapsulation.

IP packet—an IP header plus payload; e.g., an IP header plus a transport-layer segment.

IPCP (Internet Protocol Control Protocol)—a PPP Network Control Protocol (NCP) which negotiates IP addresses and other parameters necessary for the proper operation of IPv4 over the PPP link.

IPv4—version 4 of the Internet Protocol.

IPv6—version 6 of the Internet Protocol; the successor to IPv4.

ISAKMP (Internet Security Association and Key Management Protocol)—along with the Oakley key determination protocol specifies the Internet-standard protocol for key management in support of the Internet security protocols (the Authentication Header and the Encapsulating Security Payload).

ISO (International Organization for Standardization)—an international body that produced the OSI Reference Model and various networking protocol standards.

key—a chunk of binary data used in cryptographic systems. (See also secret key, public key, and private key.)

key management—the process of distributing cryptographic keys to the appropriate parties without letting them fall into the hands of Bad Guys.

L2TP (Layer Two Tunneling Protocol)—an emerging Internet standard for tunneling PPP frames through the Internet or through private links.

LAN (Local Area Network)—a link spanning a relatively small geographic distance, typically on the order of meters to hundreds of meters.

layer—the combination of a protocol and the service it provides.

layer-2 tunnel—the path followed by a link-layer frame (e.g., PPP frame) while it is encapsulated within the payload portion of a network-layer packet.

LCP (Link Control Protocol)—a phase of PPP in which the peers establish, configure, and test the link-layer connection.

link—a medium over which nodes can communicate at the link layer; i.e., the layer immediately below IP. Examples include: Ethernets (simple or bridged); PPP links; X.25, Frame Relay, or ATM networks; and Internet (or higher) layer "tunnels," such as tunnels over IP itself.

link MTU (Maximum Transfer Unit)—the maximum size of an individual frame that a link-layer protocol is capable of transferring.

link-layer address—an identifier used to indicate the source and destination of a link-layer frame.

link-local address—an IPv6 address which allows communications only among nodes on the same link. Packets containing link-local addresses may not be forwarded by routers.

logical addresses—addresses, such as those used by network-layer protocols, that are independent of physical or link-layer addresses (e.g., IP addresses).

longest prefix match—a rule for routing IP packets which requires that the matching route with the longest prefix-length be used in preference to any other matching routes.

loopback encapsulation—a pathological condition in which a router recursively encapsulates a packet to itself without the packet ever being emitted through a physical interface.

match—a packet matches a routing table entry when the left-most Prefix-Length bits of the packet's IP Destination Address are equal to the entry's Target field.

medium—a communication facility over which bits can be transferred at the physical layer; i.e., the layer below the link layer. Examples include: copper wire, optical fiber, and radio channels.

members—the set of receivers of a multicast group.

message digest—a fixed-size cryptographic "fingerprint" of an arbitrarily large message.

Minimal Encapsulation—an optional form of IPv4 in IPv4 tunneling that may be supported by home agents, foreign agents, and mobile nodes. Minimal Encapsulation has 8 or 12 less bytes of overhead than does IP in IP Encapsulation.

mobile computing—the ability to use the same computer in many locations as opposed to a single, fixed location.

mobile host—a mobile node that maintains connectivity only for itself (versus a mobile router).

Mobile IP—a scalable, robust, and secure protocol for providing node mobility in the Internet. Mobile IP is the standard for Internet mobility and is defined in RFCs 2002-2006.

mobile network—a collection of hosts and routers that are fixed with respect to each other but are collectively mobile, as a unit, with respect to the rest of the fixed portion of the Internet.

Mobile Node—a node which is capable of mobility; i.e., a node which can change its point-of-attachment from one link to another while maintaining all existing communications and using only its (permanent) IP home address.

mobile router—a mobile node that maintains connectivity for an entire mobile network as opposed to a single mobile host.

mobility—the ability of a node to change its point-of-attachment from one link to another while maintaining all existing communications and using the same IP address at its new link.

multicast packet—a packet destined to many nodes; namely, every member of the multicast group.

multicast routing—a router capable of forwarding multicast packets.

multicast routing protocol—a protocol used by multicast routers to exchange information about the locations of multicast group members.

multiprotocol router—a router capable of forwarding packets of many network-layer protocols.

NCP (Network Control Protocol)—a phase of PPP in which the peers negotiate the parameters needed to run one or more network-layer protocols over the PPP link. (See also IPCP.)

Neighbor Discovery—a set of IPv6 protocols that describe how nodes discover and interact with neighboring nodes on their current link.

neighbors—nodes attached to the same link.

nested encapsulation—a condition in which a tunneled packet enters a second (outer) tunnel before exiting the first tunnel. Unlike recursive encapsulation, nested encapsulation is non-pathological and is required in many circumstances (e.g., a home agent uses nested encapsulation to deliver broadcast packets to a mobile node that has registered a foreign agent care-of address).

netmask—a 32-bit number in which each bit determines whether the corresponding bit in an associated IP address comprises the network-prefix portion (1's) or the host portion (0's). (See also prefix-length.)

network layer—Layer 3 of the OSI Reference Model, which is responsible for moving packets from an original source to the ultimate destination through an arbitrary topology of routers and links.

network-prefix—a bit string that consists of some number of initial bits of an IP address. The network-prefix is identical for all nodes on the same link.

network-prefix route—a routing table entry that matches more than one but less than all possible destinations. A network-prefix route has a Prefix-Length between 1 and 31 bits, inclusive.

node—a host or a router.

nomadic node—a node which is capable of nomadicity. (See nomadicity.)

nomadicity—the ability of a node to change its point-of-attachment from one link to another but not without terminating all ongoing communications at its old link and then starting new communications at its new link (with a new IP address).

non-repudiation—proving that a source of some data did in fact send data that he might later deny sending.

nonce—a random number included by a node in a cryptographic computation to prevent replay attacks.

Notification—the process by which a mobile node informs its home agent and various correspondent hosts of its current care-of address in Mobile IPv6.

Oakley—a key determination protocol which when integrated with ISAKMP is likely to become the Internet standard key management protocol.

OSI (Open Systems Interconnection)—a 7-layer reference model for computer communications. (See also the definition of each of the following layers: physical, data link, network, transport, session, presentation, and application.)

other protocol—a protocol other than IP.

packet—header plus payload (see IP packet).

PAP (Password Authentication Protocol)—a username/password-based authentication protocol used in PPP.

passive eavesdropping—an attack in which a Bad Guy listens to the packets being exchanged across a link in order to obtain confidential information contained in those packets. In contrast, an active attack is one in which the Bad Guy actually sends packets.

path MTU (Maximum Transfer Unit)—the smallest of the individual link MTUs comprising the path between an original source and an ultimate destination.

payload—the portion of a segment, packet, or frame containing data passed down from a higher-layer protocol or application.

peers—two protocol entities of the same type communicating across a network (e.g., the *Internet Protocol (IP)* entities within a host and a neighboring router).

physical interface—an interface that connects a node to a physical medium (e.g., an Ethernet interface). (See also virtual interface.)

physical layer—Layer 1 of the OSI Reference Model, which is responsible for transferring raw bits of information across a particular communications medium.

plaintext—data that is not encrypted.

port—a 16-bit (2-byte) integer which allows the receiving TCP and UDP protocol entities to determine which of many possible higher-layer applications is supposed to receive the data portion of any segment that arrives over the network.

PPP (Point-to-Point Protocol)—a link-layer standard for encapsulation of packets of many different protocols over point-to-point links, such as telephone lines.

prefix-length—the number of bits which comprise the network-prefix portion of an IP address.

presentation layer—Layer 6 of the OSI Reference Model, which is responsible for defining the syntax and encoding of data types such that computers of different operating systems and hardware types are capable of interoperating over a network.

private key—one of two mathematically related keys in public-key cryptography which must be kept secret from all but its owner. A private key is used by its owner to decrypt messages and to produce digital signatures.

protocol—a set of rules and procedures governing how two or more computers cooperate to accomplish a specific set of functions over a network.

protocol entity—a hardware or software module within a network device which implements a specific protocol.

proxy ARP—an *ARP Reply* message sent by a designated node on behalf of some other node that is unable or unwilling to respond to *ARP Request* messages itself. For example, a home agent proxy ARPs for a mobile node that has registered a care-of address on a foreign link.

public key—one of two mathematically related keys in public-key cryptography which may be given to anyone. A public key is used to encrypt messages and to verify digital signatures.

QoS (Quality of Service)—the attributes of the service provided by a protocol on behalf of higher-layer protocols, such as speed, delay, delay variance, and reliability.

real-time—data in which the time-of-arrival of individual packets is as important as, perhaps more so than, whether the data arrives error-free. Examples include audio and video.

reassembly buffer—an area of memory within a node where the individual fragments of an IP packet are accumulated until the original, unfragmented packet can be restored.

recursive encapsulation—a pathological condition in which tunneled packets continually reenter the same tunnel (an additional time) before exiting. (See also nested encapsulation.)

Registration—the process by which a mobile node informs its home agent of its current care-of address and in some cases requests service from a foreign agent.

relaying—the process by which a node receives transport-layer or application-layer data from a first node, processes the received data, and later transmits that data to a second node. In contrast with forwarding, a relaying node consumes the arriving network-layer packet and generates a new network-layer packet to carry the relayed data (e.g., a foreign agent relays a *Registration Request* from a mobile node to a home agent).

reliable—an error-free, in-order quality of service provided by a lower-layer protocol on behalf of a higher-layer protocol.

replay protection—prevention against a Bad Guy's storing a copy of an authenticated or encrypted message and retransmitting that message at a later time.

RFCs (Request For Comments)—a series of documents which contains Internet Standard protocols as well as a large variety of other interesting and often useful information of relevance to the Internet community.

round-trip time—an estimate of how long it takes a segment, packet, or frame to travel from the original source to the ultimate destination and for an acknowledgment to be returned to the source.

route (*noun*)—an entry in a routing table (see host-specific, network-prefix, and default routes).

route *(verb)*—to forward a packet from one interface to another.

route optimization—the process by which correspondent hosts are informed of a mobile node's care-of address such that these correspondents may tunnel packets directly to the mobile node. Such packets need not be routed through the mobile node's home agent and therefore tend to follow a more optimal path.

router—a network-layer device that forwards packets not explicitly addressed to itself (e.g., an IP router).

routing—the process of selecting a Next Hop and an outgoing Interface over which an IP packet should be forwarded.

routing loop—a pathological condition in which a packet circulates continuously among a set of routers because of inappropriate or incorrect routing table entries in one or more of the routers. The purpose of the IP Time to Live field is to cause a router to eventually discard a packet that is caught in a routing loop.

routing protocol—a protocol used between routers to exchange information about the location of destinations in a network (e.g., OSPF, RIP, BGP).

routing table—a software or hardware entity within a host or router that it uses to select a Next Hop and an outgoing Interface for packets that it transmits.

routing table entry—an entry in a routing table consisting of a Target, a Prefix-Length, and the Next Hop and Interface to which packets matching that Target and Prefix-Length should be forwarded.

RS-232—a physical-layer protocol often used to connect computers to modems.

RSVP (Resource reSerVation Protocol)—a protocol by which a receiver requests a specific Quality of Service from the network on behalf of an application, usually an application sending real-time traffic.

secret key—a shared value in secret-key cryptography that is known only by the two or more parties which wish to communicate securely.

security—the branch of computer science which deals with protecting computers, network resources, and information against unauthorized access, modification, and/or destruction.

segment—a transport-layer header plus payload; a segment often forms the payload portion of an IP packet.

service—the set of functions performed by a given protocol on behalf of higher-layer protocols.

Service Agent—as defined by the Service Location Protocol, software running on server that responds to requests from User Agents.

session layer—Layer 5 of the OSI Reference Model, which is responsible for providing rich, application-oriented services to the higher layers (e.g., checkpointing of large file transfers).

site-local address—an IPv6 address which allows communications only among nodes within an organization. Packets containing site-local addresses may not be forwarded by routers that connect the organization to the rest of the IPv6 Internet.

SKIP (Simple Key-management for Internet Protocols)—a key-management protocol based on the Diffie-Hellman key determination algorithm that provides inline-keying.

sliding window—a window which advances as acknowledgments are received.

slow start—an algorithm in TCP which prevents a node from overwhelming the network with segments at the beginning of a connection or just after a period of congestion.

SLP (Service Location Protocol)—a protocol used by a host to dynamically find the network address of services on a network (e.g., printers, file servers, etc.).

snoop—the process by which a link-layer entity peeks within the TCP header contained within a frame to determine whether the frame duplicates another frame in the link-layer window.

soft state—a set of variables maintained by a tunnel entry-point in order to relay ICMP messages generated within the tunnel to the ultimate source of an offending packet.

stack—a diagram that identifies the individual protocols operating at various layers.

stateful address autoconfiguration—a method by which a node can obtain an IPv6 address, usually involving leasing the address from a server. Examples include DHCPv6 and PPP's IPCP for IPv6.

stateless address autoconfiguration—a method by which a node can obtain an IPv6 address simply by concatenating a network-prefix learned from Router Discovery with an interface token.

stream—the data which flows across a reliable, transport-layer connection; e.g., the data transferred over a TCP connection.

stream-oriented—describes information that flows as an unstructured sequence of bytes.

suite—a set of individual protocols, at all layers of the stack, which generally operate together (e.g., the Internet's TCP/IP Suite of Protocols, the AppleTalk Suite of Protocols, etc.)

TCP (Transmission Control Protocol)—a reliable, full-duplex, stream- and connection-oriented, transport protocol used throughout the Internet.

TCP/IP Suite of Protocols—the Internet-standard suite of protocols used throughout the Internet and private intranets world-wide.

timestamp—a measure of the current time and date included by a node in a cryptographic computation to prevent replay attacks.

topologically correct address (routable address)—an IP address to which packets can be delivered using existing IP routing mechanisms, usually without requiring host-specific routes. Examples include a care-of address (always); and a mobile node's home address when the mobile node is connected to its home network.

topology—the layout of a network; specifically, the interconnection between hosts, routers, and links in the network.

transport layer—Layer 4 of the OSI Reference Model which is responsible for moving segments containing higher-layer data from source to destination. Reliable transport-layer protocols such as TCP guarantee error-free and in-order delivery of higher-layer data. Others, such as UDP, provide little more than multiplexing capability over and above what IP itself provides.

triangle routing—refers to the path followed by a packet from a correspondent host to a mobile node which must first be routed via the mobile node's home agent. (See also route optimization.)

tunnel—the path followed by a first packet while it is encapsulated within the payload portion of a second packet.

UDP (User Datagram Protocol)—an unreliable, connection-less transport protocol used throughout the Internet. UDP is little more than an application-layer interface to IP.

unicast—a packet destined to a single host or router.

User Agent—as defined by the Service Location Protocol, software running on a client computer that locates service on behalf of applications.

V.n—a generic term that refers to any of the "V" series of modem standards produced by the CCITT (e.g., V.34).

virtual interface—an interface that performs encapsulation or decapsulation but, unlike a physical interface, does not connect a node to a physical medium.

VPN (Virtual Private Network)—a single, logical network consisting of many physical networks separated by a public network.

VTP (Virtual Tunneling Protocol)—a protocol for establishing dynamic layer-2 or layer-3 tunnels through a public infrastructure for the purposes of outsourcing remote dial-in.

WAN (Wide Area Network)—a link spanning a relatively large geographic distance, typically on the order of kilometers to thousands of kilometers.

window—in TCP, the maximum number of segments that a node may send to its peer before stopping and waiting for acknowledgments.

you-are-kidding-yourself—a security solution that can be defeated easily by eavesdropping or by simple decoding methods.

References

Requests for Comments

[RFC 768]   Postel, J., *User Datagram Protocol*, RFC 768, August 1980.

[RFC 791]   Postel, J., *Internet Protocol*, RFC 791, September 1981.

[RFC 792]   Postel, J., *Internet Control Message Protocol*, RFC 792, September 1981.

[RFC 793]   Postel, J., *Transmission Control Protocol*, RFC 793, September, 1981.

[RFC 826]   Plummer, D., *Ethernet Address Resolution Protocol: Or converting network protocol addresses to 48.bit Ethernet address for transmission on Ethernet hardware*, RFC 826, November 1982.

[RFC 854]   Postel, J. and Reynolds, J., *Telnet Protocol specification*, RFC 854, May 1983.

[RFC 951]   Croft, W. and Gilmore, J., *Bootstrap Protocol*, RFC 951, September 1985.

[RFC 959]   Postel, J. and Reynolds, J., *File Transfer Protocol*, RFC 959, October 1985.

[RFC 1034]   Mockapetris, P., *Domain names—concepts and facilities*, RFC 1034, November 1987.

[RFC 1035]   Mockapetris, P., *Domain names—implementation and specification*, RFC 1035, November 1987.

[RFC 1055]   Romkey, J., *Nonstandard for transmission of IP datagrams over serial lines: SLIP*, RFC 1055, June 1988.

[RFC 1058]   Hedrick, C., *Routing Information Protocol*, RFC 1058, June 1988.

[RFC 1112]   Deering, S., *Host Extensions for IP Multicasting*, RFC 1112, August 1989.

[RFC 1144] Jacobson, V., *Compressing TCP/IP headers for low-speed serial links*, RFC 1144, February 1990.

[RFC 1191] Mogul, J., and Deering, S., *Path MTU Discovery*, RFC 1191, November 1990.

[RFC 1256] Deering, S., *ICMP Router Discovery Messages*, RFC 1256, September 1991.

[RFC 1321] Rivest, R. *The MD5 Message-Digest Algorithm*, RFC 1321, April 1992.

[RFC 1332] McGregor, G., *The PPP Internet Protocol Control Protocol (IPCP)*, RFC 1332, May 1992.

[RFC 1334] Lloyd, B. and Simpson, W., *PPP Authentication Protocols*, RFC 1334, October 1992 (obsoleted by RFC 1994).

[RFC 1583] Moy, J., *OSPF Version 2*, RFC 1583, March 1994.

[RFC 1661] Simpson, W., *The Point-to-Point Protocol (PPP)*, RFC 1661, July 1994.

[RFC 1644] Braden, R., *T/TCP—TCP Extensions for Transactions Functional Specification*, RFC 1644, July 1994.

[RFC 1700] Reynolds, J. and Postel, J., *Assigned Numbers*, RFC 1700, October 1994.

[RFC 1701] Hanks, S., Li, T., Farinacci, D., and Traina, P., *Generic Routing Encapsulation (GRE)*, RFC 1701, October 1994.

[RFC 1723] Malkin, G., *RIP Version 2 Carrying Additional Information*, RFC 1723, November 1994.

[RFC 1771] Rekhter, Y. and Li, T., *A Border Gateway Protocol 4 (BGP-4)*, RFC 1771, March 1995.

[RFC 1813] Callaghan, B., Pawlowski, B., and Staubach, P., *NFS Version 3 Protocol Specification*, RFC 1813, June 1995.

[RFC 1819] Delgrossi, L., Berger, L., *Internet Stream Protocol Version 2 (ST2) Protocol Specification—Version ST2+*, RFC 1819, August 1995.

[RFC 1825] Atkinson, R., *Security Architecture for the Internet Protocol*, RFC 1825, August, 1995.

[RFC 1826] Atkinson, R., *IP Authentication Header*, RFC 1826, August 1995.

[RFC 1827] Atkinson, R., *IP Encapsulating Security Payload (ESP)*, RFC 1827, August 1995.

[RFC 1828] Metzger, P. and Simpson, W., *IP Authentication using Keyed MD5*, RFC 1828, August 1995.

[RFC 1851] Karn, P., Metzger, P., and Simpson, W., *The ESP Triple DES Transform*, RFC 1851, September 1995.

[RFC 1877] Cobb, S., *PPP Internet Protocol Control Protocol Extensions for Name Server Addresses*, RFC 1877, December 1995.

[RFC 1883] Deering, S. and Hinden, R., *Internet Protocol, Version 6 (IPv6) Specification*, RFC 1883, January 1996.

[RFC 1884] Hinden, R. and Deering, S., *IP Version 6 Addressing Architecture*, RFC 1884, January 1996.

[RFC 1885] Conta, A. and Deering, S., *Internet Control Message Protocol (ICMPv6) for the Internet Protocol Version 6 (IPv6)*, RFC 1885, January 1996.

[RFC 1889] Schulzrinne, H., Casner, S., Frederick, R., and Jacobson, V., *RTP: A Transport Protocol for Real-Time Applications*, RFC 1889, January 1996.

[RFC 1905] Case, J., McCloghrie, K., Rose, M., and Waldbusser, S., *Protocol Operations for Version 2 of the Simple Network Management Protocol (SNMPv2)*, RFC 1905, January 1996.

[RFC 1918] Rekhter, Y., Moskowitz, B., Karrenberg, D., de Groot, G. J. and Lear, E., *Address Allocation for Private Internets*, RFC 1918, February 1996.

[RFC 1928] Leech, M., Ganis, M., et al., *SOCKS Protocol Version 5*, RFC 1928, March 1996.

[RFC 1945] Berners-Lee, T., Fielding, R., and Nielsen, H., *Hypertext Transfer Protocol—HTTP/1.0*, RFC 1945, May 1996.

[RFC 1970] Narten, T., Nordmark, E., and Simpson, W., *Neighbor Discovery for IP Version 6 (IPv6)*, RFC 1970, August 1996.

[RFC 1971] Thomson, S. and Narten, T., *IPv6 Stateless Address Autoconfiguration*, RFC 1971, August 1996.

[RFC 1972] Crawford, M., *A Method for the Transmission of IPv6 Packets over Ethernet Networks*, RFC 1972, August 1996.

[RFC 1984] IAB and IESG, *IAB and IESG Statement on Cryptographic Technology and the Internet*, RFC 1984, August 1996.

[RFC 1994] Simpson, W., *PPP Challenge Handshake Authentication Protocol (CHAP)*, RFC 1994, August 1996.

[RFC 2002] Perkins, C., *IP Mobility Support*, RFC 2002, October 1996.

[RFC 2003] Perkins, C., *IP Encapsulation within IP*, RFC 2003, October 1996.

[RFC 2004] Perkins, C., *Minimal Encapsulation within IP*, RFC 2004, October 1996.

[RFC 2005] Solomon, J., *Applicability Statement for IP Mobility Support*, RFC 2005, October 1996.

[RFC 2006] Cong, D., Hamlen, M., and Perkins, C., eds., *The Definitions of Managed Objects for IP Mobility Support using SMIv2*, RFC 2006, October 1996.

[RFC 2018] Mathis, M., Mahdavi, J., Floyd, S., and Romanow, A., *TCP Selective Acknowledgment Options*, RFC 2018, October 1996.

[RFC 2023] Haskin, D. and Allen, E., *IP Version 6 over PPP*, RFC 2023, October 1996.

[RFC 2058] Willens, S., Rubens, A., Simpson, W., and Rigney, C., *Remote Authentication Dial In User Service (RADIUS)*, RFC 2058, January 1997.

[RFC 2065] Eastlake, D. and Kaufman, C., *Domain Name System Security Extensions*, RFC 2065, January 1997.

[RFC 2068] Fielding, R., Gettys, J., Mogul, J., Frystyk, H., and Berners-Lee, T., *Hypertext Transfer Protocol—HTTP/1.1*, RFC 2068, January 1997.

[RFC 2107] Hamzeh, K., *Ascend Tunnel Management Protocol—ATMP*, RFC 2107, February 1997.

[RFC 2113] Katz, D., *IP Router Alert Option*, RFC 2113, February 1997.

[RFC 2131] Droms, R., *Dynamic Host Configuration Protocol*, RFC 2131, March 1997.

[RFC 2136] Vixie, P., Thomson, S., Rekhter, Y., and Bound, J., *Dynamic Updates in the Domain Name System (DNS UPDATE)*, RFC 2136, November 1996.

[RFC 2165] Veizades, J., Guttman, E., Perkins, C., and Kaplan, S., *Service Location Protocol*, RFC 2165, June 1997.

ISO Standard

[ISO8473] *Protocol for Providing the Connectionless-mode Network Service*, International Standard 8473, ISO/IEC JTC 1, Switzerland, 1986.

Articles and Books

[Atki96] Atkinson, J., *Wiretapping and Outside Plant Security—Wiretapping 101*, Granite Island Group, December 1996. Available on the Web at: http://www.tscm.com/.

[BakBad95]   Bakre, A. and Badrinath, B., *I-TCP: Indirect TCP for Mobile Hosts*, Proc. 15th International Conf. on Distributed Computing Systems (ICDCS), May 1995.

[BKVP96]   Bakshi, B., Krishna, P., Vaidya, N., and Pradhan, D., *Improving Performance of TCP over Wireless Networks*, Department of Computer Science, Texas A & M University, Technical Report 96-014, May 1996.

[BSAK95]   Balakrishnan, H., Seshan, S., Amir, E., and Katz, R., *Improving TCP/IP Performance over Wireless Networks*, Proc. 1st ACM International Conf. on Mobile Computing and Networking (Mobicom), November 1995.

[Bellovin96]   Bellovin, S., *Problem Areas for the IP Security Protocols*, AT&T Research, 6th Usenix Security Symposium, San Jose, California, July 22-25, 1996.

[CacIft95]   Caceres, R. and Iftode, L., "Improving the Performance of Reliable Transport Protocols in Mobile Computing Environments," *IEEE Journal on Selected Areas in Communications,* 13(5), June 1995.

[Come95]   Comer, D., *Internetworking with TCP/IP,* Vol. 1, *Principles, Protocols, and Architecture*, 3d ed., Prentice Hall, Upper Saddle River, NJ, 1995.

[Daye97]   Dayem, R., *Mobile Data & Wireless LAN Technologies*, Prentice Hall, Upper Saddle River, NJ, 1997.

[DifHel76]   Diffie, W. and Hellman, M., "New Directions in Cryptography," *IEEE Transactions on Information Theory,* Vol. IT-22, Nov. 1976, pp. 644-654.

[GarWil95]   Garg, V. and Wilkes, J., *Wireless and Personal Communications Systems (PCS): Fundamentals and Applications*, Prentice Hall, Upper Saddle River, NJ, December 1995.

[Huitema95]   Huitema C., *Routing in the Internet*, Prentice Hall, Upper Saddle River, NJ, March 1995.

[Huitema97]   Huitema C., *IPv6: The New Internet Protocol*, 2d ed., Prentice Hall, Upper Saddle River, NJ, 1997.

[iDEN96]   *iDEN™ Technical Overview: Notes on the iDEN System*, Instruction Manual 68P81095E55-A, Motorola Inc., August 1996. (Also see http://www.mot.com/LMPS/iDEN/.)

[John93]   Johnson, D., *Mobile Host Internetworking Using IP Loose Source Routing*, Technical Report CMU-CS-93-128, School of Computer Science, Carnegie Mellon University, February 1993.

[KoRaAl94]   Kojo, M., Raatikainen, K., and Alanko, T., *Connecting Mobile Workstations to the Internet over a Digital Cellular Telephone Network*, Proc. Mobidata Workshop, November 1994.

[KaPeSp95] Kaufman, C., Perlman, R., and Spencer, M., *Network Security: Private Communication in a Public World*, Prentice Hall, Upper Saddle River, NJ, 1995.

[Lee95] Lee, W., *Mobile Cellular Telecommunications: Analog and Digital Systems*, 2d ed., McGraw-Hill, New York, 1995.

[Murr97a] Murray, C., *What It Means to Be a Libertarian: A Personal Interpretation*, Broadway Books, New York, 1997.

[Murr97b] Murray, K., *Electronic Eavesdropping & Industrial Espionage*, Murray & Associates, March 1997. Available on the Web at: http://expertpages.com/news/eleeaves.htm.

[NeCr95] Needham, M. and Crisler, K., *QCRA—A Packet Data Multiple Access Protocol for ESMR Systems*, 45th IEEE Vehicular Technology Conference, July 1995.

[Pear97] Pearce, M., *TCP Performance Over Wireless Channels*, Motorola Internal Report, January 1997.

[Perk93] Perkins, C., "Providing Continuous Network Access to Mobile Hosts Using TCP/IP," *Computer Networks and ISDN Systems,* Vol. 26, 1993. Also Proceedings of 4th Joint European Networking Conference, Trondheim, Norway, May 1993.

[Perl92] Perlman, R., *Interconnections: Bridges and Routers*, Addison-Wesley, Reading, MA, 1992.

[Ranum95] Ranum, M., *Internet Firewalls Frequently Asked Questions*, V-One Corporation, 1995. Available on the Web at: http://www.v-one.com/newpages/faq.htm

[Redman97] Redman, P., "The Development of Integrated Solutions To Combat Cellular Fraud," *YankeeWatch Wireless Mobile Communications,* Vol. 4(1), February 1997.

[Schneier95] Schneier, B., *Applied Cryptography: Protocols, Algorithms, and Source Code in C*, 2d ed., John Wiley & Sons, New York, 1995.

[SiAnOp90] Sidhu G., Andrews, R., and Oppenheimer, A., *Inside AppleTalk,* 2d ed., Addison-Wesley, Reading, MA, May 1990.

[Stall95] Stallings, W., *Protect Your Privacy: The PGP User's Guide*, Prentice Hall, Upper Saddle River, NJ, 1995.

[Ster92] Sterling, B., *The Hacker Crackdown: Law and Disorder on the Electronic Frontier*, Bantam Doubleday Dell, New York, 1992.

[Stev94] Stevens, W., *TCP/IP Illustrated,* Vol. 1, Addison Wesley, Reading, MA, 1994.

[Tane96]   Tanenbaum, A., *Computer Networks*, 3d ed., Prentice Hall, Upper Saddle River, NJ, 1996.

[TaWaBa97]   Taylor, M., Waung, W., and Banan, M., *Internetwork Mobility: The CDPD Approach*, Prentice Hall, Upper Saddle River, NJ, 1997.

[Tuchman79]   Tuchman, W., "Hellman Presents No Shortcut Solutions to DES," *IEEE Spectrum,* 16(7), July 1979, 40-41.

[Viol96]   Violino, B., "The Security Facade," *InformationWeek,* October 1996.

[YavBag94]   Yavatkar, R. and Baghwat, N., *Improving End-to-End Performance of TCP over Mobile Internetworks*, Mobile 94 Workshop on Mobile Computing Systems and Applications, December 1994.

Internet Drafts

[draft-berger-rsvp-ext-07.txt]   Berger, L. and O'Malley, T., *RSVP Extensions for IPSEC Data Flows*, Internet Draft—work in progress, March 1997.

[draft-calhoun-vtp-ext-l2-00.txt]   Calhoun, P., *Virtual Tunnel Protocol: Layer 2 Protocol Extension*, Internet Draft—work in progress, July 1996.

[draft-calhoun-vtp-protocol-00.txt]   Calhoun, P. and Wong, E., *Virtual Tunneling Protocol (VTP)*, Internet Draft—work in progress, July 1996.

[draft-ietf-dhc-dhcpv6-10.txt]   Bound, J., and Perkins, C., *Dynamic Host Configuration Protocol for IPv6 (DHCPv6)*, Internet Draft—work in progress, May 1997.

[draft-ietf-ipngwg-ipv6-tunnel-07.txt]   Conta, A. and Deering, S., *Generic Packet Tunneling in IPv6 Specification*, Internet Draft—work in progress, December 1996.

[draft-ietf-ipsec-inline-isakmp-01.txt]   Sommerfeld, B., *Inline Keying within the ISAKMP Framework*, Internet Draft—work in progress, March 1997.

[draft-ietf-ipsec-isakmp-07.txt]   Maughan, D. et al., *Internet Security Association and Key Management Protocol (ISAKMP)*, Internet Draft—work in progress, February 1997.

[draft-ietf-ipsec-isakmp-oakley-03.txt]   Harkins, D. and Carrel, D., *The resolution of ISAKMP with Oakley*, Internet Draft—work in progress, February 1997.

[draft-ietf-ipsec-oakley-01.txt]   Orman, H., *The Oakley Key Determination Protocol*, Internet Draft—work in progress, May 1996.

[draft-ietf-ipsec-skip-07.txt]   Aziz, A., Markson, T., and Prafullchandra, H., *Simple Key-Management for Internet Protocols (SKIP)*, Internet Draft—work in progress, August 1996.

[draft-ietf-mobileip-ft-req-00.txt] Gupta, V. and Glass, S., *Firewall Traversal for Mobile IP: Goals and Requirements*, Internet Draft—work in progress, January 1997.

[draft-ietf-mobileip-firewall-trav-00.txt] Gupta, V. and Glass, S., *Firewall Traversal for Mobile IP: Guidelines for Firewalls and Mobile IP entities*, Internet Draft—work in progress, March 1997.

[draft-ietf-mobileip-integrated-00.txt] Li, T. and Rekhter, Y., *Integrated Mobility Extension*, Internet Draft—work in progress, March 1994.

[draft-ietf-mobileip-ipv6-02.txt] Johnson, D. and Perkins, C., *Mobility Support in IPv6*, Internet Draft—work in progress, November 1996.

[draft-ietf-mobileip-optim-05.txt] Johnson, D. and Perkins, C., *Route Optimization in Mobile IP*, Internet Draft—work in progress, November 1996.

[draft-ietf-mobileip-tunnel-reverse-02.txt] Montenegro, G., *Reverse Tunneling for Mobile IP*, Internet Draft—work in progress, March 1997.

[draft-ietf-pppext-ipcp-mip-01.txt] Solomon, J. and Glass, S., *Mobile IPv4 Configuration Option for PPP IPCP*, Internet Draft—work in progress, May 1997.

[draft-ietf-pppext-l2f-03.txt] Valencia, A., Littlewood, M., Kolar, T., *Layer Two Forwarding (Protocol) "L2F"*, Internet Draft—work in progress, December 1996.

[draft-ietf-pppext-l2tp-03.txt] Hamzeh, K., Kolar, T., Littlewood, M., Pall, G., Taarud, J., Valencia, A., and Verthein, W., *Layer Two Tunneling Protocol "L2TP"*, Internet Draft—work in progress, March 1997.

[draft-ietf-pppext-pptp-00.txt] Hamzeh, K., Pall, G., Verthein, W., Taarud, J., and Little, W., *Point-to-Point Tunneling Protocol*, Internet draft—work in progress, June 1996.

[draft-ietf-rsvp-md5-03.txt] Baker, F., *RSVP Cryptographic Authentication*, Internet Draft—work in progress, May 1997.

[draft-ietf-rsvp-tunnels-interop-00.txt] Krawczyk, J., *Designing Tunnels for Interoperability with RSVP*, Internet Draft—work in progress, March 1997.

[draft-ietf-rsvp-spec-16.txt] Braden, R., Zhang, L., Berson, S., Herzog, S., and Jamin, S., *Resource ReSerVation Protocol (RSVP)—Version 1 Functional Specification*, Internet Draft—work in progress, June 1997.

[draft-ietf-spki-cert-req-00.txt] Ellison, C., *SPKI Requirements*, Internet Draft—work in progress, March 1997.

[draft-ietf-spki-cert-structure-01.txt] Ellison, C., Frantz, B., and Thomas, B., *Simple Public Key Certificate*, Internet Draft—work in progress, March 1997.

[draft-ietf-tls-ssh-00.txt] Ylonen, T., *SSH Transport Layer Protocol*, Internet Draft—work in progress, June 1996.

[draft-ietf-tls-ssl-version3-00.txt] Freier, A., Karlton, P., and Kocher, P., *The SSL Protocol Version 3.0*, Internet Draft—work in progress, November 1996.

[draft-ietf-wts-shttp-04.txt] Rescorla, E. and Schiffman, A., *The Secure Hyper-Text Transfer Protocol*, Internet Draft—work in progress, March 1997.

[draft-montenegro-firewall-sup-00.txt] Montenegro, G. and Gupta, V., *Firewall Support for Mobile IP*, Internet Draft—work in progress, September 1996.

Other

[CA9621] *TCP SYN Flooding and IP Spoofing Attacks*, CERT Advisory CA-96.21, September 1996, available on the World Wide Web at: ftp://info.cert.org/pub/cert_advisories/CA-96.21.tcp_syn_flooding.

[802.11] *Wireless LAN Medium Access Control (MAC) & Physical Layer (PHY) Spec. vD5*, IEEE Catalog Number DS2972, May 1996.

Index

Public-key authentication, 136-39
  digital signatures, 136, 137-39
    and message digests, 138
    and non-repudiation, 138-39
Public-key certificate, 140-41
Public-key encryption, 130-32

Q
Quality of Service, IP, 284-85

R
R bit, 88-89, 170
Real-time Internet applications, 283
Real-time traffic, 273, 282-92
  example of, 282-83
  how Mobile IP affects, 288-91
  Internet application categories, 283
  and IP, 284-85
  mobile nodes as receivers of, 289
  mobile nodes as senders of, 290-91
  Resource reSerVation Protocol (RSVP),
    285-88, 300
Real-time Transport Protocol (RTP), 288
Recursive encapsulation, preventing,
  117-18, 122-23
Redman, Phillip, 201
Registration, 72-82, 304
  Mobile IP, 72-82, 108-9
  with other protocols, 222-23
Registration Lifetime field:
  ICMP Router Advertisement, 67
  Mobility Agent Advertisement
    Extension, 68
Registration procedure, tunneling, 61
Registration Reply, 73-75, 109, 162-63, 186,
  222, 240, 304
Registration Requests, 73-75, 103-4, 107,
  109, 160-63, 186, 187, 209, 211-12,
  222, 225-26, 240, 266-67, 304
  bogus, 84-85
  and foreign agents, 80, 81-82
  and home agents, 80-81
  and mobile nodes, 78-79, 82
  and shorthand notation, 191-92
Rekhter, Yakov, 221
Remote Authentication Dial In User Service
  (RADIUS), 238-39
Remote dial-in, 236-37
Replay attacks, 163
Replay protection, 136

Requests For Comments (RFCs), 5-6, 303
  Mobile IP standards documents, 48
Resource reSerVation Protocol (RSVP),
  285-88, 292, 300, 307
  Path message, 286-87, 289
  Resv message, 287, 289
Retransmissions, TCP, 275
Reverse tunneling, 98, 212-13, 306
Round-trip time, definition of, 275
Route optimization, 101-2
Routers, 14, 15, 56
Routing, 14-15
Routing Header, 250
Routing Information Protocol (RIP), 28, 49
Routing loop, 19
Routing protocols, 14, 26
  and routing updates, 51
Routing table entry creation, 26-29
  advertising reachability, 28-29
  dynamic routing protocols, 27-28
  ICMP Redirects, 27
  statically configured routing entries,
    27
Routing tables, 21-22
  entries in, 21-22
    categories of, 23
    creation of, 26-29
  integration via virtual interfaces, 92-95
  for mobile networks, 229-33
    foreign agent's routing table
      entries, 231-33
    home agent's routing table entries,
      230-31
  multiple entries in, 22-24
  sample, 22-23
Routing updates, 28, 51

S
Scalability, and IP routing, 29, 48
SCP (Secure remote file CoPy), 166
Secret-key algorithms, 128, 129
Secret-key authentication, 133-36
  integrity checking, 136
  and message digests, 134-35
  procedure, 133-34
  replay protection, 136
  timestamps, 135
Secret-key encryption, 130
Secure HyperText Transfer Protocol (S-HTPP),
  144